Planning Reform in the New Century

By

Daniel R. Mandelker, FAICP
Editor

Proceedings of the conference held at the School of Law,
Washington University in Saint Louis

December 3-4, 2004

Sponsored by the university's Center for Interdisciplinary Studies
Cosponsored by the American Planning Association

PLANNERS PRESS
AMERICAN PLANNING ASSOC
Chicago, Illinois
Washington, D.C.

D1361217

Copyright 2005 by the American Planning Association
122 S. Michigan Ave., Suite 1600, Chicago, IL 60603

ISBN (paperback edition): 1-932364-10-2
ISBN (hardbound edition): 1-932364-11-0
Library of Congress Control Number 2005929228

Printed in the United States of America

Interior composition and copyediting by Joanne Shwed, Backspace Ink
Cover design by Susan Deegan

Contents

Preface

Daniel R. Mandelker

In December 2004, the Center for Interdisciplinary Studies at the Washington University School of Law and the American Planning Association (APA) sponsored a conference on "Planning Reform in the New Century." We called the conference to examine major issues in land-use planning and land-use policy made all the more urgent by proposals for model planning legislation recently published by the APA. The conference also met just after Oregon voters adopted a statute that makes clear the precarious nature of planning reforms, even those that seemed to enjoy widespread support. The statute threatens Oregon's state planning program by requiring uncertain compensation for land-use regulations and decisions.

The Oregon vote was a wake-up call, but there are other indicators that planning has reached a critical turning point. Problems we have tried to solve for decades, such as the affordable housing problem, have not been solved. Programs we thought had succeeded, like growth management programs, need a new vision and a new direction. State legislation that powers the system by authorizing land-use planning and regulation is decades old and is not adequate for a new century. Model legislation proposed by the APA brings new ideas and challenges to law-makers, public officials, and citizens.

The issues raised by these new demands on land-use planning include statutory reform, housing affordability, growth management, and the role of the comprehensive plan in guiding land-use decisions. To consider these issues, we brought together a distinguished group of planners, lawyers, and law professors with wide knowledge and expertise in land-use planning and planning law, and divided them into six panels to address the major topics that planning reform presents. We did not ask them to summarize the law on the topics they addressed or to update us on the latest in planning practice. We asked them, instead, to look at the issues their topics presented and give us their perspective on what the problems are, what successes and failures we have had, and what policies and programs we need in order to deal with these issues more effectively. All of the panelists met this challenge, and we have collected their papers in this volume along with comments on their presentations by commentators for each of the panels. We have also included additional comments by observers who participated in the conference.

A major theme to emerge from the conference is that many land-use programs we adopted with great expectations are at midpoint, face problems, and need revision. Some have had unexpected consequences and some have not found the structure and policies they need to make them successful. We also learned that problems we have tried to solve, such as the housing affordability problem, also need new concepts and new strategies. We cannot continue to look to state leadership for planning reform. Local government may have to take the leadership role, and achieving progress at the local level can be daunting.

THE PANELISTS

The conference was divided into six panels. Panel I, "Political Leadership in Planning Statute Reform," looked at political leadership in the reform of planning statutes. The APA's model planning legislation will require state legislators to confront major changes in the statutory structure for their planning systems and land development codes. Statutory reform must also occur in local government through local legislation that adopts new programs or that implements state legislation at the local level.

This volume includes a paper from the first panel by John R. Nolon (see Chapter 1), a law professor at Pace University School of Law, where he teaches property, land-use, and environmental law, and is counsel to the Land Use Law Center and director of the Joint Center for Land Use Studies. The center has provided needed leadership on land-use issues in New York State through outreach programs, conferences, and publications. He is also a visiting professor in environmental law at Yale School of Forestry & Environmental Studies. John is also the author of numerous monographs and articles on land-use and environmental law topics.

As he states in his paper, he "begins with a brief look at the system's familiar dysfunctions, continues with a lengthier examination of positive examples of reform, emphasizes the importance of coalition building in the reform process, and ends with the observation that reform efforts should be organized by the task of creating essential connections among the governments involved." In an important section of his paper, John presents "several examples of land-use law reform that demonstrate clear roles for each level of government and shows how these roles can be coordinated to create a more integrated approach to land-use planning and regulation."

Panel II, "A Survey & Critique of Contemporary Efforts/Growing Smart," surveyed and provided a critique of contemporary efforts at statutory reform, and focused on the model legislation proposed by the APA. Stuart Meck (see Chapter 3) was the first panelist. Until the summer of 2005, he was a senior research fellow with the APA's research department and was the principal investigator for the Growing Smart^SM project that produced the new model planning and zoning legislation in its *Legislative Guidebook*.[1] Stuart is a former national president of the APA and has had a distinguished career as author and coauthor of articles and other publications on a wide range of planning issues. He is also the coauthor of a treatise on Ohio land-use law.

Stuart's paper discusses "(1) the evolution of planning statute reform in the U.S. through its classification into three periods; (2) an assessment of what recent planning statute reform has accomplished, as gauged by academic research; and (3) a discussion of a philosophy that should guide contemporary planning statute reform efforts." Stuart reviews what planning statute reform has accomplished, and discusses the quality of plans and their implementation, the impact on urban sprawl and urban form, the impact on housing affordability and the production of affordable housing, and the efficiency of the permit process and judicial review.

He then discusses the philosophy that should guide statutory reform efforts. One of his suggestions is his recommendation that statutes should be detailed and precise rather than general and open-ended as in the standard zoning and planning enabling acts. He believes that precise direction is needed because users of the statute at the local government level will be laypersons, and they should be able to pick up the statute and know what is required.

John Delaney (see Chapter 4), a land-use attorney from the Maryland suburbs of Washington, DC, has represented developers, utilities, and institutions in a wide variety of land-use matters. John has long been a leading figure in land-use law nationally, and he played an important role in the development of the APA model legislation, attending meetings of the project advisory committee where his advice and counsel were a major influence. He is a member of the adjunct faculty at American University Washington College of Law and coauthor of *Handling The Land Use Case: Land Use Law, Practice & Forms*.[2]

John addresses a number of problems he sees as critical in the APA model legislation. He addresses eight major needs he sees as essential if smart growth is to succeed:

1. The need to reform the development review process so that it will become stable, predictable, and certain;

2. The need for greater involvement of the state in planning and development review;

3. The need to end the "tilt" against residential uses in land-use plans and regulations;

4. The need for a process that balances job growth with housing for the workforce;

5. The need for a meaningful remediation alternative to litigation when addressing obvious inequitable regulatory burdens on specific properties;

6. The need to immediately address the chaotic common law of vested rights—one of the most serious threats to the orderly planning and financing of development;

7. The need to stem the burgeoning use of initiatives and referenda to preclude affordable housing; and

8. The need to end the abuse of moratoria in the development review process.

Panel III, "Sprawl and Urban Growth," addressed sprawl and smart growth, a high priority issue on the nation's planning agenda. The APA model legislation has a number of recommendations on smart growth issues, including urban growth boundaries. Bob Freilich (see Chapter 6), a land-use attorney now practicing in Los Angeles, is a major figure in the development of growth management programs nationally and has represented more than 200 cities, states, and counties on land-use issues. He is the author of a book on growth management, *From Sprawl to Smart Growth: Successful Legal, Planning, and Environmental Systems*[3] and litigated the famous *Ramapo*[4] decision that still provides major constitutional support for growth management programs.

Bob's first recommendation is that it is necessary "to assure that a comprehensive plan fulfills its 80-year-old prophecy of becoming the constitution guiding all development regulations and the development approval process."

He believes that comprehensive planning is necessary as a basis for growth management and to prevent ad hoc and possibly arbitrary decision-making. Bob criticizes the Growing Smart[SM] model legislation because it retreated from the mandatory planning principle. He also disagrees with the decision in the model legislation to provide detailed and specific authority, and argued that "Cities, counties, and regional agencies require simple, direct, and general authority in order to carry out appropriate smart growth management." Bob believes that courts will interpret broadly based authority to provide the needed statutory basis for local programs, and that "may more severely restrict local government authority than confirm it." He also addresses takings and public use issues as they affect broader economic initiatives to achieve smart growth management.

Gerrit-Jan Knaap (see Chapter 7), who is professor of urban studies and planning and director of the National Center for Smart Growth Research & Education at the University of Maryland, has written extensively on growth management programs, including coauthored books. In his paper, he first discusses the origins of the smart growth movement and the recommendations in the Growing Smart^{SM} legislation for growth management. Gerrit then reviews the Maryland smart growth program, which provides financial incentives for growth management programs, and national initiatives for smart growth. He then discusses five principles and strategies he believes growth management should adopt, and reviews national trends that can indicate whether smart growth has succeeded. Gerrit concludes that "evidence on development patterns, consumer preferences, and public policies suggests that not much is trending in the direction of smart growth," and offers a number of insights to explain why this is so.

Panel IV, "The Role of the Comprehensive Plan," considered the role of the comprehensive plan in the planning process and its role in providing planning policy for use decisions. Making comprehensive plans mandatory, and requiring land-use codes and decisions to be consistent with a comprehensive plan, is a major planning reform that has occurred in recent decades. It is still a minority reform; only a limited number of states require mandatory planning and consistency. This panel asked what the mandatory planning and consistency reform has done and whether it has achieved its objectives. Both panelists are practicing lawyers, and both come from states where mandatory plans and consistency are required.

Ed Sullivan (see Chapter 9) is a practicing attorney in Portland and a leader in its land-use bar, and teaches planning law at Northwestern College of Law and Portland State University. Ed is a major advocate of mandatory planning and consistency, and his articles have been a major influence in the law that governs the consistency doctrine. His paper raises critical questions about how mandatory planning and the consistency doctrine have worked in practice.

Ed first reviews the history of the mandatory planning movement and how courts have treated comprehensive plans, and concludes that courts are accepting the view that plans are mandatory and that zoning must be consistent with them. He then discusses the difficulties the interpretation of comprehensive plans presents, and suggests how plan interpretation may be made easier by adopting a philosophy, or approach, to interpretation, and by using tools that are available to make interpretation easier. Ed concludes by discussing the important question of judicial deference and how it should guide judicial review of plans and consistency issues.

Tom Pelham (see Chapter 10) is an influential Florida land-use attorney who served as secretary of the Florida Department of Community Affairs (the state agency that supervises the state's land-use program, which includes mandatory planning and consistency requirements). Florida has had a mandatory planning and consistency requirement for some time, and Tom reviews lessons from the Florida experience.

Tom explains how the Florida system has achieved the intended purposes of the planning model, and how Florida has expanded that model through state standards and state review of comprehensive plans. He then discusses important lessons to be drawn from the unintended consequences that have occurred from Florida's adoption of this planning model, which have led to major changes in Florida's local government and planning systems. They include the judicialization of the local land-use decision-making process, the changing role of the local legislator, the meaning of consistency, the interpretation of the local plan, and the polarization of state-local relations. He believes all these issues need to be addressed in any reform of planning legislation.

Panel V, "Housing and Regulatory Streamlining," dealt with housing affordability questions. Anthony Downs (see Chapter 12) is one of the nation's leading urban scholars. He is a senior fellow at The Brookings Institution in Washington, DC, and a visiting fellow at the Public Policy Institute of California in San Francisco. For years, Tony has been a leading student of housing affordability issues, and his writings provide the critical scholarship on housing affordability programs. His paper discusses the problem of removing regulatory barriers to affordable housing.

Tony concludes that many local governments deliberately adopt regulations that raise the cost of housing, and that it is a waste of time to urge local governments to act differently. Tony then discusses the issues raised by the housing affordability problem, which he considers serious, and describes five ways in which it occurs. He contends that structural conditions (e.g., greater citizen participation in decision-making and fragmented control over land-use decisions) and dynamic conditions (e.g., fast regional growth and the axioms of the smart growth movement) have produced the regulatory barriers that make it difficult to provide affordable housing, as well as the immense increase in homeowner wealth caused by a sizable rise in home prices. He then discusses the tactics that are available to attack housing affordability problems.

Charles Daye (see Chapter 13) is a Henry P. Brandis Professor of Law, School of Law, at the University of North Carolina at Chapel Hill, where he teaches housing and community development, and is the senior editor of a law school casebook, *Housing and Community Development*,[5] now in its third edition. Charlie has long been active in housing discrimination issues and has written extensively on them, including racial discrimination in land-use regulation. Charlie brings a new dimension to the discussion of race and class problems in housing. He develops a housing social efficiency analysis to deal with these problems which, in his judgment, are nowhere near solved.

To get a perspective on this analysis, Charlie discusses the multiple dimensions of housing and points out that "housing is at the intersection where we encounter housing-related issues when we look at the social problems we face in virtually any domain toward which we travel." He notes it is hard to get and hold a consensus on solving race and class issues in housing, and suggests a new framework for social efficiency analysis that can get us out of this gridlock.

Panel VI, "Evaluating the Impacts of State and Local Programs," evaluated the effects of state and local programs. The first speaker was Shirley Abrahamson (see Chapter 15), Chief Justice of the Wisconsin Supreme Court. Chief Justice Abrahamson is president of the Conference of Chief Justices, chair of the board of directors of the National Center for State Courts, and a member of the council of the American Law Institute.

She first notes that land-use cases are an important part of an appellate court's docket, and claims that courts are "the bulwark between the government and the individual" in land use as in other cases. She "finds a battle raging regarding governing regulation of property between an ideology that emphasizes individualism" and one that "emphasizes environmental considerations and communal health and welfare." Chief Justice Abrahamson recommends that the role of the legislature and the courts in the land-use field should be analyzed, and concludes with a number of observations on land-use cases, including a comment that the distinction between quasi-judicial and legislative land-use actions is an important one that will need clarification, and that amicus briefs are very helpful if they take a different position from that taken by the parties.

Michael Berger (see Chapter 16), a noted California land-use attorney who also specializes in eminent domain and other varieties of real property litigation, also spoke on this panel. He is active both as a lecturer and legal commentator on land use and eminent domain, and devotes most of his time to appellate practice, including several appearances before the Supreme Court in land-use takings cases.

Mike provides a final wake-up call. He argues that it is time to take a "hard look" at how planning is practiced and at the constitutional consequences of planning decisions. After revealing his personal biases and discussing land-use regulation in California, Mike concludes that "we already have too much planning; we need less, not more." He then provides biting criticism of the organized planning community with numerous examples, followed by case studies from California where Mike believes planning and regulation have gone wrong. He does not believe that planning is all bad, however, but finds an "unfortunate zealousness" that permeates city halls in this field.

COMMENTS BY OBSERVERS

A number of observers attended the conference as participants. This volume includes papers by two of these observers. Robert Einsweiler (see Chapter 18) is past president of the APA. During his career, Bob focused primarily on urban growth management, strategic planning, environmental policy, and transportation planning. He worked in the public sector, ran his own consulting firm, and taught at the University of Minnesota and the Lincoln Institute of Land Policy.

Bob comments on a number of themes raised in the conference. The first is whether detailed enabling legislation will lead to better planning. Bob does not believe it will, and concludes that specifying plan content may cause planners to lose sight of major issues in planning and development control. The second part of his paper examines a framework for considering competing views of how land is used. He develops a conceptual framework for looking at this issue that considers the relative balance between the community and the individual in land-use decisions. He then applies this framework to examples such as Oregon's compensation measure, the recent *Tahoe-Sierra*[6] takings case in the Supreme Court, and the affordable housing issue, and concludes with comments on what the appropriate role for planning enabling legislation should be.

Rachelle Alterman (see Chapter 19) holds the David Azrieli Chair in Town Planning at the Faculty of Architecture and Town Planning, Technion—Israel Institute of Technology. She is internationally recognized as an authority on comparative land policy, planning law, and planning theory. Rachelle provides an international perspective. Her paper offers a critically important discussion on the role of cross-national learning in land-use law reform. She first notes that American land-use law, from an international perspective, is in a class of its own because it grew through a "bottom-up" evolution that is different from the European model. With this history in mind, she then notes several strengths and weaknesses embedded in land-use law and practice in the United States.

Rachelle first notes several strengths in the American system, including the absence of a federal law that allows room for decentralized innovation, built-in competition among alternative land-use instruments that leads to survival of the fittest, a growing export of American programs, and federal legislation that affects many areas related to land use. Rachelle then notes the absence of a federal land-use law as one of the weaknesses and targets for reform, as well as other issues including the ambivalent status of comprehensive plans, the large differences in state laws born in "The Quiet Revolution," and the low import rate of planning-law concepts from other countries.

CONCLUSION

The new century presents many opportunities for planning reform. Many of these opportunities, and the problems and issues that will have to be faced, are discussed in the papers in this volume. We believe they contain a critical blueprint for approaching questions of planning reform in the new century.

NOTE ON *KELO*

In an interesting development that occurred just as this book was being completed in June 2005, the U.S. Supreme Court issued a ruling in *Kelo v. City of New London*,[7] the last of four important planning cases the Court decided during its 2004-2005 session. Several contributors to this book refer to *Kelo*. In its five-to-four opinion in this case, the Court ruled that taking private property for the purpose of economic development does satisfy the "public use" requirement of the Fifth Amendment.

The Court gave unanimous support to planning in the other three cases: *Lingle v. Chevron*,[8] *City of Rancho Palos Verdes v. Abrams*,[9] and *San Remo Hotel v. City and County of San Francisco*.[10] Perhaps most important was *Lingle*, in which the Court upheld Hawaii's rent control law—and in doing so, rejected the "substantially advances" test first set out in 1980 in *Agins v. City of Tiburon*.[11] Justice Sandra Day O'Connor, writing for the Court in *Lingle*, noted that "today we correct course" and hold that the substantially advances language is "not an appropriate test for determining whether a regulation effects a Fifth Amendment taking."

DANIEL R. MANDELKER NOTES

1. Stuart Meck (gen. ed.), *Growing Smart^{SM} Legislative Guidebook: Model Statutes for Planning and the Management of Change* (Chicago: American Planning Association, 2002).
2. John J. Delaney, Stanley D. Abrams, and Frank Schnidman, *Handling The Land Use Case: Land Use Law, Practice & Forms* (3d ed.) (Rochester, NY: Thomson-West, 2005).
3. Robert H. Freilich, *From Sprawl to Smart Growth: Successful Legal, Planning, and Environmental Systems* (Chicago: American Bar Association, 1999).
4. *Golden v. Planning Bd. of the Town of Ramapo*, 285 N.E.2d 291 (N.Y. 1972).
5. Charles E. Daye et al., *Housing and Community Development* (3d ed.) (Durham, NC: Carolina Academic Press, 1999).
6. *Tahoe-Sierra Preservation Council v. Tahoe Regional Planning Agency*, 535 U.S. 302 (2002).
7. *Kelo v. City of New London*, 125 S.Ct. 2655.
8. *Lingle v. Chevron*, 125 S.Ct. 2074.
9. *City of Rancho Palos Verdes v. Abrams*, 125 S.Ct. 1453.
10. *San Remo Hotel v. City and County of San Francisco*, 125 S.Ct. 2491.
11. *Agins v. City of Tiburon*, 447 U.S. 255.

List of Tables

List of Acronyms

AESOP	Association of European Schools of Planning
APA	American Planning Association
BANANA	Build Absolutely Nothing Anywhere at Any Time
CIP	capital improvement program
COAH	[State of New Jersey's] Council on Affordable Housing
CZMA	Coastal Zone Management Act
DOT	Department of Transportation
EAR	evaluation and appraisal report
EU	European Union
GMA	[Florida's] Growth Management Act
GPA	Georgia Planning Association
HUD	[U.S. Department of] Housing and Urban Development
IHDA	Illinois Housing Development Authority
IJA	Institute for Judicial Administration
IMLA	International Municipal Attorneys Association
ISTEA	Intermodal Surface Transportation Efficiency Act
JCTC	Job Creation Tax Credit [program]
NGA	National Governors Association
NIMBY	Not In My Back Yard
PFA	Priority Funding Area
PUD	planned-unit development
RPI	residential/professional/institutional
RRCC	Rockland Riverfront Communities Council
SCPEA	Standard City Planning Enabling Act

SIG	special interest group
STPP	Surface Transportation Policy Project
SZEA	[Standard] State Zoning Enabling Act
TDR	transfer of development rights
TND	traditional neighborhood development
TRPA	Tahoe Regional Planning Agency
UEDD	Urban Economic Development Division
UGB	urban growth boundary
US EPA	U.S. Environmental Protection Agency
US GAO	U.S. Government Accounting Office
WDFW	Washington Department of Fish and Wildlife

Law Review Abbreviations

ALI-ABA	American Law Institute-American Bar Association
Ariz. L. Rev.	Arizona Law Review
Fla. St. U. L. Rev.	Florida State University Law Review
Fordham Urb. L.J.	Fordham Urban Law Journal
Ga. L. Rev.	Georgia Law Review
Harv. BlackLetter L.J.	Harvard BlackLetter Law Journal
Harv. Envtl. L. Rev.	Harvard Environmental Law Review
Harv. L. Rev.	Harvard Law Review
J. Affordable Housing & Commun. Dev. L.	Journal of Affordable Housing & Community Development Law
JAPA	Journal of the American Planning Association
J. Hous. Res.	Journal of Housing Research
J. Land Use & Envtl. L.	Journal of Land Use and Environmental Law
J. Plng. Ed. & Res.	Journal of Planning Education and Research
J. Plng. Envtl. L.	Journal of Planning and Environment Law
J. Plng. Lit.	Journal of Planning Literature
J. Urb. & Contemp. L.	Journal of Urban and Contemporary Law
J. Urb. Econ.	Journal of Urban Economics
Law & Contemp. Probs.	Law and Contemporary Problems
Mich. L. Rev.	Michigan Law Review

Mun. Fin. J.	Municipal Finance Journal
N.C. Cent. L.J.	North Carolina Central Law Journal
N. Ill. U. L. Rev.	Northern Illinois University Law Review
NIMLO Mun. L. Rev.	National Institute of Municipal Law Officers Municipal Law Review
Ohio St. L.J.	Ohio State Law Journal
Or. L. Rev.	Oregon Law Review
Pace Envtl. L. Rev.	Pace Environmental Law Review
Pace L. Rev.	Pace Law Review
Pepp. L. Rev.	Pepperdine Law Review
Rutgers L. Rev.	Rutgers Law Review
Stan. L. Rev.	Stanford Law Review
Stetson L. Rev.	Stetson Law Review
St. John's L. Rev.	St. John's Law Review
Third World Pl. Rev.	Third World Planning Review
U. Balt. L. Rev.	University of Baltimore Law Review
U.C.L.A. L. Rev.	University of California at Los Angeles Law Review
U. Colo. L. Rev.	University of Colorado Law Review
U. Detroit J. Urban L.	University of Detroit Journal of Urban Law
Urb. Law.	Urban Lawyer
Urb. Law Ann.	Urban Law Annual (formerly the Journal of Urban and Contemporary Law; now Washington University Journal of Law & Policy)
Urb. Stud.	Urban Studies
Vt. L. Rev.	Vermont Law Review
Wash. L. Rev.	Washington Law Review
Wash. U. J.L. & Pol'y	Washington University Journal of Law & Policy
Wash. U. J. Urb. & Contemp. L.	Washington University Journal of Urban & Contemporary Law (now Washington University Journal of Law & Policy)
W. New Eng. L. Rev.	Western New England Law Review
Wis. L. Rev.	Wisconsin Law Review
Wm. and Mary L. Rev.	William and Mary Law Review

I

Political Leadership in Planning Statute Reform

CHAPTER 1

**Paradigms of Positive Change:
Reordering the Nation's Land-Use System**

John R. Nolon (panelist)
Pace University School of Law

CHAPTER 2

**Planning Reform in the
New Century—A Century Ago**

Fred Bosselman (commentator)
Chicago-Kent College of Law

1

Paradigms of Positive Change: Reordering the Nation's Land-Use System

John R. Nolon

INTRODUCTION

The general perception of the American land-use system is that it is disorganized, disorderly, and inefficient. The nation's landscape is coherent but, when dissected by the jurisdictions of federal, state, and local governments, its physical development becomes woefully fragmented. Imagine, for example, trying to implement a cogent plan for flood prevention in the Mississippi watershed. In the Upper Mississippi Basin alone, there are six federal agencies, 23 state agencies in five states, and 233 local governments involved in concocting a recipe for mitigating damage caused by flooding. Nationally, there are up to 40,000 local governments that have some legal authority to control private land use, 50 states adopting laws and spawning agencies with significant influence on the land, and countless federal laws and regulations administered by dozens of federal agencies directing their attention to how the land is used.

All of these influences are legitimate; each level of government has serious interests that must be protected and advanced. The defect in the system is its lack of coherence. In examining how the system should be reformed and assessing particular examples of land-use law reform, attention must be paid to the issue of how greater coordination can be achieved.

This article begins with a brief look at the system's familiar dysfunctions, continues with a lengthier examination of positive examples of reform, emphasizes the importance of coalition building in the reform process, and ends with the observation that reform efforts should be organized by the task of creating essential connections among the governments involved.

LESSONS IN DYSFUNCTION AND DISCONNECTION

The history of our nation's land-use system is freighted with discontinuity, dysfunction, and tumultuous disconnections. This persists within all components of the system from its grassroots engagements to its removed state and federal interventions. A few illustrations suffice to make the point.

At the local level, the NIMBY (Not In My Back Yard) reaction is so pervasive that it has become a household word: the acronym speaks for itself. The land-use decision-making process somehow encourages neighbors to oppose developments nearby. This is usually an automatic, rather than a thoughtful, reaction. The unintended consequence of this serious discontinuity is to shift development pressures elsewhere, often to the countryside. Comprehensive land-use plans cannot be implemented without developers who build in conformance with the community's vision. Developers and their financiers, however, are pushed away by NIMBYism rather than drawn into partnerships with local plans and planners.

State tax policies that rely heavily on local property taxes to fund education and pay municipal service costs create fierce competition among municipalities, all of whom seek industrial and commercial projects that promise higher assessed values and fewer schoolchildren. This state policy also leads to local land-use laws that zone out affordable types of housing, causing alarming housing price spirals in many metropolitan areas and denying housing opportunities to workers needed by the businesses that are zoned in. Fiscal zoning causes both municipal border wars and housing discrimination; it is as ubiquitous and dysfunctional as NIMBYism, if not as well understood.

Federal interstate highway funding and low-cost mortgage programs famously fueled the forces of sprawl in the 1950s and 1960s that are with us still.[1] There is little evidence that these federal projects and programs bore any relationship with, or even considered, state and local policies regarding environmental protection, farmland preservation, or housing development.

To justify his proposed National Land Use Planning Act in the early 1970s, Senator Henry M. Jackson pointed to the conflicts and confusion concerning critical economic and environmental programs at the national, state, and local levels. One example, of many he cited, involved three agencies of the federal government that were working at cross purposes in the Florida Everglades. One of them was preserving the area as a park, the other altering the landscape for flood control, and the third funding airport construction. One of these was responding to the request of a local Florida government, the other a county, and the third the state. None knew what the others were planning or doing.[2]

Encouraged by the federal Coastal Zone Management Act (CZMA), the South Carolina legislature adopted its Beachfront Management Act, which resulted in regulations prohibiting all development on David Lucas's two barrier island beachfront lots in the Isle of Palms, whose zoning permitted single-family homes on relatively small lots. This led to the seminal holding of the U.S. Supreme Court that a land-use regulation that denies any economic use of the land is a per se taking.[3]

The purchase of homes built close to the beach on barrier islands would not be possible for most homebuyers without mortgage financing, which is dependent on casualty insurance. Private casualty companies refuse to insure property losses in such locations. Curiously, such insurance is available under federal flood insurance programs and a state-created, shared-risk insurance pool in South Carolina—programs made available by the two governments whose legislation led to the regulation of which Lucas complained.[4] Today, the frustrated efforts of the Environmental Protection Agency—under the all-important Clean Water Act, which requires local land-use authorities to respect pollution standards for federally impaired waters and to manage stormwater runoff—are contemporary manifestations of this same disconnect.[5]

It is clear that there is confusion over the role that each level of government should play regarding land-use planning and regulation. In addressing the subject of law reform in this area, a critical issue is to clarify what the role of each level of government should be and how these roles should be coordinated. The Sustainable Use of the Land Project, conducted by the Lincoln Institute of Land Policy, resulted in a book that is perhaps the last significant review of land-use control in America.[6] The study concluded with the presentation of a land-use agenda that provides guidance for the future of land-use policy.[7]

According to its reform agenda, local governments must take the lead role in securing good land use, state governments must establish the ground rules on matters that affect more than one locality, and federal policies and actions must be coordinated to properly influence the direction and pace of development affected by the land-use machinery of state and local governments. This agenda recognizes the validity of top-down and bottom-up influences in the system, ratifies the centuries' old tradition of local planning and project approval, endorses the need for clear policy direction and local capacity building at the state level, and acknowledges the need to secure national interests in the process.

CASE STUDIES IN COMPETENCE AND CONNECTIVITY

This section examines several examples of land-use law reform that demonstrate clear roles for each level of government and shows how these roles can be coordinated to create a more integrated approach to land-use planning and regulation. The examples may help frame the discussion about an agenda for reforming land use in America in general and suggest a strategic direction for that agenda to follow.

Federal Action

A positive example of coordinating federal, state, and local influences is the CZMA, adopted by Congress in 1972. Congress recognized that state and local institutional arrangements for planning and regulating land and water uses in coastal areas were inadequate and adopted an integrated approach that encouraged responsible economic, cultural, and recreational growth in coastal zones.[8]

Drafters of the CZMA realized that, in order for a coastal management program to be successful, administration needed to take place at a local rather than at a national level, aided by a strong state role. Since many of the problems surrounding coastal areas are geographically specific, drafters reasoned that state and local governments should control coastal policy consistent with national objectives. Thus, the CZMA did not create a centralized federal agency to dictate coastal zone management, but rather articulated national policies and then established a process for the development of state coastal zone management programs.[9]

Rather than mandate state involvement, the CZMA provided incentives to encourage state participation. It offered states that meet consistency requirements effective regulatory control of their coastal areas; provided federal funds for coastal planning, projects, and program administration; and promised that federal actions would respect state and local coastal plans and policies. This approach of articulating national policies, encouraging and supporting state action, and recognizing the important role of local governments was important to the program's success and was probably the reason it was adopted by a Congress sensitive to state prerogatives in the land-use area.

This connected national strategy, under the CZMA, operates effectively at the grassroots level in New York where the Department of State, through its Division of Coastal Resources and Waterfront Revitalization, provides grants to coastal communities to prepare local waterfront revitalization plans, and encourages intermunicipal land-use agreements among localities that share coastal resources such as harbors, bays, and riverfronts. The division's combination of funding resources, technical assistance, and emphasis on intermunicipal approaches to coastal resource protection has been a catalyzing force in creating intermunicipal agreements regarding the protection of Long Island Sound, Hudson River, Manhasset Bay, and Oyster Bay–Cold Spring Harbor.[10]

In Florida, the Waterfronts Florida Partnership Program works with communities to develop plans for local waterfront revitalization and offers an initial grant to make a visible improvement in the waterfront, which the community must match with a 20 percent contribution.[11]

In Michigan, the Department of Environmental Quality allocates grants to municipalities through the Michigan Waterfront Redevelopment Grant Program.[12] A requirement of this grant program is that the project must increase public access to the waterfront.

Washington State's Coastal Zone Management Program was initiated under the CZMA in 1976—the first such program in the country. The state's Shorelands and Environmental Assistance Program is administered by the state's Department of Ecology and, in 2004-2005, it awarded grants to 11 cities and counties for comprehensive shoreline master program updates and inventories.[13]

State Action

There is abundant evidence that state legislatures and agencies are adopting laws and taking actions to connect with local land-use decision-makers and to build local capacity and encourage or require local actions compatible with state policy objectives. Here is a sampling of recent examples of state legislative actions that integrate state and local land-use policy:

• In 1999, the State of Wisconsin adopted smart growth legislation that directs every city to enact a comprehensive smart growth plan by 2010.[14] Each plan must incorporate specific smart growth elements, including agricultural, natural resource, intergovernmental cooperation, and land-use plan elements. Traditional neighborhood developments (TNDs) are encouraged. The TND ordinance adopted by the City of River Falls, Wisconsin, exemplifies a local government's successful implementation of this state smart growth initiative.[15]

• Michigan mandates the adoption of local land-use regulations to combat erosion.[16] A state commission adopts recommendations, guidelines, and specifications for erosion control. Local governments then pass ordinances based on the commission's program and have primary responsibility for the administration and enforcement of plan and permit procedures for land-disturbing activities.

• Iowa's state-mandated erosion control program is locally designed and enforced.[17] The state gives conservation districts broad guidelines for adopting erosion control ordinances. Adopted regulations are subject to approval by a state committee.

• The zoning enabling law in Connecticut requires that local zoning ordinances "shall provide that proper provision be made for soil erosion and sediment control."[18]

• The Illinois legislature adopted the Local Planning Technical Assistance Act in 2002. The law's purpose is to provide technical assistance to local governments for the development of land-use ordinances, promote and encourage comprehensive planning, promote the use of model ordinances, and support planning efforts in communities with limited funds.[19] The Department of Commerce and Community Affairs is authorized to provide technical assistance grants to be used by local governmental units to "develop, update, administer, and implement comprehensive plans, subsidiary plans, land development regulations . . . that promote and encourage the principles of comprehensive planning."[20]

• In Massachusetts, the legislature adopted a statute that directs its Department of Housing and Community Development to provide assistance to communities in solving local land-use, housing, and development problems both individually and intermunicipally. The department is directed to help with data, studies, coordination with other state agencies, and training for local land-use decision-makers.[21] The state has established the Citizen Planner Training Collaborative, which provides land-use training by professionals on a regular basis throughout the state.[22]

• The State of Washington has been at the forefront of developing local protection for fish and wildlife habitats. The state's Growth Management Act of 1990 implements what the Washington Department of Fish and Wildlife (WDFW) calls a bottom-up approach to land-use planning.[23] It requires all counties, cities, and towns in the state to classify and designate resource lands and critical areas, including fish and wildlife habitats, and to adopt development regulations for them.[24] The WDFW has created detailed checklists to assess the wildlife potential of urban areas and to aid local governments in reviewing the elements of their development regulations and comprehensive plans.

• In 1999, Utah adopted the Quality Growth Act, which establishes a state Quality Growth Commission to advise the legislature on smart growth issues, provide planning assistance to local governments, and administer a state program for the preservation of open space and farmland.[25] In 1997, the Envision Utah Public/Private Partnership was established to guide the state in creating a quality growth strategy. The organization conducted a series of studies, forums, and media events over the next five years, involving thousands of residents and hundreds of stakeholder groups. In addition to supporting state smart growth legislation, Envision Utah has helped to unify the planning goals of the citizenry and constituent local governments and to provide local officials with "quality growth efficiency tools" to help them determine the consequences of current zoning and land-use patterns and the legal strategies available to adjust them to the evolving planning vision.[26]

Several states have adopted statutes that create urban growth areas. These statutes aim to achieve the essential goal of smart growth: to contain growth in defined and serviceable districts. They are guided by various objectives, including the creation of cost-effective centers, preservation of agricultural districts, promotion of affordable housing, protection of significant landscapes containing critical environmental assets, and the preservation of open lands for the future. Not all of these state growth management statutes are regional in nature.

• Maine requires local land-use plans to identify areas suitable for absorbing growth and other areas for open space protection.

• Minnesota authorizes, but does not require, localities to designate urban growth areas in local and county comprehensive plans.

- The Oregon growth management statute, adopted in 1973, is the most directive of its kind.[27] It creates a state agency known as the Land Conservation and Development Commission, articulates a number of statewide land-use planning goals, requires local governments to adopt comprehensive plans consistent with state-designated urban growth boundaries, and requires local plans to be approved by the commission. The statute also created the Metropolitan Service District (Metro) to supervise the intermunicipal urban growth boundary in the greater Portland area. In 1979, the statute was amended to create the Land Use Board of Appeals to review local land-use decisions. Litigation under this regime has not attacked its legality but mainly the validity of particular planning decisions that affect individual parcels. Strong public support and an enduring coalition of growth management advocates have blocked several attempts to repeal or significantly modify this initiative. Ballot Measure 37, however, adopted in November 2004 by an impressive margin, threatens the Oregon initiative by granting property owners compensation for the enactment or enforcement of land-use laws that diminish their land values.[28]

Regional and Intermunicipal Action

The Standard City Planning Enabling Act, promulgated by the Advisory Committee on City Planning and Zoning in 1928, provided for regional planning by authorizing local planning commissions to petition the governor to establish a regional planning commission and to prepare a master plan for the region's physical development. Provisions were included in the planning enabling act for communication between the regional and municipal planning commissions with the objective of achieving a certain degree of consistency between local and regional plans.

Much of the country, at one time or another, was brought within the jurisdiction of some form of regional planning organization due to a variety of influences. The most powerful of these was the promise of funding for regional efforts under federal housing, water, and public works programs. Predominant among these organizations were voluntary, area-wide, regional councils of government; multistate river basin compacts; and regional economic development organizations.

With few exceptions, these regional bodies have stopped far short of preemptive land-use planning and regulation. They have become, however, effective vehicles for communication, education, collaboration, and networking. An early study of the positive effects of voluntary regional councils of governments found that "the most significant contribution of councils is that they have furthered the concept and interests of regionalism."[29] Among their most significant contributions is the effect they have of educating local land-use officials. In these regional bodies, they learn about the common problems and mutual dependence of localities that share the same economic or housing market area or that have regulatory power over river basins and watersheds, which cannot be protected without intermunicipal cooperation.

Under New York's Town, Village, and General City Law, local governments are specifically authorized to enter into intermunicipal agreements to adopt compatible comprehensive plans and zoning laws as well as other land-use regulations.[30] Local governments also may agree to establish joint planning, zoning, historic preservation, and conservation advisory boards and to hire joint inspection and enforcement officers. Several dozen intermunicipal land-use councils have been created under this authority.

State statutes in New York also enable county governments to assist constituent localities in land-use matters.[31] Cities, towns, and villages may enter into intermunicipal agreements with counties to receive professional planning services from county planning agencies. In this way, municipalities lacking the financial and technical resources to engage in professional planning activities can receive assistance from county planning agencies to carry out their land-use planning and regulatory functions. Pursuant to these amendments, a county planning agency can act in an advisory capacity, assist in the preparation of a comprehensive plan, assist in the preparation of land-use regulations, and participate in the formation of individual or joint administrative bodies. Counties in New York are now signatories on several intermunicipal land-use agreements involving local governments in watershed, riverfront, harbor, and other land-use partnerships.

Using this broad legal authority in New York, the Rockland Riverfront Communities Council (RRCC) was created in 2002. It comprises the towns of Clarkstown, Haverstraw, Orangetown, and Stony Point; the villages of Grand View, Haverstraw, Nyack, Piermont, South Nyack, Upper Nyack, and West Haverstraw; the Palisades Interstate Park Commission; and the County of Rockland. The council is organized under an intermunicipal agreement and is charged with exploring ways to obtain funding and carry out programs for conservation, development, and other land-use and water-related activities along the Hudson River. Its goals are to protect, enhance, and utilize the unique assets of the Hudson River; to enhance and promote historic preservation; to educate the public on environmental issues; to provide public access to the Hudson River where possible; to preserve and protect natural, historic, and cultural resources; and to encourage economic development that is sustainable.

The incentive funding provided to the RRCC was part of an experimental funding program initiated by the State of New York. In 2001, the state created the Quality Communities Demonstration Grant Program, offering $1.15 million on a competitive basis to local governments for their quality community, or smart growth, projects. The Department of State, which administers the program, made it clear that localities were more likely to receive grants if they joined with neighboring communities in developing smart growth strategies.

Over 180 applications were received, totaling over $17 million in requests, and over 80 percent of the applications were intermunicipal in nature.[32] This type of intermunicipal cooperation is unprecedented in New York and is attributed largely to the state's decision to make funding available on a priority basis to intermunicipal smart growth projects.

Local Action

Communities have a number of mechanisms they can use to connect the participants in land-use decision-making. Case studies[33] of citizen participation in local planning in the New York communities of Dover and Warwick are examples of effective public involvement in formulating comprehensive plans and land-use regulations. New York's planning enabling act stresses the importance of citizen participation in comprehensive planning in all cases and provides a special mechanism to ensure that all stakeholder groups may be involved in drafting the plan. It provides for the formation of a special board to prepare the plan involving one member of the local planning board, to which representatives of interest groups may be appointed, and requires the board to have meetings with the public at large.

Even with respect to controversial development projects, effective communication processes can be created between developers and those who will support and oppose their projects during the land-use review process. These techniques provide an opportunity for those involved to negotiate solutions face to face, rather than simply influence the adjudicative body as adversaries. In our work in the Hudson Valley, trained local land-use leaders have helped developers form concept committees involving the developer and community stakeholders. Local land-use laws have been amended to provide for a preapplication submission and process that does not trigger the time periods required by state or local law for the review and approval of the proposal. State enabling acts allow for the project review process to be put on hold for a short time while the applicant negotiates with interested parties.

The idea of a preapplication process was hotly resisted by developers, their counsel, and likely project opponents (the so-called NIMBYs). Over time, however, developers learned that they are not required to abandon their "as-of-right" development option by entering into the process, and neighbors learned that results might be achieved that were better than the likely outcome of a disputed administrative proceeding before the planning board. Several successful case studies are now available to demonstrate the benefits of this consensus-based approach.

• In the case of *Santa Margarita Area Residents Together v. San Luis Obispo County*,[34] all principal stakeholders affected by a proposal to develop the Santa Margarita Ranch participated in a preapplication mediation about the development. The mediation arrived at a consensus regarding the number and location of housing units, the preservation of agricultural land, and open space conservation easements. This became the basis for a development agreement between the developer and the county. The court upheld the agreement as valid, finding that the agreement retained the county's authority to exercise its discretion in approving the developer's application under existing zoning rules.

• In *Medeiros v. Hawaii County Planning Commission*,[35] the court enthusiastically endorsed mediation of a land-use dispute with these words: "[S]ince it allows the interested parties the opportunity to meet with the developers on a one-to-one basis and to attempt to resolve their differences, mediation may, as a practical matter, provide the residents and property owners with greater impact on the decision than a contested case."

• The concurring opinion by Justice Bryson in *Fasano v. Board of County Commissioners of Washington County*,[36] Supreme Court of Oregon, is also instructive: "The basic facts in this case exemplify the prohibitive cost and extended uncertainty to a homeowner when a government body decides to change or modify a zoning ordinance or comprehensive plan. . . . No average homeowner or small business enterprise can afford a judicial process such as described above nor can a judicial system cope with or endure such a process in achieving justice. The number of such controversies is ascending."

COALITION BUILDING AND POLITICAL REFORM

At the local, state, and federal levels, innovative land-use laws have been adopted that respond to the pressures of change in ways that integrate stakeholders at the local level, build on the competencies and resources of multiple levels of government, and exhibit successful approaches that suggest a strategic path toward the reform of our national land-use system. By looking at a few examples in a bit more depth, we can probe how these changes have happened and better understand how to emulate and encourage them.

Dover, New York

The Town of Dover sits along the eastern edge of New York's Hudson Valley at the northern boundary of the New York metropolitan area. A rural community with fewer than 10,000 residents, it is intersected by a large and critical freshwater wetland system and Route 22, a major state transportation arterial. It shares with its neighbors two distinct aquifers that supply much of the region's water.

With reasonable housing costs in a tight housing market, Dover has received an impressive number of applications for large residential subdivisions. The town is located to the north of, and just beyond, the New York City drinking water watershed where industrial land uses and facilities are strictly regulated by New York City's Department of Environmental Protection to protect the city's drinking water. This, coupled with its considerable sand and gravel resources, attracted many heavy industries, including mining and deposition businesses, to the town. These potential new land uses are perturbations: they pose a great threat to the community's aquifers and create traffic, produce schoolchildren and particulate contamination, and cause other impacts that are inconsistent with the town's rural and residential character.

These circumstances were anticipated by local leaders over a decade ago. In 1991, a committee with members from several stakeholder groups was appointed to revise the community's ancient comprehensive plan. At this early stage, Dutchess County's Planning Department encouraged town leaders to act, as did the staff of a county-wide land trust. Physical studies were done, a survey of town residents was completed, and the results were incorporated into the amended plan, adopted in 1993. A critical hydrogeological study completed by the town was funded by the Hudson River Valley Greenway Communities Council, a state agency charged with voluntary regional planning activities in the valley. In the new plan, the town committed itself to take a variety of actions to protect its natural resources and community character.

Because of continued intensive development pressures, the town board adopted a moratorium in 1997, which was drafted by land-use students working through a law school externship program, and defended the moratorium with help provided by a law school litigation clinic. In 1999, Dover adopted its new zoning and further amended its comprehensive plan to provide for greater protection of natural resources.

The new zoning ordinance included provisions for cluster development and resource conservation zones to preserve open space and discourage building where it would be incompatible with the landscape. Additionally, the new code created a Floodplain Overlay District, a Stream Corridor Overlay District, a Mixed Use Institutional Conversion Overlay District, and an Aquifer Overlay District.[37] The Aquifer Overlay District ultimately provided the solution that defeated a highly controversial proposed landfill proposal for a construction and demolition debris processing operation. A series of legal challenges against the town ensued; in each case, Dover's actions, which were defended by the law school clinic, were validated by the courts.

During the course of this process of citizen involvement, comprehensive plan revision, and zoning amendment, 11 of the community's leaders—elected and appointed board members and citizens—attended and graduated from the Land Use Leaders Alliance Training Program, an intensive four-day experience. The program, conducted by law school staff attorneys and funded in part by the Hudson River Valley Greenway Communities Council (a state agency), instructs participants on how to use the dozens of innovative land-use strategies authorized by state law. It also trains them in the process of community decision-making and on methods of bringing the community to consensus on how to resolve complex land-use issues and the tensions they inspire.

Warwick, New York

Warwick is located at the western edge of the New York metropolitan area, defined by rich farmland and rural vistas. The Ramapo Mountain range to its east served, until recently, as a barrier to sprawl. Historically, most of the settlers in the area resided in three incorporated villages within the town, with most of the land within the town's land-use jurisdiction devoted to farming or forests. The town's 1999 comprehensive plan states that, despite its rural past, its population is projected to increase by almost 30 percent between 1990 and 2005.[38]

As early as 1965, the town and its three villages were working together on land-use issues. In that year, they adopted a common comprehensive plan that articulated a shared vision for future land use. In 1987, that plan was amended in anticipation of further growth pressures and community change. By 1999, a new plan was adopted that reflected citizen goals for future growth as determined by public opinion polls, steering committee sessions, and informational meetings. In 1994, a grassroots coalition of Warwick citizens (known as Community 2000), who were concerned with further evidence of growth pressures, requested another review of the plan.

The local legislature responded by appointing a 17-member Master Plan Review Coordinating Committee in July 1994 to study the current plan and make recommendations for its revision; this was not done casually. Community 2000 hosted a series of public forums and town-wide meetings to engage the greater public in exercises designed to create a vision for the future of Warwick. Over 500 residents were involved by the citizens group and agreed, generally, that they wanted the town to retain its rural character, agricultural lands, and scenic beauty. Twenty-two leaders who emerged during this process were appointed to serve on the committee and were charged with making recommendations regarding a new land-use plan.

In 1995, the committee submitted its report to the town board, recommending actions to preserve the town's rural character and natural resources. Additional public hearings were held and, in 1997, the town formed a special comprehensive plan committee to begin preparing the new comprehensive plan. This board continued to involve the public and reached outside the community for help. It hosted regular public meetings and interviewed local, county, and state officials.

In 1997, Cornell University conducted a cost of services study, which showed the positive impact on the town budget of agricultural operations and the high cost to the town of low-density residential development. Cornell also assisted the town in interviewing farmers and found that 85 percent wished to remain in the agricultural business. Between 1997 and 1999, the town received four large grants from the New York State Department of Agriculture and Markets for the purchase of development rights on agricultural lands.

Beginning in 1997, leaders involved in the town's land-use planning were accepted as participants in the Land Use Leaders Alliance Training Program, exposing them to available legal strategies and community decision-making processes. By 2002, over a dozen local leaders had graduated from this four-day program, including members of the town board, zoning board of appeals, comprehensive plan committee, conservation advisory board, planning board, local developers, and citizen leaders.

In 1999, the town board adopted a new comprehensive plan, which clearly anticipated future land-use changes, described their detrimental impacts, and called for the adoption of a number of innovative land-use laws and strategies available to the town board. These included the adoption of a purchase of development rights program and a density transfer system, both aimed at preserving agricultural lands. A month later, the town board appointed a Citizen Code Revision Committee to draft regulations recommended by the plan.

Based on this considerable effort, Warwick was selected for a Countryside Exchange program by the Glynwood Center, a nonprofit organization that supports land preservation in rural areas. The program engaged seven experts in community planning, conservation, and economic development from several countries to review local policies and laws and make recommendations. Their findings confirmed that Warwick's current zoning code encouraged sprawl; they recommended remedial action.

In 2000, the town board placed an open space bond referendum on the town ballot. This followed an extensive study conducted by a law school land-use research team on the legal authority of municipalities in New York to use their financial authority to issue bonds for open space preservation purposes. The referendum was controversial in two of the three villages, whose residents wondered whether the benefits in the town were worth the tax increase within their villages, which were somewhat isolated from the agricultural lands to be preserved. The ballot passed by a very slim margin as a result of strong village opposition.

Following the election, village leaders threatened to challenge the ballot's legality, oppose applications for state grants, and in other ways derail the bond issue and open space plan. A law school mediator was engaged to resolve the dispute; by mid-2001, the town and its three villages reached a mutually acceptable agreement on the bond issue. The town agreed to allocate bond money ratably for village open space protection and the village leaders agreed to support farmland protection in the town.

The town board assumed control of the zoning review in early 2001, enacted a moratorium on subdivision review, received a $75,000 quality community grant from the Department of State, conducted a buildout analysis of the current zoning, secured the pro-bono legal assistance of a senior staff attorney from the Department of State, and, by December, adopted new zoning designed to effectuate the comprehensive plan's objectives. The new zoning contained several new districts, including a land conservation district, an agricultural protection overlay district, a ridgeline overlay district, a traditional neighborhood overlay district, and a senior housing floating zoning district. It also prescribed low-density or clustered development in rural areas and allowed for mixed uses in the town's hamlets.

In September 2002, the town received an Outstanding Planning Project Honorable Mention from the American Planning Association (APA) and a Quality Communities Award for Excellence from New York Governor George Pataki. In that same year, the Town and Village of Warwick signed an inter-municipal agreement regarding annexation. Assisted by a law school technical assistance program, village and town leaders agreed to adopt a floating zoning/incentive zoning system, which would allow annexation and provide developers in the annexed territory additional development density on the annexed land in exchange for significant cash payment. These funds were dedicated to additional land acquisition in the town that serves the village's watershed and viewshed areas.

New York State

In both Dover and Warwick, it was essential that local leaders understood the legal authority that they possessed to adopt effective land-use strategies to react to change. This sheds light on the role of the New York state legislature which, between 1990 and 2004, responded to this local need by adopting dozens of land-use law amendments that carefully organized, significantly clarified, and considerably expanded local land-use authority.

These changes in state land-use enabling laws were made incrementally, beginning with needed organizational changes and then moving on to more innovative matters. They were based on the input of citizens, local leaders, developers, and others affected by land-use decisions gleaned from numerous regional roundtables conducted by the legislature. Widespread concern regarding local land-use problems was instrumental in convincing reluctant legislators to take land-use law reform seriously.

Specific amendments were crafted by a carefully selected group of stakeholders, state agency representatives, practitioners, academics, local government representatives, and other land-use experts, assembled as the state Land Use Advisory Committee. The process was led by the Legislative Commission on Rural Resources, headed by a leading member of both the New York Senate and Assembly and staffed by an executive director skilled at consensus building. All bills were submitted to both houses at the same time on behalf of the bipartisan commission.

The first law recommended by the commission and adopted by the legislature clarified provisions regarding the adoption of a town or village's first zoning law.[39] This was adopted in 1990; four bills were passed in 1991. They concerned procedures for adopting land-use laws, the appointment and function of zoning boards of appeal, the standardization of criteria for the issuance of variances, joint appointments to local and county planning boards, and zoning incentives for developers in exchange for public benefits.

Twenty additional bills were enacted between 1992 and 1996, touching on the mundane and the exceptional. They included provisions that assist planning boards to properly calculate density when approving clustered subdivisions, guidance on the appointment of planning board members, and clarifications of the procedures and standards for site plan approval. During this time, amendments were added that encourage highly innovative, intermunicipal land-use planning, regulation, and enforcement; that allow planning boards to require developers to cluster lots in a subdivision; and that clearly explain the importance of comprehensive plans, their components, and the participation of the public in their creation.

Over a dozen new laws were adopted between 1997 and 2004, including provisions that clarify the authority of localities to adopt planned unit development ordinances, the formation of county planning boards and regional councils, and the formation of agricultural districts and their coordination with local zoning laws. Bills being considered in the current legislative session address intermunicipal tax sharing, mediation of land-use disputes, mandatory training for local planning and zoning board members, and provisions that encourage inclusionary zoning.

Wisconsin

Response to land-use crises, anticipation of future problems, and strategic coalition building are all evident in Wisconsin,[40] leading up to the adoption of its smart growth legislation in 1999.[41] The law requires Wisconsin municipalities that engage in actions that affect land use to adopt comprehensive plans by 2010. The plan requires these local plans to contain nine enumerated elements. Grants are authorized to local governments to prepare and implement their land-use plans, but eligibility for grants is limited to communities whose plans evidence intergovernmental cooperation, identify smart growth areas, contain implementation plans, and address 14 planning goals articulated by the state. Interestingly, the law engages the University of Wisconsin to develop model laws for local adoption.

This bill is traceable to events that began in the mid-1990s, which involved a citizens group, two industry groups, the influence of judicial decisions, an academic institution, the governor, and the state legislature. Armed with traditional land-use authority, local governments in Wisconsin were unprepared for the economic boom and increased development pressures in the early and mid-1990s. In some cases, their actions were exclusionary, rejecting affordable housing and mixed-use development decisions. Based on state law at the time, two controversial decisions of this type were sustained by the courts.[42]

These decisions alerted the Wisconsin Builders Association and the Wisconsin Realtors Association of the need for improved planning legislation and motivated them to work with more traditional advocates for land-use reform. 1000 Friends of Wisconsin, an environmental advocacy group, got involved because of increasing citizen complaints about local land-use decisions from local citizens.

Republican Governor Tommy Thompson responded in 1994 by issuing Executive Order No. 236, which created the State Interagency Land Use Council.[43] The council's charge was to develop a renewed vision for land use in Wisconsin, recommend consistent land-use policy objectives for state agencies, and establish a framework for state agency participation in land-use discussions currently under discussion by other state-level bodies. The council created the Wisconsin Strategic Growth Task Force and the governor appointed a former head of the Wisconsin Realtors Association as its chair—a leader who had strong personal interest in land-use issues and saw the task force as a mechanism to broadly address land-use decision-making. Also appointed to the council were homebuilders, environmentalists, real estate professionals, academics, land-use experts, and state and local government officials.

The task force issued a final report on July 1, 1996.[44] It concluded that primary responsibility for land use should remain at the local level but that the state needed to encourage and guide local land-use planning. It recommended that the state create a multilevel land-use framework to produce comprehensive plans and implementation programs including intergovernmental cooperation, mandatory adoption of comprehensive plans, and mandatory compliance of land-use laws with land-use plans. The council also recommended that the University of Wisconsin should be involved in accomplishing these land-use objectives.

The university then initiated a broad-based, consensus-building effort. Included in the planning group were the Wisconsin Town's Association, Wisconsin Builders Association, Wisconsin Alliance of Cities, Wisconsin Counties Association, Wisconsin Realtor's Association, Wisconsin Road Builders Association, Wisconsin Chapter of the APA, 1000 Friends of Wisconsin, and others. The governor agreed that, if the group could come to consensus on a framework for land-use decision-making, he would support and advance their recommendations. After a series of meetings, the recommendations ultimately contained in the smart growth legislation were framed into a proposed bill and submitted to the governor.

The bill was presented to the Joint Finance Committee of the Wisconsin legislature, which then took several months to review and negotiate its provisions. Reports were that the Republican members of the committee would oppose the bill on property rights grounds. Task force members friendly with these opponents gradually worked out an agreement designed to preserve their positions without compromising the essential components of the proposed legislation.

The result of this collaboration between the coalition and members of the legislature resulted in the passage of Wisconsin's smart growth legislation. Since it was adopted, approximately 100 municipalities have completed work on their comprehensive plans and another 600 communities are in the process of formulating and adopting theirs. The state has awarded nearly $1 million in planning grants to support these activities.[45]

Opposition to the legislation has come from property rights groups and some municipalities. Bills submitted to the legislature to repeal the law have been blocked and legitimate local concerns responded to through legislative amendments. The result of the coalition's process and consensus has been to convert land-use reform opponents to supporters of land-use planning while remaining responsive to legitimate concerns and difficulties experienced.

CONCLUSIONS: WHAT DIRECTION FOR LAND-USE LAW REFORM?

These stories from the local, state, and federal levels depict stakeholders in the land-use system organizing themselves in the process of law reform. This was the case in Dover's aquifer protection overlay zone, Warwick's annexation zoning, Wisconsin's smart growth legislation, New York's recodification effort, Utah's regional planning process, and the federal CZMA—paradigms of positive change. In all cases, the ethic of local control persists as a dominant force and an anchoring concept.

When our federal republic was formed, there was no evidence of national or state land-use control—only local, based on an ancient tradition derived from the medieval municipal corporation. In our colonial, preindustrial, industrial, and modern eras, the legacy of localism prevailed. Federal and state reform efforts need to redouble their efforts to provide broad authority to local governments; build the capacity of local officials to develop, adopt, and implement strategies appropriate to their circumstances; and guide local energies so that state and federal interests are achieved.

In Wisconsin, we observe realtors, developers, local officials, and environmentalists who are working to understand what is needed in the 21st century, given the state's historical reliance on local control. They engaged in a serious and protracted process of inquiring whether their individual group's self-interest could be promoted while accommodating those of the other stakeholders. In the end, they not only found an answer—a change in the system that reformed it in a positive way—but they built a continuing coalition that is tending to the reform and adjusting it to meet coalition members' interests in the implementation stage. Reform efforts need to be patient in this way, include all stakeholders, encourage them to seek mutually beneficial solutions, and, in the process of deliberating, seek solutions that would not be possible without the resources and commitment of them all.

Obvious parallels to the Wisconsin story are seen in the Land Use Advisory Council in New York, the powerful grassroots coalitions within the towns of Dover and Warwick, and among the communities cooperating in the RRCC. Additional connected networks of leaders are gradually organizing within other municipalities and among adjacent communities in New York's Hudson Valley, where they have been encouraged to collaborate by being trained together and provided incentives for such positive behavior under grant programs of two state agencies (the Department of State and the Hudson River Valley Greenway Communities Council).

Productive connections are being created between state and local governments in a host of ways as state policies and local authority are clarified and local governments are assisted in addressing local problems (e.g., soil erosion in Michigan, Iowa, and Connecticut; and habitat protection in Washington). In Maine, Wisconsin, Minnesota, and Oregon, local governments are either encouraged or required to define urban growth boundaries and support proper land uses there, changing the historical pattern of land development spawned by Euclidian zoning. In Illinois, Massachusetts, and New York, local land-use leaders are being trained and are provided technical assistance under programs established or funded by state agencies. State and federal agencies and universities are helping by distributing best management practices and exemplary local ordinances to local leaders alerted to the possible dangers of change.

Through reforms like these, which test and settle proper roles, build vertical and horizontal connections, and increase the rate of effective communication, we are learning slowly how to knit together our national land-use system through law reform.

JOHN R. NOLON NOTES

1. See Henry R. Richmond, *From Sea to Shining Sea: Manifest Destiny and the National Land Use Dilemma*, 13 Pace L. Rev. 327, 329-30 (1993).
2. See John R. Nolon, *National Land Use Planning: Revisiting Senator Jackson's 1970 Policy Act*, Land Use Law & Zoning Digest, Vol. 48, No. 5 (May 1996), at 4.
3. *Lucas v. South Carolina Coastal Council*, 112 S.Ct. 2886 (1992).
4. See John R. Nolon, *Footprints in the Shifting Sands of the Isle of Palms: A Practical Analysis of Regulatory Takings Cases*, J. Land Use & Envtl. L., Florida State University College of Law, Vol. 8., No. 1 (Fall 1992), n. 58, at 10.
5. See John R. Nolon, *In Praise of Parochialism: The Advent of Local Environmental Law*, 26 Harv. Envtl. L. Rev. 365, 366-372 (2002).
6. See Henry L. Diamond and Patrick F. Noonan, *Land Use in America* (Chicago: Island Press, 1996).
7. Id. at 100.
8. See 16 U.S.C.A. § 1451(b), (h) (2004).
9. See 16 U.S.C.A. § 1452(2) (2004).

10. See John R. Nolon, *Grassroots Regionalism Through Intermunicipal Compacts*, 73 St. John's L. Rev. 1011, 1034 (1999).

11. Waterfronts Florida Partnership Program, Florida Department of Community Affairs, Division of Community Planning (http://www.dca.state.fl.us/fdcp/dcp/waterfronts/index.cfm) (visited Oct. 21, 2004).

12. Waterfront Redevelopment, Michigan Department of Environmental Quality (http://www.michigan.gov/deq/0,1607,7-135-3311_4110_4229-11504--,00.html) (visited Oct. 21, 2004).

13. See Washington State Department of Ecology, Coastal Zone Management Grants (http://www.ecy.wa.gov/programs/sea/grants/czm/index.html).

14. Wis. Stat. § 66.1027 (2004).

15. River Falls, Wisconsin, Municipal Code, Chapter 117.112, "Traditional Neighborhood Development."

16. See, e.g., Ann Arbor, Mich., Title V Zoning and Planning, Chapter 63, "Stormwater Management and Soil Erosion and Sedimentation Control," § 5.650.

17. Iowa Code § 161A.1 et seq. (2003).

18. Conn. Gen. Stat. § 8-2(a) (2003).

19. 20 Ill. Comp. Stat. Ann. 662/5 (2004).

20. Id. at 662/15.

21. Mass. Gen. Laws Ann., Chapter 23B, § 3 (West, 2004).

22. Massachusetts Citizen Planner Training Collaborative (http://www.umass.edu/masscptc/about.html) (visited Oct. 21, 2004).

23. Wash. Rev. Code § 36.70A (2004).

24. Id. at § 36.70A.045.

25. Utah Code Ann. § 11-38-101 et seq. (2004).

26. See Envision Utah (http://www.envisionutah.org) (visited Nov. 1, 2004).

27. Or. Rev. Stat. §§ 197.005 (2003); see also Henry R. Richmond, *From Sea to Shining Sea: Manifest Destiny and the National Land Use Dilemma,* 13 Pace L. Rev. 327, 338-41 (1993).

28. The ballot title and text of Measure 37 are available at the Web site of the Oregon Secretary of State (http://www.sos.state.or.us/elections/nov22004/guide/meas/m37.html). Measure 37 is entitled "Governments must pay owners, or forgo enforcement, when certain land-use restrictions reduce property value." The summary of the measure contained on the ballot reads: "Currently, Oregon Constitution requires government(s) to pay owner 'just compensation' when condemning private property or taking it by other action, including laws precluding all substantial beneficial or economically viable use. Measure enacts statute requiring that when state, county, metropolitan service district enacts or enforces land-use regulation that restricts use of private property or interests therein, government must pay owner reduction in fair market value of affected property interest, or forgo enforcement."

29. Nelson Wikstrom, *Councils of Governments: A Study of Political Incrimination* (Chicago: Nelson-Hall, 1977), at 130-131.

30. See N.Y. Town Law § 284 (Supp. 1996); N.Y. Village Law § 7-741; and N.Y. Gen. City Law § 20g (Supp. 1996).

31. The 1993 amendments modified N.Y. Gen. Mun. Law §§ 119-u, 239-d, as well as N.Y. Gen. City Law § 20-g, N.Y. Town Law § 284, and N.Y. Village Law § 7-741 (McKinney 2004).

32. Telephone interview with Carmella Mantello, Assistant Secretary of State (May 2, 2000).

33. John R. Nolon, *Golden and Its Emanations: The Surprising Origins of Smart Growth*, 35 Urb. Law. 15, 36, 44 (Winter 2003), No. 1.

34. 100 Cal. Rptr.2d 740 (2000).

35. 8 Haw. App. 183, 797 P.2d 59 (1990).

36. 507 P.2d 23 (Ore. 1973).

37. Town of Dover, N.Y., Zoning Law (adopted April 29, 1999).

38. See §§ 1.1 and 1.2 of Town of Warwick, N.Y., "Comprehensive Plan" (adopted Aug. 19, 1999).

39. N.Y.S. Legislative Commission on Rural Resources, Senator Patricia K. McGee, Chair, *Community Planning & Land Development Laws Enacted 1990-2003.*

40. See Brian Ohm, *Reforming Land Planning Legislation at the Dawn of the 21st Century: The Emerging Influence of Smart Growth and Livable Communities,* 32 Urb. Law. 181, 206 (2000).

41. Wis. Stat. § 66.1001 (West, 2004); A.B. 133, Gen. Assem., 1999 Reg. Sess. (Wis. 1999).

42. See *Lake Bluff Hous. Partners v. City of South Milwaukee,* 540 N.W.2d 189 (Wis. 1995); *Lake City Corp. v. City of Mequon,* 558 N.W.2d 100 (Wis. 1997).

43. State of Wisconsin, Office of the Governor, Exec. Order No. 236 (Sept. 15, 1994).

44. State of Wisconsin, State Interagency Land Use Council, *Planning Wisconsin: Report of the Interagency Land Use Council to Governor Tommy Thompson* (July 1, 1996).

45. State of Wisconsin, Department of Administration, Office of Land Information Services (http://doa.wi.gov) (visited Oct. 26, 2004).

2

Planning Reform in the New Century —A Century Ago

Fred Bosselman

In 1904, many people were making plans for the new century. As a way of commenting on some of the papers being delivered here in 2004, I thought it might be useful to talk for a few minutes about the context of planning a century ago.

It was the formative years of the progressive movement[1] and the heyday of the City Beautiful movement.[2] Teddy Roosevelt had just been elected president,[3] and here in Missouri Joseph W. Folk had been elected governor on a reform platform.[4] Optimism about the new century was in plentiful supply,[5] particularly here at Washington University, which in 1903 had just celebrated the 50th anniversary of its founding.[6]

St. Louis is an appropriate venue to discuss the status of planning in 1904. The Louisiana Purchase Exposition (otherwise known as the St. Louis World's Fair) was in progress. Included in the fair was a Congress of Arts and Scholars, an assembly of domestic and foreign scholars that was called "the most notable assembly of scholars the modern world had seen."[7]

Unlike its predecessor in Chicago a decade earlier, the St. Louis fair focused not just on spectacular buildings but on local streetscapes and model parks.[8] Working with Albert Kelsey on the design of the fair was a young landscape architect named John Nolen, who went on to become one of the leaders of the city planning movement that developed towards the end of that decade.[9] Frank Lloyd Wright, who was completing what many call his first masterpiece, the Larkin building in Buffalo,[10] was one of those who was influenced by designs that he had seen at the fair.[11] President Roosevelt, who was promoting conservation and setting aside large stretches of federal land for protection,[12] visited the fair and called it "a perfect whirl."[13]

Planning of that period often emphasized the construction of parks and public buildings.[14] In 1904, a citizens' committee in St. Louis recommended the planning of a civic center. Three years later, the first city plan for St. Louis was presented, and it was one of the first to stress concepts like neighborhood development and waterfront renewal, not just grandiose civic centers.[15] On the other side of the state, George Kessler was in the midst of developing his highly regarded plans for the Kansas City park system.[16]

In 1904, city planning was beginning to take hold in many parts of the country. Daniel Burnham's new Union Station in Washington opened that year—the centerpiece of a revision of the old L'Enfant plan.[17] Burnham himself was in San Francisco in 1904 working on a visionary plan for that city—a plan that unfortunately was shelved two years later after the earthquake.[18] Philadelphia mapped plans for the famous Franklin Parkway and surrounding museums and parks in 1904.[19] In that same year, the New York City Improvement Commission issued its preliminary report on a plan for the city, which culminated in their proposed plan three years later.[20] In addition, Dwight Perkins prepared a park plan for Chicago in 1904 that was eventually largely incorporated in Burnham's plan five years later.[21]

Coinciding with the interest in the city beautiful was the beginning of concern about the conditions in which poor urban residents lived.[22] Books such as *The Tenement House Problem*, published in 1903,[23] reflected conditions exposed by Jane Addams and other activists in the settlement house movement.[24] In 1904, the New York Court of Appeals upheld the constitutionality of a city ordinance that required existing tenement houses to install flush toilets.[25] The extension of water and sewer systems brought major advances in sanitation.[26] Some economists began to see the need for incorporation of the ideas of the progressive movement into classical economics; Richard T. Ely's *Studies in the Evolution of Industrial Society* was published in 1903.[27]

In England, Ebenezer Howard was combining social and aesthetic ambitions in his ideas for garden cities. The first garden city, Letchworth, was under construction in 1904.[28] In that same year, Patrick Geddes, who became one of the intellectual leaders of planning, prepared his first city plan in Britain.[29]

In the United States, lawyers and planners were beginning to emulate the kinds of regulatory measures that Europeans had long used to place limits on private development.[30] Regulation of nuisance-type uses had been prevalent in the United States in the 19th century,[31] but now cities began to implement more widespread building controls.[32] Boston adopted its first general height limits in 1904, later to be upheld by the Supreme Court.[33] By 1904, Chicago had covered much of the city with a network of frontage consent ordinances that restricted uses in residential neighborhoods. (When they were later stricken by the courts, it led to the beginning of the zoning movement.)[34]

The intellectual legal foundation for such regulations was cemented in 1904 with the publication of Ernst Freund's magnificent treatise *The Police Power.*[35] "A vast amount of police legislation is justified on" the preservation of life, health, and property, Freund wrote, "and the state is readily conceded more incisive powers than despotic governments would have dared to claim in former times."[36] His treatise became the leading authority for decades and Freund himself became a powerful advocate for the city planning movement.[37]

The book that has been characterized as the bible of the new planning movement[38]—Charles Mulford Robinson's *Modern Civic Art, or the City Made Beautiful*—had just been published in 1903.[39] Although it was not until 1909 that the idea of a national city planning movement coalesced in the form of the first national conference on city planning,[40] the separate strands that formed the movement were already widely evident by 1904.

The first five years of the 20th century were a time of great technological change for cities as railroads brought industrialization throughout the country.[41] Electricity was being widely distributed in urban areas.[42] Mass transit systems were under construction in many cities.[43] The automobile was no longer an eccentric toy—a hit song of 1905 would have people singing, "Come away with me Lucille in my merry Oldsmobile"[44] and the discovery of huge oil fields in the southwest was making its use affordable.[45]

At the St. Louis World's Fair, crowds oohed and aahed at the magnificent displays of electric light, and a competition for a hundred thousand dollar "grand prize for aeronautical achievement" attracted "metallic lighter-than-air cylinders, pterodactyl-like contraptions flapping bamboo wings, aluminum and silk sky-cycles, and huge cigars and saucers and tetrahedrons that defied gravity with varying success ..." but failed to win the proffered prize.[46]

These technologies created a feeling of the inevitability of "progress" that was pervasive during the first few years of the 20th century.[47] Of course, the stock market crash of 1907 and the war of the next decade tempered that optimism, and we now know that the course of planning in the United States has not been smooth. Although planning accomplished a great deal during the last century, today some people blame inadequate planning for pollution, social anomie, energy imbalance, urban sprawl, and many other difficulties that today's Americans endure.[48]

We should ask ourselves: Have the weaknesses of the planning system that existed in the 20th century been ameliorated, giving us grounds for a revival of optimism about the future of 21st century planning? A complete analysis of that question would far exceed the scope of my task here today. So I will close by citing what I believe to be two of the biggest problems that overwhelmed last century's planning.

1. When people in 1904 thought about planning, they were thinking about plans for public works. However, city planners soon lost out to the civil engineers in the battle for control of public works. At the city level, at least, the planners ended up being the people who tried to rein in the private development that followed the public projects that the engineers planned and built. Gradually, that problem has been ameliorated, at least in some metropolitan areas, by regional institutions that both planned and built the major regional infrastructure such as highways, sewers, ports, and airports, but it is still a struggle in many places in this country.

2. Some 35 years ago, Norman Williams wrote a short article that concisely summed up a roadblock to successful planning that existed in 1904 and remains in 2004.[49] He summarized his argument in his treatise on *American Land Planning Law*. "The dominant role of the local real property tax system in American land-use controls must be clearly understood," he wrote.[50] Because "different types of land use vary widely both in the tax revenue they produce and in the services required by their occupants, the financial consequences of any proposed land use are a matter of real importance to the municipality."[51]

This week's issue of *The Economist*[52] highlights the consistent failure of litigation that has tried to fight the pattern of educational discrimination brought about by the property tax system. Despite decisions by a significant number of state supreme courts holding the present system unconstitutional, there has been little progress in reaching agreement on alternatives. If we could make progress in this area, and remove the incentive for municipal government to base their planning policies on fiscal considerations, we would greatly increase the chances of success for planning in the new century.

In regard to the first of these two issues, I can share some of John Nolon's optimism (see Chapter 1) that we now have the tools that facilitate effective local planning; in regard to the second issue, I am afraid I share the frustration of Ricca Slone (another speaker at the conference) with the inability of legislatures to resolve such contentious issues.

FRED BOSSELMAN NOTES

1. N. E. H. Hull, Roscoe Pound, and Karl Llewellyn, *Searching for an American Jurisprudence* (Chicago: University of Chicago Press, 1997), 28-31.
2. See William H. Wilson, "The Ideology, Aesthetics and Politics of the City Beautiful Movement," in Anthony Sutcliffe, ed., *The Rise of Modern Urban Planning, 1800-1914* (New York: St. Martin's Press, 1980), 165 [hereinafter "Wilson" with page reference].
3. Edmund Morris, *Theodore Rex* (New York: Random House, 2001), 363 [hereinafter "Morris" with page reference].
4. Stephen L. Piott, *Holy Joe: Joseph W. Folk and the Missouri Idea* (Columbia, MO: University of Missouri Press, 1998).
5. Wilson, 174-75.
6. Donald W. Meinig, *The Shaping of America: A Geographical Perspective on 500 Years of History, Vol. 3* (New Haven: Yale University Press, 1998), 318.

7. Howard Mumford Jones, *The Age of Energy: Varieties of American Experience, 1865-1915* (New York: Viking Press, 1971), 280.
8. Mel Scott, *American City Planning Since 1890: A History Commemorating the Fiftieth Anniversary of the American Institute of Planners* (Berkeley: University of California Press, 1969), 69-71 [hereinafter "Scott" with page reference]; John E. Burchard and Albert Bush-Brown, *The Architecture of America: A Social and Cultural History* (Boston: Little, Brown & Company, 1961), 274 [hereinafter "Burchard/Bush-Brown" with page reference].
9. Scott, 69-71.
10. Burchard/Bush-Brown, 260-62, 291.
11. Ada Louise Huxtable, *Frank Lloyd Wright* (New York: Viking Adult Books, 2004), 78.
12. Samuel Eliot Morison, *The Oxford History of the American People* (New York: Oxford University Press, 1965), 819-20.
13. Morris, 367.
14. Wilson, 166-169.
15. M. Christine Boyer, *Dreaming the Rational City: The Myth of American City Planning* (Cambridge, MA: MIT Press, 1983), 23, 51-52; Richard E. Fogelsong, *Planning the Capitalist City: The Colonial Era to the 1920s* (Princeton, NJ: Princeton University Press, 1986), 160-161 [hereinafter "Fogelsong" with page reference]; Scott, 73.
16. Scott, 13-15; Fogelsong, 113-14, 122; Wilson, 165, 167.
17. Burchard/Bush-Brown, 277.
18. Fogelsong, 154-56; Scott, 64-65.
19. Scott, 60.
20. Scott, 57; Fogelsong, 159.
21. Scott, 100-102.
22. Delores Hayden, *Redesigning the American Dream: Gender, Housing and Family Life* (2d ed.) (New York: W. W. Norton, 2002), 36-39 [hereinafter "Hayden" with page reference].
23. Robert W. DeForest and Lawrence Veiller, *The Tenement House Problem* (New York: Macmillan, 1903).
24. Hayden, 46-48.
25. *Tenement House Dept. of the City of New York v. Moeschen*, 179 N.Y. 325, 72 N.E. 231 (1904).
26. Sam Bass Warner, Jr., *The Urban Wilderness: A History of the American City* (New York: Harper and Row, 1972), 25-27 [hereinafter "Warner" with page reference].
27. Richard T. Ely, *Studies in the Evolution of Industrial Society* (New York: The Macmillan Company, 1903). See also Morton J. Horwitz, *The Transformation of American Law 1870-1960* (New York: Oxford University Press, 1992), 165-167.
28. Dugald MacFayden, *Sir Ebenezer Howard and the Town Planning Movement* (Manchester: Manchester University Press, 1970), 43; Fogelsong, 184-85.
29. Helen Meller, "Cities and Evolution: Patrick Geddes as an International Prophet of Town Planning Before 1914," in Anthony Sutcliffe, ed., *The Rise of Modern Urban Planning, 1800-1914* (New York: St. Martin's Press, 1980), 199, 200.
30. See, e.g., Benjamin C. Marsh, *An Introduction to City Planning: Democracy's Challenge to the American City* (New York: privately printed, 1909).
31. See generally William J. Novak, *The People's Welfare: Law and Regulation in Nineteenth-Century America* (Chapel Hill: University of North Carolina Press, 1996).
32. Scott, 75.
33. *Welch v. Swasey*, 214 U.S. 91 (1909).
34. Fred P. Bosselman, *The Commodification of "Nature's Metropolis": The Historical Context of Illinois' Unique Zoning Standards*, 12 N. Ill. U. L. Rev. 527, 570-572 (1992).
35. Ernst Freund, *The Police Power: Public Policy and Constitutional Rights* (Chicago: Callaghan & Co., 1904), 109.
36. Id.

37. Seymour Toll, *Zoned American* (New York: Grossman, 1969), 137-139.

38. Wilson, 171.

39. Charles Mulford Robinson, *Modern Civic Art, or the City Made Beautiful* (New York and London: PG Putnam's Sons, 1903).

40. Scott, 95.

41. Burchard/Bush-Brown, 295; Warner, 88-92.

42. Warner, 85-86. See generally Harold L. Platt, *The Electric City* (Chicago: University of Chicago Press, 1991).

43. Warner, 33-34.

44. Clay McShane, *The Automobile* (Westport, CT: Greenwood Publications, 1997), 19-39.

45. Fred Bosselman, Jim Rossi, and Jacqueline Weaver, *Energy, Economics and the Environment* (New York: Foundation Press, 2000), 317-18.

46. Morris, 365.

47. Wilson, 174-75.

48. See, e.g., Dolores Hayden, *A Field Guide to Sprawl* (New York: W. W. Norton & Company, 2004), 16.

49. Norman Williams, *The Three Systems of Land Use Control*, 25 Rutgers L. Rev. 80 (1970).

50. Norman Williams, Jr., and John M. Taylor, *American Land Planning Law* (St. Paul, MN: Thomson-West, 1988).

51. Id.

52. "Who needs a bad teacher when you can get a worse judge?" *The Economist*, Nov. 25, 2004 (http://www.economist.com/printedition/displayStory.cfm?Story_ID=3429003).

3

Notes on Planning Statute Reform in the United States: Guideposts for the Road Ahead

Stuart Meck

INTRODUCTION: GETTING INVOLVED WITH DANGER

Urban planners should stop fooling around with trivialities and instead get involved with danger, the late Kevin Lynch, the preeminent theorist on city form, is reputed to have declared. I recalled Lynch's advice one Sunday afternoon in September 2004. I sat in the auditorium of Wilmette Junior High School where the local League of Women Voters for Chicago's North Shore was sponsoring a symposium on the new Affordable Housing Planning and Appeal Act[1] that the Illinois General Assembly had enacted the previous year, much to my surprise. The auditorium was nearly full and not everyone was as pleased as I was that the law, which I had helped draft, had passed.[2]

The act was based on a model statute contained in the *Growing Smart[SM] Legislative Guidebook*[3] (hereinafter "the Guidebook") by the American Planning Association (APA), for which I served as the principal investigator and general editor. The Guidebook model was in turn an adaptation of the housing appeals laws of three New England states. These laws provide a vehicle to appeal directly—either to a state-level board (in Massachusetts and Rhode Island) or to a court (in Connecticut)—local decisions either denying or imposing unreasonable conditions on affordable housing projects when the local government did not have a minimum percentage of low- and moderate-income housing.[4]

Nick Brunick, an attorney with a Chicago-based public interest group, Business and Professional People in the Public Interest, had done most of the initial drafting. I had helped out Brunick on two sections: the procedures for calculating what constituted affordable housing and the housing plan requirement. I will address these below because they are a departure from the appeals laws of the other states, and they represent part of the topic of this article, which is the philosophy that should guide planning statute reform in the U.S.

The focus of the League of Women Voters symposium was about what the North Shore municipalities should do about the law, since all of them—with the exclusion of the City of Evanston, which has a diverse housing stock—had not been exempted from its application. A group called New Trier Neighbors wanted to fight the law in court or get it repealed.[5] The Neighbors were at the symposium in force and they cast a mood of brooding menace (much grumbling and sullen arm crossing, accompanied by the setting of jaws).

A flyer distributed by the group—stacks were set out by a table outside the auditorium—warned that the law was "an unfunded state mandate" and predicted that compliance costs "will be in the hundreds of millions of dollars." Residents of the new affordable housing, assuming it would be built, would be "forcibly evicted" if their household income rose above the affordability levels, the flyer claimed. The law was about "takeover of local zoning and the unjustified usurpation of local government authority."[6]

A Chicago-area attorney, Ronald Cope, had written an article[7] deriding the law and contending that it usurped local zoning authority. Cope stated that the law "appears to be a continuation of the social agenda embarked upon in the *Metropolitan Housing [Development Corporation v. Village of Arlington Heights*[8]] case,"[9] a decision in which the U.S. Supreme Court ruled that proof of racially discriminatory intent or purpose was necessary to show a violation of the Constitution's equal protection clause. Interestingly, Cope recognized that the Illinois General Assembly, in the new law, had "mandated municipalities to engage in affirmative action toward integration,"[10] integration that presumably was *both* racial and economic. "Whether it is necessary to have integrated housing in well-to-do suburbs is a policy issue which should be clearly framed and then decided by the state legislature." The act, he wrote, "serves a particular social agenda at the expense of the authority of local government, particularly in the sensitive area of zoning."[11]

The symposium featured Cope, state senator Jeff Schoenberg (a co-sponsor of the law),[12] Nick Brunick, Gail Schecter (an affordable housing advocate), and the presidents of the village boards of trustees of Wilmette, Winnetka, and Glencoe—all North Shore communities that were nearly built out. Cope reiterated the arguments in his article, contending the act was a "bad law," to the applause of the New Trier Neighbors and their allies.

The big surprise was the attitude of the village board presidents. Wilmette's president indicated that her village clearly intended to comply with the law and had taken steps to complete a housing plan. She acknowledged that it was difficult to find affordable housing in Wilmette but that the village was committed to diversity. While they were uncomfortable about the law, concerned about lack of guidance from the Illinois Housing Finance Agency (which had responsibilities for the law's administration), and questioned how affordable housing could be constructed in areas where the housing prices and property values were so high, the presidents of Glencoe and Winnetka still indicated that their villages would take steps to comply, albeit grudgingly, and prepare housing plans. Other local governments on the North Shore, they stated, were probably going to comply as well.

For me, the symposium had a satisfactory, even optimistic conclusion.[13] I left thinking about the significance of what I had heard, particularly with respect to my task in preparing this article. The state legislature decided to make affordable housing and how local zoning codes provide for it a statewide issue. A narrowly drafted law, with a high-minded purpose, is passed that seemed to sidestep the substantive and procedural land mines of similar statutes in other states. Despite some unpleasantness by the law's opponents, local elected officials in several affected communities stated their commitment to implementation. Democracy, I presumed, was working its rough magic.

We have had more than eight decades of experience with state enabling legislation for planning and land use in this country, and we certainly recognize the problems with it. The Illinois Affordable Housing Planning and Appeal Act is just one part of that experience. What central themes emerge from the assessment of this law and the others that states have enacted to manage the planning and use of land? What do we know and how can we apply what we know to the challenges of the future? Should we start, as Kevin Lynch suggested, by getting involved with danger, and tackling tough, politically sensitive issues like siting affordable housing in well-to-do suburbs?

The remainder of this article will cover three topics:

1. The evolution of planning statute reform in the U.S. through the classification into three periods;

2. An assessment of what recent planning statute reform has accomplished, as gauged by academic research; and

3. A discussion of a philosophy that should guide contemporary planning statute reform efforts.

THE THREE PERIODS OF PLANNING
STATUTE REFORM IN THE U.S.

Planning statute reform in the United States can be roughly divided into three periods, with each period signifying a different view of the responsibilities of state and local government and their respective interests.[14] The boundaries of these periods are fuzzy and, arguably, something that occurred in one period can be credited to another. The discussion below is about central themes or trends; notes at the end of this chapter refer the reader to additional monographs and journal articles on specific state programs.

The Standard Acts and Their Progeny

The Standard State Zoning Enabling Act (SZEA) and the Standard City Planning Enabling Act (SCPEA) (together, "the Standard Acts"),[15] drafted by an advisory committee of the U.S. Department of Commerce under Secretary Herbert Hoover, formed the bases for most of the state enabling acts in this nation. The SZEA was drafted during the period 1922 to 1926. The SCPEA appeared in an interim form in 1927 and was published in a final version in 1928.

The SZEA authorized municipal governments to zone, required the local legislative body to establish a temporary zoning commission to advise it on the initial development of the zoning regulations (where there was an existing city planning commission, it could serve as the zoning commission), and set up a board of zoning adjustment that would authorize hardship variances and grant special exceptions. It also included provisions for enforcement.

The SCPEA covered six subjects:

1. Establishment of the municipal planning commission, which was empowered to prepare and adopt the master plan;

2. A description of the master plan (in the SCPEA, a zoning plan was to be part of the master plan);

3. Provision of adoption of a master street plan and subsequent control of building in mapped but unopened streets;

4. Control of land subdivision;

5. Provision for approval by the planning commission of public improvements before approval by the legislative body (although the SCPEA permitted an override of commission vetoes); and

6. Provisions for the creation of a regional planning commission, for the making of a regional plan, and for the adoption of that plan by any municipality in the region that desired to do so.

As Professor Mandelker has observed,[16] the SZEA built carefully on the nuisance concept in land-use cases, and its drafters noted that the courts draw lines to determine the established residential districts, which are protected from invading offensive uses. In large measure, the SZEA was less about planning for land use and more about the segregation of land uses in an urban or urbanizing setting. Indeed, it treated land use as an urban and a local issue, with no regard for land use in rural areas or for the larger regional setting of the municipal government. The fact that the U.S. Department of Commerce tackled zoning first was an indicator of its priority and the SZEA was more popular than the SCPEA. The U.S. Department of Commerce tracked the SZEA's adoption and, by 1930, the department could report that 35 states had adopted legislation based on it.

There were at least three motivations in drafting the Standard Acts. The first two were clear and the third somewhat less apparent, even though it too was framed with an ostensible concern for orderly growth and protection of property values. The first motivation was to respond to the tremendous growth boom after World War I, when many American cities, particularly those on the east coast, were literally being reconstructed as a consequence. Business and political leadership in American cities wanted to reach for something to respond to perceived overbuilding and sharp land-use conflicts during the boom years of the 1920s. Commerce Secretary Hoover believed that American cities needed the tools to manage this growth and protect investments in homes without violating property rights—hence his support for planning and zoning.

The second motivation was to establish a uniform national framework for zoning at a time when zoning was being challenged in federal and state courts. In the early 1920s, no one knew for certain whether zoning was constitutional. The drafters of the SZEA knew that a threshold issue would be whether the delegation of power to local units of government was an express one, even in states where municipalities received their authority from constitutional, as opposed to statutory home rule, authority. Thus, it was important that states specifically delegate the power to plan and regulate land use in order that the lack of delegation could not be the basis for a court voiding a local government's zoning ordinance.

The last motivation was a desire to exclude—no question about it—and create a legal framework for exclusion, disguised in use segregation, with the single-family home at the top of the zoning hierarchy. Some of the exclusionary intent was racial, and some was related to a burgeoning immigrant population in metropolitan areas and the prospect that immigrants would live in tenements and apartments.[17]

The period after World War I was a time of escalation in anti-immigrant sentiment in the U.S. To some degree, this was part of the political context for the rapid spread of zoning. In response to the anti-immigration movement, Congress enacted two immigration laws, one in 1921 and the other in 1924. They set quotas for nationality groups based on their percentage of the American population as of 1910 and 1890, respectively. The 1921 law was an interim measure fixing the figure at 3 percent. The 1924 law, the Johnson-Reed Act, set the quota at 2 percent, which effectively allotted about 85 percent of the quota to immigrants from northwestern Europe, keeping out those pesky central and eastern Europeans and Russians.[18]

Urban historians David R. Goldfield and Blaine Brownell noted that, in New York City, the specific problem was the rapid growth of the garment industry, which had expanded out of its cramped Lower East Side location northward to other residential and commercial districts. "The expansion," they wrote, "was coming perilously close to Fifth Avenue, where the city's luxury shopping district was located. The Fifth Avenue Association, composed of the avenue's shop owners, demanded that the city prevent the incursion of the garment industry, with its towering buildings, Jewish immigrant workers, and the inevitable refuse left by industry."[19] The solution, of course, was zoning, which New York enacted in 1916, becoming the first U.S. city to do so. "Not only by segregating different classifications of land uses such as commercial from residential, but also by differentiating types of residential structures such as single-family and apartment dwellings," said Goldfield and Brownell, "zoning determined who was going to live where."[20]

Another urban historian, Sam Bass Warner, Jr., has commented that, "Just as zoning had given wealthy retailers of Fifth Avenue a means of defense against encroaching garment factories, so subsequent zoning gave suburbanites a defense against 'undesirable' activities and people."[21]

The state statutes that were the progeny of the Standard Acts served the needs of a suburbanizing America through much of the 1950s. However, the era of the Standard Acts came to an end in the early to mid-1960s, when some state governments began to reexamine their enabling legislation and the inadequacies of the acts were revealed, particularly in the areas of planning and the protection of dormant state interests.

In 1960, William Doebele, a planning professor at Harvard University, completed the first post-war study of a state's enabling legislation, in this case for the State of New Mexico.[22] Commissioned by the state planning office, Doebele submitted discussion drafts of 14 acts for consideration by the New Mexico legislature. While most of the proposals dealt with issues specific to the state, one section expressly addressed a central weakness of the SCPEA, on which the New Mexico legislation had been based. That weakness was the confusing language describing a plan and the ambiguous role of a plan in support of a zoning decision.

"In the opinion of leading commentators, both in the legal and planning profession," Doebele wrote, "no state has enacted enabling legislation adequately defining the proper content of the Master or General Plan."[23] The language in the New Mexico act, he stated, "was out of accord with the best current thinking of the planning profession on this subject, and from a legal point of view, is ambiguous and unclear."[24] Doebele pointed to the SCPEA as the culprit: "These faults spring principally from the fact that the Master Plan concept was first evolved in the 1920's and the statutory language used in New Mexico and so many other states was developed at that time."[25]

Doebele went on to propose much more detailed language on the content of the general plan, as it was termed in New Mexico, some of it derived from the California enabling legislation, and a two-part process for preparing the plan. Doebele's general plan was different from "the master plan" contained in the SCPEA. His proposed legislation listed several functional elements—for land use, population and building intensity, circulation and transportation, economic and fiscal—as well as optional elements.[26]

The planning process involved the formulation of a "preliminary general plan report," a broad-brush presentation of problems, opportunities, and choices for direction of development. This report, which was to be the subject of a separate public hearing, was intended to allow the legislative body and planning commission to agree on a central direction for the plan. It was to be followed by a more detailed "final general plan report," containing all the specific plan elements, and was also to be subject to a public hearing, then adoption by the planning commission and certification to the legislative body.[27]

Doebele also sought to give the general plan more binding power than it had in the Standard Acts. He proposed an innovative burden-shifting approach to relate to the general plan to implement ordinances such as zoning and subdivision. In any litigation or dispute involving zoning or subdivision control, the adoption of the plan could be introduced as evidence supporting the reasonableness of the ordinance.[28] Doebele saw this as a compromise between authorizing the adoption of certain minimum types of land-use controls and authorizing the adoption of land-use controls but only where a general plan had to be prepared first. Where the plan was introduced as evidence, the plaintiff in land-use litigation bore the greater burden of proof because, as Doebele wrote, "the controls must inevitably rest on a firmer foundation" than the case without a plan.[29]

Other states, notably Connecticut and Wisconsin, undertook studies in the 1960s, and they provide a transition to the next period of statutory reform.[30] The Connecticut study, prepared by the American Society of Planning Officials (one of the predecessor organizations of the APA) and the Chicago law firm of Ross, Hardies, O'Keefe, Babcock, McDugald, and Parsons, proposed changes that strengthened the relationship of zoning to planning, authorized new techniques and changes in the structure of planning, and corrected inconsistencies and ambiguous provisions, including definitions, in the Connecticut statute.[31]

The Wisconsin study, prepared by University of Wisconsin law professor Jacob Beuscher and attorney (and now professor of law at the University of Maine) Orlando Delogu is significant because of its early emphasis on state supervision of critical areas and special protection of lands where major infrastructure was proposed.[32] It recommended the creation of a state interagency land-use council. The council's function was to develop state-level land-use controls for highway, wetland, shoreland, floodplain, and open space protection and promulgate them by administrative rule. Under the proposal, day-to-day administration of the controls would be left to line agencies most directly concerned with the state interest protected by the control. The state highway commission was also to be given the authority to preserve highway corridors, save highway interchanges from misdevelopment, and protect scenic amenities along highways.

The Quiet Revolution

The year 1971 saw the publication of a pivotal and influential report, *The Quiet Revolution in Land Use Control*, by attorneys Fred Bosselman and David Callies, prepared for the Council on Environmental Quality.[33] In that report, Bosselman and Callies identified examples of state legislation that had in essence taken back regulation of land use from local governments and asserted dormant state interests. These new statutes valued land as a resource as well as a commodity, they wrote, out of recognition that land serves vital ecological, aesthetic, and social functions (e.g., provision of affordable housing) but also has importance as an economic good, whose value land-use regulation traditionally sought to maintain, if not enhance.[34]

The report looked at nine states and regions in detail[35] and a dozen others in a more limited fashion.[36] The legislation that the report analyzed was largely concerned with environmental planning and regulation for areas such as wetlands and coastal areas, and the establishment of new institutional structures for planning such as the Twin Cities Metropolitan Council (although one state, Massachusetts, was profiled for its affordable housing appeals act).[37]

The new Quiet Revolution statutes supplanted local control because of questions about how well local governments could manage these resources. The SZEA, Bosselman and Callies noted, was an enabling act and was:

> "... directed at delegating land use control to the local level, historically the city level where the problems which called into being first arose. It has become increasingly apparent that the local zoning ordinance, virtually the sole means of land use control in the United States for over half a century, has prove woefully inadequate to combat a host of problems of state significance, social problems as well as problems involving environmental pollution and destruction of vital ecological systems which threaten our very existence."[38]

Bosselman and Callies also observed that the new state systems that they described did not result in complimentary overhauls of local planning and land-use regulation. In most cases, the new systems completely bypassed them, which required the developer, who is subject to both systems, to go through two separate and distinct administrative processes, "often doubling the time required and substantially increasing the costs required to obtain approval of the development proposal."[39] The reason for the creation of duplicating procedures, they wrote, was to eliminate potential enemies of new legislation; local control was left intact. In many states, the motives behind the state regulatory system were solely to prohibit development that would otherwise occur. "To persons who have this motive," they wrote, "the duplication can only operate to prevent and not to encourage development."[40]

The Wisconsin Shoreland Protection Program, enacted as part of the state's Water Resources Act of 1966, offers a good example of the Quiet Revolution legislation, although it retained a measure of local control. Here, the motivation was to protect the scenic beauty of lakes and rivers in Wisconsin, whose shorelines were being threatened by commercial development (e.g., taverns, souvenir shops, and grocery stores), displacing shore cover and wildlife habitats.[41]

The legislation authorized shoreland protection zoning, and counties were empowered to enact separate zoning ordinances affecting all unincorporated land within 1,000 feet of a lake, pond, or flowage, and 300 feet of a navigable river or stream, or the landward side of a floodplain, whichever distance is greater.[42] The act placed responsibility for administering the act with a division of the Wisconsin Department of Natural Resources, which was to produce a model ordinance. If a county failed to adopt an ordinance meeting the minimum standards to meet the act's objectives by a certain date, then the department must adopt such an ordinance that would apply in a recalcitrant county.[43]

Bosselman and Callies observed that the Shoreland Protection Program's thrust was to place at the county level primary responsibility for protection of shoreland resources but always under state supervision to ensure that the regulation met state standards. The counties' response, at the time of the writing of the report, showed widespread compliance, with the state attempting to maintain an amicable relationship with them. Still, the question remained, they said, over how effectively and diligently counties were administering the new regulations.[44]

Writing a quarter of a century later about the conclusions of *The Quiet Revolution* and surveying the states that had joined the revolution since 1971, David Callies, now a professor of law at the University of Hawaii, reflected that local zoning had not withered away, that there had been "precious little permit simplification," and that the environmental decade of the 1970s that had spawned the legislation continued "unabated into the 1980s although in a somewhat different form."[45] Finally, he observed that growth management had become "the accepted rubric embracing state and local land use development and regulatory reform."[46]

Growth Management

Two court cases in the 1970s—one from the east coast and the other from the west coast—provided the springboard for the growth management movement in the U.S. *Golden v. Town of Ramapo*[47] from New York State upheld a phased development time system in which the approval of residential development was linked to the provision of public infrastructure in accordance with an 18-year capital improvement program; the developer had the choice of waiting for the infrastructure, some of it to be provided by other governmental units, to be installed, or of installing infrastructure at his/her own cost ahead of schedule. In California, the Ninth Circuit upheld a building permit allocation system in *Construction Industry Association of Sonoma County v. City of Petaluma.*[48] Here, Petaluma established a building permit allocation system under which only a certain number of building permits would be awarded in a city for a given year through a permit award competition.

The growth management movement, which is still underway, is characterized by legislation containing a number of features:

• Recognition that land use has a temporal dimension to it: The growth management movement thus focused on timing, as well as the location and character of development.

• The principle that public services and infrastructure should support urban development, and that these services and facilities should be provided at the time the development's impact is experienced, rather than postponed to some point in the future: A related principle is the distinction that different levels of development require different levels of service, and that those service levels can be established quantitatively, which has led to the adoption of adequate public facilities or concurrency ordinances, and which tie local government approval of development to the availability and adequacy of public facilities.

• The acknowledgement that public investment stimulates development and the effort to use the power of investment to direct development positively rather than react to it.

• An attempt to reduce the consumption of land and make development more compact: This is where urban growth areas, which establish minimum land-use density and intensity levels, an adequate land supply to meet expected growth for periods of up to 20 years, and supporting infrastructure, come in. In employing urban growth areas, the assumptions about how land is to be used, and at what densities and intensities, must be clearly stated and linked to economic and population forecasts.[49]

• In some states, an attempt to establish minimum levels of competence for local planning and land-use regulations, through requirements of the adoption of plans and regulations that satisfy state statutes and regulations and periodic review.

• In some states, the infusion of local comprehensive planning with state goals through the creation of systems of vertical and horizontal integration, sometimes based on formal review and approval of local plans and regulations to determine whether plans and regulation reflect those goals.

I classify the systems in Vermont, Florida (a set of related laws), Oregon, New Jersey, Maine, Rhode Island, Washington, Tennessee, and Wisconsin as falling into the growth management category, although the features outlined above are not present in all of them, especially the degree of state oversight.[50]

A variant was the well-known 1997 Smart Growth Act from Maryland, where the state attempted to use the power of state investment to direct growth to "Priority Funding Areas" (PFAs) listed in the statute itself (including all of the state's municipalities) or designated by counties, and that met certain density and public facility requirements for water and sewer.[51] Here, the intention was to send a signal to the private sector that state infrastructure investments would only be available within such areas, although local governments and private developers could fund infrastructure on their own outside the PFAs.

WHAT HAS PLANNING STATUTE REFORM ACCOMPLISHED?

Over the past decade, planning researchers have attempted to nail down with quantitative analysis the impact of various state programs. Much of the attention has been directed at Oregon, where the existence of sophisticated geographic information systems and relatively clear state goals has made the task of measurement easier. This section summarizes some of the leading studies that concern the effect of state mandates on the quality of plans and their implementation, on urban sprawl and urban form, and on housing affordability. Their results are not always consistent, depending on the precise nature of the research approach.

Quality of Plans and Their Implementation

A 1997 study by Raymond Burby and Peter May, *Making Governments Plan*,[52] looked at the consequences of requiring local governments to plan and the effect on local development management. They compared three states (California, Florida, and North Carolina, but for the coastal regional only) with planning mandates of varying strength and sophistication with three states (Texas, Washington, and North Carolina, for the mountain region only) without planning mandates.

The focus in these states is on planning for hazard protection. The study, which used a quasi-experimental design, found that plans in states with comprehensive planning mandates addressed hazard management goals more thoroughly than plans in states without such mandates; thus, state planning mandates are an important factor in determining the quality of local comprehensive plans.[53] Moreover, the study found that higher-quality plans are more likely to be implemented than lower-quality plans.[54]

A study by Robert Deyle and Richard Smith of local government compliance with state planning mandates in Florida came to somewhat different conclusions,[55] although they are not surprising for those who understand how large bureaucracies function. Deyle and Smith examined compliance with mandates for coastal storm hazards by reviewing final, state-approved comprehensive plans prepared by nine counties and nine cities across Florida. They found highly variable compliance by the communities, with compliance different for different categories of mandates. Thus, compliance with mandates, and therefore plan content, were influenced by the manner in which the state administrative agency (in this case, the Department of Community Affairs) decided to pursue its responsibilities, including how well it monitored and enforced the state laws concerning the substantive contents of plans. At bottom, they wrote, the Florida mandate was "selectively implemented" and storm hazard planning requirements "were not rigorously enforced."[56]

In a content analysis of 23 local comprehensive plans produced under Wisconsin's 1999 Smart Growth Act, Mary Edwards and Anna Haines found that local governments tended to comply with the mechanical requirements of the act but failed on the particulars.[57] For example, the act requires that plan elements include nine elements that meet certain detailed specifications. The local plans included the nine elements but did not always satisfy the standards for the elements contained in the statute. "For example," they wrote, "many failed to address brownfields at all even if it was only to say that the community did not have any brownfields within its jurisdiction."[58] Eight of the 23 land-use elements lacked land-use projections, certainly a serious omission. Similarly, the plans were sketchy on implementation measures and schedules. Only one plan delineated potential funding resources for each activity required for plan implementation.

Edwards and Haines also analyzed whether plans contained goals that addressed 11 nationally accepted smart growth principles; again, they found that most of the plans came up short. For example, only one of the 22 plans addressed making development decisions predictable, fair, and cost effective, and only five addressed mixed-use development. On the other hand, 17 plans addressed the preservation of open space, farmland, and critical environmental areas; 16 plans mentioned creation of a range of housing choice and opportunity.[59]

Impact on Urban Sprawl and Urban
Form Including Urban Growth Boundaries

A 2002 study by John Carruthers was a comparative analysis of state growth management programs and whether or not they reduced urban sprawl.[60] Carruthers looked at a cross-section of 283 metropolitan counties, observed at four points in time (1982, 1987, 1992, and 1997). These were all of the metropolitan counties located in Arizona, California, Colorado, Florida, Georgia, Idaho, Nevada, New Mexico, North Carolina, Oregon, Tennessee, Texas, Utah, and Washington.

The econometric analysis found that state growth management programs with strong consistency requirements and enforcement mechanisms held much promise for reducing urban sprawl, while programs that do not require consistency and/or have weak enforcement mechanisms may inadvertently contribute to it (see discussion in the note at the end of this chapter).[61] In

Georgia and California, he theorized, the reason for less dense urban development and higher property values arise out of a purely locally oriented approach to land-use planning, where the state lacks any effective coercive mechanism for enforcing its policies and that no consistency—including internal consistency—is required for local governments.[62]

There have been a number of studies of urban growth areas, which are features of the Oregon and Washington systems. A 1991 study of four areas in Oregon (Bend, Brookings, Medford, and Portland), conducted for the Oregon Department of Land Conservation and Development,[63] found that urban growth could be largely contained within urban growth boundaries (UGBs). In the Portland area, only 5 percent of residential growth occurred outside the UGB. However, in the Bend area, 57 percent of the residential development occurred outside the UGB; in the Brookings area, 37 percent; and in the Medford area, 24 percent.

Indicators of livability—although the study admitted they were incomplete—suggested some areas for concern: traffic congestion and real housing prices increased in all case study areas, but air quality improved. Though parkland was being acquired in some case study areas, the amount of developed parkland was probably not increasing as fast as population, the study showed. Moreover, fast-growing communities, the study found, appeared to be able to fund their sewer and water needs but not their street and road needs. Actual developed densities within the UGBs varied considerably among the four case studies. The report recommended an extensive series of measures to improve the operation of UGBs, including minimum densities (in addition to maximums) in residential zones, strict schedules and unambiguous standards for UGB expansion, state programs to assist with the funding of local public services, and the prohibition or limitation of nonfarm dwellings in exclusive farm or forest zones.

A 1991 study conducted by 1000 Friends of Oregon and the Home Builders Association of Metropolitan Portland[64] examined the implementation of Oregon's statewide housing goal in the Portland area through the metropolitan housing rule for the Portland area, adopted by the Oregon Land Conservation and Development Commission (Ore. Admin. Rules §§ 660-07-000 et seq.). That rule requires local plans to provide adequate land zoned for needed housing types and to ensure that land within the metropolitan Portland UGB accommodates the region's population growth.

Under the rule, each of the region's three counties and 24 cities must develop plans that allow for a new construction mix that includes at least 50 percent multifamily or attached single-family units and that allows development to occur at certain minimum target housing densities. This ranges from 10 dwelling units per buildable acre in the City of Portland to six to eight dwelling units per buildable acre in suburban areas.

The study found that the rule resulted in increasing the availability of affordable housing and making homeownership more attainable by diversifying the stock of single-family housing sites to include smaller lots. Further, the rule's implementation reduced the amount of land consumed by development during the 1985-89 study period. Had planned residential development occurred in the urban growth area at lower prehousing-rule densities, it would have consumed an additional 1,500 acres of planned residential land— an area over 2 square miles in size.

A comprehensive 1992 assessment of the Oregon program by Professors Gerrit-Jan Knaap and Arthur Nelson[65] concluded that UGBs:

1.   Facilitated intergovernmental coordination among cities, counties, and state agencies;

2.   Affected current land values (generally higher inside the boundary than outside) and allocation; and

3.   Had limited ability to manage urban growth.

Knaap and Nelson noted that, while development at urban densities had been contained within UGBs, development densities within them were lower than planned and development densities outside UGBs were higher than planned.

Jerry Weitz and Terry Moore examined development inside UGBs in three communities in Oregon (Florence, McMinnville, and Medford) for a study period of 1990-1995.[66] Their analysis found that recent development inside UGBs tended to be contiguous to the urban core rather than dispersed. This finding, they wrote, was consistent with Oregon's policies for urban form, which stress strong justification for the principles of contiguous development.

Economist Anthony Downs looked at the impact of the Portland UGB on housing prices in comparison with housing prices in other metropolitan areas to determine whether UGBs cause home prices to rise faster there than elsewhere.[67] He conducted a detailed analysis of home price movements from 1980 to 2000, finding that Portland home prices did not rise as rapidly from 1980 to 1990 as other metropolitan areas, that home prices rose rapidly in Portland only from 1990 to 1994 or 1996, and that home prices in several other regions without UGBs were also rising rapidly. Downs conducted multiple regression analyses of 85 large metropolitan areas that showed that a dummy variable measuring the effect of Portland's UGB had statistically significant effects on home prices only in the first half of the decade. He stated that it was erroneous to conclude from Portland's experience that UGBs inevitably cause prices to rise.

Yan Song and Gerrit-Jan Knaap examined the consequences of the Oregon policies in Washington County, the western portion of the Portland metropolitan area.[68] They evaluated development patterns and trends in the area by computing several measures of urban form and examining them over time. Their results suggested that neighborhoods in Washington County have increased single-family dwelling unit density since the 1960s, internal street connectivity and pedestrian access to commercial areas has improved since the early 1990s, external connectivity continues to decline, and mixing of land uses remains limited.

These results, they wrote, "characterize a trend in urban form toward denser, more internally connected and more pedestrian friendly and yet relatively homogenous neighborhoods with poor external connectivity are rather encouraging for the neighborhoods, but less so for the region. At the regional scale, we speculate, better land use mixing and regional connectivity is [sic] constrained by economies of scale in commercial land uses and transportation infrastructure. . . . In sum, Portland is winning the war on urban sprawl at the neighborhood scale, or at least appears to have won some important battles; but progress remains elusive at the regional scale."[69]

Impact on Housing Affordability and Production of Affordable Housing

Jerry Anthony looked at the impact of Florida's Growth Management Act (GMA) on housing affordability.[70] Using two indices of housing affordability, with data from all 67 counties, and after controlling for alternate hypotheses, his study found that the act had a statistically significant effect in decreasing the affordability of single-family homes. While this is a negative impact of the legislation and its administration, Anthony believes the solutions to the problem lay in more specificity in the housing requirements in the act, better enforcement of the act and its rules (this is consistent with Carruthers's findings, described above), increase in the density of housing, and the provision of increased funding for affordable housing.

For example, he noted, the GMA was supposed to encourage compact development through the application of the concurrency principle, which requires that all infrastructure needed to service a development is available before it is completed and occupied. "Yet even today," he wrote, "most communities in the state have large-lot zoning and maximum-density rules. To ensure compact development, the GMA should require local zoning ordinances and subdivision regulations to include more intensive minimum-density zoning for *all* new development."[71]

In a 2003 study on regional approaches to affordable housing that I coauthored with my colleagues Rebecca Retzlaff and James Schwab,[72] we evaluated a number of long-standing state-level programs, including fair-share programs in New Jersey and California, and housing appeals laws in Massachusetts, Connecticut, and Rhode Island—the three laws that provided the bases for the Illinois appeals law described above. The results were mixed in terms of program participation and quite modest in terms of production of affordable housing.

The fair-share housing program in New Jersey, prompted by the New Jersey Supreme Court's 1975 and 1983 Mount Laurel anti-exclusionary zoning decisions, had, as of 2001, resulted in 48 percent of cities and towns participating. Since the state began monitoring progress in 1990, the opportunity (which could include prezoning sites for affordable housing as part of a local housing plan) had been made available for 60,731 affordable housing units, and new unit construction totaled 28,855 as of 2000.[73]

In California, which has had a fair-share program for all local governments since 1980 that involves the state and regional planning agencies, there simply were no statewide totals on the number of units of affordable housing constructed that allows comparison with total need. The state and regional planning agencies did not collect that information—a critical flaw in the system.[74] Thus, it was impossible to draw conclusions about whether production made an impact on regionally established fair-share goals.

The Massachusetts affordable housing appeals act, between its inception in 1969 and 1999, had resulted in some 18,000 affordable housing units being built with comprehensive permits, the vehicle by which a state housing appeals board authorized construction. As of April 2002, 27 (7.7 percent) of the state's 351 communities had achieved the 10 percent goal of housing stock for affordable housing.[75]

The Connecticut law was enacted in 1989. In 1990, when the state started compiling the initial list of local governments that were exempt from the law's operation because they achieved the 10 percent goal, 25 communities were exempt. Between 1990 and 1998, a total of 10,084 affordable units were added to the housing stock base of the 144 towns subject to the act. As of October 2001, 32 Connecticut cities and towns were exempt from the act.[76]

The Rhode Island law was enacted in 1991. In January 1992, when Rhode Island began tracking housing achievement under the law, 7.09 percent (29,324 units) of the state's housing was classified as affordable; five towns, of the 39 in the state, were exempt from the act by virtue of meeting the 10 percent housing affordability goal. The state's affordable housing stock increased by 19 percent from 1992-2001, but there was no change in the number of towns exempt from the act.[77]

Efficiency of Permit Processes and
Judicial Review: An Overlooked Area

One area that has escaped evaluation almost completely is the efficiency of local government development review processes[78] and judicial review systems for land-use appeals. Except by anecdote and the occasional court case, we don't really know much about the internal, daily workings of most state land-use systems.

One exploratory law journal article, by Arthur Nelson, did attempt to analyze the differences between appeals systems in Oregon, Georgia, New Jersey, and Florida.[79] He found that local government decisions on developments could take as long as two years in Georgia, Florida, and New Jersey, but only

120 days in Oregon. Excluding appeals to higher courts, a state court order on an appeal of a local government's land-use action could take between two to seven years in Georgia, two to six years in Florida and New Jersey, and less than one year in Oregon.[80] Excluding Oregon, these are long times to get a local development permit or obtain a court decision on an appeal.

Summing Up

What do the studies described above reveal? First, good comprehensive planning seems to make a difference in implementation. Second, the effect of an external monitoring entity—a state agency with rule-making power—depends on the diligence with which the agency addresses its job and how it interprets the statutes. Third, it is extremely hard to stop sprawl, and the design of the planning system makes a great deal of difference in whether you are able to do so, especially as it affects the internal characteristics of urban form such as neighborhood connectivity. Fourth, constraints on urban expansion through UGBs do not inevitably result in higher home prices, as compared to other metropolitan areas without UGBs; as Anthony Downs concludes, there is no simple relationship between containment programs and housing prices.[81] Fifth, attempting to produce affordable housing on a statewide basis through statutory reform is not easy either, and you must have a system in place in which compliance with state-established goals can be determined. Finally, we do not really know much about the internal workings of permit review processes because there has been almost no research on that topic, but we do know more about the process of judicial review; Oregon, almost alone, has managed to shorten the process of permit issuance and land-use appeals.

WHAT PHILOSOPHY SHOULD GUIDE STATUTORY REFORM INITIATIVES?

So what should our philosophy about reform be? As a backdrop, let me make some fearless and somewhat bleak predictions about what we *cannot* expect in the next 20 years.

- I do not think we are going to stop urban sprawl, despite some limited empirical evidence to the contrary[82] and despite hikes in the price of gasoline. We may make some inroads here and there, as Baby Boomers age and want to live in denser environments, or because people want to live near transit lines—where they exist—to avoid long commutes; however, in the United States, we are not going to see a dramatic restructuring of metropolitan areas, at least as the result of changes in planning laws. This is not to say that we should give up and that we shouldn't keep plugging away. Rather, it is a practical recognition of how many small things and how many actions by local government and the private market that a planning system would have to affect over a long period of time to make a difference in the consumption of land. Our low-density, autodependent pattern of growth is ingrained in American society and it will take a lot of hard hits to dislodge it. I wonder if we are up to the challenge.

• I do not think that some of the other factors influencing land-use change—notably local government reliance on property[83] and sales taxes, which results in zoning for high revenue-producing land uses such as big-box retail and auto dealerships—are going to change much either. We have been talking about this problem for a long, long time, and I see no notable trends on the horizon, or even below it, that lead me to believe a tax revolution that will neutralize the fiscal impacts of land use is in the offing.

• Regional planning doesn't offer much hope (although I would like to be more optimistic on this point)[84] with some rare exceptions—again, like the Metro, which oversees planning for the three-county area in Portland, Oregon, and for the Metropolitan Council in the Twin Cities.[85] There are few really dynamic regional agencies in the U.S., in my opinion, and, regardless of their dynamism, local governments loathe ceding them any significant land-use planning authority. There are regional agencies that are earnestly trying, but the odds are stacked against them.

• Despite the review of earlier initiatives above, I don't particularly see state government becoming a vigorous activist in new state growth management experiments, and overseeing sophisticated vertically and horizontally integrated planning systems. Again, we will experience initiatives here and there—like the efforts of Maryland Governor Parris N. Glendening, who aggressively pushed smart growth until his successor basically disassembled the program—but nothing permanent will occur. It is too hard for state governments to sustain the level of effort over the long term to make a material change in land use and the density of metropolitan areas. Planning systems that depend on the charisma and drive of a governor have a limited life span.

My philosophy for planning statute reform[86] is as follows:

• *We need to stick to the fundamentals.* Before moving on to propose grand planning and regulatory schemes, we should really understand how an individual state system, as interpreted and implemented at the local level, actually works. It takes more than a few public hearings to discover this. In my opinion, the fundamentals are:

   o Definitions of a comprehensive plan;
   o The specific set of planning and land-use powers that local governments are delegated by the state;
   o The clear and consistent relationship of the comprehensive plan to zoning, subdivision, and other regulatory tools;
   o The openness of the process by which land-use decisions are made;
   o The documentation that land-use decision-makers produce that explains how they determined whether a rezoning or other development approval would be granted; and

○ The processes of permitting, and administrative and judicial review, including their duration.

The understanding of the system should be gained through interviews, case studies, and review of previous reform studies, case law, and attorney general opinions—something that most reform efforts fail to do.[87] Only after we have done our homework should we fix what's broken about the fundamentals. In most states, people know what's broken, like a subdivision statute that allows unlimited platting without any type of public review. One just has to probe a little harder to discover and document it.

• *When we draft new statutes, we must be detailed and precise and not assume, as the authors of the Standard Acts did in the 1920s, that the courts will be there to interpret them where they are vague.* We also cannot assume that a state agency will be there promptly with guidance documents and administrative rule-making. Statutes should stand by themselves.

The users of planning statutes will be laypersons. They ought to be able to pick up the statutes and understand what kind of plan document is called for, how the various parts of a plan relate to one another, what the notice for a public hearing should be, and how long you have to decide on whether to issue a development permit. Legislation that details the types of analyses that must underpin plans, describes the substantive contents of plan elements, and characterizes the types of implementation measures can ensure that thorough, systematic, and useful documents emerge from the planning process.[88]

• *Where we create new responsibilities for local governments and state agencies, or revise existing ones, we ought to be careful to spell out what they need to do, so that, at least for critical tasks, there is little, rather than more, discretion.* Thus, the system should be *self-executing* and not depend on external forces, such as litigation or rule-making, to define what to do.

Let me give you an example. I described above the Illinois Affordable Housing Planning and Appeal Act. One of the sections I helped draft was the procedure by which the Illinois Housing Development Authority (IHDA) would use to calculate the threshold numbers of year-round affordable housing units and compare them to the total number of housing units in each community in the state.

The provisions I developed with Attorney Nick Brunick provided air-tight definitions and a step-by-step procedure for the limited arithmetic involved. This was intended to prevent the agency from acting puzzled about what action to take, as bureaucracies often do in controversial situations, and delay implementation of the act over concerns about the meaning of terms, the gathering of data, and the issuance of rules.

Moreover, we broadened the definition of affordable housing, in contrast to the three other states with appeals statutes. In the Illinois law, affordable housing, for the purposes of establishing the 10 percent threshold, could either be market-rate housing that was affordable, or state- or federally assisted housing. This effectively increased the pool of units, providing a more realistic picture of the mix of housing stock in the state, and blunted the argument that the only way affordable housing could be counted is if it were subsidized. The act did not provide for the appeal of the individual housing goals as calculated by the IHDA.

We decided to allow local governments that were not exempt to have some control over their destiny by requiring them to complete housing plans, whose contents were similarly detailed in the act, in order to prevent confusion about exactly what the local government's responsibilities were.[89] Thus, if a local government had less than 10 percent affordable housing, it first had to complete a plan and submit it to the IHDA by April 2005.

The housing plan provision was included to allow a local government affected by the act to think about where it wanted affordable housing to be located and to identify possible incentives that could be offered to developers. In the plan, the local government had to acknowledge what the numerical goal for affordable units was, but it could formulate alternate strategies for achieving the goal. It also had to adopt the plan, and submit it to the IHDA, which didn't have to take any action except receive it—no completeness review, and no discretion to reject it or accept it with conditions.

- *We ought to have deadlines for land-use decisions, which in some quarters is a concept viewed with alarm.* There are those who believe that the land-use decision-making system should not have a beginning, a middle, or an end, and that local governments should be able to be coy about whether or not they have reached a final decision for the purposes of judicial review. I don't agree with that. Each phase in the development review system should have time limits, with as much predictability and certainty as reasonably possible. There is something Kafka-esque, uncivil, and impolite about a planning system that never ends, and where permit applications get caught in a mobius strip of endless reviews. Similarly, I favor strong vesting requirements, so that the rules cannot be changed in the middle of the game.[90]

- *In the absence of state supervision of planning systems, we should have broad standing requirements.* This may be an anathema to developers and home builders, but I believe broad standing requirements are essential to enforce plans and ensure competence, consistency, and honesty by local governments. Third-party interest groups can be a powerful corrective force to ensure that planning systems are operating properly and, while they can also generate abuse, I think the benefits they offer exceed the detriments.

- *We need to make certain that our public officials charged with overseeing planning systems are properly trained.* This is extremely important in order to ensure that the systems function fairly and efficiently. You can no longer take the risk of putting someone on a planning commission or a board of zoning appeals and assume that he or she will learn on the job, and that mistakes or bad faith behavior can be easily overlooked. There is too much at stake in modern land-use litigation for that.

Mandatory orientation training and continuing education are an answer. Since 2001, four states—all of them in the south and southeast—have enacted laws that require planning officials—and, in some cases, planners themselves—to participate in such training.[91] The laws reflect a heightened concern on the part of state legislatures about the knowledge and competence of local planning officials. I hope this trend spreads.

• *We need to dedicate our planning systems to ensuring that there is an adequate supply of affordable housing and that the barriers to it are removed.* This is a topic that has been the subject of countless studies and reports, with very little nationwide progress and a good deal of political backsliding. After World War II, our nation managed to do this, but we have lost our way, and now affordable housing is the exception rather than the rule.

Consequently, we now seem to need special procedures and controls to produce it. Even with them, progress is slow and painful. That's unfortunate. We have done a remarkable job at improving measures to protect the environment from harm over the past 35 years or so, but our commitment to a decent, affordable home for all Americans has flagged, and our planning and land-use systems are partly to blame. Pursing this objective is, of course, getting involved with danger, but what is life without a little of that?

STUART MECK NOTES

1. 310 ILCS 67/15 et seq. (2004).
2. The Illinois law, Public Act 93-595 (2003) as amended by Public Act 93-678 (2004),
   is intended to encourage local governments to incorporate sufficient affordable housing into their communities—the first time the State of Illinois has acted to make such a requirement part of public policy. It requires all counties and municipalities with insufficient affordable housing, as defined by the law, to adopt an affordable housing plan. The act also states that housing developers that have applications for affordable housing developments—any project with 20 percent or more affordable housing—that are either denied by or approved with infeasible conditions by local governments with insufficient affordable housing may appeal local decisions to a state housing appeals board, which is to be established by 2009. Local governments with sufficient affordable housing, set by the statute as 10 percent or more of total year-round housing units, are exempt from the provisions relating to the development of an affordable housing plan and to the State Housing Appeals Board.

   The statute defines affordable housing as housing that costs no more than 30 percent of a household's income. Rental units must be affordable to households with incomes of 60 percent of area median household income, and owner-occupied units must be affordable to households with incomes of 80 percent of area median household income.

   Under the law, the Illinois Housing Development Authority (IHDA) is charged with developing a list of exempt and nonexempt communities and serving as a repository for housing plans. In July 2004, the IDHA finally released the list of communities. Of the 1,287 municipalities and 102 counties in Illinois, 49 municipalities were determined to be nonexempt and had to develop housing plans. An additional 10 municipalities had less than 10 percent of affordable housing but were exempt because they have populations below 1,000. All of the nonexempt local governments are in the six-county Chicago Primary Metropolitan Statistical Area. Lake and Cook Counties have the most nonexempt municipalities, with 18 and 16 respectively; followed by DuPage County with seven nonexempt municipalities; and then Kane, McHenry, and Will Counties with three or fewer. In Illinois, 52.9 percent of all year-round housing units are classified as affordable. Kelly King Dibble, Executive Director, IHDA, "Procedures for Implementation of Public Act 93-595/Public Act 93-678 (The Affordable Housing Planning and Appeal Act, as amended)," Memorandum (Aug. 11, 2004).

3. Stuart Meck (gen. ed.), *Growing Smart^SM Legislative Guidebook: Model Statutes for Planning and the Management of Change* (Chicago: American Planning Association, 2002). For a recent review of the impact of this book on planning statute reform in the U.S., see Patricia E. Salkin, "The Guidebook is Making a Difference," SK002 ALI-ABA 593 (2004).

4. Mass. Gen. Laws, Chapter 40B, §§ 20-23 (2004); Conn. Gen. Stat. Ann., Chapter 126a, § 8-30(g) (2004); R.I. Gen. Laws, Chapter 53, §§ 45-53-1 et seq. (2004).

5. Andrew Shroedter, "Group pushes for repeal of state housing law," *Wilmette Life*, July 22, 2004.

6. New Trier Neighbors, "So Tell Me Again: Why is the 'Affordable Housing' Act Necessary?" Flyer (n.d., 2004).

7. Ronald S. Cope, *The Affordable Housing Planning and Appeal Act—The New Illinois Affirmative Action Housing Program* (unpublished, 2004) (http://www.lwvwilmette.org/AHCopedoc.pdf) (visited June 2, 2005).

8. 429 U.S. 252, *on remand*, 558 F.2d 1283 (7th Circ. 1977).

9. Cope, note 7, *supra*, at 11-12.

10. Id. at 3.

11. Id. at 12.

12. Other lead co-sponsors included: Senator Harry Walsh (D–Chicago); Senator Iris Martinez (D–Chicago); Representative Ricca Slone (D–Peoria); Representative Harry Osterman (D–Chicago); and Representative Julie Hamos (D–Evanston).

13. Another positive note was the attitude of *Wilmette Life*, one of the newspapers serving the area. In an editorial, the newspaper stated:

    > "New Trier Township needs more diverse housing stock, but the thought of even considering planning for that has brought opposition from some residents fearful of change . . .
    >
    > "Rather than work to ensure areas designated in mandated plans are appropriate for affordable housing, or to seek ideas for making some of the housing stock affordable, New Trier Neighbors want to repeal a law aimed at requiring municipalities to address the issue. It will not be easy for these communities to pursue affordable housing options, but it is essential that they do so." "Remove Fear from Debate on Housing," *Wilmette Life*, July 22, 2004.

14. For a survey of model planning statutes and important early studies, see Stuart Meck, "Model Planning and Zoning Enabling Legislation, A Short History," in *Modernizing State Planning Statutes: The Growing Smart^SM Working Papers*, Vol. I, Planning Advisory Service Report No. 462/463, 1 (Chicago: American Planning Association, March 1996). Some of the discussion in this section is based in part on this article.

15. U.S. Department of Commerce, Advisory Committee on Zoning, *A Standard State Zoning Enabling Act* (rev. ed.) (Washington, DC: U.S. Department of Commerce, 1926); U.S. Department of Commerce, Advisory Committee on Planning and Zoning, *A Standard City Planning Enabling Act* (Washington, DC: U.S. Department of Commerce, 1928). For a background on the drafting of the Standard Acts, see Ruth Knack, Stuart Meck, and Israel

Stollman, *The Real Story Behind the Standard Planning and Zoning Acts of the 1920s*, 48 Land Use Law & Zoning Digest, No. 2, 3 (1996).

16. Daniel R. Mandelker, *Land Use Law* (3d ed.) (Charlottesville, VA: Michie, 1993), 113-114.

17. See Robert H. Whitten, "Zoning and Living Conditions," in *Proceedings of the Thirteenth National Conference on City Planning* (Pittsburgh, PA: The Conference, May 9-11, 1921), 22. Whitten, a nationally known zoning consultant, who developed a racially exclusionary zoning ordinance for Atlanta, declared:

> "Coming back to the main criticism that zoning tends inevitably toward the segregation of the different economic classes, I admit the fact but do not consider this result either anti-social or undemocratic in its tendency . . .
>
> "The zoning movement in so far as it may be said in small measure to facilitate the natural trend toward a reasonable segregation of economic classes is neither undemocratic or [sic] anti-social. Such effect of zoning is merely incidental. A reasonable segregation is normal, inevitable and desirable and cannot be greatly affected, one way or the other, by zoning." Id. at 27-28.

See also Barbara J. Flint, *Zoning and Residential Segregation: A Social and Physical History, 1910-1940* (dissertation) (Chicago: University of Chicago, December 1977); Kenneth Baer, *The National Movement to Halt the Spread of Multifamily Housing, 1890-1926*, 58 JAPA, No. 1, 39 (Winter 1992); Yale Rabin, "Expulsive Zoning: The Inequitable Legacy of Euclid," in Charles M. Haar and Jerold S. Kayden, eds., *Zoning and the American Dream: Promises to Keep 101* (Chicago: American Planning Association, 1989); Christopher Silver, *The Racial Origins of Zoning: Southern Cities from 1910-40*, 6 Planning Perspectives 189 (1991) (noting, at 193, that Virginia's enabling legislation circa 1910-11 allowed cities to zone their entire area according to race). Compare with Larry R. Ford, *Cities and Buildings: Skyscrapers, Skid Rows, and Suburbs* (Baltimore: Johns Hopkins University Press, 1994), Chapter 5 (describing the diffusion of the tenement occupied by immigrants and the gradual replacement by apartments intended for the middle and upper classes).

18. John Higham, *Strangers in the Land: Patterns of America Nativism 1860-1925* (New York: Atheneum, 1973), 308-324; John Higham, *Send These to Me: Jews and Other Immigrants in Urban America* (New York: Atheneum, 1975), 54-55.

19. David R. Goldfield and Blaine Brownell, *Urban History in America* (2d ed.) (Boston: Houghton Mifflin, 1990), 278. See also Seymour Toll, *Zoned American* (New York: Grossman, 1969); S. J. Makielski, Jr., *The Politics of Zoning: The New York Experience* (New York: Columbia University Press, 1966); Raphael Fischler, *The Metropolitan Dimension of Early Zoning: Revisiting the 1916 New York City Ordinance*, 64 JAPA, No. 2, 170 (Spring 1998).

20. Goldfield and Brownell, note 19, *supra*, at 278.

21. Sam Bass Warner, Jr., *The Urban Wilderness: A History of the American City* (New York: Harper & Row, 1972), 31.

22. William A. Doebele, Jr., *Recommended Enabling Legislation for Regional, County and Municipal Planning in the State of New Mexico*, prepared for the State Planning Office, State of New Mexico (September 6, 1960). While New Mexico eventually did make changes to its enabling acts, the innovative language proposed by Doebele was not incorporated into statutes.

23. Id. at 93.

24. Id. at 94.

25. Id., citing, at n. 4, the SCPEA and observing §§ 14-2-18, 20, and 22 of N.M. S.A. (1953 Comp.) were taken "almost verbatim" from §§ 6 to 9 of the SCPEA.

26. Id. at 102-108.

27. Id. at 99-101, 109-112.

28. Id. at 123-126.

29. Id. at 126.

30. See Meck, note 14, *supra,* for a review of some of these studies.

31. American Society of Planning Officials, *New Directions in Connecticut Planning Legislation: A Study of Connecticut Planning, Zoning, and Related Statutes* (February 1966).

32. Jacob Beuscher and Orlando Delogu, *Land Use Controls, Wisconsin Development Series,* prepared for the Wisconsin Department of Resource Development [1965?].

33. Fred Bosselman and David Callies, *The Quiet Revolution in Land Use Control* (Washington, DC: Council on Environmental Quality and Council of State Governments, 1971).

34. Id. at 314-315.

35. Hawaii, Vermont, San Francisco Bay, Twin Cities Metro Council, Massachusetts, Maine, Wisconsin, and the New England River Basin.

36. Tahoe Regional Planning Agency; Hackensack Meadowlands Development Commission; Adirondack Park Agency; Delaware Coastal Zone Act; Colorado Land Use Act; Washington Land Planning Commission; Alaska Joint State–Federal Natural Resources and Land Use Planning Commission; wetland and shoreland laws in North Carolina, Rhode Island, Connecticut, Maryland, and Georgia.

37. Mass. Gen. Laws, Chapter 40B, §§ 20-23 (enacted in 1969).

38. Bosselman and Callies, note 33, *supra,* at 3.

39. Id. at 320.

40. Id.

41. Id. at 235.

42. Id. at 236, citing Wisc. Stat. Ann. § 59.971(4).

43. Id. at 238, citing Wisc. Stat. Ann. § 59.971(6).

44. Id. at 254-255.

45. David L. Callies, "The Quiet Revolution Revisited: A Quarter Century of Progress," in *Modernizing State Planning Statutes: The Growing Smart^{SM} Working Papers*, Vol. I, Planning Advisory Service Report No. 462/463, 19 (Chicago: American Planning Association, March 1996). See also Frank J. Popper, *Understanding American Land Use Regulation Since 1970: A Revisionist Interpretation,* 57 JAPA, No. 3, 291 (Summer 1988).

46. Callies, note 45, *supra,* at 19.

47. 30 N.Y.2d 359, 334 N.Y.S.2d 138, 285 N.E.2d 291 (1972), *appeal dismissed,* 409 U.S. 1003, 93 S.Ct. 440, 34 L.Ed.2d 294 (1972). For an update, see Julienne Marshall, *Whatever Happened to Ramapo?,* 69 Planning, No. 11, 4 (December 2003).

48. 522 F.2d 897 (9th Cir., 1975), *cert. denied,* 424 U.S. 934, 96 S.Ct. 1148, 47 L.Ed.2d 342 (1975).

49. See, e.g., Arthur C. Nelson, *Planner's Estimating Guide: Projecting Land-Use and Facilities Needs* (Chicago: American Planning Association, 2004).

50. Vermont (Environmental Board and District Environmental Commissions Act, 1970 Vt. Laws 250, current version at Vt. Stat. Ann. tit. 10, §§ 6001-6108); Florida (The State Comprehensive Planning Act of 1972, 1972 Fla. Laws, Chapter 72-295, current version at Fla. Stat. §§ 186.001-186.031, 186.801-186.911; Florida Environmental Land and Water Management Act of 1972, 1972 Fla. Laws, Chapter 72-317, current version at Fla. Stat. §§ 380.012-.27; Land Conservation Act of 1972, 1972 Fla. Laws, Chapter 72-300, current version at Fla. Stat. §§ 259.01-.101; Water Resources Act of 1972, 1972 Fla. Laws, Chapter 72-299, current version at Fla. Stat. §§ 373.013-.619; Local Government Comprehensive Planning Act, 1975 Fla. Laws, Chapter 75-257, current version at Fla. Stat. Ann. §§ 163.3161-.3215); Oregon (Land Use Planning Coordination Act, 1973 Or. Laws, Chapter 80, current version at Or. Rev. Stat., Chapter 197.005-.860); New Jersey (New Jersey State Planning Act, N.J. Rev. Stat. §§ 52:18A-196-52:18A-207; Fair Housing Act, N.J. Rev. Stat. §§ 52:27D-301 to 52:27D-329); Maine (Comprehensive Planning and Land Use Act, Me. Rev. Stat. Ann. tit. 30A, §§ 4301-4469); Rhode Island (Comprehensive Planning and Land Use Regulation Act, R.I. Gen. Laws §§ 45-22.2-1-45- 22.2-14); Washington (The Growth Management Act, Wash.

Rev. Code §§ 36-70A); Tennessee (Growth Management Act, Public Chapter 1101, Tenn. Stat. Ann. (1998)); and Wisconsin (1999 Wis. Act 9 (1999)). The Rhode Island law is a personal favorite because of the clarity of the drafting.

51. "Smart Growth" and Neighborhood Conservation Act, Chapter 759, 1997 Md. Laws 4335. See also a related law establishing "visions" for Maryland to be incorporated into local comprehensive plans (although affordable housing is not one of them): Economic Growth, Resource Protection, and Planning Act, 1992 Md. Laws, Chapter 437.

52. Raymond J. Burby and Peter J. May, *Making Governments Plan: State Experiments in Managing Land Use* (Baltimore: Johns Hopkins University Press, 1997).

53. Id. at 113.

54. Id. at 127, 132-133.

55. Robert E. Deyle and Richard Smith, *Local Government Compliance with State Planning Mandates: The Effectiveness of State Implementation in Florida,* 64 JAPA, No. 4, 457 (Autumn 1998).

56. Id. at 467.

57. Mary Edwards and Anna Haines, *Wisconsin's "Smart Growth" Planning Law: Is it Resulting in "Smart Growth" Plans?*, presented at the Association of Collegiate Schools of Planning conference, Portland, Oregon, Oct. 23, 2004 (unpublished). For a discussion of the Wisconsin law, see Brian W. Ohm, *Reforming Land Planning Legislation at the Dawn of the 21st Century: The Emerging Influence of Smart Growth and Livable Communities,* 32 Urb. Law. 181 (2000); Manan M. Yajnik, *Challenges to "Smart Growth": State Legislative Approaches to Comprehensive Growth Planning and the Local Government Issue,* 2004 Wis. L. Rev. 229 (2004) (comparison between Wisconsin and Maryland).

58. Edwards and Haines, note 57, *supra,* at 18.

59. Id. at 12.

60. John I. Carruthers, *The Impacts of State Growth Management Programs: A Comparative Analysis,* 39 Urb. Stud., No. 11, 1 (2002).

61. Carruthers discussed five states in particular. In California, which requires cities and counties to produce plans but has no vertical or horizontal consistency requirement, the analysis showed that the system over time has worked to decrease densities, raise property values, and indirectly slow population growth. "Through land market processes," he wrote, "growth was forced into relatively restrictive areas on the urban fringe." Id. at 1975.

In Florida, the planning mandate, which requires plans at the municipal, county, and regional levels, has proved to be "surprisingly ineffective" and "has worked to increase the extent of urbanizable land." Id.

Georgia's planning mandate, which encourages but does not require local governments to produce plans consistent with those developed by regional planning organizations, has, on the basis of the analysis, "been completely ineffective from the standpoint of growth management." The program, adopted in 1989 and conceived as a response to sprawl in the Atlanta region, has led to less dense development and higher property values. Id. at 1976.

Oregon's planning mandate is based on vertical and internal consistency and urban growth boundaries and, according to Carruthers, "has produced results that live up to the expectations of growth management." Id. Oregon's program was the only one that has produced more compact urban areas, he wrote. Id. at 1977. Because of its emphasis on accommodating urban land, he observed, the state's program had not had a significant impact on property values. Id. at 1976.

Washington's program, adopted in 1960, was the newest of those analyzed. It requires internal consistency for all local governments, horizontal consistency among the adjacent counties and, like Oregon, uses urban growth boundaries. The program, Carruthers found, had had little impact since its adoption: density, urbanized land area, and property values remained unaffected, which he theorized were a factor of the program's youth. Id. at 1977.

62. Id. at 1976.
63. ECONorthwest with David J. Newton Associates and MLP Associates, *Urban Growth Management: Case Studies Report,* prepared for Oregon Department of Land Conservation and Development, v-vii (Jan. 1991).
64. 1000 Friends of Oregon and the Home Builders Association of Metropolitan Portland, *Managing Growth to Promote Affordable Housing: Revisiting Oregon's Goal 10, Executive Summary* (Portland, OR: 1000 Friends of Oregon, Sept. 1991), 10.
65. Gerrit-Jan Knaap and Arthur C. Nelson, *The Regulated Landscape: Lessons on State Land Use Planning from Oregon* (Cambridge, MA: Lincoln Institute of Land Policy, 1992), 66-68.
66. Jerry Weitz and Terry Moore, *Development inside Urban Growth Boundaries: Oregon's Empirical Evidence of Contiguous Urban Form,* 65 JAPA, No. 4, 424 (Autumn 1998).
67. Anthony Downs, *Have Housing Prices Risen Faster in Portland than Elsewhere?* 13 Housing Policy Debate 1, 7 (2002).
68. Yan Song and Gerrit-Jan Knaap, *Measuring Urban Form: Is Portland Winning the War on Sprawl?,* 70 JAPA, No. 2, 210 (Spring 2004).
69. Id. at 223.
70. Jerry Anthony, *The Effects of Florida's Growth Management Act on Housing Affordability,* 69 JAPA, No. 3, 282, 292 (Summer 2003).
71. Id. at 292. [Emphasis in original.]
72. Stuart Meck, Rebecca Retzlaff, and James Schwab, *Regional Approaches to Affordable Housing,* Planning Advisory Service Report No. 513/514 (Chicago: American Planning Association, Feb. 2003).
73. Id. at 32. See N.J. Fair Housing Act, N.J. Rev. Stat. §§ 52:27D-301-52:27D-329.
74. Meck, Retzlaff, and Schwab, note 72, *supra,* at 42. The California housing element law can be found at Cal. Gov't. Code §§ 65583 et seq. (2004).
75. Id. at 142. For a good assessment of the Massachusetts law, see Sharon Krefetz, *The Impact and Evolution of the Massachusetts Comprehensive Permit and Zoning Appeals Act: Thirty Years of Experience with a State Legislative Effort to Overcome Exclusionary Zoning,* 22 W. New Eng. L. Rev. 381 (2001).
76. Meck, Retzlaff, and Schwab, note 72, *supra,* at 152.
77. Id. at 148.
78. For a good analysis of local building and land-use permitting in New York City, see Jerry J. Salama, Michael H. Schill, and Martha E. Stark, *Reducing the Cost of New Housing Construction in New York City: A Report to The New York City Partnership and Chamber of Commerce, The New York City Housing Partnership and The New York City Department of Housing Preservation and Development* (New York: Center for Real Estate and Urban Policy, 1999) (http://www.law.nyu.edu/realestatecenter/CREUP_Papers/Cost_Study/NYCHousingCost.pdf) (visited Nov. 21, 2004).
79. Arthur C. Nelson, *Comparative Judicial Land-Use Appeals Processes,* 27 Urb. Law. 251 (Spring 1995).
80. Id. at 265.
81. Anthony Downs, *Have Housing Prices Risen Faster in Portland than Elsewhere?* 13 Housing Policy Debate 1, 30 (2002).
82. James W. Hughes and Joseph J. Seneca, *The Beginning of the End of Sprawl?,* Rutgers Regional Report, Issue Paper No. 21 (May 2004) (finding a "powerful new residential trend" in the three-state New York metropolitan area in which the region's core is growing at a much greater rate than the suburban ring since 1994).
83. See Meck, note 3, *supra,* at 14-4 to 14-6. See also Rolf Pendall, *Do Land-Use Controls Cause Sprawl?* 26 Environment and Planning B: Planning and Design, No. 4, 555 (1999) (finding that regions whose local governments rely on ad valorem property taxes to fund services and infrastructure tend to sprawl more than those that rely on a broader tax base).

84. For some earlier pessimism on the effectiveness of regional planning agencies, see Richard F. Babcock, "Let's Stop Romancing Regionalism," in *Billboard, Glass Houses, and the Law, and Other Land Use Fables* (Colorado Springs, CO: Shepard's, 1977), 11. Commented Babcock: "Most regional plan commissions are political bastards, the offspring of a loveless dalliance between cynics and dreamers, with no general government willing to acknowledge more than a foster parent relationship." Id. at 15.

85. For a case affirming the Twin Cities Metropolitan Council's statutory authority to require a city to conform its comprehensive land-use plan to the council's system plans when the council determined that the city's plan may have a substantial impact on or contain a substantial departure from council's regional system plans, see *City of Lake Elmo v. Metropolitan Council*, 685 N.W.2d 1 (Minn. 2004).

86. See also Patricia E. Salkin, *Political Strategies for Modernizing State Land Use Statutes*, 44 Land Use Law & Zoning Digest, No. 8, 6 (Aug. 1992).

87. In planning statute reform studies that I have coauthored for the APA, I have tried to use small group interviews, questionnaires, and analyses of court decisions to get at the inner workings of planning statutes and local decision processes. See Stuart Meck and Marya Morris, *A Critical Analysis of Planning and Land-Use Laws in Montana: A Report of the American Planning Association Research Department for the Montana Smart Growth Coalition* (Chicago: American Planning Association, Jan. 2001); Stuart Meck and Marya Morris, *New Directions: Recommendations for Planning, Zoning, and Subdivision Law in Michigan* (Ann Arbor, MI: Michigan Society of Planning, March 2004).

88. On this point, see Stuart Meck, *Present at the Creation: A Personal Account of the APA Growing Smart[SM] Project*, 54 Land Use Law & Zoning Digest, No. 3, 3, at 8 (March 2002).

89. The housing plan had to consist of at least the following:

"(i) a statement of the total number of affordable housing units that are necessary to exempt the local government from the operation of this act;

"(ii) an identification of lands within the jurisdiction that are most appropriate for the construction of affordable housing and of existing structures most appropriate for conversion to, or rehabilitation for, affordable housing, including a consideration of lands and structures of developers who have expressed a commitment to provide affordable housing and lands and structures that are publicly or semi-publicly owned;

"(iii) incentives that local governments may provide for the purpose of attracting affordable housing to their jurisdiction; and

"(iv) a goal of a minimum of 15 percent of all new development or redevelopment within the local government that would be defined as affordable housing in the act; or a minimum of a 3 percentage point increase in the overall percentage of affordable housing within its jurisdiction; or minimum of a total of 10 percent of affordable housing within its jurisdiction." 310 ILCS 67/25 (b) (2004)

When developers later submit proposals for affordable housing developments to the local government under the Illinois act, the assumption was that the plan would serve as a direction-giving device on where such housing should go, and in what amounts, and serve as a defense when the local government denied proposals that were not consistent with it, proposals that could be subsequently appealed to the state-level board. Apart from the plan, there was no mandate that local government subsidize affordable housing or take any other specific actions involving the spending of money. All of the action to build affordable housing would come from either the private sector or nonprofit groups.

90. See Meck, note 88, *supra*, at 9.

91. Kentucky (K.R.S. § 147A.027); Tennessee (Tn. Code Ann. § 13-3-101 (j), § 13-4-101(c), § 13-7-106 (b), § 13-7-205 (c)); South Carolina (S. C. Code Ann. §§ 6-29-1310 et seq.); Louisiana (La. Rev. Stat. § 33:103.1).

4

Development Review Wars: Failing the Fairness Test

John J. Delaney

INTRODUCTION

What follows are thoughts and reflections from the perspective of a practitioner of land-use law in Montgomery County, Maryland, and an ardent observer of how it is done elsewhere.[1] Maryland has been recognized as one of the four "most important" and "most interesting" states for its zoning jurisprudence, a body of case law which "tend[s] to be rather unsympathetic to developers' claims" and "strikingly sympathetic to neighbors."[2] However, Maryland courts have strictly construed "aggrievement" standards in determining issues of third-party standing in site-specific land-use cases.[3]

The above comments are made in the interest of full disclosure in light of what is to come regarding this author's concerns about the generally confused state of the planning and development review processes in many jurisdictions throughout the country.[4] While recognizing that land-use planning and regulation has historically been a *political* process, it is nevertheless disconcerting to observe the extent to which fair and predictable decision-making has been skewed by that reality. In the absence of serious reforms, such as those discussed below, achieving smart growth in the prevailing, open-ended development review environment will likely be an impossible task.

This paper identifies eight major "needs" for "growing smart" to succeed, namely:

1. The need to reform the development review process so that it will become stable, predictable, and certain;

2. The need for greater involvement of the state in planning and development review;

3. The need to end the "tilt" against residential uses in land-use plans and regulations;

4. The need for a process that balances job growth with housing for the workforce;

5. The need for a meaningful remediation alternative to litigation when addressing obvious inequitable regulatory burdens on specific properties;

6. The need to immediately address the chaotic common law of vested rights—one of the most serious threats to the orderly planning and financing of development;

7. The need to stem the burgeoning use of initiatives and referenda to preclude affordable housing; and

8. The need to end the abuse of moratoria in the development review process.

These and ancillary issues are summarized in the sections to follow.

THE NEED TO REFORM THE DEVELOPMENT REVIEW PROCESS

Smart growth cannot be achieved without "smart process." This was recognized long ago by the late Richard Babcock, the "godfather" of land-use attorneys, who called for nationwide statutory reform to establish balanced adjudicatory procedures at the local government level. He noted that before communities "can indulge in the luxury of debate on design" [they must] face up to the issue of fair play in municipal administration.[5] Similar sentiments for a stable development review process have echoed increasingly from smart growth advocates in recent years. For example, the Smart Growth Network cites among its 10 "Smart Growth Principles" the "need to make development decisions predictable, fair and cost effective." For smart growth to flourish, the Network asserts that "state and local governments must make an effort to make development decisions that support innovation in a more timely, cost-effective and predicable way for developers."[6]

Recognizing the Two District Phases of the Land-Use Regulatory Process: A Threshold Issue

As a general principle, applicants for land-use approvals are interested in a process that is stable, predictable, and certain, so that they will know where they stand and when a final decision will be forthcoming. The degree of difficulty of the process, although very important, is not the primary concern.

Too often, achievement of these goals is being frustrated because land-use regulations in many states fail to recognize and incorporate the vast differences between the two major phases of the land-use regulatory process, namely *comprehensive planning and zoning* on the one hand and *post-zoning development review* on the other. They are fundamentally different processes: one is essentially *legislative* in character; the other, in many jurisdictions, is regarded as *adjudicatory* or *quasi-judicial*. Public hearings are an essential element of both. Yet, just who the "public" should be in each process, and the extent to which it should participate therein, are *threshold questions* that have not been adequately understood or addressed.

We believe that the *Growing Smart[SM] Legislative Guidebook* (hereinafter "the Guidebook") by the American Planning Association (APA), although well documented with scholarly research and containing many positive features,[7] has not gone far enough in addressing this threshold issue. This may be attributable to an expansive vision of "planning" as an ongoing continuum of regulatory activity, forever in flux as it searches for compromise and consensus. Whether or not this is true, the Guidebook's *preferred* post-zoning development review process:

- Is virtually *open ended*;
- *Tends to favor opponents* of development over applicants;
- Institutionalizes "NIMBYism"[8]; and
- *Affords easier access to court for opponents* of development than for applicants.

Some of these issues can be addressed or ameliorated through judicious use of other options or alternatives provided in the Guidebook.[9]

Comprehensive Planning and Zoning

As noted, comprehensive planning and zoning are generally policy-making legislative proceedings, involving preparation and adoption of comprehensive plans and subplans as well as the comprehensive zoning ordinance text and map. They are often exhaustive in scope; well publicized; usually involve many public hearings, meetings, and work sessions (sometimes over a period of years); and culminate in the adoption of land-use laws and policies that affect the community at large.[10] The long-established tradition in many communities of fostering widespread public participation and testimony in these proceedings should be continued and encouraged. Public involvement at the comprehensive planning/zoning stage is often much more extensive and substantive than it is, for example, in the typical "rule-making" process at the federal and state government levels, where only minimal notice is often provided.

Post-Zoning Development Review

Third-Party Standing: The "Aggrievement" Standard

As noted, post-zoning, site-specific development review proceedings (i.e., a hearing on a subdivision, site plan, or conditional use application) *implement* the plan. They are generally quasi-judicial or adjudicatory in nature, particularly when a public hearing is required, and are normally conducted by administrative agencies that are responsible for determining adjudicative facts (i.e., *facts specific to the parties, their properties, and activities*).

In most cases, "third-party standing" (i.e., the *legal right* to testify and present evidence in such proceedings) should not be extended to the public at large, but should focus instead upon *aggrieved parties,* meaning residents of adjacent properties, the immediate neighborhood, and their civic association who are *prima facie* aggrieved,[11] or other persons (whose property is more remotely located from the subject property) who can demonstrate that they may suffer special harm or injury from the proposed use, over and above its expected impact upon the public generally.[12]

Many, if not most, jurisdictions use the "person aggrieved" standard to determine one's standing to participate as a "third party" in a development review proceeding.[13] However, the Guidebook has not adopted this widely accepted aggrievement standard as its primary test for determining third-party standing in a development review proceeding. (It is merely an "option.")

The Guidebook's preferred option would leave open a broad opportunity for nonaggrieved persons (i.e., persons *not* suffering any *special* harm or injury but merely a generalized "harm or injury") to participate in development review proceedings. For example, under the Guidebook's preferred standard, virtually any member of the public could participate in a site-specific proceeding without having to demonstrate aggrieved status under the "special harm or injury" test (§§ 10-101 and 10-207(5)). Thereafter, such persons would *retain standing to seek judicial review* of the agency's decision under the Guidebook's relaxed standing provisions.[14]

Of course, determination of aggrievement on a case-by-case basis is a question of fact for the court.[15] Were a court to make this determination on the basis of the preferred definition in the Guidebook, it would have to confer standing upon:

• "all other persons" who participated by right in the agency review or who were parties to a record hearing on a development permit application, without any showing of aggrieved status (§ 10-607(4)); and

• "any other person, neighborhood council, community organization or governmental unit," *even if they did not participate in the agency proceedings,* merely on a showing that they are "aggrieved" under the Guidebook's expansive definition of that term (§ 10607(5)).

This evidences a major *philosophical divide* between third-party standing rules heretofore followed in most jurisdictions and the Guidebook's preferred, more relaxed standard. As noted, the Guidebook's approach seems to reflect a perspective of many in the public sector who favor an open-ended process that is easily accessible to the general public at all stages, and where consensus and compromise are seen as preeminent virtues to be espoused. Such a philosophy may well be appropriate at the comprehensive planning/zoning stage, where broad-based policies and laws affecting the use and development of land within the community are forged; however, it has no place in a post-zoning *adjudicatory* development review process where these policies and laws are being *implemented and applied* to specific sites.

By analogy, formulating new policies and laws regarding tort reform is everyone's business. The trial in the local courthouse on Mrs. Smith's tort action against Mr. Jones is usually not. Imposing what is essentially an open-ended development review process at the post-zoning stage is grossly unfair to applicants. Further, by elongating and ultimately undermining that process, it defers the achievement of smart growth goals. Accordingly, when third-party standing is discussed at the state and local government levels, the Guidebook's preferred definition of "aggrieved" (§ 10-101) should be resisted in favor of the Guidebook's alternative "special harm or injury" option, which is the traditional standard for establishing third-party standing in post-zoning development review proceedings.

Rearguing Settled Issues

Unfortunately, the post-zoning, site-specific development review proceeding is often used as a forum for rearguing broad public policy issues that have been decided at the comprehensive planning/zoning stage. This is an abuse of the process and often contributes to extensive delay. Issues decided at the comprehensive planning/zoning stage (e.g., use, density, or intensity), or the phasing of development, should ordinarily *not* be revisited in the post-zoning, site-specific development review proceeding *unless* the application does not comply with previously adopted legislative/policy determinations of these issues. For example, if a proposed 20-lot subdivision is within the density contemplated in the plan and allowed on the zoning map, the issue of density should rarely, if ever, arise at the hearing on the subdivision application.[16]

It is critical for the integrity of the process that this principle be *codified* in state planning and zoning enabling laws and local ordinances. Without such codification, there will be little protection or political cover for decision-makers who must face the onslaught of often well-organized, entrenched residents of areas planned for growth. These persons inevitably have an economic stake in maintaining the status quo (i.e., restricting the supply of new housing—particularly higher-density housing) and consistently resist applications for new development—particularly higher-density residential development—even if it conforms with the plan.[17] One way to protect the integrity of the development review process would be to *amend state planning and zoning enabling acts* to provide that, within a specified number of years following adoption/amendment of a comprehensive or local plan, "major issues decided in the plan, shall not be reargued or reconsidered in any post-zoning, site specific proceeding."[18]

Judicial Review: Supplementation of the Record

Courts conducting "record reviews" of land-use decisions should exercise judicial restraint, particularly with respect to agency findings of fact on evidentiary matters. They should not allow the record to be supplemented with additional substantive evidence on appeal, or take other actions that would usurp the traditional decision-making authority of local government in the land-use approval process. Historically, reviewing courts have limited their review of an agency action to the question of whether that action is arbitrary, capricious, unreasonable, or illegal. When the agency record is not complete, or is too flawed to enable a court to review the agency decision, the proper practice is to remand the matter to the agency for rehearing and redetermination.[19]

However, in an optional provision (§ 10-613(i)(d)) closely mirroring the expanded standing provisions described herein in the section entitled "Third-Party Standing: The 'Aggrievement' Standard," the Guidebook would liberally allow for expansion of the record by the reviewing court. The optional provision states that the court "may supplement the record with additional evidence" [if it relates to] "*matters indispensable to the equitable disposition of the appeal.*" This open-ended provision could easily be abused. Parties would be able to introduce new studies, new testimony, and new exhibits that were never made available to the local government that issued the land-use decision in the first place. Neither would the applicant have had an opportunity to challenge, verify, or modify this new evidence in a deliberative process before the responsible agency. Such a provision could turn courts into planning and zoning appeals boards, allowing them not only to second guess a local government decision but to determine cases based upon extra-record evidence, with no deference to local concerns.

Treatise writers and court decisions have narrowly construed the role of courts on judicial review.

> "The local government, not the court, should be the final decision-maker in land use cases. Generally, the judge's role in land use litigation is to provide a forum for serious and disinterested review of the issues, sharply limited in scope but independent of the immediate pressures which often play upon the legislative and administrative decision-making processes."[20]

These authorities and numerous reported cases reflect the overwhelming consensus that an appellate court should not be second-guessing the merits of an administrative finding and, except for corrections of ministerial errors or minor mistakes, it should use its remand authority when required findings on the evidence are flawed or missing.

Piecemeal Rezoning: A Proposal to Resolve the "Legislative vs. Adjudicatory" Conundrum?

We pause at this point to discuss "piecemeal rezoning," a procedure that ideally should be rare, and that cannot truly be characterized as either "comprehensive" zoning *or* "post-zoning" development review. The nature and character of piecemeal rezoning has long been a subject of debate. We offer a resolution to that debate, one based upon a well-reasoned decision of Maryland's high court, which avoids the shoals underlying the two currently prevailing—and somewhat doctrinaire—points of view.

Landowners sometimes find it necessary to *return* to the zoning process in order *to amend the underlying law* governing the use of their property. For example, in a situation where a desired use of property is not feasible under existing zoning, variances are not available, and waiting for the next comprehensive rezoning cycle is not a viable option, the filing of a "piecemeal" application to rezone the property may be the only practical means of obtaining redress.

The nature of this process, also known as the "local map amendment" process, has evoked considerable discussion, debate, and *confusion* in recent decades. For example, is rezoning by local map amendment—like comprehensive rezoning —"legislative" in character, thereby enjoying a strong presumption of correctness that can be overturned upon judicial review only if found to be arbitrary or capricious under a deferential rational basis test? While most state courts answer "yes" to this question,[21] a growing minority of courts, following the lead of the Oregon Supreme Court, have adopted the view that the piecemeal rezoning *decision* is *judicial* or *quasi-judicial* in nature.[22] Therefore, the presumption of validity normally afforded to legislative acts does *not* apply.

The Fasano *Case*

In *Fasano*, the Supreme Court of Oregon ruled that a decision by the local government's legislative body in a piecemeal rezoning case was "an exercise of *judicial* rather than legislative authority."[23] To reach this conclusion, the court had to sidestep the state legislature's express delegation of its "power to amend zoning ordinances"[24] (clearly a legislative function) to the governing body of the county. The court explained:

> "[W]e feel we would be ignoring reality to rigidly view all zoning decisions by local governing bodies as legislative acts to be accorded a full presumption of validity and shielded from less than constitutional scrutiny by the theory of separation of powers. Local and small decision groups are simply not the equivalent in all respects of state and national legislatures. There is a growing judicial recognition of this fact of life."[25]

Approximately a dozen state courts have followed the rationale of *Fasano*.[26]

The **Hyson** *Case*

Several years before *Fasano*, Maryland's highest court, in *Hyson v. Montgomery County*,[27] sought to avoid issues arising from separation of powers principles that are inherent in the "legislative vs. quasi-judicial" debate over piecemeal rezoning. It declined to adopt either the inflexible rule that local map amendments are purely legislative, or its fanciful opposite that a delegated portion of the state's *legislative* power to a local government, when exercised by the local government's legislative body, somehow "morphs" into a *judicial* or *quasi-judicial function*. Instead, the court steered a middle course, first by reaffirming its repeated holdings that the actual acts of rezoning are legislative or quasi-legislative in nature. However, it further held that when state law or local ordinance require a public hearing on an application for rezoning and "prescribe within constitutional limitations the mode of conducting the hearing"[28] [it is] "improper and inaccurate to characterize the *whole proceeding* . . . as quasi-legislative or quasi-judicial in nature."[29]

County ordinances required, among other things, that any interested party could testify at the rezoning hearing; that a written transcript be maintained; that the transcript and exhibits were to be considered a part of the record; and that the county council's decision was to be based upon the evidence of record. In the court's view, these provisions required the council to resolve "disputed questions of adjudicative facts" concerning particular parties.[30] In determining these facts, the council "was performing a quasi-judicial function," even though its final decision granting or denying the application "was quasi-legislative in character."[31] Moreover, a "reasonable right of cross examination" must be allowed.[32]

Simply put, *Hyson* holds that the act of rezoning is legislative, thus enjoying a presumption of correctness. However, if a hearing is required and procedural safeguards are provided by state or local government legislation, the court will look *behind* the decision—at the *conduct of the hearing*—to ensure that the procedural due process rights of the parties have not been violated. This appears to be a viable approach to resolving a vexing constitutional issue that finds its roots in the separation of powers doctrine.[33] The majority rule—that piecemeal rezoning is legislative—seems overly broad, while the *Fasano* rule invokes a slight of hand (that the exercise of delegated *legislative* authority somehow becomes a *judicial* activity) and effectively turns the court into a zoning board. The *Hyson* rule protects the integrity of the legislative prerogative in piecemeal rezoning, while also recognizing the need for enhanced procedural due process rights for the parties to the hearing. Each of the three approaches has advantages and disadvantages. These are briefly summarized in Table 4-1.

Table 4-1. Advantages/Disadvantages of Each Approach

	Advantages	Disadvantages
Legislative approach (most states)	• Is less time-consuming and less costly. • Zoning power in local legislative body is retained. • Piecemeal rezoning as essentially a political process is recognized.	• Court review is significantly restricted. • Greater opportunity for abuse by local legislatures exists.
Quasi-judicial approach, Oregon *(Fasano)*	• Closer scrutiny by the courts is promoted. • Greater procedural due process protections for participants exist. • Protects rezoning from abuses arising from the local political process.	• Is least protective of local legislative prerogatives. • Requires courts to become "super zoning boards." • More lengthy proceedings, which will likely require hearing examiners, occur. • Is more costly for government and development.
Bifurcated approach (decision legislative; proceedings quasi-judicial), Maryland *(Hyson)*	• Presumption of correctness of tribunal decision is retained. • Greater procedural due process protections for participants exist. • Partially insulates piecemeal rezoning from abuses arising from the local political process.	• Court review is somewhat restricted. • More lengthy proceedings, which will likely require hearing examiners, occur. • Is more costly for government and development.

THE NEED TO GROW SMART THROUGH A PROCESS THAT BALANCES JOB GROWTH WITH HOUSING FOR THE WORKFORCE

Smart Growth: Easier Said Than Done

Musings of a Suburban Alderman in the Path of Growth[34]

Our growth management plans are set.
We have run the regulatory course.
The arch enemy we have met.
Indeed, it is our own work force!

They want to live near where they work.
But they play us for abject fools.
For with that comes another "perk."
Their children will attend our schools.

> Should we zone for jobs, large lots, plains of grass?
> Thus avoiding that taxing load.
> And tell that pesky working class
> To "keep on moving down the road."
>
> Or should we zone for density
> To balance new jobs with housing for all?
> And show that planning need not be
> The sweet siren song for suburban sprawl.

Smart growth is supposed to be about encouraging and facilitating growth in designated growth envelopes, not merely about prohibiting or restricting growth outside of these envelopes. State and local governments committed to smart growth are often inclined to focus on the relatively easy tasks, such as designating open space areas, sensitive or critical areas, agricultural preserves, and historic districts. These "soft" decisions are usually politically popular and enjoy widespread community support.

However, the converse is not true regarding the "hard" decisions about *accommodating growth in planned growth areas*, particularly with respect to providing housing for the community's workers and combating sprawl. As a result, these decisions are not being made in a timely fashion or are being postponed altogether. Smart process is essential if these twin goals are to be achieved in a region's planned growth areas. At the outset, the legal framework within which the land-use regulatory process is conducted must be understood and evaluated. This is particularly relevant with regard to the issue of balancing a region's planned job growth with housing.

The "Balanced Growth Checklist": Discerning Whether the State and the Developing Local Government are Committed to Balancing Job Growth with Housing for the Workforce

Workforce housing has emerged as a major issue across the country.[35] It is not the purpose of this paper to address this issue in detail, as it is included in the discussions of a separate panel. However, in the case of a developing community, it is important to know at the outset whether there is a *climate for reform* in that community. Are the state and local governments receptive to growing smart (i.e., to combating sprawl and balancing that community's new job growth with sufficient housing for its workers and their families)?

The following checklist of questions is intended to serve as a guide in discerning an answer to this question.[36] As a general matter, *state* plans and land-use laws, including planning and zoning enabling acts—along with a *local government's plans*, regulations, and policies—should be examined to determine whether the operative land-use regulatory framework in that community is likely to promote *balanced growth*. It is not enough to review only the plans and ordinances of the local government. Balanced growth is a *regional* issue.[37] Thus, state planning and regulatory oversight are essential to achieving regional solutions to this problem. By "balanced growth," we mean: (1) authorizing residential uses in planned growth areas at sufficiently high densities to facilitate workforce housing while protecting environmentally sensitive areas, and (2) discouraging sprawl. As will be seen, the Guidebook addresses some of these issues.

The "Balanced Growth Checklist"

- *Initiatives and Referenda:* Is an initiative or referendum process in place or readily available? Initiatives and referenda are often directed at affordable housing and are proving to be a major problem.[38] The Guidebook has not faced up to this problem. It proposes model laws that would allow initiatives to proliferate in states where they are not already permitted in the state constitution and sanctions *neighborhood plebiscites*—a dubious concept that has been frowned upon by the Supreme Court and state courts.[39]

- *The State Planning and Zoning Act:* Does the state planning and zoning enabling act, plan, or other document (1) adopt a *regional approach* to housing, with state oversight and/or standards for achieving *fair share goals* for workforce housing, or (2) include a statement of purpose, a "vision statement," or a mandate strongly asserting the need for housing in general, and *conveniently located affordable housing* in particular?[40]

- *The Comprehensive Plan:* Does the local government's comprehensive plan include a *housing element* and an *affordable housing element*?[41]

- *Capital Improvement Program and Budget:* Do the local government's capital improvement program (CIP) and budget provide for or mandate *funding to timely implement the comprehensive plan* recommendations regarding roads, schools, and other infrastructure needed to support planned growth, including residential development?[42] Does the state's CIP *prioritize* the use of state funds for infrastructure and public amenities in *planned growth areas*?

- *Zoning Ordinance Text and Map:* Do the local zoning ordinance text and zoning map allow residential uses at *sufficiently high densities* in planned growth areas to *support workforce housing* (i.e., apartments, townhouses, and single-family dwellings on small lots)?

- *Minimum Densities in Major Growth Areas:* To promote efficient use of land, are "minimum densities" required in, for example, central business districts and other planned major growth areas, such as areas adjacent to public transportation hubs and subway stations, or is the zoning map dominated by large-lot "sprawl" zoning?[43]

- *Discriminating Against Residential Uses:* In many jurisdictions, "growth management" really means "*residential* growth management." Do the local government's policies or regulations discriminate against or limit residential uses, including affordable housing, in comparison to other uses such as office, retail, or industrial? For example:

- ○ Do the *growth management plan and regulations restrict residential development* while imposing few, if any, restrictions upon nonresidential development?[44]
- ○ Does the *adequate public facilities ordinance apply to all categories of development or only to residential development?*[45]
- ○ Is there a history of imposing *development moratoria* primarily upon *residential development*, while other use categories (e.g., office, retail, and industrial) are not significantly affected?
- ○ Are *development taxes/impact fees imposed disproportionately* upon new residential development while existing residential and nonresidential uses get a "free ride"?[46]

• *Prioritizing "Smart Growth" Development Applications:* Do development review regulations and procedures pertaining to subdivision, site plan, and related post-zoning reviews provide flexibility and prioritize the processing of affordable housing applications on sites located in planned, high-density growth areas?

• *Buildable Residential Land Inventories:* Is the local government required to maintain an inventory of buildable residential land and establish a land-market monitoring system to periodically evaluate the supply and availability of buildable land?[47]

REMEDIATION: A NEEDED ALTERNATIVE TO LITIGATION WHEN ADDRESSING INEQUITABLE REGULATORY BURDENS ON LANDOWNERS

A meaningful, nonbinding remediation or mitigation mechanism is urgently needed to provide a viable alternative to litigation and to allow local governments to equitably redress (within the applicable zoning envelope) situations in which federal, state, or local regulations have imposed "inequitable regulatory burdens" upon a specific parcel of land which, in fairness and justice, should be borne by the public as a whole.

Remediation is best suited to large parcels of land where the cumulative effect of land-use restrictions has significantly reduced the permissible "development envelope" under existing zoning and where the traditional "area variance" is not a workable solution. The restrictions need not necessarily have resulted in a regulatory taking to qualify for remediation. Rather, the concept is to bring about an equitable solution when regulations designed to promote the public welfare have a markedly disparate impact upon a narrow segment of the community.

The need to provide for a remediation mechanism in planning and zoning enabling acts is demonstrable. This mechanism should be nonbinding, flexible, and open to the public, and should also incorporate standards for approval, including findings that address the underlying health-safety-welfare concerns, which gave rise to the restrictions on the property in the first place, and a requirement that the proposed development conform with the applicable master plan and zoning.

For example, if a burdened property consists of 100 acres and applicable zoning would allow up to 200 residential lots (but regulatory restraints have severely reduced its potential yield), a favorable decision on a remediation request must not result in more than 200 lots being approved. As noted below, if, at the end of the day, the remediation request is disapproved or approved only in part, and litigation ensues, the government entity's findings regarding the existence or absence of an inequitable burden on the property would not be binding upon it.

Features of Remediation

Listed below are some of the features of the remediation mechanism:

• It is a *nonbinding* alternative process that can reduce the need for litigation, particularly in borderline regulatory taking cases.

• It does not rely upon use variances.

• It utilizes the vast experience of local governments acquired over many decades of regulating land use in addressing site-specific problems.

• The procedure is *voluntary* and can occur as part of the local government's existing development review process, such as during subdivision review.

• A *public hearing* is required.

• The local government *retains discretion* to approve the remediation request in whole or in part, or to deny it.

• The local government's findings regarding the existence or absence of an inequitable burden on the affected property *are not binding* upon it or the landowner in any subsequent litigation that may arise concerning the use, density, or intensity of development of the property.

Requirements for Approval of Remediation

To approve a remediation request, the local government would be required to find that:

• The use, density, or intensity of development upon the landowner's property has been *inequitably burdened* by regulatory actions;[48]

• The *conditions* of approval *address* the *public interest concerns* that gave rise to the restrictions on the property;

• Approval will result in development that is *consistent with the comprehensive plan*; and

• The resulting use, density, or intensity *will not exceed* that which is authorized for the entire tract under *applicable zoning*.

The Guidebook contains a limited remediation mechanism.[49]

THE COMMON LAW OF VESTED RIGHTS: A HODGEPODGE OF OUTDATED CONFLICTING RULES UNSUITED TO THE COMPLEXITIES OF MODERN-DAY PLANNING AND DEVELOPMENT

The land-use regulatory review process is often lengthy and multifaceted. It can involve numerous approvals, including rezoning and an array of post-zoning approvals such as subdivision, record plat, site plan, conditional uses, and numerous permits, including stormwater management, grading, demolition, foundation, and building permits. These land-use approvals are often followed by significant development activity such as engineering, land dedications, payment of regulatory exactions, fees and taxes, grading, and infrastructure installation. These activities can impose major financial obligations upon developers and lenders, long before the first building permit for the project has been issued. Yet, in 60 percent of the states, a landowner has no common-law vested right to rely on prebuilding permit approvals in the event of an intervening change in law that deletes the use or reduces the previously approved density.

In many jurisdictions, the development review process has become increasingly unpredictable, repetitive, costly, and fraught with peril. The late Justice William J. Brennan, Jr., in his famous "plurality dissent" in the *San Diego Gas* case, quoted from the following advice given by a California municipal attorney to his peers, to illustrate the extreme seriousness of the problem faced by applicants for land-use approvals:

> "IF ALL ELSE FAILS, MERELY AMEND THE REGULATION AND START OVER AGAIN.

> "If legal preventive maintenance does not work, and you still receive a claim attacking the land use regulation, or if you try the case and lose, don't worry about it. All is not lost. One of the extra 'goodies' contained in [a recent California Supreme Court case] appears to allow the City to change the regulation in question, even after trial and judgment, make it more reasonable, more restrictive, or whatever, and everybody starts over again.

> "See how easy it is to be a City Attorney. Sometimes you can lose the battle and still win the war. Good luck."[50]

Projects that have received repeated agency reviews and approvals may nevertheless be denied final permit approval based upon a myriad of reasons. These usually involve an intervening change in law that is often attributable to a volatile political climate, resulting in the election of public officials whose views on growth are significantly different from those of their predecessors. When the rules affecting approvals of use or density change in the middle of the process, it is often difficult to find solace in the state's vesting laws. In a great many states, vesting rules are court-made and often result in "late vesting" scenarios (i.e., no matter how many prior approvals a project may have received, the developer has no vested right to the use, density, or intensity shown on his approved plans, regardless of the resources spent or obligated in reliance upon these approvals).

Courts generally apply two basic standards in determining whether a right has been acquired to complete a project as originally conceived before the proposed rule or actual change in regulations. One standard, known as the "vesting rule," applies principles of common and constitutional law, focusing upon whether real property rights that cannot be taken away by subsequent government regulation have been acquired.[51] The second standard, known as the "estoppel rule," derives from equity and focuses upon whether it would equitable to allow the government to repudiate its prior conduct. It employs a balancing approach under which a local government may be estopped from changing regulations when:

> "[a] property owner (1) in good faith, (2) relying upon some act or omission of government; (3) has made such a substantial change in position or has incurred such extensive obligations and expenses that it would be highly inequitable and unjust to destroy the right he acquired."[52]

The Late Vesting Rule

In approximately 30 states, there is no vested right to develop a pending project in the face of an intervening change in law affecting use, density, intensity, or other development rights, unless building permits have been issued for each of the buildings in the project. Some states require more than mere issuance of a building permit—namely, actual commencement of construction authorized by the permit.[53]

The traditional late vesting rule is out of date and unfair.[54] It fails to recognize the complexity of the modern regulatory environment, or the difference between a single building project on the one hand and long-term or multi-building projects on the other. For example, in the *Avco* case,[55] the developer of a 5,000-acre, phased planned-unit development (PUD) was held not to have achieved vested rights regarding a 74-acre parcel designated for multiple family use, even though the PUD had been approved years before and nearly $3 million had been expended or obligated by the developer in planning and site improvements, including the conveyance of parkland to the county at a below-market price.

The court's decision was based upon the traditional late vesting rule followed in California that work performed and liabilities incurred to vest one's rights must be pursuant to a valid building permit. However, in support of its reasoning, the court cited only cases involving conventional *single-building developments,* in contrast to Avco's *multiphased project* where enormous front-end development costs had been incurred before the first building permit was issued. Nevertheless, the court asserted that there were only "minor factual variations" between Avco's situation and the cited cases.[56]

Legislative Reforms

As a result of these problems, 15 states have attempted to deal with the issue of vested rights through legislation.[57] This has taken the form of laws *codifying vested rights* and laws authorizing local governments and landowners/developers to execute *development agreements* as part of the development approval process.

States Codifying Vested Rights

States that have codified vested rights include:

Arizona	Maine	Pennsylvania
Colorado	Massachusetts	Texas
Connecticut	New Jersey	Vermont
Florida	North Carolina	Virginia
Kansas	Oregon	Washington

A number of these states recognize vested rights based upon the filing of a complete application that is in accordance with regulations in effect at the time of filing. This is essentially one of the options in the Guidebook that has gone to great lengths to address the vesting issue.[58] Other states confer vested rights as of the date of a prebuilding permit development approval, such as approval of a preliminary subdivision plan, record plat, or site plan.

States Authorizing Development Agreements

Development agreements have emerged as a valuable tool in stabilizing the development review process. Thirteen states, beginning with California, have enacted development agreement legislation as a further response to the difficulties encountered in common law late vesting rules.[59]

An obvious hurdle in this regard is the issue of bargaining away the police power. (See discussion herein of a significant court decision on this issue in the section entitled "Is Government 'Bargaining Away' Its Police Power?") For many years, ad hoc agreements between local governments and applicants for land-use approvals have been viewed dimly by most courts as a surrender or a bargaining away of the police power, and thus have been invalidated as being contrary to uniformity requirements and public policy.[60]

However, the development agreements laws in effect in the states listed below contain guidelines and criteria designed to address this issue. For example, they require that a development agreement may be approved only after a *public hearing*, and establish a number of *standards* that must be met by local governments and private parties that desire to enter into such agreements. One of these is that an agreement must contain a statement describing how the proposed development will conform to the *applicable laws and the comprehensive plan of the jurisdiction. Phasing* of development based upon availability of public facilities may also be required. Moreover, the local government retains the right to *suspend or terminate* an agreement when such action is essential to protect public health, safety, or welfare.

States authorizing development agreements include:[61]

Arizona	Louisiana	Oregon
Colorado	Maryland	Virginia
Connecticut	Minnesota	Washington
Florida	Nevada	
Hawaii	New Jersey	

Public Sector Benefits

The development agreement can be an attractive mechanism in resolving the concerns of both the public and private sectors regarding conditional land-use approvals. From the perspective of the public sector, the Supreme Court's decision in *Dolan v. City of Tigard*[62] must be taken into account when conditioning permit approvals or imposing exactions. In *Dolan,* the Supreme Court held that there must be "rough proportionality" between a regulatory exaction and the "projected impact" of the proposed development. Further, the burden of proof is on the government—not the landowner/developer—to demonstrate rough proportionality.

The development agreement offers the government entity an opportunity to negotiate exactions or permit conditions and thus avoid *Dolan*-mandated closer court scrutiny of exactions that might otherwise have to be imposed during the development review process. At the same time, the development agreement provides a greater degree of certainty that infrastructure and other public amenities needed to support new growth will in fact be provided on a timely basis.

Private Sector Benefits

Similarly, the development agreement assures greater predictability and stability for developers and lenders in uncertain and volatile regulatory environments by providing a "freeze period" during which the laws and regulations enacted subsequent to project approval will not affect the approved use, density, or intensity of the development *unless exigent circumstances subsequently arise,* which affect public health, safety, or welfare to such a degree as to warrant suspension or termination of the agreement. Thus, it is not surprising that representatives of local government and builders associations have supported development agreements legislation.

Is Government "Bargaining Away" Its Police Power?

A significant California decision has raised hopes that development agreements authorized pursuant to state law will answer this question in the negative. In *Santa Margarita Area Residents Together v. San Luis Obispo County Board of Supervisors*,[63] believed to be the first case of its kind, a California appellate court squarely addressed the issue of bargaining away police power in the context of development agreements executed pursuant to the California Development Agreements statute. The court expressly rejected a claim that the challenged development agreement effectively contracted away the police power of the zoning board, resulting in a surrender of the board's right to exercise its police power in the future.[64]

The statute allowed any city or county to enter into an agreement with the developer to develop a property. It included "requirements that a development agreement may be approved only after a public hearing . . . and must be consistent with the general plan and any specific plan . . ., a provision permitting annual review by the government entity and termination for non-compliance . . . and a statement that the agreement is subject to referendum. . . ."[65]

The defendant county had entered into an agreement that effectively "froze" the zoning of the named property for five years in return for a commitment from the developer to provide a construction plan. The court held that, since the project must at all times be constructed in accordance with the general plan of the county, there was no surrender of the police power.

The California Supreme Court declined to review the *Santa Margarita* decision. Thus, there is judicial precedent for the conclusion that development agreements, properly prepared and executed pursuant to standards contained in state enabling laws, will not violate historic proscriptions against bargaining away police power.

Suggestions for Common Law Reform

The following reforms are proposed for states that do not have vested rights statutes or development agreements legislation, particularly those states adhering to the late vesting "building permit plus construction" rule.[66]

It is recommended that reviewing courts consider the following factors:

• *The late vesting rule, based upon commencement of construction pursuant to a valid building permit, should not be applied in cases involving long-term, multibuilding projects.* The late vesting rule requiring construction of *a building* pursuant to *a building permit* has no place in long-term buildout cases where, in reliance upon repeated development approvals long before the first building permit is issued, significant resources may have been obligated for prebuilding permit development. These expenditures often far exceed those required for a single building permit. They include expenditures for planning, engineering, and constructing essential project components such as lots, roads, infrastructure, and public amenities. These are improvements without which a viable "building" would not have been possible in the first place.

• *The single permit/single building rule should not be the focal point in determining whether there has been reliance and changed position in multi-building projects.* Construction of a single building on a single lot pursuant to a single building permit in large projects, where there may be dozens or hundreds of buildings to be built, adds little to the equation of "substantial reliance." As noted, the developer's position has *already changed* as a result of major land development work carried out in reliance upon and compliance with required prior development approvals.

• *After multiple prebuilding permit approvals of a long-term project, the local government should not be allowed to change its mind in the absence of a compelling public interest.* Through a series of land-use approvals (e.g., approval of concept plans; subdivision plans; site plans; acceptance of dedications for roads and public amenities; and issuance of permits for grading, street, and utility construction), the local government acquires an ever-increasing knowledge of the specifics of a proposed development and its likely impacts (i.e., knowledge about the use, density, layout, infrastructure, and amenities).

Moreover, *with each such exercise of the police power, findings are made by the government that its action will promote the public health, safety, and welfare.* Thus, it is arbitrary and incredible for the government entity to later argue that its prior approvals should *not* have been relied upon, and that they can be repudiated with impunity prior to issuance of a building permit. Such arguments should be rejected, except in the very rare instance where a direct and imminent threat to public health or safety is posed by the development (i.e., when contamination of the public water supply would result). (Even in these rare cases, the "emergency" should be real and the exercise of the developer's vested rights should only be *postponed* for a reasonable period, *not terminated.*)

It must be remembered that the government entity, in addition to being one of the two essential parties to the development review process, is also the "referee." It can change the rules in the middle of the game, even to the point of exculpating its own bad faith. Thus, at the very least, the government should be required to justify its changed position under a *higher standard of judicial review*, for example, that its change of position is necessary to promote a *compelling governmental interest.*[67]

• *The "whole parcel" rule should be applied in determining vested rights cases.* When a planned segmented development of contiguous parcels under common ownership has been approved and is being developed as a single unit under a coordinated plan of development, the principle of "nonsegmentation" should be applied to protect the owner's right to complete the unfinished sections. Thus, a claim of vested status based upon partial development of the "parcel as a whole" should be upheld.[68] If, as the Supreme Court has held, a regulatory takings claim should be evaluated under the whole parcel theory, taking into account development activity on a contiguous site, so too should a claim of vested rights logically be reviewed under the same criterion. It should not be rejected merely because construction has not yet commenced upon *all* contiguous segments of the parcel.[69]

* ***Government misconduct should not be rewarded.*** A landowner cannot normally claim a vested right based upon a building permit issued as a result of mistake of fact or in violation of law. Similarly, a landowner or developer, whose failure to timely obtain a building permit or commence construction is the direct result of prior *improper* or *unlawful* actions by government, should not be denied vested status.[70] Government accountability should not be ignored in such cases.

MORATORIA: THE GROWING ABUSE OF A NEEDED POLICE POWER TOOL

Once upon a time, the moratorium was generally regarded as a regulation of last resort, to be imposed only in response to an unanticipated emergency affecting the public health or safety. Two decisions by the Court of Appeals of New York—both involving sewerage facilities—exemplify this view. In one, the court held that where a problem is general to the community and not caused by a specific landowner, it is impermissible to single out that person to bear the financial burden attributable to that general condition.[71] In an often-quoted related case five years later, the New York high court established a three-pronged rule for validating moratoria:

> "To justify interference with beneficial enjoyment of property [under its police powers,] a municipality must establish that it has acted in response to *dire necessity,* that its action is reasonably calculated to alleviate or prevent the crisis condition, and that it is presently taking steps to rectify the problem."[72]

Public Policy Arguments Against Moratoria

In addition to the legal arguments that can be raised against moratoria, there are a number of public policy reasons as well. These include:

* The moratorium is, at best, a temporary, ad hoc, short-term measure. It simply preserves the status quo (e.g., water pollution) and usually contributes little toward the long-term solution of the underlying problems.

* Moratoria can be *disruptive to the economic base* of the development industry and the community. It is particularly *inequitable to small builders* who are less prepared to stand economic strains over a long term.

* Moratoria inevitably *generate a "panic" atmosphere*, leading in turn to increased land speculation and inflation, thereby militating against a number of desirable goals such as market stability and maintenance of an adequate supply of moderately priced housing.

- Except in cases involving dire emergencies or serious threats to the public health or safety, moratoria *should not be imposed* on the issuance of development approvals *in designated "smart growth" areas.*[73]

- The moratorium may for the short-term actually *increase building activity* as builders scurry to beat a rumored moratorium deadline or vest grandfather rights in a prior order.

Legal Arguments Against Moratoria

Among the legal arguments that can be made against moratoria are the following:

- *Lack of Authority under State Law:* Although the laws in some states expressly authorize local governments to impose moratoria, this is not universally the case, and implied authority should not always be assumed.[74]

- *Equal Protection:* Is the moratorium applied evenly? Does it apply to *all* categories of development in a similar manner, or is it applicable *only to selected categories*, such as *residential*?

- *Procedural Due Process:* Has there been adequate notice and an opportunity to be heard? How are *pending* land development applications being treated? Are there any *waiver provisions*?

- *Substantive Due Process:* The same question as with equal protection applies regarding *all categories* of land use being *treated similarly.* Also, what is the *nature of the "emergency"* (e.g., pollutants threatening the local aquifer or merely the need for "more time to plan")?

Abatement of Real Property Taxes While a Moratorium is Pending

Pending termination of a moratorium, affected landowners should seek prompt assessment review and relief from payment of real estate taxes and related charges.[75]

"Planning Moratoria" and the Effect of the *Tahoe-Sierra* Case

Some public agencies have expansively applied moratoria, based upon dicta in the Supreme Court's *Tahoe-Sierra*[76] decision, both to lengthen time periods and stretch the "dire necessity" standard to include "planning moratoria." These efforts should be resisted through clarifying state legislation and aggressive court challenges.

Tahoe Sierra: *A Narrow Question Narrowly Decided*

Tahoe-Sierra involved a *facial* challenge to a moratorium in a *regulatory takings* context. In the words of the Supreme Court, the lot owners in the hills surrounding Lake Tahoe faced an "uphill battle" that was made "especially steep" by their claim that the *mere enactment* of the regulation effected a per se taking of their properties for public use without just compensation.[77]

The essence of the Court's ruling was that it would not be receptive to a *per se takings* rule. That "narrow inquiry" was all that *Tahoe-Sierra* addressed.[78] No equal protection or due process issues were considered by the Court. Nor were any issues of legal authority for the moratoria under state law adjudicated. However, even in the narrow context of regulatory takings law, the Court stated that, had the lot owners challenged the *application* of the moratorium to their individual properties (i.e., had they applied for building permits and been denied), "some of them might have prevailed" under a *Penn Central* analysis.[79] Further, the Court warned that moratoria in excess of one year should be viewed with "special skepticism."[80]

Planning Moratoria Remain Especially Suspect Under the "Dire Necessity" Test

To ward off the facial challenge of the lot owners in *Tahoe Sierra*, public planning advocates succeeded in getting the Court to observe in dicta that "moratoria ... are an essential tool for successful development."[81] Even if this extraordinary statement were true, it does not overrule the common law of most states pertaining to moratoria. To be valid, they must be authorized under state law with standards prescribed for their use. Further, they should be of temporary duration and subject to the three-pronged "dire necessity" test promulgated in *Belle Harbor* and *Almquist*.[82] Under no circumstances should the dicta in *Tahoe Sierra* be relied upon to avoid the dire necessity test or to enable a moratorium to escape close judicial scrutiny.

CONCLUSION

Smart growth and balanced growth are likely to remain illusive goals under the prevailing political and regulatory climates in which development review is conducted throughout America. Resolution of some of these obstacles would be facilitated if the regulatory reforms discussed above were implemented. Based upon political and regulatory realities, including *the lack of an adequate state role in*—and thus a *viable regional approach to*—planning and land-use regulation in many jurisdictions, it appears doubtful that meaningful smart or balanced growth will occur on a large scale.

JOHN J. DELANEY NOTES

1. Many innovative approaches to land-use planning and regulation have been spawned or nurtured in Montgomery County (a suburb of Washington, DC) and its highly respected planning agency, the Maryland–National Capital Park and Planning Commission. Some of these are the floating zone in the 1960s, rural-open space zoning with a major transferable development rights program in the 1970s and 1980s, and mandated moderately priced housing in the 1980s.

2. See Norman Williams, Jr., and John M. Taylor, *American Land Planning Law* (rev. ed.) (St. Paul, MN: Thomson-West, 2003), Vols. 1 § 7:2, 221-222 and § 7:6, 229-230. These comments were first written by Professor Williams over three decades ago and, while Maryland case

law is still important and interesting, it has become somewhat less imbalanced in recent years. As discussed herein in the section entitled, "Piecemeal Rezoning: A Proposal to Resolve the 'Legislative vs. Adjudicatory' Conundrum?," an important achievement of the state's highest court was its fashioning of a unique and viable response to the age-old question: "Is piecemeal rezoning legislative or quasi-judicial?"

3.   See, e.g., *Bryniarski v. Montgomery County Board of Appeals*, discussed in note 11, *infra*, and further discussion of aggrievement in the section entitled, "Rearguing Settled Issues," *infra*.

4.   Please excuse the author's references to his own prior works. Since this paper focuses upon the author's opinions, the purpose in so doing is to save time and space.

5.   Richard F. Babcock, *The Zoning Game: Municipal Practices and Policies* (Madison: The University of Wisconsin Press, 1966), 154, 157.

6.   Smart Growth Network, *Getting to Smart Growth* (Washington, DC: International City / County Management Association and the Smart Growth Network, Jan. 2002), Chapter 9, 69-70. Smart Growth Online (http://smartgrowth.org).

7.   Stuart Meck (gen. ed.), *Growing Smart^SM Legislative Guidebook: Model Statutes for Planning and Management of Change* (Chicago: American Planning Association, 2002) (the "Guidebook"). Some of the positive features included in the Guidebook are:

   • Requirements that *exactions and impact fees be proportional* to the *impact* of the proposed development (§§ 8-601(4) and 8-602(5));

   • Provisions requiring local governments adopting a concurrency management ordinance to *annually prepare a local capital improvements program and adopt a local capital budget* (§ 8603(7));

   • Requirement that *adequate public facilities ordinances* must apply to *all categories* of development, not just residential development (§ 8603(8));

   • Authorization (albeit overly limited) of *Development Agreements* (§ 8-701);

   • Provisions requiring establishment of a *land market monitoring system*, periodically evaluating the *supply and availability of buildable land* when urban growth areas are included in the local government's comprehensive plan (§ 7204.1); and

   • A number of helpful process reforms, such as defining when an agency decision shall be deemed "final" (§§ 10-603, 10-203, and 10-210), but some of these are offset by requirements for exhaustion of administrative remedies, limited aggrievement standards for third parties, and rules allowing liberal supplementation of the record by the court on judicial review.

8.   "NIMBY" is a popular acronym for "Not In My Back Yard."

9.   In many of the Guidebook's proposed model laws and ordinances, alternative options are also presented. Through careful use of these optional provisions, objectionable features of particular model statutes or regulations can often be overcome. Examples of helpful options, as well as options of concern, are discussed throughout this paper.

10.   See Daniel R. Mandelker, *Land Use Law* (5th ed.) (Newark, NJ: LexisNexis Matthew Bender, 2003), §§ 3.01-3.02; Charles M. Haar, *In Accordance with a Comprehensive Plan*, 68 Harv. L. Rev. 1154-1155 (1955).

11.   See, e.g., *Bryniarski v. Montgomery County Board of Appeals*, 230 A.2d 289, 293-296 (Md. 1967) (adjoining, confronting, or nearby properties are deemed *prima facie* to be specially damaged and, therefore, aggrieved).

12.   Id. Depending upon local custom and practice, lack of legal standing would not necessarily preclude nonaggrieved persons from participating in the proceedings, but this would be a matter of grace, not of right, and such persons would *not* have legal standing as a "third party."

13.   Treatise writers concur. For example:

   "Almost all state statutes contain the 'person aggrieved' provision but only a minority extend standing to taxpayers . . .

"Under the usual formulation of the rule, third-party standing requires 'special' damage to an interest or property right that is different from the damage the general public suffers from a zoning restriction. Competitive injury, for example, is not enough. This rule reflects the nuisance basis of zoning, which protects property owners only from damage caused by adjacent incompatible uses. Although the special damage rule is well entrenched in zoning law, a few courts have modified it. New Jersey has adopted a liberal third-party standing rule which requires only a showing of 'a sufficient state and real adverseness.'" Daniel R. Mandelker, *Land Use Law* (5th ed.) (Newark, NJ: LexisNexis Matthew Bender, 2003), § 8.02 at 8.3-8.4. [Emphasis added; citations omitted.]

"The requirement that a person must be 'aggrieved' in order to appeal from the board of adjustment to a court of record was originally included in the Standard State Zoning Enabling Act that has been adopted by most of the states." See Kenneth H. Young, *Anderson's American Law of Zoning* (4th ed.) (Deerfield, IL: Clark Boardman Callaghan, 1997), § 27.09.

14. In contrast, applicants for development approval who are *denied* must travel a more difficult road to obtain judicial review. Despite the Guidebook's well-conceived "ripeness" reforms in §§ 10-201, 10-202, 10-203, 10-210, and 10-603, a denied applicant must exhaust three additional *administrative remedies* after the initial denial, in order to have standing in court. These are: (1) appeal for administrative review (§ 10-209); (2) apply for a conditional use (§ 10-502); and (3) seek a variance (§ 10-503). In many jurisdictions, exhaustion of these remedies can add years to the process, even *before* one has standing to seek judicial review. On the other hand, a third party, as described above, wishing to seek judicial review of a development *approval* would at most be required to exhaust only the first of these administrative remedies (i.e., appeal for administrative review), which action has the effect of staying the applicant's right to implement the approval (unless the approving agency issues a certification, reviewable by a court, that staying the approval will cause immediate harm or peril to life or property) (§ 10-209(1) and (3)).

15. Eugene McQuillin, *The Law of Municipal Corporations* (3d ed.) (Rochester, NY: Thomson-West, 2003, revised volume), § 25.318.15.

16. Of course, topographical conditions or other site constraints may (in the absence of cluster provisions, best management practice guidelines, or other flexible mechanisms) affect the density yield of a specific site.

17. This issue is discussed in detail by the author in an article entitled *Addressing the Workforce Housing Crisis in Maryland and Throughout the Nation*, 33 U. Balt. L. Rev. No. 2, 153, 165-166, 171 (Spring 2004).

18. For example, the enabling act could provide:

   "Within six years following adoption/amendment of a comprehensive or local plan, where the zoning map is in accordance with the plan, major issues decided in the plan, including but not limited to land use, density, intensity, or [other], shall not be reargued or reconsidered in any proceeding on a site-specific development application unless the use, density, or intensity proposed for the site is not in accordance with the plan, or exceeds that which is authorized in the applicable zone."

19. *Carbone v. Weehawken Township Planning Bd.*, 421 A.2d 144 (N.J. Super. 1980); see also E. C. Yokley, *Yokley's Law of Subdivisions* (2d ed.) (Charlottesville, VA: Michie Co., 1981), § 69(c); see also Kenneth H. Young, *Anderson's American Law of Zoning* (4th ed.) (Deerfield, IL: Clark Boardman Callaghan, 1997), § 27.29, at 605: ("Reviewing courts say they are not super zoning boards and that they will not weigh the evidence.")

20. Norman Williams, Jr., and John M. Taylor, *American Land Planning Law* (St. Paul, MN: Thomson-West, 1988), § 4.05, at 100. [Emphasis added.]

21. See, e.g., *Cabana v. Kenai Peninsula Borough*, 21 P.3d. 833 (Alaska 2001) (holding that piecemeal rezoning is a legislative act from which there is no right of appeal whatsoever); see generally Corpus Juris Secundum, § 2-3.
22. See *Fasano v. Board of County Comm'rs of Washington County*, 507 P.2d 23 (Ore. 1973).
23. Id. at 29.
24. Id. at 26.
25. Id.
26. See John J. Delaney, Stanley D. Abrams, and Frank Schnidman, *Handling The Land Use Case: Land Use Law, Practice & Forms* (3d ed.) (Rochester, NY: Thomson-West, 2005), § 5:11, 5-16, n. 4. The Oregon Supreme Court appears to have modified its *Fasano* ruling in regard to its applicability to large parcels of land. See *Neuberger v. City of Portland*, 607 P.2d 722 (Ore. 1980).
27. 217 A.2d 578 (Md. 1966).
28. Id. at 583.
29. Id. at 584. [Emphasis added.]
30. Id. at 583-584.
31. Id. at 584-585.
32. Id. A respected concurring judge argued in *Hyson* that zoning and rezoning are legislative in character, rejecting the concept that they could "by some mysterious means" become quasi-judicial or quasi-legislative. The state legislature and the local legislative body could provide for procedural protection in the rezoning process, but these were matters of legislative grace rather than constitutional right. Thus, in his view, the council was exercising a "restricted legislative function, not a quasi-judicial function." Id. at 594. Judge Wilson K. Barnes, dissenting.
33. *Hyson* was strongly reaffirmed by the Maryland high court in *Bucktail LLC v. The County Council of Talbot County*, 723 A.2d 440, 446-447 (Md. 1999). The *Hyson* decision led to the establishment of the zoning hearing examiner system in Maryland. The late Rita C. Davidson, attorney for the appellant in this breakthrough case, went on to become one of the first zoning hearing examiners in the state, and thereafter became the first woman to ascend to the Court of Appeals of Maryland, the state's highest court.
34. Reprinted in modified form from a paper by the author in the ALI-ABA "Land Use Institute" Course Materials (2003), 564.
35. See, e.g., Peter Whoriskey, "Investing In Sprawl" (a comprehensive three-part series describing the problems of workforce housing and sprawl in the suburbs of Washington, DC), *Washington Post*, Aug. 8, 9, 10, 2004, at A1; "Voters Reject San Francisco Plan To Encourage Workforce Housing," *Planning*, May 2004, at 36 (describing the 70 percent to 30 percent defeat by San Francisco citizens of a ballot initiative to provide housing affordable to median income working family households).
36. This checklist is based upon a similar evaluation by the author in *Addressing The Workforce Housing Crisis in Maryland and Throughout the Nation*, note 17, *supra*.
37. See, e.g., "Investing In Sprawl," note 35, *supra*.
38. See, e.g., *City of Eastlake v. Forest City Enterprises*, 426 U.S. 668 (1976); *City of Cuyahoga Falls v. Buckeye Community Hope Foundation*, 538 U.S. 188 (2003). These are two egregious cases in which popular votes against proposed affordable housing developments were upheld by the Supreme Court. In *Cuyahoga Falls*, the Court even sanctioned community-wide referenda on *nonlegislative* decisions of local governing bodies in site-specific cases, stating that such referenda would advance First Amendment interests. The Guidebook—unwisely in our view—appears to condone if not promote initiatives and referenda mechanisms in states where they are not already authorized in the state constitution.
39. The Guidebook allows new land development regulations (and zoning changes) to be initiated either by petition of owners of record lots constituting "51% of the area that is to be the subject of the proposed ordinance" (i.e., by neighborhood plebiscite), or optionally by

petition of a minimum percentage of "bona fide adult residents" of the local government jurisdiction. (§ 8-103(1)(d)(e).)

Treatise writers and other respected authorities agree that zoning by the initiative process is destabilizing to orderly planning and undermines settled planning and zoning decision-making. See, e.g., Nicholas M. Kublicki, *Land Use by, for, and of the People: Problems with the Application of Initiatives and Referenda to the Zoning Process,* 19 Pepp. L. Rev. 99, at 104, 105, 155, 157-158 (1991); David S. Broder, *Democracy Derailed—Initiative Campaigns and the Power of Money* (New York: Harcourt, 2001). The author is a senior columnist for the *Washington Post.*

See also the excellent discussion of the negative impact of referenda upon comprehensive plan in *Township of Sparta v. Spillane,* 312 A.2d 154 (N.J. Super. 1973). While initiatives are sanctioned in the constitutions of a minority of states, they should not be encouraged to proliferate via statutory mechanisms such as those in the Guidebook. Similarly, plebiscites of neighborhoods to effect zoning changes are destabilizing and are unlawful in many states. See, e.g., *Benner v. Tribbit,* 57 A.2d 346 (Md. 1948). The Supreme Court has also expressly condemned this practice as an unconstitutional "delegation" of power to neighbors who opposed a proposed home for the elderly. See *Washington ex rel Seattle Trust Co. v. Roberge,* 278 U.S. 116 (1928).

40. For an important case on the benefits of regional state oversight and mandates on housing, see *City of Lake Elmo v. Metropolitan Council,* 685 N.W.2d 1 (Minn. 2004). Twin Cities regional planning authority had the power to require the city to conform its comprehensive plan to the authority's regional system plans, including the minimum density requirements of the regional system plan for development in urban areas.

41. The Guidebook devotes extensive attention to housing issues. See generally Chapters 4 and 7, including § 7-207 (Housing Element in Local Comprehensive Plans).

42. The Guidebook (§ 8-603(7)) contains model language encouraging the use of mandates to require timely funding of infrastructure, schools, and public amenities in the local government CIP.

43. See, note 40, *supra,* for an important case upholding minimum density requirements in designated urban areas.

44. The Guidebook forthrightly addresses this issue. See §§ 8-601(4) and 8-603(8); see also § 8-602(5).

45. Two widely heralded growth management cases exemplify this problem. See, e.g., *Golden v. Planning Bd. of the Town of Ramapo,* 285 N.E.2d 291 (N.Y. 1972) (noting that the timed development control ordinance applied only to residential development); see also, e.g., *Const. Indus. Ass'n of Sonoma County. v. City of Petaluma,* 522 F.2d 897 (9th Cir. 1975) (noting that growth cap ordinance applied only to residential development).

46. Id. See also, *Addressing The Workforce Housing Crisis,* note 17, *supra,* at 168.

47. The Guidebook recommends the use of residential-based inventories and land-market monitoring systems. See § 7-204.1.

48. "Inequitable burden" would be a defined term focusing primarily on principles rooted in equity rather than law. A landowner need not have suffered a taking of his land in order for it to be "inequitably burdened."

49. Guidebook, § 10-504. However, the Guidebook's model is limited solely to negotiated development agreements and requires a third-party mediator. Many other mechanisms in addition to development agreements are available and might well have been included in the Guidebook, especially since to date only about 25 percent of the states have authorized their local governments to execute development agreements. See notes 59 and 61 and accompanying text, *infra.* Moreover, some local governments are reluctant to subject their police power decisions to review or "arbitration" by a mediator or other third party. A restricted form of development agreement is authorized in § 8-701. Alternative remediation mechanisms are available in the author's files.

50. *San Diego Gas & Electric Co. v. City of San Diego*, 450 U.S. 621, 656, n. 22 (1981) (Brennan, J. dissenting). Quoting Longtin, *Avoiding and Defending Constitutional Attacks on Land Use Regulations (Including Inverse Condemnation)*, in 38B NIMLO Mun. L. Rev. 192-193 (1975). [Emphasis in original.]

51. See, e.g., *Avco Community Developers, Inc. v. South Coast Regional Comm'n.*, 553 P.2d 546 (Cal. 1976), *cert. denied*, 429 U.S. 1083 (1977).

52. *Hollywood Beach Hotel Co. v. City of Hollywood*, 329 So.2d 10, 16 (Fla. 1976).

53. See J. J. Delaney and E. J. Vaias, *Recognizing Vested Development Rights As Protected Property In Fifth Amendment Due Process and Taking Claims*, 49 J. Urb. & Contemp. L. (1996), Washington University of St. Louis School of Law, updated under same name in ALI-ABA, *Inverse Condemnation and Related Governmental Liability Course Materials* (April 22-24, 2004).

54. For example, Maryland's high court has repeatedly denied vested rights claims, even in circumstances where the landowner's failure to acquire the requisite building permit and commence construction was the direct result of previously adjudicated or acknowledged unlawful conduct by the government. See *Sycamore Realty Co. Inc. v. People's Counsel of Baltimore County*, 684 A.2d 1331, 1336 (Md. 1996) ("courts are loath to impose estoppel against the government when it is acting in a governmental capacity"); *Prince George's County v. Blumberg*, 418 A.2d 1155 (Md. 1980); *Montgomery County v. District Land Corp*, 337 A.2d 712 (Md. 1975); *Rockville Fuel & Feed Co. v. Board of Appeals*, 291 A.2d 672 (Md. 1972).

55. Note 51, *supra*.

56. 553 P.2d at 551. The case of *Consaul v. City of San Diego*, 231 Cal. App. 3d 131 (1991), appears to have modified *Avco* to a degree, providing some hope of more reasoned analyses in future vesting cases.

57. See Daniel R. Mandelker, *Land Use Law* (5th ed.) (Newark, NJ: LexisNexis Matthew Bender, 2003), § 6.22, citing Stuart Meck (gen. ed.), *Growing Smart*[SM] *Legislative Guidebook: Model Statutes for Planning and Management of Change* (Chicago: American Planning Association, 2002), § 8-501. The relevant vesting statutes of the states in question are cited in these works.

58. See § 8-501(a). The other Guidebook option, § 8-501(b), confers vested rights at the time of issuance of a "development permit," a broadly defined term that could include, among other things, approvals of subdivision plans, site plans, and building permits. The Guidebook's definition of "development permit" lists a number of approvals, including a "building permit" (§ 10-101). Thus, the revised second alternative in § 8-501(b) can also be construed as authorizing a late vesting rule—similar to the common law vesting rule in effect in approximately 30 states—that would not confer vested status on a project until after a building permit has been issued, and significant and ascertainable construction thereunder has occurred. This would be a draconian imposition of the rule in today's multilayered regulatory environment because it ignores the often numerous development approvals that a project may have previously received and implemented. If applied in this manner, the revised section relating vested status to significant and ascertainable development pursuant to a development permit would not effect meaningful reform and instead would only embalm the status quo. (Ironically, the Guidebook's definition of "development permit" does not include preliminary subdivision plans.) However, the Guidebook also includes several *prebuilding permit approvals* within its definition of "development permit," including final subdivision plat, conditional use, and site plan. Any of these could serve as an appropriate milestone for vesting.

59. For a comprehensive treatment of development agreements, see David L. Callies, Daniel R. Curtin, Jr., and Julie A. Tappendorf, *Bargaining for Development* (Washington, DC: Environmental Law Institute, July 2003), § III. See also Daniel R. Curtin, Jr. and Scott A. Edelstein, *Development Agreement Practice in California and Other States*, 22 Stetson L. Rev. 761 (1993); Theodore C. Taub, *Development Agreements*, ALI-ABA "Land Use Institute" Course Materials (August 1991), 555.

60. See, e.g., *Attman/Glazer P.B. Co. v. Mayor and Aldermen of Annapolis*, 552 A.2d 1277 (Md. 1989); *Peoples Counsel for Baltimore County v. Beachwood I Ltd. Partnership*, 670 A.2d 484 (Md. App. 1995).

61. See *Bargaining For Development*, note 59, *supra*, at 92 (n. 576).

62. 512 U.S. 374, 114 S.Ct. 2309 (1994).

63. 84 Cal. App. 4th 221, 100 Cal. Rptr. 2d 740 (2d Dist. 2000), *reh'g denied* (Nov. 15, 2000), *review denied* (Jan. 17, 2001).

64. Id. at 232.

65. Id. at 229.

66. See, e.g., J. Delaney, *Vesting Verities and the Development Chronology: A Gaping Disconnect?* 3 Wash. U. J.L. & Pol'y 603, 621-623 (2000).

67. See Charles L. Siemon and Wendy U. Larsen, with Douglas R. Porter, *Vested Rights: Balancing Public and Private Development Expectations* (Washington, DC: Urban Land Institute, 1982).

68. See *K&K Constr. Inc., et al. v. Department of Natural Resources*, 575 N.W. 2d 531 (Mich. 1998); *Forest Properties v. United States*, 177 F. 3d 1360 (F. Cir. 1999).

69. See *Penn Central Transp. Co. v. City of New York*, 438 U.S. 104, 130 (1978) ("In deciding whether a particular governmental action has effected a taking, this Court focuses . . . both on the character of the action and on the nature and extent of the interference with rights in the parcel *as a whole*." [Emphasis added.]). See also *K&K* and *Forest Properties*, note 68, *supra*.

70. Maryland courts routinely overlook previously adjudicated or acknowledged government misconduct in such cases. See note 54, *supra*.

71. *Westwood Forest Estates v. Village of South Nyack*, 244 N.E.2d 700 (N.Y. 1969).

72. *Belle Harbor Realty Corp. v. Kerr*, 323 N.E.2d 697, 699 (N.Y. 1974). [Emphasis added.] See also *Almquist v. Town of Marshan*, 245 N.W.2d 819, 826 (Minn. 1976).

73. The Guidebook squarely addresses this issue as an optional provision in § 8-604(4).

74. See, e.g., *Naylor v. Township of Hellam*, 773 A.2d 770 (Pa. 2001) (no implied authority in state planning enabling law for local governments to halt the land-use approval process); *Board of Supervisors v. Horne*, 215 S.E.2d 453 (Va. 1975) (interim zoning imposing an 18-month freeze on applications for site plan and preliminary subdivision plat approval invalidated).

75. See, e.g., *Smokerise, Inc. v. Washington Suburban Sanitary Comm'n, et al.*, 400 F. Supp. 1369 (D. Md. 1975) (agency could not continue to collect front foot benefit charges for use of sewerage facilities during the course of a moratorium preventing such use).

76. *Tahoe Sierra Preservation Council, Inc. v. Tahoe Regional Planning Agency, et al.*, 535 U.S. 302, 122 S.Ct. 1465 (2002).

77. 535 U.S. at 320, 122 S.Ct. at 1477. The narrow question presented, as written by the Court, was ". . . whether a moratorium on development imposed during the process of devising a comprehensive land use plan constitutes a *per se* taking of property requiring compensation under the takings clause . . ." (535 U.S. at 306). [Emphasis in original.]

78. Id. at 316, 122 S.Ct. at 1476.

79. Id. at 335, 122 S. Ct. at 1485, referring to *Penn Central Transp. Co. v. City of New York*, 438 U.S. 104, 98 S.Ct. 2646 (1978).

80. Id. at 342, 122 S.Ct. at 1487. The Guidebook authorizes moratoria of up to 18 months or longer. §§ 8-604(8) and 10.

81. Id. at 339, 122 S.Ct. at 1487. Far from being a "tool" for successful development, "planning moratoria" are a symptom of failed planning. A moratorium is an "essential tool" only when it can be justified by dire necessity, such as the need to address an imminent threat to the public health, safety, or welfare. It is noteworthy that the APA staff, in deliberations preceding adoption of the Guidebook, originally favored abolishing planning moratoria but later changed its position. Planning moratoria are now authorized under § 8-604(3), Alternative 1(b).

82. See notes 71 and 72, *supra*, and accompanying text.

CHAPTER

5

Comments on Delaney and Meck Papers

Jerry Weitz

It is my privilege to be here today to respond to the papers prepared by John Delaney (see Chapter 4) and Stuart Meck (see Chapter 3) on the topic of "A Survey & Critique of Contemporary Efforts/Growing Smart." My role in this panel is to look for commonalities in the two papers and note where the authors appear to part company, though I don't want to dwell on those differences. I also summarize key features of each paper and then add my own perspective to substantiate some of their key points.

Both of the authors share a concern about the development review process; both place some emphasis on, and generate concern for, affordable housing; and both call for regional approaches to affordable housing. Both authors are generally skeptical about overcoming obstacles to implementing smart growth.

Two key differences of opinion are also evident. The first relates to the use of (or support for) moratoria. John Delaney sees potential for abuse with moratoria. Stuart Meck and the American Planning Association supported the *Tahoe-Sierra* decision.[1]

John Delaney's paper is an excellent paper that covers a broad array of topics. It is comprehensive and I learned a lot from it. It also has some interesting ideas. I enjoyed hearing John's presentation and wish we had another hour for him to speak so that we hear more of the finer points. His paper has already influenced my work in writing zoning ordinances.

Delaney raises some significant criticisms about the *Growing Smart*[SM] *Legislative Guidebook*[2] (hereinafter the "Guidebook"). Most of these appear valid to me; he makes persuasive arguments. Delaney is careful, however, to qualify his criticism. Most if not all of the time, he finds the alternative to regulation he prefers in the Guidebook—it is just that the alternative recommended in the Guidebook is not always the one he prefers. For instance, Delaney finds that at least the appeals part of the process recommended in the Guidebook is too open-ended and therefore unfair.

One of Delaney's most important points is that there are two distinct phases of the regulatory process: (1) comprehensive planning and zoning; and (2) the post-zoning development review process. He calls it, for short, "rearguing settled issues." I share John's concern that local governments intermingle these two steps of the process when they should remain separate. I can relate my own experience in Georgia where every local zoning decision now seems to involve site plan review at the zoning stage.

Delaney's paper discusses the differences between legislative versus quasi-judicial zoning and land-use map amendments, and notes how various states and court rulings differ on this subject. Delaney calls it "piecemeal zoning." I have to share my own preference, after seeing "legislative" rezonings in Georgia, and how bad they can be, versus local government processes in Washington State, where rezonings are treated as on-the-record, quasi-judicial hearings pursuant to the 1995 Regulatory Reform Act. The process is much better in Washington State. Interestingly, Delaney introduces a middle ground between the Oregon *Fasano* decision[3] and the legislative approach to piecemeal zoning used in most states. That is the *Hyson* case[4] from Maryland.

I love the poem, "Musings of a Suburban Alderman in the Path of Growth."[5] It is definite recommended reading. I encourage everyone to look at it.

Delaney also poses an idea for remediation, or the need for an alternative to litigation in settling land-use disputes. This seems like a bold recommendation coming from an attorney! Better or interim steps prior to litigating are needed. I'm not sure I buy the full idea—hook, line, and sinker—as proposed by Delaney, but he has qualified it enough that I would probably agree with his points. One of the keys to that agreement is his requirement that claims of inequitable burdens will not receive relief if they are inconsistent with the comprehensive plan.

His paper also discusses development agreements that are enabled in some 13 states now plus California. I think that development agreements hold one of the keys to large-scale, mixed-use development. Development agreements will need to be authorized in more states. I have tried to persuade some Atlanta attorneys on the point that development agreements are not authorized in Georgia, but without enabling legislation there may be obstacles.

Perhaps one of the few points on which I would disagree with Mr. Delaney is the notion that taxes should be abated while a moratorium is pending. I'm not sure I agree! Delaney's conclusion is pretty skeptical, but for good reason: One cannot have meaningful smart growth without regulatory reform.

Turning to the paper by Stuart Meck, I focus my remarks on his conclusions. Much of the first part of Meck's paper is an excellent historical account of planning statutes, including a recap of Bosselman and Callies' work, the Standard Acts, and the state studies in New Mexico and Connecticut, all of which proved to be valuable steps forward in statute reform. Meck is not optimistic, though he includes a pep talk that we should not quit our efforts. He offers a bitter pill, one that I'm sure is hard for him to swallow, yet he readily admits it: There will probably not be wholesale reform of statutes. That observation must be hard for Stuart to admit, given his seven or eight years of work on the Guidebook. True, the Guidebook has been useful to many states, so let's not—and Stuart would not let us—consider it irrelevant in future reform efforts.

Meck emphasizes some of the successes of growth management. There are many research efforts in the literature, cited in Stuart's paper, that are now focusing on the outcomes—the successes—of growth management. His paper cites Burby and May, Knaap, Pendall, John Carruthers, and Jerry Anthony, who have contributed important findings on whether state growth management programs make a difference. Perhaps he's emphasized only the positives; Burby and May found that, yes, growth management matters, but the footnote to that study is that it doesn't matter very much.

I have to share Meck's concerns with the rather pitiful state of regional planning. We have Portland's Metro and the Twin Cities' Regional Council, but where's the diffusion of innovation? Both authors and I would probably agree that a broader role is needed for states, especially in affordable housing.

Stuart also makes a good point about the fiscalization of land use. This is a key obstacle that must be overcome if smart growth is to succeed. Nobody is optimistic on this point. Meck emphasizes training for planning commissioners and elected officials, and notes that four southeastern states have required training. He sees this as a good trend and I agree.

Now, I offer my own thoughts in brief. I think that the role of the business community in promoting smart growth is critical. As an example, in Atlanta, I cite the Metro Atlanta Chamber of Commerce and its formation of a Quality Growth Task Force. The chamber has built on prior successes in the area of transportation and water and is now moving the smart growth agenda along where it couldn't go before. The regional institution is much too timid to take on that role. My limited research into other regions is that it is the business community carrying the torch of smart growth now. I have witnessed in Georgia a movement away from strict compliance-based reviews of local comprehensive plans. Georgia appears to be moving from rigorous standards for local plans to not requiring such rigid reviews, and toward an emphasis on—

let's call it—a more "quality growth" approach. I wonder if other state agency plan review staffs are feeling the same way and whether this signifies a trend.

NIMBY[6] is one of the most potent obstacles to smart growth. As the authors have argued, we need regional approaches to affordable housing. I agree that more emphasis should be placed on the development review process by instilling fairness and shortening unfair delays. Delaney's paper is quite useful in that regard. Meck calls for deadlines for all development decisions, so I believe he is in agreement on that point. Delaney hits the "nail on the head" in his observation that we have achieved the "soft" decisions of smart growth but have not addressed the "hard" ones like affordable housing.

Finally, on the topic of local planning mandates, I conclude that local planning mandates have improved the quality of plans. However, we must ask ourselves, "Are they worth it?" Meck cites research from Florida and Wisconsin's 1999 Smart Growth Act on this point. He notes how Florida's Department of Community Affairs seems to be growing weary of compliance reviews, and that local governments in Wisconsin perhaps have had no sincere intentions of completely following the planning rules. Hence, I'm beginning to wonder whether the old paradigm of compliance-based reviews will continue.

I regret having to conclude on a negative note, especially since, as another speaker already pointed out, we need to be optimistic given the students that are present here today. However, the papers' authors and I share some significant skepticism with regard to the degree to which our prospects for smart growth will improve in the short run.

JERRY WEITZ NOTES

1. *Tahoe-Sierra Preservation Council v. Tahoe Regional Planning Agency*, 535 U.S. 302 (2002).
2. Stuart Meck (gen. ed.), *Growing Smart^SM Legislative Guidebook: Model Statutes for Planning and the Management of Change* (Chicago: American Planning Association, 2002).
3. *Fasano v. Board of County Commissioners of Washington County*, 507 P.2d 23 (Ore. 1973).
4. *Hyson v. Montgomery County*, 217 A.2d 578 (Md. 1966).
5. Reprinted in modified form from a paper by the author in the ALI-ABA "Land Use Institute" Course Materials (2003), 564.
6. "NIMBY" stands for "Not In My Back Yard."

6

Smart Growth Planning: America's Future in the 21st Century

Robert H. Freilich

ACKNOWLEDGMENT

Once before I had the privilege of paying homage to Dan Mandelker at the time that the Washington University School of Law held a festschrift in his honor. On that occasion, I wrote the concluding article of the resulting symposium extolling Dan's career. In my judgment, Dan is the dean of all American land-use law professors, not by reason of his chronological years but due to his continuous substantive contribution, boundless energy, and infectious enthusiasm. We all owe a great debt of gratitude for the contributions that Dan has made to illuminate land-use planning.

THE ROLE OF PLANNING

In examining "planning reform" in America today, the first fundamental task facing the planning and law professions is to assure that a comprehensive plan fulfills its 80-year-old prophecy of becoming the constitution guiding all development regulations and the development approval process. What seems so simple blinds most of the special interest academics, professionals, and governments active in land-use planning today.

It is discouraging to note how so many who profess to be planners[1] fail to understand that basic proposition. Much of Dan's work has been addressed to the need for comprehensive planning.[2] Contrast an early icon in the field who could see nothing in land use except a zoning game,[3] to the modern anti-planning property rights,[4] Sage Brush, and Wise Use movements.[5]

Everyone in America does planning. "Planning," in my definition, simply means the use of man or woman's intelligence with a little bit of forethought. Corporations have billion dollar corporate planning departments to determine what they're going to make, who will make it, where it will be made, and how it will be marketed. Merrill Lynch sells a $2 billion planning program for estate planning. We plan for the education of our children, retirement, and death. The federal government since September 11, 2001, is involved in the most extraordinary planning effort: the development of a unified intelligence network of information about the world of terrorism.

However, when local government attempts planning, property rights advocates call it "communism." A local government comprehensive land-use plan is not a five-year Stalinist plan. I am presently preparing a regional plan for the Boise metropolitan area, with six cities, Ada County, and the Ada County Highway District participating, to determine the form and pattern of regional growth, including development of corridors, centers, walkable master planned communities, job force, and affordable housing and revitalization of older areas. Parked on the doorstep of one of the public hearing sites was an old sports utility vehicle painted red, with a huge sign on it that said, "Zoning is America's Communism."

Nevertheless, if local governments fail to utilize comprehensive planning, citizens legitimately become extremely defensive about ad hoc decision-making. From NIMBYs (Not In My Back Yarders) to BANANAs (Build Absolutely Nothing Anywhere at Any Timers), citizens fear growth if they cannot determine whether a project is the first of one or the first of a hundred. Unfortunately, many groups from the property rights movement to the federal government itself mock these legitimate citizen concerns when they put forward platforms based on the notion that all planning and zoning is inherently exclusionary.[6] Blaming exclusionary practices in zoning on comprehensive planning is not rational.[7] Exclusionary practices can be excised from community practices through affordable housing strategies without destroying planning and zoning.[8]

Exclusionary and ad hoc tendencies in zoning will be better controlled if renewed efforts are made in this century to insure that individual parcel rezoning is treated as administrative and not legislative under the principle that the comprehensive plan establishes policy and individualized rezoning simply applies the policy.[9] Unfortunately, *Fasano's* brilliant foresight has met a mixed reaction among the two key growth states,[10] and recently has been in retreat.[11] By treating rezoning decisions as quasi-judicial or administrative, the overutilization of referenda and initiative will be limited to true policy questions,[12] and both the developer and neighboring interests will be afforded more meaningful judicial review based on substantial evidence and accompanied by procedural due process.[13]

I developed the Ramapo Plan and successfully defended it before the New York Court of Appeals and the U.S. Supreme Court.[14] The Ramapo Plan utilized zoning, subdivision regulation, and capital improvement programming to time and sequence growth based on the availability of adequate public facilities at the time of development, initiating growth management and smart growth in America.[15]

Ramapo shifted the whole nature of land-use planning in America:

> "The *Ramapo* decision shifted the balance of power from the developer to public use agencies. The developer no longer has an absolute right to proceed with development, irrespective of whether public facilities can reasonably accommodate the development. Instead, the developer can be made to wait a reasonable period to allow public facilities to catch up or expend funds to ripen the land for development. At the same time the *Ramapo* case has expanded the judicial view of just what incidental public costs affiliated with development may be shifted to the developer—the *Ramapo* decision and rationale also permanently altered the courts' perception of the land use regulatory process, and paved the way for subsequent decisions that have favored public regulation over the developer's immediate right to develop property. . . ." Rohan, 1 Zoning and Land Use Controls § 4.05 (1984).

Ramapo has led to tier systems and regional growth plans nationwide from San Diego to Baltimore and from Seattle to Miami during the 1980s and 1990s to counter urban sprawl.[16]

Nevertheless, for 30 years, critics on the left and right, focusing only on affordable housing, have irresponsibly attacked state, regional, county, and city growth management and smart growth plans for the control of sprawl.[17]

On the contrary, growth management and smart growth communities have been the major providers of affordable housing in America if only for the reason that such plans will inevitably be attacked for alleged exclusionary effects on affordable housing and must therefore contain significant housing elements to meet such challenges.[18]

Moreover, smart growth and growth management plans must be based upon a rigorous comprehensive plan including an affordable housing element together with capital facility, environmental, open space, agriculture, economic development, transit, transportation, energy, historic preservation, design, safety, noise, and educational elements. Without a comprehensive treatment of all of the needs of a community and all of the disciplines focused on solutions, smart growth management cannot be accomplished. Ramapo was the first suburban town in New York State to voluntarily develop, as part of its planning, over 800 integrated public and subsidized housing for low-income families and had to defend these programs in the courts.[19] As the New York Court of Appeals stated:

"[Ramapo] utilized its comprehensive plan to implement its timing controls and has coupled these with provisions for low and moderate income housing on a large scale."[20]

Utilization of comprehensive planning is critical to the solution of America's regional and urban problems. Every effort in the 21st century must be made to obtain legislative and judicial support for the principle that only implementation of sound comprehensive planning underlies all efforts to utilize techniques to solve urban problems.[21]

The *Growing Smart^SM Legislative Guidebook*[22] (hereinafter "the Guidebook") by the American Planning Association (APA) has advanced many excellent proposals for revision of state planning and zoning laws including Professor Mandelker's Chapter 10, which calls for enlargement of procedural safeguards. It has also provided support for growth management techniques including, *inter alia*, the timing and sequencing of capital improvement planning linked to adequate facility ordinances and development rights transfer to save agricultural land.

Without these principles, planning can only be weakened despite an excellent roster of optional growth management tools. If planning is left optional and nonbinding by the APA in its proposed legislation, we can be assured that it will be so treated by state legislatures.

As Myres McDougal wisely stated in criticizing the Restatement of Property, "To perform a superb inventory of the Augean stables is not to cleanse them."[23]

AUTHORITY

Cities, counties, and regional agencies require simple, direct, and general authority in order to carry out appropriate smart growth management. An inherent defect of the Guidebook is that it offers myriads of choices to state legislatures but feels constrained to spell out each specific grant of authority as if the ill-advised 19th century Dillon's Rule is still a guiding principle in 21st century America.[24]

To counter such a narrow view, some recent decisions have utilized a basically simple premise. The authority to plan and to implement the plan has already been delegated through the standard state planning and city zoning enabling acts (or recently enacted equivalents). Cities and counties should therefore have the authority to implement planning power without any need to have express statutory authority for each technique utilized.

In 1976, I was the principal planning and legal consultant in developing the Minneapolis–St. Paul Metropolitan Council Development Framework. The Town of Marshan, located in Dakota County, was placed in Tier IV of the development framework, which mandated that urban growth be deferred until after the 20-year period of the plan, and that agricultural land and rural character be preserved. Subsequent to the enactment of the development framework, but before the town could amend its own comprehensive plan and zoning regulations to implement the framework, two subdivision applications proposing over 400 units in prime agricultural land were filed. The town adopted a moratorium to defer consideration of the applications until it could revise its plan and regulations. A lower court found the moratorium to be a regulatory taking, but I was successful in having it reversed in the Minnesota Supreme Court.[25]

The critical issue was authority. The state's county and city planning enabling acts authorized use of moratoria. The Town Act was silent on moratoria. The district court relied upon Dillon's Rule to find the moratoria unauthorized. The Supreme Court reversed, based upon an article I had written in 1971,[26] which suggested that the standard township planning enabling act provides the requisite authority to plan and to implement the plan, including moratoria and interim controls designed to protect the planning process.[27]

Similar concerns have surfaced with regard to the use of impact fees. Many states have adopted express impact fee enabling legislation; in a number of those states, the state legislation places severe limits on the authority of local governments.[28] A few state courts have concluded that, absent such express legislation, cities and counties may enact impact fee ordinances under the provisions of the standard planning and zoning enabling acts and/or home rule providing for capital facility elements and adequate provision of transportation, school, park, sewer, water, drainage, and other improvements.[29]

Nevertheless, many local government attorneys, fearful of providing memoranda of law asserting broad public authority, have sought specific state legislation for such programs; unfortunately, such legislation may more severely restrict local government authority than confirm it. Recently, that was the experience of the Texas Municipal League, whose authorizing legislative proposals ended up, under intense homebuilding lobbying, with severely depleted authority under a catastrophically bad piece of legislation,[30] despite having broad judicial authority under the general planning acts.[31]

UTILIZATION OF BROADER ECONOMIC INITIATIVES TO ACHIEVE SMART GROWTH MANAGEMENT

The spate of inverse condemnation lawsuits, statutory compensation restrictions on government regulation (Florida's Bert Harris Act and Oregon's recent Measure 37), and state supreme court decisions increasing scrutiny over economic development and redevelopment projects under the Fifth Amendment and state constitutional public use clauses have raised the specter of diminishing government planning and regulation despite increasingly significant central city, housing, environmental, energy, natural resource, sprawl, and infrastructure deficiency problems.

Takings Claims

Most takings claims involve permanent restrictions on environmentally constrained lands. Government often fails to utilize economic techniques to eliminate these takings claims. Greater use of mandatory cluster zoning, transfers of development rights (TDRs), mitigation fees, and open space assessment district compensation will usually be successful in defeating *Lucas*[32] or *Penn Central*[33] takings claims for agricultural lands, historic preservation, floodplains, hillsides, wetlands, or coastal management.[34] Similarly, I was able to reverse a decade of judicial holdings that preservation of the future right-of-way of transportation corridors was a per se facial take by convincing the Florida Supreme Court that such takings claims were premature and would require an as-applied review of these same economic techniques as part of administrative exhaustion and finality.[35]

Public Use Challenges

Utilization of condemnation for large-scale development and redevelopment projects has come under increasing scrutiny in state courts. In a recent decision,[36] overruling the excessive use of eminent domain 20 years earlier to wipe out a Detroit neighborhood of 4,100 homes to build a General Motors plant, the Michigan Supreme Court held that an economic development project cannot in and of itself constitute a public use simply because it provides employment and fiscal benefits.[37] Nevertheless, the court indicated that, if the government retains either regulatory, contractual, or ownership controls, public use will be found.[38]

It becomes critical then for local governments in achieving economic development to utilize a series of steps to achieve proper public use:

1.   Insure that mixed-use, walkable projects replace conventional, economically segregated development. These mixed-use, new urbanism projects require that government utilize complex development agreements in order to retain significant regulatory and contractual controls. Current law approves development agreements against illegal delegation to private interests if the government retains regulatory land-use controls.[39]

2.   Government needs to utilize greater public-private development in a whole series of economic development projects (e.g., transit stations, riverfront, and transportation corridors) in which government retains significant ownership through assemblage of the land with long-term leasehold dispositions.[40] Public-private economic development is absolutely critical for the continued renewal and revitalization of central cities and suburbs and through which proper planning and regulatory controls can be sustained.[41]

3. Blight and redevelopment studies must be kept up to date, be supported by appropriate findings and, most importantly, have plans that incorporate as wide an area as possible involving multiple developers.[42]

4. Requiring that condemnees be given the opportunity to participate in the project through contributing the land, provided they comply with the redevelopment plan, will assure appropriate public use.[43]

Neighborhood Infill

Planners must achieve greater ability to convince neighborhood residents that infill development, both residential and mixed use, can be accomplished with proper compatibility and preservation of the character of the neighborhood. Objections will often occur based on traffic congestion, loss of property values and, occasionally, subliminally on racial and ethnic fears.

The use of some surprising techniques can overcome many of these objections. The fear, discussed earlier, where residents cannot determine whether a project is the first of one or a hundred, can be met with better neighborhood and area planning. Too often, this aspect of planning is lost due to inadequate budgeting and staff involvement, primarily in development application processing. The use of numerical quotas, accepted in critical environmental and growth management systems,[44] proved to be very effective by this author in developing the Champaign, Illinois, In-Town Development Project in which, after determining the actual need for townhouse development, a quota of four square blocks of townhouse development was imposed on an 88-square-block area. Neighbors and property owners responded by finding eight square blocks.

Most interesting of all is the use of insurance to maintain neighborhood property values to meet concerns that higher densities will result in lowering property values.[45] Other measures are the greater use of design standards and new urban, walkable, mixed-use district overlays to reduce traffic congestion.[46]

CONCLUSION

Planning reform in the 21st century will necessitate reinforcement of the comprehensive plan as the constitution of the land-use regulatory process, coupled with direct planning authority to develop the plan and implement it. Achieving these simple and basic goals with flexible economic techniques will resolve most of the numerous challenges posed by constitutional litigation. It will enable state and local governments to effectively produce results in providing the smart growth management needed to control sprawl; protect environmentally sensitive land; produce new, urban, mixed-use communities; revitalize neighborhoods; create transit-oriented development to reduce air pollution and transportation congestion; and meet the social, housing, and economic needs of citizens.

ROBERT H. FREILICH NOTES

1. Planning, unlike architecture, law, engineering, accounting, or medicine, is a profession without certification or licensing so that anyone with a bent towards land use in any form is free to call himself a planner.
2. See Daniel R. Mandelker, *The Role of the Comprehensive Plan in Land Use Regulation*, 74 Mich. L. Rev. 900 (1976); Daniel R. Mandelker and Edith M. Netter, "Comprehensive Plans and the Law," in Stuart Meck and Edith M. Netter, ed., *A Planner's Guide to Land Use Law* (Chicago: American Planning Association, 1983) at 17; Charles M. Haar, *In Accordance with a Comprehensive Plan*, 68 Harv. L. Rev. 1154 (1955); Charles M. Haar, *The Master Plan, An Impermanent Constitution Consultation*, 20 Law & Contemp. Probs. 353 (155); Edward Sullivan, *The Plan As Law*, 24 Urb. Law. 881 (1992).
3. See Clifford L. Weaver and Richard F. Babcock, "The Plan and Planning," in Stuart Meck and Edith M. Netter, eds., *A Planner's Guide to Land Use Law* (Chicago: American Planning Association, 1983), 25 (reporting Babcock's indictment of planning); see also Richard F. Babcock, *The Zoning Game: Municipal Practices and Policies* (Madison: The University of Wisconsin Press, 1966); Joseph DiMento, *The Consistency Doctrine and the Limits of Planning* (Cambridge, MA: Oelgeschlager, Gunn, and Hain, 1980).
4. See Institute of Bill of Rights Symposium, *Defining Takings: Private Property and the Future of Government Regulation*, 38 Wm. and Mary L. Rev. 749 (1997).
5. See Anita Miller, *America's Public Lands: Legal Issues in the New War for the West*, 24 Urb. Law. 894 (1992); Robert H. Freilich et al., *Supreme Court Review: The New Conservative Paradigm Impacts State and Local Government*, 23 Urb. Law. 499, 608 (1991).
6. See the Kemp report by the Advisory Commission to the U.S. Department of Housing and Urban Development entitled *Not In My Back Yard: Removing Barriers To Affordable Housing* (1991).
7. See Patricia E. Salkin, *Barriers to Affordable Housing: Are Land Use Controls The Scapegoat?* Land Use Law & Zoning Digest, at 3 (April 1993).
8. S. Mark White, *Affordable Housing: Proactive and Reactive Planning Strategies*, Planning Advisory Service Report No. 441 (Chicago: American Planning Association, 1992).
9. See *Fasano v. Board of County Commissioners of Washington County*, 507 P.2d 23 (Ore. 1973), pioneered by Edward Sullivan, who appeared at this conference (see Chapter 9 in this book).
10. Compare *Board of County Commissioners v. Snyder*, 627 So. 2d 469 (Fla. 1993) with *Arnel Development Co. v. City of Costa Mesa*, 620 P.2d 565 (Cal. 1980).
11. See *Cabana v. Kenai Peninsula Borough*, 21 P.3d 833 (Alaska 2001).
12. See Robert H. Freilich and Derek B. Guemmer, *Removing Artificial Barriers To Public Participation In Land Use Policy: Effective Zoning and Planning By Initiative and Referendum*, 21 Urb. Law. 511 (1989).
13. *Whitted v. Canyon County Board of Commissioners*, 44 P.3d 1173 (Id. 2002).
14. See *Golden v. the Planning Board of the Town of Ramapo*, 285 N.E.2d 291 (N.Y. 1972), *appeal dismissed for want of a substantial federal question*, 409 U.S. 1003 (1972).
15. John Nolon, *Golden and Its Emanations: The Surprising Origins of Smart Growth*, 35 Urb. Law. 15 (2003); Thomas Pelham, *From the Ramapo Plan to Florida's Statewide Concurrency System: Ramapo's Influence on Infrastructure Planning*, 35 Urb. Law. 113 (2003).
16. See Robert H. Freilich, *From Sprawl to Smart Growth: Successful Legal, Planning and Environmental Systems* (Chicago: American Bar Association, 1999) (describing San Diego; Minneapolis–St. Paul; Baltimore County and Region; Lexington-Fayette County; Palm Beach County; Washington Four County Puget Sound Area (Seattle to Tacoma); Miami-Dade County; and a host of other tier systems). Utilizing a four-tier system: (1) the urbanized built-up area; (2) a planned urbanizing area using *Ramapo's* timed and sequenced growth for the 20-year life of plans; (3) the future urbanizing area proscribing urban growth during the 20-year life of the plan; and (4) a permanent rural/agricultural/environmentally

sensitive lands area. These plans are able to incorporate full growth, meet all affordable housing needs, and revitalize Tier I downtown and existing built-up areas by eliminating subsidies for new growth on the fringe through charging full cost for infrastructure needs generated by new growth.

17. Herbert Franklin, *Controlling Growth, But For Whom? The Social Implications of Development Timing* (Washington, DC: The Potomac Institute, 1973); Fred Bosselman, *Can the Town of Ramapo Pass a Law to Bind the Rights of the Rest of the World?* 1 Fla. St. U. L. Rev. 234 (1973); Heidi Guth, *Ramapo Looking Forward: Gated Communities, Covenants and Concerns,* Urb. Law. 177 (2003); William A. Fischel, *Exclusionary Zoning and Growth Management,* 40 Wash. U. J. Urb. & Contemp. L. (1991).

18. Stuart R. Shamberg and Adam L. Wekstein, *The Local and Regional Need for Housing and the Ramapo Plan,* 35 Urb. Law. 165 (2003): "Golden v. Town of Ramapo marked an important step in the evolution from an insular judicial point of view as being strictly local in nature to a philosophy recognizing it as a regulatory requirement that must consider the housing needs of the regional residents . . . thus the Court considered [assimilation] of population and related housing growth in the region [as a critical] factor in reaching its result."

19. See *Greenwald v. Town of Ramapo,* 317 N.Y.S.2d 839 (App. Div. 2nd Dept. 1970); *Farrelly v. Town of Ramapo,* 317 N.Y.S.2d 837 (App. Div. 2nd Dept. 1970); and *Fletcher v. Rowney,* 323 F.Supp. 18 (S.D.N.Y. 1971).

20. *Golden,* id., note 15, *supra,* at 153; see The National Commission on Urban Problems (Douglas Commission, 1968): "New types of controls—including timing and location of development—are needed if basic metropolitan scale problems [of controlling sprawl] are to be solved."

21. See *Udell v. Haas,* 235 N.E.2d 897 (N.Y. 1968): "In our view sound zoning principles were not followed in this case . . . because zoning can only be a vital tool for maintaining a civilized form of existence . . . if it conforms to a well considered or comprehensive plan [in which] consideration is given to the needs of the community as a whole."

22. Stuart Meck (gen. ed.), *Growing Smart[SM] Legislative Guidebook: Model Statutes for Planning and the Management of Change* (Chicago: American Planning Association, 2002).

23. Myres S. McDougal, *Future Interests Restated: Traditions Versus Clarification and Reform,* 55 Harv. L. Rev. 1077, 1115 (1942).

24. The traditional rule governing local regulatory authority, known as Dillon's Rule (named after a drunken chief judge of the Iowa Supreme Court in the mid-19th century, who was later convicted of securities fraud after resigning his judicial post), provides that local governments possess only the powers expressly delegated to them by the state legislature and those extremely limited ministerial powers that are necessarily implied and encompassed within the expressed power. See, e.g., *Hoepker v. City of Madison Planning Commission,* 563 N.W.2d 145 (Wis. 1977) (municipalities have no inherent or home rule power to enact land-use regulations; any power they have is derived from state enabling statutes and strictly construed).

25. See *Almquist v. Town of Marshan,* 245 N.W.2d 819 (Minn. 1976).

26. Robert H. Freilich, *Interim Development Controls: Essential Tools For Implementing Flexible Planning and Zoning,* 49 U. Detroit J. Urban L. 65 (1971).

27. The 1971 article was also recently cited by the U.S. Supreme Court in *Tahoe-Sierra Preservation Council, Inc. v. Tahoe Regional Planning Agency,* 535 U.S. 302 (2002), as a principal authority in finding that a 31-month moratorium designed to protect the planning process did not constitute a regulatory taking.

28. Martin L. Leitner and Susan P. Schottle, *A Survey of State Impact Fee Enabling Legislation,* 25 Urb. Law. 491 (1993).

29. *Contractors and Builder's Association v. City of Dunedin,* 329 So.2d 314 (Fla. 1976) (home rule); *Call v. City of West Jordan,* 606 P.2d 217 (Utah 1980) (standard planning enabling act).

30. Tex. Loc. Gov't Code § 394.024 (1993).

31. *City of College Station v. Turtle Rock*, 680 S.W.2d 802 (Tex. 1984).

32. *Lucas v. South Carolina Coastal Council*, 505 U.S. 1003 (1992).

33. *Penn Central Transp. Co. v. City of New York*, 438 U.S. 104 (1978).

34. Robert H. Freilich and Linda K. Davis, *Saving The Land, The Use of Modern Techniques of Growth Management To Preserve Rural and Agricultural America*, 13 Urb. Law. 27 (1981). See *City of Hollywood v. Hollywood, Inc.*, 432 So.2d 1332 (Fla. App. 1983) in which I utilized TDRs to save a 2.5-mile oceanfront beach from inverse condemnation claims; Robert H. Freilich and Wayne Senville, *Freilich and Senville Takings, TDRs and Environmental Fairness: The Hollywood North Beach Case*, 35 Land Use Law & Zoning Digest 4 (June 1983).

35. See *Palm Beach County v. Wright*, 641 So.2d 50 (Fla. 1994) (reversing judgment of per se taking through use of flexible zoning techniques).

36. *County of Wayne v. Hathcock*, 684 N.W.2d 765 (Mich. 2004), overruling *Poletown Neighborhood Council v. City of Detroit*, 304 N.W.2d 455 (Mich. 1981).

37. A number of other courts have reached similar conclusions: *Southwestern Illinois Development Authority v. National City Environmental, L.L.C.*, 768 N.E.2d 1 (Ill. 2002) (taking for racetrack parking expansion void unless public entitled to use or control property); *Berry v. City of Reno*, 107 S.W.3d 128 (Tex. App. 2003) (public must have right of use in the business or undertaking); *Condemnation of 110 Washington Street*, 767 A.2d 1154 (Pa. Commw. Ct. 2001) (delegation to private developer is void where developer has power to determine whether condemnation occurs). These cases are summarized in Robert H. Freilich and Robin Kramer, *Condemnation For Economic Development Violates the Public Use Clause: The Michigan Supreme Court Overturns The Historic Poletown Decision*, Planning and Zoning Law Rep. (St. Paul, MN: West-Thomsen, Nov. 2004).

38. In *Kelo v. City of New London*, 843 A.2d 500 (Conn. 2004), the Connecticut Supreme Court, however, upheld an economic development project despite an absence of blight so long as the public purpose contributes to the revitalization of the city. The U.S. Supreme Court has accepted certiorari. 125 S. Ct. 27 (2004). This author has contributed an amicus brief on behalf of 15 law professors, supporting the city's position and requesting the Court to reject the petitioner's call for higher scrutiny, provided the local government retains regulatory, contractual, or ownership control.

39. *Santa Margarita Area Residents Together v. San Luis Obispo County*, 100 Cal. Rptr. 2d 740 (Cal. App. 2000).

40. See Michael S. Bernick and Amy E. Freilich, *Transit Villages and Transit Based Developments: The Rules Are Becoming More Flexible—How Government Can Work With The Private Sector To Make It Happen*, 30 Urb. Law. 1 (1998).

41. Robert H. Freilich and Brenda A. Nichols, *Public Private Partnerships in Joint Development: The Legal and Financial Anatomy of Large Scale Urban Development Projects*, 7 Mun. Fin. J. 5 (1986).

42. *Charleston Urban Renewal Authority v. Courtland Co.*, 509 S.E.2d 569 (W. Va. 1998); *Aposporos v. Urban Redevelopment Comm'n.*, 790 A.2d 1167 (Conn. 2002).

43. See Cal. Health & Safety Code § 33339; *Huntington Park Redevelopment Agency v. Duncan*, 190 Cal. Rptr. 744 (Cal. App. 1983); *cert. denied*, 464 U.S. 895 (1983).

44. *Schenk v. City of Hudson*, 114 F.3d 590 (6th Cir. 1997); *Pardee Construction Co. v. City of Camarillo*, 208 Cal. Rptr. 228 (Cal. Sup. Ct. 1984); *Wilkinson v. Pitkin County* (Aspen), 872 P.2d 1269 (Colo. App. 1993).

45. Direct racial integration quotas are forbidden, *U.S. v. Starrett City Associates*, 840 F.2d 1096 (2d Cir. 1988), but insurance for neighborhood residents against the lowering of property values has been both upheld and successful. See The Illinois Urban Property Insurance Act, Chapter 215 ILCS, upheld in *Clayton v. Village of Oak Park*, 453 N.E.2d 937 (Ill. App. 1983).

46. See Robert J. Sitkowski and Brian W. Ohm, *Enabling The New Urbanism*, 34 Urb. Law. 935 (2002).

7

A Requiem for Smart Growth?

Gerrit-Jan Knaap

INTRODUCTION

In the days following the 2004 presidential election, there was much consternation in Democratic circles. George W. Bush won again, the Republicans picked up seats in the House and Senate, and the Republican majority seemed to have grown in depth and strength. Pundits and progressives were already wondering, "Could the Democrats ever recapture the hearts of an American public now apparently obsessed with security, morality, and personal charm?"

Among academic and professional planners, there was similar concern. Although John Kerry had never been a champion of smart growth, it was clear that the prospects for smarter growth were far greater in an administration headed by Kerry than one headed by Bush. Smart growth had not fully disappeared in the federal agenda in the first Bush administration, but the momentum had clearly waned. Further, the discussion in the planning chat rooms and list serves focused on the blue and red maps, which made clear that Republicans dominated not only the central and southern states but also the rural and suburban areas of most every state in the union. The subject line of one long conversation on the PLANET list serve said "sprawling Republicans," which conveyed the alarm: The new American majority was deeply rooted in urban sprawl.

In the wake of these political events, it is reasonable to ask, "Can smart growth survive another term of President Bush? If so, what must be done to regain the momentum and capture the favor of an ever-growing conservative majority?" In this period of national reflection, therefore, I consider the state of smart growth and its prospects for the near-term future. I start with a brief history of its evolution, continue with an examination of recent trends, and follow with an assessment of whether smart growth will change those trends. I conclude with recommendations for how smart growth might adapt to the new political realities.

A BRIEF HISTORY OF SMART GROWTH

The birth of smart growth is difficult to pinpoint. Antecedents include the growth controls of the 1960s and the growth management revolution of the 1970s and 1980s. Smart growth also shares principles with contemporaneous movements identified by the terms "new urbanism" and "sustainable development." I will not attempt to parse the distinctions implied by these terms. Still, clear discussion begins with definition.

According to the U.S. Environmental Protection Agency (US EPA), smart growth is "development that serves the economy, the community, and the environment. It changes the terms of the development debate away from the traditional growth/no growth question to how and where should new development be accommodated" (Smart Growth Network 2004). Towards this end, the US EPA established in 1996 and continues to fund a network of organizations dedicated to smart growth principles. Thanks in large part to this network, smart growth is now part of the lexicon of planners, policy-makers, and almost everyone with an interest in urban issues (US EPA 2004).

Though the origins of the term are unclear, the rapid ascendance of smart growth can be traced to three key projects (Burchell et al., 2000):

1. In the mid 1990s, the American Planning Association (APA) launched Growing Smart[SM], an ambitious project that, in 1997, produced the *Growing Smart[SM] Legislative Guidebook: Model Statutes for Planning and the Management of Change* (hereinafter the "Guidebook") (Meck 2002).

2. In the same year, the Natural Resources Defense Council and the Surface Transportation Policy Project (STPP) published *The Toolkit for Smart Growth* (Natural Resources Defense Council and the STPP 1997), which promoted compact growth, mixed land uses, and transit-oriented development.

3. Also in 1997, the State of Maryland passed the Neighborhood Conservation and Smart Growth initiative (hereinafter the "Smart Growth Act"), which encouraged Brownfield Redevelopment, a Live Near Your Work housing assistance program, which concentrated state-funded infrastructure in Priority Funding Areas (PFAs), preserved Rural Legacy lands, and spatially concentrated Job Creation Tax Credits (JCTCs).

Since then, smart growth programs—at least in name—have been promoted by groups that range from the Sierra Club to the National Association of Home Builders.

Growing Smart in Chicago

Work on the Guidebook began in the research department of the APA in October 1994 (Meck 2003). The genesis of the project came from two sources. In

1991, a U.S. Department of Housing and Urban Development (HUD) advisory committee on affordable housing recommended that HUD "work with government and private industry groups, such as the American Bar Association, and American Planning Association . . . and others to develop consensus-based model codes and statutes for use by State and local governments" (US HUD 1991).

Also in 1991, the APA created a task force to draft new model planning and zoning enabling legislation because it was "concerned about the number of bills to [reform] planning and land development control being introduced in state legislatures without an overall body of evaluative research to offer guidance" (Lewyn 2003: 8-9). Initial funding for the project came from HUD and the Henry Jackson Foundation, and subsequently from several other federal agencies, the Annie E. Casey Foundation, the Siemans Corporation and the APA itself. The project was guided by a large "directorate," which included representatives of many national interest groups and organizations.[1]

As the Guidebook's subtitle suggests, its purpose is to offer "Model Statutes for Planning and the Management of Change." The intent was to supplant the Standard State Zoning Enabling Act (SZEA) of the 1920s and the American Law Institute's Model Land Development Code of 1976, which were widely viewed as out of date. According to the Guidebook, for example, the SZEA inadequately addresses the state's role in land-use regulation, environmental issues such as land preservation, citizen participation, and judicial oversight.

In contrast to the SZEA, which presented a single model for every state, the Guidebook presents alternative strategies and statutes from which state legislators can choose. It offers models for regional planning agencies, urban growth boundaries, adequate public facilities ordinances, impact fees, and more. It does not specifically promote the agenda now known as "smart growth," though it includes many of the tools prescribed by smart growth advocates and offers excerpts from Maryland's Smart Growth Act as one possible alternative.

The Guidebook was published in 2002 but was a source of controversy long before its publication. Technical issues such as "standing" and "moratoria" stimulated considerable debate among members of the directorate and slowed production. A group of property rights advocates requested HUD Secretary, Mel Martinez, to halt publication and convinced Congressman Steve Chabot (R–Ohio) to conduct an oversight hearing under the auspices of the House Judiciary Committee. *Professional Builder* magazine announced it would give the APA its Professional Achievement Award for the Guidebook, but later declined to make the award.[2] Despite the controversy, most members of the directorate still stand by the project and, according to Stuart Meck (its principal author), 15 states have passed or considered bills that incorporate language directly from the final publication (Meck 2003).

Smart Growth in Maryland

Like the growth management programs of all other states, Maryland's smart growth programs reflect the geographic, political, and historical features of land-use issues in the state. The historical roots of Maryland's smart growth program date to 1933, when Maryland established the nation's first State Planning Commission. By 1959, the commission staff became the State Planning Department and, by 1969, was elevated to cabinet status as the Department of Planning. A steady stream of planning legislation followed: the State Planning Act of 1974, the Chesapeake Bay Critical Areas Act of 1984, the failed growth management effort of the state's 2020 Commission in 1991, and the Economic Growth, Resource Protection, and Planning Act (hereinafter "the Planning Act") of 1992.

Maryland's Planning Act required local governments to prepare comprehensive land-use plans, to incorporate six visions[3] and a sensitive-areas element in their plans, to encourage economic growth and regulatory streamlining, and to review their plans every six years. Once a plan is adopted, local governments may approve development projects that include state funds, only if they are consistent with the plan. The state also may not fund a public works or transportation project unless the project is consistent with the applicable local plan. The Maryland Department of Planning must provide written commentary on the sensitive elements of all plans, but local governments need not incorporate the state's recommendations in the plan.

In 1996, following an extensive listening campaign, many meetings, and frequent forums, the governor's office developed five initiatives that have made Maryland recognized as the undisputed leader of smart growth policy reforms:

1. *PFAs:* State subsidies for new roads, water, and other infrastructure will be available only for projects that are either within municipalities, within the I-495 and I-695 beltways, or within other locally designated areas that meet certain criteria set by the state.

2. *Rural Legacy Program:* The state provides funds for local governments and land trusts to purchase properties and development rights in rural areas threatened by encroaching development to preserve agriculture, forests, and natural resource lands in contiguous blocks, corridors, or greenways.

3. *Brownfields/Voluntary Cleanup Programs:* The state provides financial incentives and technical assistance to eligible participants in the cleanup and redevelopment of underutilized or abandoned industrial properties that are, or are perceived to be, contaminated.

4. *Live Near Your Work Program:* This program promotes linkages between employers and nearby communities by offering incentives to enable employees to buy homes in proximity to their workplaces.

5. *JCTC Program:* Employers who create 25 or more new, full-time jobs within a PFA are eligible for state income tax credits.

From the outset, Governor Parris N. Glendening sought to develop a strategy that favored incentives over regulations, preserved local autonomy, could be rapidly implemented, would not create a new bureaucracy, and had modest budgetary impacts (Cohen 2002). For the most part, the five smart growth programs meet these requirements.

Planning and development regulation remains primarily the domain of local governments. There is no state land-use plan. The Department of Planning, and its budget, already existed; hence, no new agency was needed. Further, the administration of the programs was assigned to different state agencies: the PFA program to the Department of Planning; the Rural Legacy program to the Department of Natural Resources; the Brownfields/Voluntary Cleanup Programs to the Department of Business and Economic Development and the Department of Environment, respectively; the Live Near Your Work program to the Department of Housing and Community Development; and the JCTC program to the Department of Business and Economic Development. This assignment of programs to multiple agencies not only saved costs, but also built widespread support within state government.

Smarter Still in Washington, DC

Although the axis of smart growth runs through Annapolis and Chicago, much of what is now known as "smart growth" was cultivated inside the beltway. Though the Guidebook was written in Chicago, the APA has an office in Washington, the project was funded by HUD, and most members of the directorate have offices in DC. Glendening and Al Gore were no strangers, and the smart growth advocates in Annapolis worked closely with smart growth advocates in Washington. It is no coincidence that Maryland is the only state member of the US EPA's smart growth network. This doesn't imply that smart growth did not have advocates all over the nation, but it is certainly fair to say that smart growth was no quiet revolution spreading covertly from Burlington (Vermont) to Salem (Oregon) to Honolulu (Hawaii).

The federal government also played a significant role in the promotion of smart growth. Although the U.S. Government Accounting Office (US GAO 1999) reported that the federal influence of urban sprawl is ambiguous, the federal government has always had a significant influence of land use in the United States. In 2000, a panel of experts listed the Interstate Highway Act and the Federal Housing Administration mortgage program as the two most influential determinants of metropolitan growth patterns in the post-war period (Fishman 2000). In the 1990s, however, the federal government took on a new role in land-use policy-making—a role that combined the federal interest in transportation and air quality with local land-use planning.

The seeds of smart growth in Washington were planted by the STPP, "a diverse, nationwide coalition working to ensure safer communities and smarter transportation choices that enhance the economy, improve public health, promote social equity, and protect the environment" (STPP 2004).

Established in 1990, the STPP was instrumental in the passage of the Intermodal Surface Transportation Efficiency Act (ISTEA), which in 1991 made the receipt of transportation funds by local governments contingent on conformance with the Clean Air Act.[4] Further, the ISTEA "challenges officials to reduce vehicle emissions, to reduce the number of single-occupant vehicles, and to make alternatives such as transit and bicycles a more viable part of the transportation network" (Jensen 2003). Through these provisions, the ISTEA established the explicit interest of the Department of Transportation (DOT) and the US EPA in state and local land-use planning and decision-making.

The passage of the ISTEA led to the creation of the Urban Economic Development Division (UEDD) (now the division of Development, Community, and Environment) within the US EPA Office of Policy, Economics and Innovation. Under the leadership of Harriet Tregoning (who later became Maryland's Secretary of Planning and, subsequently, the Special Secretary for Smart Growth in the Glendening administration), the UEDD created the Smart Growth Network, providing funding for a variety of smart growth activities. This network, partially administered by the International City/County Management Association, consists of some 36 organizations, most of them not-for-profit interest groups, several trade organizations, two federal agencies (the US EPA and the National Oceanic & Atmospheric Administration) and one state (Maryland). Partners of the network are active all over the nation, but the headquarters of most are located in Washington, DC.

KEY PRINCIPLES AND STRATEGIES

Of the 36 partners of the Smart Growth Network, each probably has a different definition of smart growth. Still most ascribe—in various degrees—to these 10 principles:

1. Mix land uses.
2. Take advantage of compact building design.
3. Create a wide range of housing opportunities and choices.
4. Create walkable neighborhoods.
5. Foster distinctive, attractive communities with a strong sense of place.
6. Preserve open space, farmland, natural beauty, and critical environmental areas.
7. Strengthen and direct development toward existing communities.
8. Provide a variety of transportation choices.
9. Make development decisions predictable, fair, and cost effective.
10. Encourage community and stakeholder collaboration in development decisions.

In many respects, however, these goals are similar to the goals of growth management, new urbanism, sustainable development, or just good planning.

What's more, goals often reveal little about the activities and strategies that organizations pursue. In contrast to its antecedents, however, the smart growth movement can be characterized by the following principles and strategies:

- Incentives for implementation;
- Insurgency and advocacy;
- Integrated transportation and land-use policy;
- Innovative policy instruments; and
- Institutional reform.

Incentives for Implementation

To the extent that Maryland provides the model of smart growth strategies, incentives are the instruments that drive implementation. The strategy of the Glendening administration was to promote a set of policies that would not raise strong opposition by Maryland's powerful counties. Incentives were the answer.

Under Maryland's Smart Growth Act, local governments can grow anywhere they want, but state funds for accommodating development are available only within PFAs. Property owners need not clean up and redevelop their properties, but the state provides grants for doing so. Residents can live anywhere, but the state and local governments provide grants for those who purchase homes near their work. Farm and forestland can be developed, but the state will buy land or development rights from those who refrain from development. Businesses can expand anywhere, but the threshold for state tax credits for job creation is lower for businesses that expand in PFAs.

Incentives, or market orientations, are features of many other smart growth policy instruments. Transferable development rights do not by themselves restrict development in rural areas but grant farmers the opportunity to trade development rights in rural areas for development rights in urban areas. Density bonuses enable developers to develop at higher densities if they provide local governments with affordable housing units, dedicated parklands, or other forms of compensation. Transportation-efficient mortgages enable low-income residents who purchase homes near transit stations to claim transportation cost savings as part of their capacity to make mortgage payments. Impact fees allow developers to develop in areas with inadequate public services when they pay their share of the cost of public service improvements. Historic preservation tax credits provide incentives for the preservation of historic buildings and the redevelopment of inner-city neighborhoods. Most of these market-oriented instruments were not part of the earlier growth management programs but represent central tools for smart growth implementation.

Insurgency and Advocacy

The focus of smart growth advocates on insurgency and advocacy was clearly intentional. Although smart growth had the blessing of the Clinton-Gore administration, the authority of federal agencies to participate in land-use decision-making is limited. Further, smart growth was conceived in the era of sound bites, the Internet, and spin. Thus, the UEDD division of the US EPA, itself unable to do so, sought to influence local land-use policy by funding advocacy and insurgency by its network members. The stated mission of the network is (Smart Growth Network 2004):

- Raising public awareness of smart growth and the implications of development decisions for the economy, the community, and the environment;
- Promoting smart growth best practices through educational publications and other venues;
- Developing and sharing information, innovative policies, tools, and ideas;
- Fostering collaboration among network partners and members who represent various interests to apply smart growth approaches to resolve problems of the build environment; and
- Cultivating strategies to address barriers to, and to advance opportunities for, smart growth.

Towards these ends, the UEDD provided grants to many of the major players in the smart growth arena, including grants to (Samuel and O'Toole 1999):

- 1000 Friends of Oregon to establish the National Growth Management Leadership Project;
- National Association of Governors to help states develop smart growth strategies;
- Growth Management Institute for workshops, focus groups, and anti-sprawl activities;
- Center for Watershed Protection to develop smart growth zoning codes;
- Congress for New Urbanism for workshops and conferences; and
- Coalition for Utah's Future to support Envision Utah's community workshops.

Though not a charter member, foremost among the Smart Growth Network is Smart Growth America. Smart Growth America was formed in 2000 and is self-described as "a nationwide coalition promoting a better way to grow: one that protects farmland and open space, revitalizes neighborhoods, keeps housing affordable, and provides more transportation choices" (Smart Growth America 2004). Smart Growth America is an active lobbyist with close connections to the Senate Smart Growth Task Force, the House Livable Communities Task Force, the Housing Sustainable Development Caucus, and the Congressional Black Caucus Transportation Brain Trust. Smart Growth America has been instrumental in several high-profile projects, including projects that produced "The Link Between Growth Management and Housing Affordability: The Academic Evidence" and "Measuring the Health Effects of Sprawl."

In 2002, Parris L. Glendening (after two terms as governor of Maryland) and Harriet Tregoning convinced Smart Growth America to establish a subsidiary organization called the Smart Growth Leadership Institute to provide "technical and strategic assistance to communities working to achieve smart growth" (id.). With funding from the US EPA, the Smart Growth Leadership Institute is currently providing smart growth technical assistance to nine communities across the country.

Integrated Transportation and Land-Use Policy

Recognition of the link between transportation and land use is not new. Melvin Webber in 1959 wrote an essay entitled *The Engineer's Responsibility for the Form of Cities* (Webber 1959); in the early 1970s, Steve Putman and others in the U.S. DOT were experimenting with "an Integrated Transportation and Land Use Models Package" (Putman 1976). Still, in the 1990s, transportation and land-use policy became much more interconnected and the focus of two smart growth principles.

The seminal work in this area was the Land Use, Transportation, Air Quality Project spearheaded by 1000 Friends of Oregon. 1000 Friends, a pioneering land-use advocacy organization, mobilized opposition to a bypass freeway in Washington County, Oregon, in 1991. With funding from the US EPA, the Federal Highway Administration, and others, 1000 Friends led a team of planning and transportation engineering consultants in an effort to demonstrate the superiority of a land-use and transit alternative to the proposed freeway. When the highway proposal was successfully defeated, the project became a model for advocacy organizations around the nation. For better or worse, any new major transportation investment in the U.S. today—whether highway or transit—is likely to draw the attention of multiple advocacy organizations armed with studies that support both the build and no-build options.

The success of 1000 Friends of Oregon was matched, if not surpassed, by the STPP, which led the effort to pass the ISTEA in 1991 and its successor, the Transportation Equity Act for the 21st Century, in 1998. Both bills provided billions of dollars to the Congestion Mitigation and Air Quality program, which have been used for a variety of transportation and land-use projects around the nation. The idea that transportation and land use are connected is perhaps not new but, in the smart growth era, land-use and transportation policies have become deeply intertwined.

Innovative Policy Instruments

The smart growth movement also differs from its antecedents in its approach to policy instrumentation. Whereas advocates of growth management relied extensively on the standard tools of zoning, subdivision regulations, and comprehensive plans, smart growth advocates generally eschew these tools or call for their substantial reform. This is less true for the Guidebook, where recommendations for zoning reforms are only marginal. Though the Maryland Department of Planning has produced its own model land-use ordinance, comprehensive planning and zoning are still fundamental elements of land-use governance in the state.

Pressure for the reform of zoning and subdivision regulations comes primarily from the smart growth nucleus in Washington. Listed on the Web site of the Smart Growth Network are extensive lists of models and recommendations for the reform of ordinances, codes, statutes, and policies. However, this list pales in comparison to the plethora of tools, strategies, and implementation tools offered by the smart growth coalition. Indeed, the inaugural book by the STPP and the Natural Resources Defense Council was *The Toolkit for Smart Growth*. Since then, the Smart Growth Network has helped to produce *Local Tools for Smart Growth, Getting to Smart Growth: 100 Policies for Implementation,* and *Getting to Smart Growth II: 100 More Policies for Implementation.*

Institutional Reform

The call for institutional reform is pervasive throughout the smart growth coalition but is most prominent at the APA. After all, the raison d'étre of the Guidebook is the reform of state land-use statutes. Again, the Guidebook merely offers a menu of alternative approaches to statutory reform, but there is no doubt that the Guidebook favors a stronger role for state and regional governments in land-use decision-making.

Not only does the Guidebook offer models for a state planning agency, state plans, and state land-use controls, it also offers requirements for local plans and models for the establishment of regional planning agencies. The Brookings Institution, not a formal member of the Smart Growth Network but with many overlapping interests, is also a strong supporter of stronger regional participation in land-use decision-making. Calls for regional approaches and regional institutions certainly appear among the 200+ strategies for smart growth offered by the Smart Growth Network, but greater regional or state participation in land-use decision-making is not high on the network's agenda, perhaps because the network membership includes several local government organizations and is funded in large part by the US EPA.

Institutional reform was also not the central element of smart growth in Maryland. At the time that Maryland's Smart Growth Act was passed, Maryland already had a state office of planning and already required local governments to plan and zone. Maryland has no regional governments—other than the councils of governments and metropolitan planning organizations that are found everywhere. In fact, most of Maryland's smart growth reforms were restraints imposed by the state government on itself.

In essence, the thrust of smart growth in Maryland—through the designation of PFAs—is to minimize the state's funding for urban sprawl. By executive order, Governor Glendening did establish a smart growth subcabinet, which included the secretaries of the Departments of Agriculture, Budget & Management, Business & Economic Development, Environment, General Services, Housing & Community Development, Natural Resources, Transportation, the Commissioner of the Higher Education Commission, and the executive director of the National Center for Smart Growth Research & Education. Governor Glendening similarly pushed through legislation to create an Office of Smart Growth within the governor's office, headed by a special secretary for smart growth. However, under the Ehrlich administration, the special secretary was never replaced, the majority of its employees left or were dismissed, the Office of Smart Growth was downsized and subsumed within the Department of Planning, and the subcabinet rarely meets.

ARE WE GROWING SMART?

Trying to assess whether we are indeed growing smart is inherently dicey. The notion is ill defined, the dates of policy intervention are murky, and the targets of change are complex. Further, the movement is yet young. The final version of the Guidebook was published only two years ago, the Maryland Smart Growth Act was passed only seven years ago, and the first edition of *The Toolkit for Smart Growth* is only 12 years old. It is naïve to think that 60+ years of "dumb growth" can be reversed in such a short period. Still, it is at least interesting to review what has transpired since the smart growth movement began and to consider the direction of trends in urban development patterns, consumer preferences, and the efficacy of the smart growth experiment in Maryland.

Urban Development Trends

Trying to assess national development trends is always difficult. Cities are slow to change and data are notoriously stale. Fortunately, recent analyses of the 2000 census data provide some insights into what has transpired over the decade of the 1990s.

At first blush, the trends look promising. Many northeastern and midwestern cities with more than 500,000 people gained population for the first time since 1950. Chicago grew by 4 percent; New York City grew by 9 percent. Overall, the median growth rate for cities in the 1990s was 8.7 percent, more than double the median growth rate in the 1980s (Glaeser and Shapiro 2001). The pattern of growth, however, was highly uneven. Cities grew more rapidly in the west, south, and along the coastlines. Faster-growing cities had economies with smaller industrial sectors, attracted more immigrants, and featured warmer temperatures. Florida (2000) points out that faster-growing cities have higher levels of education and more cultural opportunities, high-tech jobs, and gays; Glaeser and Kahn (2001) point out that faster-growing cities have more cars.

While the population growth of metropolitan areas is good news from a smart growth perspective, the spatial pattern of population growth is less encouraging. In the 35 largest metropolitan areas of the United States, central cities grew by 7.8 percent while their suburbs grew by 16.5 percent (Lucy and Phillips 2001). Today, 50 percent of Americans live in the suburbs compared with 30 percent only 40 years ago. Within the central cities that grew, 60 percent of that growth occurred in "outer ring neighborhoods" (Katz 2002). Two-thirds of all downtown census tracts gained population, but these gains were usually offset by population losses elsewhere in the urban core (Berube and Forman 2002). Today, "boomburgs," defined as "suburbs with more than 100,000 residents," are growing at double-digit rates (Lang and Simmons 2001). In the 1990s, these places accounted for over half of the growth in cities between 100,000 and 400,000 residents.

The pattern of employment growth is even less encouraging. By 1996, less than 22 percent of employment was located within 3 miles of the city center; 35 percent of employment was located more than 10 miles from the center (Glaeser, Kahn, and Chu 2001). Employment density gradients have fallen significantly since the 1960s (Glaeser and Kahn 2000). Employment levels in "edge cities" now rival that of central cities (Garreau 1991). Even these have now been eclipsed by "edgeless cities" (Lang 2003). According to Lang, these cities—a sprawling form of office development that does not have the density or cohesiveness of edge cities—"may be the ultimate result of a metropolitan process that has been tearing apart concentrated commercial development for the better part of a century" (id.).

The spatial distributions of population and employment say little, however, about the form of urban growth. For this reason, scholars have developed a variety of innovative measures of urban form (Knaap, Song, and Holler 2004). Most, however, lack time series data and thus cannot provide measures of changes over time.

The most commonly reported measures of change in urban development patterns compare growth in urban populations with growth in urbanized areas. The Sierra Club (2004), for example, reports that between 1960 and 1990 urban areas in the United States grew twice as fast as urban populations. Fulton et al. (2001) find that between 1982 and 1997 urbanized land in the United States increased by 47 percent while urban populations increased by only 17 percent. Of the 281 metropolitan areas they examined, only 17 became denser over the same period.

Despite the release of several new indexes that reveal "who sprawls the most," the extant literature on the measurement of sprawl remains undeveloped. Metropolitan- and county-wide measures of sprawl, for example, fail to capture intrametropolitan differences and recent trends in urban form. To provide such information, Knaap and Song (Knaap, Song, and Holler 2004) measured development density, land-use mix, street network patterns, accessibility to commercial uses, and pedestrian access to commercial uses for neighborhoods of varying age in five study areas:

1. Maricopa County, Arizona;
2. Orange County, Florida;
3. Minneapolis–St. Paul, Minnesota;
4. Montgomery County, Maryland; and
5. Portland, Oregon.

They found that urban form varies a great deal between and within metropolitan areas, but that some trends appear pervasive:

• Single-family house sizes have grown continuously since 1940, but single-family lot sizes began falling in about the 1970s.

• Since about 1970, neighborhoods have become more internally connected, but external connectivity remains low in three of the five metropolitan areas.[5]

• Land-use mix within neighborhoods exhibits no obvious trends, but pedestrian access to commercial uses has consistently fallen over time.[6]

The good news is that single-family lot sizes are falling and internal connectivity is improving. The bad news is more extensive: external connectivity is deteriorating, land uses remain separated, and pedestrian accessibility to commercial uses is falling. If these trends continue, it is likely that traffic congestion, especially for nonwork trips, will only get worse.

Public Support and Consumer Preferences

Gauging public support for smart growth and smarter forms of urban development is a task fraught with potential bias and misinterpretation. One thing is certain: There has been no shortage of attempts to do so, in part, no doubt, to support the advocacy work both for and against smart growth. A Google search on "smart growth survey" yields over 130 hits; a similar search on "housing preference survey" yields over 100 hits, though many of these are directed at incoming freshmen. Perhaps not surprisingly, the results vary, depending on who is asking the questions, how the questions are asked, and when the question was posed.

There is little doubt that urban sprawl and issues of community character remain high on the list of public concerns, though obviously such concern varies considerably from place to place (Active Living Network 2004). In a national survey by the Pew Center for Civic Journalism (2000), Americans ranked traffic and urban sprawl as their number one local concern, tied with crime, and ahead of jobs and education. In the 2000 election, smart growth was an implicit element of the Gore platform, and 72 percent of growth- and open space-related ballot measures were passed (Myers and Puentes 2001). Four years later, though traffic congestion remains high among public concerns (American Public Transportation Association 2004), terrorism and economic security have largely removed smart growth from the national policy dialog.

Like popular support for other environmental issues, support for smart growth varies over the business cycle but, nearly always, urban growth is unpopular where it is rapid and desperately pursued where it is slow. However, there appear to be some constants.

First, there is widespread popular support for most of the principles of smart growth as long as there is no mention of cost. A national poll by Beldon Russonello & Stewart Research and Communications (Belden 2000) for Smart Growth America found roughly 80 percent support for the principle propositions of smart growth: focusing growth in existing communities, protecting greenspaces and farmland, and spending more money on sidewalks and other forms of pedestrian infrastructure. Similar overwhelming majorities support land-use planning, better coordination among local governments, and better growth management in the state. About half said that traffic congestion had gotten worse and about half favored public transport as a policy response.

In a poll by the National Association of Realtors (2000), 45 percent of respondents said that growth should be managed by neighborhood organizations, 45 percent said that growth should be managed by local governments, 4 percent said that growth should be managed by state governments, and 1 percent favored federal control of growth.

The evidence on consumer preferences for neighborhoods and housing is even more complex. Visual preference surveys consistently show a strong preference for leafy, well-designed neighborhoods regardless of density (Nelessen 2004). Several surveys of potential homebuyers also reveal a growing preference for high-density living (townhouses and small lots) in places that are pedestrian-friendly, have ample open space, and have convenient access to neighborhood retail (National Association of Realtors and National Association of Home Builders 2002).

Myers and Gearin (2001) further speculate that, as the population ages and fertility rates decline, the demand for smart growth and new urbanist lifestyles could grow significantly, yet the evidence to support this proposition is mixed at best. A survey by the National Association of Realtors and the National Association of Home Builders (2002) found that 42 percent of respondents would choose a "large single family house in an outlying suburban area with longer distances to work, public transportation, and shopping," while 18 percent would choose a "small single family home in the city, close to work, public transportation, and shopping."

Further, in a just-released study for the National Association of Realtors and Smart Growth America (Belden 2004), 55 percent chose the smart growth community over the sprawl community, but 45 percent chose the sprawl community with a one-way commute of over 45 minutes! Combined, these results suggest that the demand for housing in smart growth neighborhoods is not trivial and growing, but also suggest that the demand for large houses on large suburban lots—even at the expense of long commutes—is still dominant and is likely to remain so in the foreseeable future.

A number of studies have approached this question by looking at variations in housing prices. Eppli and Tu (1999) in a national study found that houses in new urbanist communities sold at a premium over houses in conventional suburban neighborhoods. They did not, however, examine what feature of a new urbanist neighborhood produced the price premium. Song and Knaap (2003) also found that houses in new urbanist communities sold at a price premium in Washington County, Oregon.

Because they collected detailed information on specific characteristics of specific neighborhoods, however, they were able to identify which features of new urbanism produced the price premium. Specifically, they found that houses sold at a premium if they were located in highly internally connected neighborhoods, if they were close to parks and open spaces, and if they had pedestrian access to commercial uses. They also found, however, that houses sold at a discount if they were located in neighborhoods that were highly externally connected, had high densities, and had a mixture of uses. Like the results of surveys and visual preference studies, these results suggest that there is a demand for some smart growth neighborhood characteristics, but that the demand for the large, single-family home as a conventional suburban neighborhood remains dominant.

The Maryland Experiment

Research on the efficacy of smart growth in Maryland has grown in recent years, largely as a result of work at the National Center for Smart Growth Research & Education. Cohen and Pruess (2002) examined the efficacy of Montgomery County's well-known transferable development rights program. Under this program, development rights in Montgomery County's agricultural reserve could be sold or transferred to areas within the existing urban envelope. Cohen and Pruess found the price of development rights falling over time, the supply of receiving areas diminishing, and the extent to which the programs preserve farmland in doubt. Further, because the program failed to target the most fertile soils as sending areas, and failed to provide adequate and timely infrastructure in receiving areas, the popularity of the program has fallen significantly.

Howland and Sohn (forthcoming) examined the effects of Maryland's PFAs on investments in sewer infrastructure from 1997 to 2002. According to Maryland's smart growth statutes, passed in 1997, the state will only invest in urban infrastructure inside PFAs. They found that, of the total amount invested in sewer infrastructure by counties, 25 percent was invested on sewer infrastructure outside PFAs; however, of the total amount invested by the state, 29 percent was invested on sewer infrastructure outside PFAs. Most of these investments were used to repair nonperforming septic systems. Still, these findings suggest that even the state has difficulty conforming with smart growth incentives—and perhaps for good reason.

Sohn and Knaap (forthcoming) examined the effects of Maryland's JCTC program, which, since 1997, provides greater credits for job creation inside rather than outside PFAs. Using data on job growth in Maryland from 1996 to 2000, they found that job growth was greater inside than outside PFAs, holding other things constant, but only for jobs in the service sector. Based on these results, they concluded that Maryland's JCTC program can help concentrate job growth in PFAs but that the contribution of the JCTC program toward such concentration is likely to be small.

The research to date, though still more exploratory than conclusive, suggests that the effects of Maryland's approach to smart growth has been marginal at best. To date, there is little evidence that the incentives provided by the state are of sufficient magnitude to stem or reverse long-standing development trends. During the Glendening administration, the state spent considerable sums purchasing open space and protecting farmland outside PFAs, but there is little evidence that growth has been contained outside PFAs or that local governments are encouraging development inside PFAs. In fact, the evidence suggests quite the opposite (Knaap et al., 2003).

Public Policy and Institutional Reform

Change in land-use policies and institutions are also difficult to assess systematically. With the flurry of activities regularly reported in smart growth newsletters and on smart growth Web sites, it is hard to imagine that new policies are not being adopted and institutions aren't being reformed. Further, according to a survey conducted by the APA (2002), "Smart growth activity in the states between 1999 and 2001 confirms that these subjects are among the top political concerns in the statehouses across the nation." As indicators of activity, the APA (id.) reports:

- More than 2,000 planning bills were introduced between 1999 and 2001 with approximately 20 percent of the bills being approved;

- 17 governors issued 19 executive orders on planning, smart growth, and related topics during the past two years, compared to 12 orders issued during the previous eight years combined;

- Eight states issued legislative task force reports on smart growth between 1999 and 2001, compared to 10 reports between 1990 and 1998;

- 27 governors (15 Republicans, 10 Democrats, and two Independents) made specific smart growth-related proposals in 2001;

- Approximately one-quarter of the states are implementing moderate to substantial statewide planning reforms: Delaware, Florida, Georgia, Maryland, New Jersey, Oregon, Pennsylvania, Rhode Island, Tennessee, Vermont, Washington, and Wisconsin;

- Approximately one-third of the states are actively pursing their first major statewide planning reforms: Arkansas, Colorado, Connecticut, Idaho,

Illinois, Iowa, Kentucky, Massachusetts, Michigan, Minnesota, Mississippi, Missouri, New Mexico, North Carolina, and South Carolina.

In a more recent assessment of the impact of the Guidebook, Salkin (2004) lists activities in 14 states and concludes, "The Guidebook is in fact influencing lawmaking and policymaking in various statehouses as some of the model language is being implemented."

The question of implementation, however, is a matter of degree. Though the list is long and the sources well documented, it is easy to misinterpret. There is no doubt that committees have been formed in the various states, and on occasion these have led to the introduction of legislation. Sometimes this legislation is passed; even then, however, the impact is often marginal. In Illinois, for example, a Local Planning Technical Assistance Act was passed in 2002 based on a model statute in the Guidebook, but the task was assigned to the Department of Commerce and Community Affairs, an agency fundamentally antagonistic to the concept of planning, and no funds were ever authorized to enable the agency to provide the assistance. As in the case of Maryland, planning reform acts with impressive names are often not quite what they seem.

The adoption of new policies at the local level is also difficult to assess; once again, however, there are signs of change. In a series of papers for the Brookings Institution, Fulton and colleagues document substantial growth in the use of urban containment policies (such as urban growth boundaries, PFAs, and urban service areas) (Pendall et al., 2002), transferable development rights (Fulton et al., 2004), and open space purchases (Hollis and Fulton 2002). The Smart Growth Web site of the US EPA lists 119 examples of smart growth policies (US EPA 2005) recently enacted at the state and local levels.

Recent research by Pendall and his colleagues, however, casts some doubt about growth in the adoption of smart growth policy instruments. Using the results of national surveys of local governments administered in 1994 and 2003, Pendall, Martin, and Wei (2004) found little evidence that sprawl-fighting measures increased in the aggregate over this period.

In general, Pendall found almost no change in the use of plans, zoning, or urban growth boundaries. In California, the use of urban growth boundaries and permit caps actually fell. Nationwide, there was a modest rise in the use of density bonuses and inclusionary zoning but a decline in the use of adequate public facilities ordinances. Perhaps the most interesting finding in the Pendall study was the degree of fluctuation in the use of smart growth policies. States Pendall (id., 12):

"Assuming the respondents answered correctly in both years, abandonment is more or nearly as common as adoption in five of eight growth management or growth-control measures: low-density only zoning (50 abandonments, 52 adoptions), permissive high density zoning (68 to 51), urban growth boundaries (70 to 79), pace control (16 to 17), and adequate public facility ordinances (54 to 35). Only

moratoria and the two affordable housing programs had substantially less abandonment than adoption between 1994 and 2003."

In sum, the evidence on development patterns, consumer preferences, and
public policies suggests that not much is trending in the direction of smart
growth. Further, the evidence from Maryland suggests that its smart growth
policies appear to be having limited effects—so far. There are, of course, two
ways to interpret these results. The first is to conclude that the need for
smarter growth continues to rise; the second is to conclude that smart growth,
to date, is not having much effect. The truth is probably some combination of
both. The question is why.

WHY AREN'T WE GROWING SMARTER?

Urban growth and transportation issues remain prominent among popular
concerns. The reform of statutes that govern land-use policy continues slowly
but steadily, and an increasing number of subdivisions exhibit new urbanist
principles, yet the obstacles to significant change in the spatial structure of
American cities remain formidable. These include social and institutional
inertia, long-term economic fundamentals, and lack of a coherent reform
strategy.

Resistance to Change

The first major obstacle is simply this: The task is monumental. Cities of the
northeastern United States are approximately 300 years old and western cities
are only slightly younger than that. While cities of the United States are
expected to add more than 90 million residents over the next three decades,
change will be difficult. Nelessen (2004), however, is optimistic. He sees the
populations of cities increasing by 50 percent over the next 30 years and can
see no reason why such growth can't lead to a significant restructuring of
metropolitan areas. Bertaud (2002) is less sanguine. He sees the current density of Atlanta, and American cities in general, as too low to sustain any form
of public transportation. For Bertaud, the die is cast; given existing development patterns, American cities are destined for dominance by the automobile
and automobile-oriented urban form.

The most formidable obstacle to smart growth is inertia. Change is hard; for
significant change in urban structure, there must be significant change in preferences, politics, institutions, and infrastructure. None of this will occur
quickly. Preferences are changing, but preferences are socially constructed—
shaped in part by demographics, social institutions, and the sprawl-industrial
complex. This complex of developers, homebuilders, financial institutions,
automobile manufacturers, and the highway construction industry all have
vested interests in the status quo.

Although there is no Status Quo Network, there is also never a shortage of response to the latest study to extol the virtues of smart growth. Perhaps the most formidable obstacles to smart growth are the millions of current home-owners in the United States. As articulated by Fischel (2001), every *homevoter* has a stake in the status quo. Rarely are the social benefits of infill, higher densities, and especially regional institutional change sufficiently compelling to draw the support of this dominant constituency.

Economic Fundamentals

Inertia, of course, can be overcome under strong, persistent, and pervasive economic pressure for change, but the economic fundamentals are mixed at best. Few these days take seriously the proposition that information and tele-communication technologies will render cities obsolete. Glaeser, Kahn, and Chu (2001) argue convincingly that information technologies and face-to-face contact are complements and not substitutes.

Cities are not obsolete; still, it is clear that firms are increasingly footloose and less attracted to city centers. According to Audirac (2002), "The form of the information age metropolis emerges as (1) polycentric and intensely extra-networked by land, air, water, and digital means to global and regional urban systems; and (2) deeply digitally and multi-modally intra-networked, albeit all the more socio-economically segregated, physically overextended, and stuck in traffic." In standard economic theory, urban decentralization (the economist's word for "sprawl") increases when incomes rise and transportation costs fall. For both of these reasons, urban areas have "sprawled" world-wide since the beginning of time. It will take a coherent strategy and powerful public policies to reverse these trends now.

Incoherent Strategies

Unfortunately, smart growth strategies have been neither coherent nor imbedded in particularly powerful public policies. The combination of incentives, institutional change, and counterinsurgency would seem sufficient to bring about significant change; in fact, they're probably not. Institutional change, perhaps the most important element, is proceeding slowly and with marginal effect.

To provide a smorgasbord approach, and appease its diverse directorate, the Guidebook seems to imply that any change is positive change. However, while the APA claims credit for shaping the language of legislation, the agendas of legislative task forces, and statutory reforms in Wisconsin and Tennessee, it played no role in the development of the best land-use programs in the nation: those in Oregon and Washington. Further, in the competition for favorable public exposure, the APA was often preempted by its adversaries and unsuccessful at generating favorable spin.

Inadequate Incentives

The incentive approach taken by Maryland also has significant limitations. Bowing to political pressures, the state failed to constrain the powers of local governments and hoped that, by limiting state spending within PFAs, buying development rights in rural areas, and creating a few incentive programs, it could significantly alter development trends in this still rapidly growing state. It has not.

Perhaps things would have been different had Democrat Kathleen Kennedy Townsend, not Republican Robert Ehrlich, followed Glendening, or if the state deficit had not removed the punch from the incentive programs, but perhaps not. Without stronger state oversight, local governments in Maryland will continue to plan and zone land for parochial benefit, often at the expense of the region. Further, incentives and market approaches assume that problems can be solved solely by adjusting prices, as though growth and development require no planning or coordination.

Counterproductive Policies

The advocacy and insurgency led by the US EPA has likely had a significant impact on popular opinion and the efficacy of smart growth advocacy organizations; however, it is not clear that the net effect has been positive. Rising concerns about sprawl and increased demands for open space, as in Maryland, can favor balkanization over regional integration. Further, it is clear that the local adoption of some policies promoted by the Smart Growth Network (e.g., urban growth boundaries, open space protection, conservation easements, and new urbanist subdivisions) can be counterproductive at the regional level. Local urban growth boundaries can deflect growth to more distant locations, and open space protections and conservation easements can lower densities. New urbanist subdivisions, while increasing internal connectivity, often decrease external connectivity. In some ways, the proliferation of smart growth policies has led to more parochialism and less smart growth.

In short, with the exception of some chapters in the Guidebook, the smart growth movement is fundamentally not rooted in planning. It is important that the public understands the consequences of sprawl and the benefits of managed urban growth. It is also important that public policies do not distort prices in favor of sprawl. However, the fundamental cause of sprawl is the lack of coordinated decision-making across sectors, over space, and through time. This cause cannot be addressed by changing prices or preferences; it must be addressed by planning.

TOWARD A MORE CENTRIST SMART GROWTH STRATEGY

Despite an unpopular war, a struggling economy, and an inarticulate candidate, the Republican Party not only retained the presidency but strengthened its control of the House and Senate. Similarly, despite rising concerns about urban sprawl, growing awareness of smart growth, and a spate of opportunities for policy reform, urban sprawl largely continues unabated. To remain competitive with their Republican rivals, Democrats must devise new strategies for winning public support. To compete effectively with urban sprawl, smart growth advocates must do the same.

Toward that end, I offer five strategies for reform.

1. *Stop perpetuating myths that alienate critical constituencies.* In attempts to gain public support and expand the umbrella, smart growth advocates perpetuate myths that support their cause. Here I address only three. First, the United States in not running out of farmland. Protecting farmland has the benefit of preserving open space and slowing haphazard urban expansion. For these reasons, it makes sense to manage urban growth. However, the argument that we need to protect farmland for food security is a canard that alienates rural constituencies and undermines the credibility of its proponents. What is needed are better plans for the use of rural lands and for the orderly conversion of farmland to alternative uses such as forests, wetlands, and natural areas.[7]

Second, urban infill and redevelopment is not less costly than the development of greenfields. If this were true, both developers and local governments would clamor for infill opportunities; they don't. Excess infrastructure capacity is rare in urban areas, and redevelopment often requires substantial infrastructure upgrades and retrofits. To preserve the health and vitality of inner cities, infill and redevelopment are worthy and important endeavors, but it is not cheap.

Third, densely developed neighborhoods are not inherently healthier than low-density neighborhoods. There is growing evidence that adults walk more for utilitarian purposes in high-density neighborhoods—and there is no doubt that many suburban neighborhoods are poorly designed for safe, nonmotorized travel—but it strains credulity to argue that children are necessarily healthier living in smaller houses and in neighborhoods with less private open space. Farmland preservationists, central city residents, and citizens concerned about public health are useful to have as smart growth advocates, and many of their arguments have merit, but extreme versions of their arguments are not credible, and they antagonize residents of rural areas, residents of suburbs, and families with children.

2. *Focus on the reform of institutions and processes, not on the promotion of lifestyles.* Of the 10 principles of smart growth, eight are substantive and two are procedural. Though the substantive principles are written in general language, there is little doubt about what they promote: compact, high-density, mixed-use, transit-oriented, and pedestrian-friendly neighborhoods. Perhaps these kinds of neighborhoods are undersupplied and do less damage to the environment, to the public purse, and to the health of its residents, but they are not the types of neighborhoods in which most Americans live or are likely to live in the near future.

What is needed, therefore, are institutions and planning processes that facilitate coordination and integration of alternative neighborhoods and lifestyles—not the promotion of one lifestyle over the other. A platform that favors the lifestyles of a minority is unlikely to succeed. What's more, the car and the lifestyle it facilitates will not soon disappear. An often forgotten fact about the history of the Oregon land-use program is that the program was created by Senate Bill 100 in 1973; the goals and guidelines were adopted in 1974.

3. *Promote the use of information and information technologies.* The Guidebook promotes land market monitoring for the management of urban growth boundaries. The Smart Growth Network also promotes the use of a variety of sustainability and other types of indicators. However, indicators are needed that provide timely information on local conditions, plans, regulations, and development decisions.

Examples include the buildout analysis led by the Massachusetts Executive Office of Environmental Affairs (2004), the work of the development capacity task force led by the Maryland Department of Planning (2004), and the National Demonstration project in land market monitoring led by the National Center for Smart Growth Research & Education (2004). These types of analyses and monitoring effects help in local government decision-making and hold local governments accountable to a larger regional constituency. Better land-use information leads to better land-use planning, which leads to better land use.

Other promising uses of information technologies in planning include scenario analysis as conducted by Portland Metro, Envision Utah, and Chicago 2020. These types of efforts are unobtrusive, facilitate public participation, and represent the cutting edge of smart growth.

4. *Strengthen and expand the use of market instruments.* Although Maryland's experiment with economic incentives has had limited success, incentives must remain a prominent feature of a centrist's strategy for smart growth. The key, however, is to use incentives large enough to affect economic decision-making when the problem is fundamentally a distortion of prices and not a need for coordination, where pricing does not undermine planning, and where incentives can be administered in a cost-effective manner.

For one or more of the reasons above, this precludes the use of PFAs, Live Near Your Work programs, and transferable development rights. Congestion tolls and impact fees, however, meet all of the above conditions. In fact, impact fees and other forms of road pricing represent the most promising and underutilized growth management tool at our disposal. For impact fees to work well, however, they should vary by the type of development, by the location of development, and with the capacity of current infrastructure. It is hard to imagine enabling legislation that allows for such variation. Thus, negotiated fees and proffers, strictly scrutinized, might be the next best approach.

5. ***Raise the profile of efforts to promote social justice.*** As the agenda of generally progressive organizations, smart growth has always supported the notion of social justice. Despite evidence to the contrary, smart growth has always been promoted as a means for providing affordable housing. However, in a widely circulated paper, Baum (2003) criticized smart growth advocates for neglecting issues of community, race, and education. Not all of his arguments are valid, and smart growth advocacy organizations have recently organized several events that highlight issues of equity and race. Still, among the listed members of the Smart Growth Network, there are no organizations that explicitly represent minorities, affordable housing, or education (Smart Growth Network 2004). Embracing such organizations may not move the network closer to the center but might expand and strengthen its base.

A REQUIEM FOR SMART GROWTH?

Despite the political climate and the formidable forces of opposition, it is premature to play a requiem for smart growth. A strong, growing, and vocal minority will not let it die and has co-opted many of its adversaries. Clearly, there remains much work to be done. Still, every organization and organism must change to survive and, if smart growth is to become more than the rallying cry of a sizable minority, it must move to the center. In this time of transition and reflection, now might be a good time to make plans to do so.

GERRIT-JAN KNAAP NOTES

1. The directorate included representatives of the APA, Council of Governors' Policy Advisors, Council of State Community Development Agencies, National Conference of State Legislatures, National Association of Counties, National Association of Regional Councils, National Association of Towns and Townships, National Governors Association (NGA) (*the NGA withdrew from the Directorate in April 2000*), National League of Cities, U.S. Conference of Mayors, Member-at-Large for the Built Environment, Member-at-Large for Local Government Law, and Member-at-Large for the Natural Environment.
2. Personal letter from Editor in Chief, Heather McCune, *Professional Builder*, to Stuart Meck, dated Dec. 30, 2002.
3. These six visions were established by the 2020 Commission in 1988: (1) development is concentrated in suitable areas; (2) sensitive areas are protected; (3) in rural areas, development is directed toward existing population centers and resource areas are protected; (4) stewardship of the Chesapeake Bay and the land is a universal ethic; (5) conservation of resources, including a reduction in resource consumption, is practiced; and (6) funding mechanisms are addresses to achieve these visions. See Cohen (2002).
4. One of the key draftsmen of the ISTEA legislation was Roy Kienitz, top aide to the late New York Senator Daniel Patrick Moynihan. Kienitz later took over as head of the STPP. Kienitz left the STPP to become planning secretary under Glendening, and is now deputy chief of staff under Ed Rendell in Pennsylvania.
5. Internal connectivity measures the proportion of nodes in the road network that are cul-de-sacs or dead ends; the greater the proportion of dead ends, the lower the internal

connectivity. External connectivity measures the distance between access points into neighborhoods; the greater the distance, the lower the external connectivity.

6. Land-use mix is measured as an entropy index of proportions of different land uses; the higher the index, the greater the mix. Pedestrian accessibility to commercial uses is measured as the percent of homes in a neighborhood within a quarter mile of a commercial use; the higher the proportion, the greater the pedestrian accessibility.

7. This point deserves more discussion than is possible here, but the general point is that smart approaches to growth management will require much more than farmland preservation and more concerted attention to both sides of the urban-rural interface.

GERRIT-JAN KNAAP BIBLIOGRAPHY

Active Living Network. 2004. *Communications Toolkit.* http://www.activeliving.org/downloads/public_opinion.pdf.

American Planning Association (APA). 2002. *Planning for Smart Growth: 2002 State of the States.* Chicago: American Planning Association.

American Public Transportation Association. 2004. Wirthlin Worldwide Public Opinion Poll. http://www.apta.com/media/releases/wirthlin.cfm.

Audirac, Ivonne. 2002. "Information Technology and Urban Form: Challenges to Smart Growth." Presented at the conference on Smart Growth and New Urbanism, College Park, MD (May 2002). http://www.smartgrowth.umd.edu/events/pdf/IT-UrbanForm&SmartGrowth.pdf.

Baum, Howell. 2003. *Smart Growth and School Reform: What if We Talked about Race and Took Community Seriously?* JAPA, 70, 1.

Belden Russonello & Stewart Research and Communications (Belden). 2004. *2004 American Community Survey: National Survey on Communities.* http://www.realtor.org/SG3.nsf/files/NAR-SGA%20Final%20(2004).pdf/$FILE/NAR-SGA%20Final%20(2004).pdf.

____. 2000. *Americans' Attitudes Toward Smart Growth.* http://www.brspoll.com/Reports/STPP%20report.pdf.

Bertaud, Alain. 2002. *Clearing the air in Atlanta: Transit and smart growth or conventional economics?* http://alain-bertaud.com/images/AB_Clearing_The_Air_in%20Atlanta_1.pdf.

Berube, Alan and Benjamin Forman. 2002. *Living on the Edge: Decentralization Within Cities in the 1990's.* Washington, DC: The Brookings Institution Living Cities Census Series.

Burchell, Robert W., David Listokin, and Catherine C. Galley. 2000. *Smart Growth: More Than a Ghost of Urban Policy Past, Less Than a Bold New Horizon,* Housing Policy Debate 11(4): 821-79.

Cohen, James R. 2002. *Maryland Smart Growth: Using Incentives to Combat Sprawl.* In G. Squires, ed., *Urban Sprawl: Causes, Consequences and Policy Responses.* Washington, DC: Urban Institute Press.

Cohen, James R. and Illana Pruess. 2002. *An Analysis of Social Equity Issues in the Montgomery County (MD) Transfer of Development Rights Program.* http://www.smartgrowth.umd.edu/research/pdf/TDRequity.text.pdf.

Eppli, M. J. and C. C. Tu. 1999. *Valuing the New Urbanism: The Impact of New Urbanism on Prices of Single-Family Homes.* Washington, DC: Urban Land Institute.

Fischel, William A. 2001. *The Homevoter Hypothesis: How Home Values Influence Local Government Taxation, School Finance, and Land-Use Policies.* Cambridge, MA: Harvard University Press.

Fishman, Robert. 2000. *The American Metropolis at Century's End: Past and Future Influences.* Housing Policy Debate 11(1).

Florida, Richard. 2000. *The Economic Geography of Talent.* Paper. Pittsburgh, PA: Carnegie Mellon University, Annals of the Association of American Geographers.

Fulton, William, Jan Mazurek, Rick Pruetz, and Chris Williamson. 2004. *TDRs and Other Market-Based Land Mechanisms: How They Work and Their Role in Shaping Metropolitan Growth.* Paper. Washington, DC: The Brookings Institution Center on Urban and Metropolitan Policy.

Fulton, William, Rolf Pendall, Mail Nguyen, and Alicia Harrison. 2001. *Who Sprawls Most? How Growth Patterns Differ Across the U.S.* Washington, DC: The Brookings Institution Survey Series.

Garreau, Joel. 1991. *Edge City: Life on the New Frontier.* New York: Doubleday.

Glaeser, Edward L. and Matthew E. Kahn. 2001. *City Growth and the 2000 Census: Which Places Grew, and Why.* Washington, DC: The Brookings Institution Survey Series.

Glaeser, Edward L., Matthew E. Kahn, and Chenghuan Chu. 2001. *Job Sprawl: Employment Location in U.S. Metropolitan Areas.* Washington, DC: The Brookings Institution Survey Series.

Glaeser, Edward L. and Jesse Shapiro. 2001. *Is There a New Urbanism? The Growth of U.S. Cities in the 1990s.* Paper. http://post.economics.harvard.edu/hier/2001papers/2001list.html.

Glaeser, Edward L. and Matthew E. Kahn. 2000. *Decentralized Employment and the Transformation of the American City.* In Gale and Pack (eds.), *Papers on Urban Affairs.* Washington: Brookings Institution Press.

Hollis, Linda and William Fulton. 2002. *Open Space Protection: Conservation Meets Growth Management.* Paper. Washington, DC: Brookings Institution Center on Urban and Metropolitan Policy.

Howland, Marie and Jungyul Sohn. Forthcoming. *Has Maryland's Priority Funding Areas Initiative Constrained the Expansion of Water and Sewer Investments?* Land Use Policy.

Jensen, Gary. 2003. *Air Quality and Transportation.* Federal Highway Administration. http://www.tfhrc.gov/pubrds/03jul/10.htm.

Katz, Bruce. 2002. *Smart Growth: The Future of the American Metropolis?* CASE paper 58. London: Centre for Analysis of Social Exclusion, London School of Economics.

Knaap, G., J. Sohn, J. Frece, and E. Holler. 2003. *Smart Growth, Housing Markets, and Development Trends in the Baltimore-Washington Corridor.* http://www.smartgrowth.umd.edu/research/pdf/ConstraintsCauseUrbanSprawl.pdf.

Knaap, Gerrit-Jan, Yan Song, and Elisabeth Holler. October 2004. *Seeing the Elephant: Multi-disciplinary Measures of Urban Sprawl.* Presented at the meetings of the Association of Collegiate Schools of Planning, Portland.

Knaap, Gerrit-Jan, Yan Song, and Zorica Nedovic-Budic. 2004. *Measuring Patterns of Urban Development: New Intelligence for the War on Sprawl.* Unpublished. College Park, MD: National Center for Smart Growth.

Lang, Robert E. 2003. *Edgeless Cities: Exploring the Elusive Metropolis.* Washington, DC: Brookings Institution Press.

Lang, Robert E. and Patrick A. Simmons. 2001. *"Boomburbs": The Emergence of Large, Fast-Growing Suburban Cities in the United States.* Washington, DC: Fannie Mae Foundation. http://www.fanniemaefoundation.org/programs/census_notes_6.shtml.

Lewyn, Michael. 2003. *21st Century Planning and the Constitution.* Boulder: University of Colorado.

Lucy, William H. and David L. Phillips. 2001. *Suburbs and the Census: Patterns of Growth and Decline.* Washington, DC: The Brookings Institution Survey Series.

Maryland Department of Planning. 2004. *Final Report: Development Capacity Task Force.* http://www.mdp.state.md.us.

Massachusetts Executive Office of Environmental Affairs. 2004. *Scope of Services for Buildout Analysis.* http://www.mass.gov/mgis/buildout.htm.

Meck, Stuart. 2003. *Growing Smart: Drafting the Next Generation of Model Planning and Zoning Enabling Legislation for the United States (and Responding to Its Critics).* Paper. Washington, DC: Brookings Institution Symposium.

_____. 2002. *Growing Smart[SM] Legislative Guidebook: Model Statutes for Planning and the Management of Change.* Washington, DC: American Planning Association.

Myers, Dowell and Elizabeth Gearin. 2001. *Current Preferences and Future Demand for Denser Residential Environments.* Housing Policy Debate 12(4): 633-659.

Myers, Phyllis and Robert Puentes. 2001. *Growth at the Ballot Box: Electing the Shape of Communities in November 2000*. Paper. Washington, DC: Brookings Institution Center on Urban and Metropolitan Policy.

National Association of Realtors. 2000. *Community and Housing Preference Survey.* http://www.realtor.org/SG3.nsf/files/CommHousePrefSurvey.pdf/$FILE/CommHousePrefSurvey.pdf.

National Association of Realtors and National Association of Home Builders. 2002. *Consumers Survey: Questions and Responses.* http://www.realtor.org/SG3.nsf/files/NARNHABSURVEY02.PDF/$FILE/NARNHABSURVEY02.PDF.

National Center for Smart Growth Research & Education. 2004. *Land Market Monitoring.* http://www.smartgrowth.umd.edu/landmarketmonitoring/index.htm.

Natural Resources Defense Council and the Surface Transportation Policy Project. 1997. *The Toolkit for Smart Growth.* New York: Natural Resources Defense Council and the Surface Transportation Policy Project.

Nelessen, Anton. 2004. *Smart Growth Primer.* Working paper. Washington, DC: National Center for Housing and the Environment.

Pendall, Rolf. 2004. *The Growth of Control?: Local land use regulations and affordable housing measures in major U.S. metropolitan areas, 1994-2003.* Presented at the meetings of the Association of Collegiate Schools of Planning, Portland, Oregon, October.

Pendall, Rolf, Jonathan Martin, and Dehui Wei. 2004. *The Growth of Growth Control.* Presented at the 45th Annual Meeting of the Association of Collegiate Schools of Planning, Portland, OR.

Pendall, Rolf, Jonathan Martin, and William Fulton. 2002. *Holding The Line: Urban Containment In The United States.* Paper. Washington, DC: Brookings Institution Center on Urban and Metropolitan Policy.

Pew Center for Civic Journalism. 2000. *Straight Talk from Americans.* http://www.pewcenter.org/doingcj/research/r_ST2000nat1.html.

Putman, Steve. 1976. *Further Results from an Integrated Transportation and Land Use Model Package.* Transportation Planning and Technology 3: 165-73.

Salkin, Patricia E. 2004. *Update on the Implementation of the American Planning Association's Growing Smart[SM] Legislative Guidebook.* Paper. Boston, MA: Land Use Institute.

Samuel, Peter and Randal O'Toole. 1999. "Smart Growth at the Federal Trough: EPA's Financing of the Anti-Sprawl Movement." Policy Analysis. 361: 1-13.

Sierra Club. 2004. http://www.sierraclub.org.

Smart Growth America. 2004. *Americans Want Smarter Growth: Here's How to Get There.* http://www.smartgrowthamerica.org/SGBOOK.pdf.

Smart Growth Network. 2004. http://www.smartgrowth.org.

Sohn, J. and G. Knaap. Forthcoming. *Does the Job Creation Tax Credit Program in Maryland Induce Spatial Employment Growth or Redistribution?* Economic Development Quarterly.

Song, Yan and Gerrit-Jan Knaap. 2003. *New Urbanism and Housing Values: A Disaggregate Assessment.* J. Urb. Econ. 54: 218-236.

Surface Transportation Policy Project (STPP). 2004. http://www.transact.org.

U.S. Department of Housing and Urban Development (US HUD). 1991. *Not in My Back Yard: Removing Barriers to Affordable Housing.* Washington, DC: Housing and Urban Development.

U.S. Environmental Protection Agency (US EPA). 2005. *Smart Growth Policies.* http://cfpub.epa.gov/sgpdb/sgdb.cfm.

____. 2004. *What is Smart Growth?* http://www.epa.gov/livability/about_sg.htm#what_is_sg.

U.S. Government Accounting Office (US GAO). 1999. *Extent of Federal Influence on "Urban Sprawl" is Unclear.* Washington, DC: U.S. Government Accounting Office.

Webber, Melvin. 1959. "The Engineer's Responsibility for the Form of Cities." *Traffic Engineering* 30, 1:11-14, 39.

CHAPTER

8

Smart Growth: A Conservative Political Movement?

Rolf J. Pendall

There are at least two important strands of conservatism in the U.S.:

1. A libertarian-laissez-faire conservatism that supposes the government should interfere as little as possible in the workings of the free market; and

2. A conservatism that supposes that the best government is that which operates at the most local level because local governments can translate the desires of residents into a package of taxes and services that most closely match their preferences.

This second strand of conservatism, which I will call "localist" conservatism, differs from the first inasmuch as it often restricts the operations of private enterprise.

Gerrit-Jan Knaap (see Chapter 7) and Robert Freilich (see Chapter 6) both convince me that smart growth is in tune with the conservative political movement. As a consequence, I'm coming to see a deeper philosophical break between growth management and smart growth than I used to see. Rather than a requiem for smart growth, we should interpret recent events as a requiem for growth management and an overture to smart growth.

This break is exemplified by the recent passage of Proposition 37 in Oregon. In that vote, which passed even in Portland's county, the citizens of one of our few blue states were forced to choose between a centralized mandate system and essentially no land-use regulation at all without compensation; they chose the latter. Arguably, the Oregon Way is—or should I say was?—just too far out of step with either strand of U.S. conservatism to endure. With mandates for local planning and fairly strict state-level interpretation of what an acceptable land-use plan and development regulations are, it's not nearly localist enough to compensate for its interference with untrammeled land markets. It's possible, accordingly, that Washington and Maine's systems of growth management will survive. In both states, at least some local governments can opt out of the system, and those that opt in face much less meddlesome reviews from state-level bureaucrats. In both states, growth management has elements of smart growth—voluntarism, incentives, and partnerships between state and local governments—which are scarce or absent in Oregon.

Both Gerrit and Bob stress the importance within smart growth of market-based measures, in particular those that require the beneficiaries of infrastructure to pay more to enjoy the privilege. I think this is right on target, and would point out that such measures are apt to endure precisely because they are in line with both strands of contemporary conservatism. On the localist side, they can be tailored by local governments to apply to as many infrastructure systems as desired (within limits set by statute, which I predict will be loosened in the coming years). Local governments can also adapt them to require not just a basic level of infrastructure but even fairly sophisticated systems, although again there are limits set by the state on the level and quality of service that can be required of new development. On the free-market side, of course, there must be a connection between the amount of the fee and the infrastructure the fee is supposed to provide.

The consonance between U.S conservatism and locally determined, market-based measures gives me some optimism about land-use patterns and "growing smart on the ground," as Gerrit puts it, but it's a regionally specific optimism. Gerrit cites my own recent work when he argues that there's not all that much change nationwide in the degree of regulation. In fact, there's a bit more change when you look at regions and states in the results of my survey, which will be ready for distribution within a couple of months.

There are regions in the U.S. where progressive and interesting things are happening to take the edge off sprawl. Arizona, California, Washington, Colorado, Maryland, and Florida all have vibrant planning systems, with definite flaws, but are experiencing at least some modification of sprawling land-use patterns. In many cases, this is precisely an outcome of "pay as you grow," imposed in an environment in which there's a lot of growth and not much infrastructure.

Impact fees are on the rise and, most impressively, zoning ordinances are being amended to allow and accommodate higher density much more often than they are becoming more exclusionary. In other words, infrastructure measures are shaping the behavior of land developers in ways that help force density higher and perhaps will even encourage more mixing of uses, if not more front porches.

Then there's the rest of the country, especially the northeast but also the midwest and parts of the south. Throughout the northeast and midwest, "pay as you grow" has also spread but hasn't spurred compactness; instead, it's sped the creation of 2-acre lots serviced by existing infrastructure (e.g., wells, septic systems, and long-established rural roads).

When most rural development happens in towns or townships as opposed to counties, local governments usually lack the technical capacity to estimate the impacts of long-term growth on infrastructure. Often there's too little growth to begin with to justify doing the studies for impact fees in these rural communities. Therefore, even when suburbs do impose fees, there are plenty of substitutes nearby who don't, so the fees encourage displacement to a more distant township rather than compact development. Many suburbs also find impact fees less appealing than raising their minimum lot sizes, matching growth to infrastructure rather than vice versa. I find it quite unlikely that this pattern will be broken any time soon, because any effective response to it is too much at odds with both laissez-faire and localist conservatism.

These results aren't entirely a creature of local governments' shifting toward market mechanisms, however, and here I want to endorse Gerrit's attention to both institutions and social equity. The states in which market-like mechanisms are less likely to produce sprawl are, not coincidentally, those with stronger housing laws.

California's housing law is a law everyone loves to hate, but California's cities have been upzoning and adopting inclusionary zoning as they do so. A study by Paul Lewis of the Public Policy Institute of California last year[1] was widely promoted as proof that the housing element system doesn't work because the cities that have good housing elements don't produce statistically higher amounts of housing than those without good housing elements. Hidden within that report was the jaw-dropping result that, in jurisdictions whose housing elements complied with state law, the share of multifamily housing gained eight percentage points more in the 1990s than it did in jurisdictions that were out of compliance.[2] Compare Colorado, which has weak housing planning, and you see much less upzoning and less dense new growth than in California.[3]

Even in the northeast, differences in housing policy result in differences on the ground. Compare Massachusetts with New Jersey. The Massachusetts affordable housing law, Chapter 40B,[4] is being applied more aggressively than ever before; as a consequence, suburban municipalities are talking seriously about comprehensive planning, mixed income, mixed use, and all those other smart growth ideas. The administration of New Jersey's Fair Housing Act has gotten progressively weaker and, as this has happened, densities have been dropping, and the most animated and sophisticated "smart growth" conversations are about buying open space.

Housing planning also connects with social equity, of course, and not just with urban form, and thus carries over into another of Gerrit's recommendations. One national organization, PolicyLink,[5] has indeed engaged the smart growth debate from a vigorous social equity perspective. PolicyLink is working hard right now on housing, in particular developing guidance for how states can coordinate all kinds of housing programs to give low-income people access to better neighborhoods. This starts with regional fair share systems, and includes funding allocation in the many state-controlled and state-administered housing programs. These already include traditional federal block-grant programs such as community development block grants and HOME, the federal low-income housing tax credit, state bond funds, and state housing trust fund monies.

The current administration will continue its attempts to shift decision-making about many other housing programs to states, including the housing voucher program. In this environment, it is crucial that planning reformers join forces with advocates for regional equity and civil rights to encourage state housing agencies to consider regional opportunity structures when they allocate housing funds.

A final comment on Gerrit's work concerns the one recommendation that I am skeptical about: promoting the use of information and information technologies. Information and information technologies will probably not change things very much on the ground, although I would very much like to have more data. Rather, things on the ground condition the acceptance and use of information technology and the generation of information.

Portland doesn't succeed because it monitors its land supply; it monitors its land supply, and succeeds, because of other institutional factors such as a generally high capacity for planning, high salaries for planners, and large enough local governments that the talent pool for local volunteer boards isn't impossibly shallow. Living in upstate New York and dealing with volunteer boards in towns of a couple thousand people, I can tell you that there is plenty of goodwill out there, and that many, many local planning boards would not act nearly as self-centeredly as economists expect them to if only they knew better. They would certainly like to be more predictable than they are; most local boards don't like meetings that last until 2 AM. The problem is that there have been very few concerted statewide efforts, not to mention a national one, to educate planning boards and their members about how to do their jobs. If these local boards don't have the capacity to use the information provided at the state level, they are likely to make very bad decisions.

A case in point is the buildout analysis. Most communities respond to buildouts by downzoning. I grant that these communities lack incentives to be more accommodating but, even if they want to accommodate growth, they often don't know how to do it well. For better or for worse, the local volunteer planning board/commission—perhaps our most durable planning institution of all—will remain a fixture in the 21st century. We would do well by thinking more about how to help them improve their practice. If we do that, perhaps we can help reduce the tendency of smart growth to produce such mixed results on the ground.

ROLF J. PENDALL NOTES

1. Paul G. Lewis, *California's Housing Element Law: The Issue of Local Noncompliance* (San Francisco: Public Policy Institute of California, 2003).
2. Id.
3. On Colorado's relatively weak housing and general plan law, see Stuart Meck (gen. ed.), *Growing Smart^SM Legislative Guidebook: Model Statutes for Planning and the Management of Change* (Chicago: American Planning Association, 2002), Chapter 7, available: http://www.planning.org/guidebook/index.htm. On the low density of new growth in Colorado, see William Fulton, Rolf Pendall, Mai T. Nguyen, and Alicia Harrison, *Who Sprawls Most? How Growth Patterns Differ Across the U.S.* (Washington, DC: Brookings Institution Center on Urban and Metropolitan Policy, 2001).
4. Mass. Gen. Laws. Chapter 40B, §§ 20-23.
5. PolicyLink (http://www.policylink.org).

The Role of the Comprehensive Plan

CHAPTER

9

Answered Prayers: The Dilemma of Binding Plans

Edward J. Sullivan

INTRODUCTION

Making any case for planning reform is only possible with an understanding of the history of the comprehensive plan and the relationship of that plan with land-use regulations and actions. For more than three quarters of a century, American planners have fought the battle for recognition and respect of comprehensive plans. For most of that time, it has been a losing battle; the public was, and still is, more comfortable with the certainties of land-use regulation, usually through zoning, than the evaluation and application of policy contained in plans. In the last quarter century, however, plans have gained that respect and recognition in a number of states. It is now time for the planning and legal professions to analyze the results of this newfound recognition and the implications of the legislative or judicial mandate that land-use regulations "carry out" or "implement" or be "consistent with" comprehensive plans.

The history of this struggle has been recounted elsewhere.[1] The first recognized land-use enabling legislation (New York in 1916) provided that zoning schemes must be "in accordance with a well considered plan."[2] Later, two model acts were prepared by the U.S. Department of Commerce for consideration by state legislatures. It is instructive to note that the first of these acts, promulgated in 1926, was the Standard State Zoning Enabling Act (SZEA),[3] which, as its name infers, enabled regulation of land use by zoning; the second, promulgated in 1928, was the Standard City Planning Enabling Act.[4] The latter model legislation allowed, but did not require, cities to adopt plans, and focused those plans largely on public works issues such as future streets and parks. The standard zoning act was adopted by three-quarters of the states, whereas the standard planning act was adopted by about half of the states.

The standard zoning act required that zoning be "in accordance with a comprehensive plan."[5] Courts faced a dilemma in the event that there was no plan or the plan was inconsistent with the challenged zoning of a parcel, resolving that question largely through a fudge—finding that the "comprehensive plan" mentioned in the standard zoning act was the overview of the zoning maps. This was done to preclude large-scale invalidation of zoning regulations. As a result, there was no necessity to have a plan or to have zoning or other regulations conform to plans.

In this planning wilderness, there were prophets who advocated both the relevance and the mandatory nature of planning. In 1954, Charles Haar, former housing secretary, wrote a remarkable article, *In Accordance with a Comprehensive Plan*,[6] that pointed out the inadequacy of the prevailing interpretation of the relationship between planning and zoning. In 1975, Daniel Mandelker published *The Role of the Local Comprehensive Plan in Land Use Regulation*,[7] which was a scholarly analysis of statutory and case law that advocated mandatory and binding comprehensive planning.[8]

Led by Hawai'i, whose planning legislation of 1961 immediately followed statehood,[9] state legislatures began to specify that plans were required and binding. California (1972), Florida (1972), and Oregon (1973) were the first wave of states in this area. In more recent times, the work of the American Planning Association in its smart growth efforts has caused many other states to join that group of states requiring binding plans. In addition, some courts have interpreted the "in accordance" language to render plans binding.[10]

As a result of this scholarly, legislative, and judicial activity, there became a number of approaches to the determination of whether land-use plans were binding. One analytical approach has been to discern three "schools" of theory on the relationship of plans and regulations[11]:

- The first "school" denies that there is any legal necessity for planning and, consequently, plans are not binding.[12]
- The second "school" asserts that plans, if they exist, are a factor in evaluating the validity of land-use regulations or actions.[13]
- The third "school" responds to the statutory changes or court decisions that establish the binding nature of plans and require plan consistency in land-use regulations or actions.[14]

Surveys of decided cases suggest that both courts and legislatures are moving away from the first school and settling upon the second and third.[15] Those states that have moved into the third category have increased and, even if a state renders the plan as a factor in the evaluation of a land-use regulation or action, the decision to apply a plan policy or land-use designation will have significant effects on local government decision-making. This chapter will deal with the implications of binding plans on that decision-making and on judicial review of the same.

WHY DOES PLAN INTERPRETATION MATTER?

Drafting, applying, and enforcing land-use regulations are no easy tasks. Nevertheless, this process has had 75+ years of accreted experience through drafting, responding to challenges and court decisions, and redrafting of regulations. Dimensional requirements of local zoning ordinances are most often stated in precise terms. Determining whether a particular use is or is not permitted in a certain zone has its own panoply of interpretive tools,[16] in addition to code interpretation or similar use provisions.

Despite being a creature of statute and at least theoretically different in each of the various states and territories, land-use regulations have a remarkably similar lexicon (e.g., "zones," "special exceptions" or "conditional uses," and "variances"). These similar terms have often led lawyers to blur the differences in the use of those terms without regard to their peculiar origin and evolution in a given jurisdiction.[17]

To complicate things further, state law is often lacking in providing direction in the day-to-day activities of land-use regulation, so the term "variance" may be defined or applied differently in adjacent cities. In that case, it would be a mistake for a court to apply, explicitly or implicitly, a definition that would erase the differences between the terms. To provide for uniformity, there have been efforts to adopt enabling legislation that would allow courts to use the case law from other states in interpreting land-use regulations.[18] However, it is safe to say that the language of land-use regulation must be interpreted to consider the many differences in state and local regulations and ordinances and to avoid generalizations in dealing with those differences.

These interpretational difficulties are exacerbated, however, in dealing with the language of plans. In the early years of land-use regulation, plans were neither required nor did they exist. Where plans did exist, they tended to be seen as nonbinding impressions of the future and to gather dust on the shelves of planning departments. Moreover, because comprehensive planning has had such a history of imprecision, generalization, and nonbinding language, such plans were not taken seriously nor were they meant to be.

If a plan were not binding, it was not a problem if the drafters used the word "should" rather than "shall," nor did it matter if a plan referred to an area not precisely defined, such as "North Downtown." Similarly, language such as "avoiding significant adverse impacts" did not give cause for focused discussion as it was not meant to be meaningful. Plans often compounded these difficulties by combining these usages, as planners (and the public agencies that employed them) strove for aspiration over precision.

However, times have changed. The surveys of the law regarding the relationship between planning and regulations and other land-use decisions demonstrate that plans are now influential, if not dispositive, in determining the validity of those regulations or actions. If influential or dispositive to courts, the language used in plans becomes much more important. Moreover, the way that planners, citizens, governing bodies, and courts *think* about plans has now changed as businesses, public interest advocates, and neighbors jockey for the language that bests helps their particular position.

Yet, planners—and the myriad of people in other walks of life who draft plans—tend to keep to the familiar generalities of the nonbinding plans.[19] For many, the suddenness of a court decision or new legislative mandate requires a yes/no decision to be made rather than avoided in vague language that offends no one. If plans are meaningful, then the "action" migrates from the regulation to the plan that is charged with guiding that action.

The next two portions of this article will discuss two aspects of plan interpretation. First, planners, lawyers, local governments, and courts must determine the approach that will be taken in plan interpretation. By "approach," we mean the philosophy of the state, particularly its legislatures and courts, toward the relationship of state and local policy to its realization in regulatory actions and decisions affecting the use of land. That approach may vary from demanding policy conformity only in those cases in which the state has specifically required the same, to deference to local plan interpretations in certain cases, to the requirement that regulations and actions not be inconsistent with policy, and to the requirement of "lockstep" conformity.

Second, there are a variety of plan interpretation tools available and courts in particular must decide which of these to use. Those tools are available by analogy to statutory and ordinance interpretation methods and carry with them some familiar means by which legislative policy is found to be carried out, or not, by local regulations and decisions.

This article does not deal extensively with another related question: how plan changes are reviewed and the methodology by which such changes are evaluated, both procedurally and substantively. Those issues are left for another day and another writing.

ALTERNATIVE APPROACHES TO PLAN INTERPRETATION

Before dealing with particular rules of interpretation of plans, the approach to that interpretation must be selected. To a great extent, the approach will be governed by the words used in the applicable statute or ordinance. The SZEA used the deceptively simple words "in accordance with a comprehensive plan" as its standard. However, as we have seen, those words did not, as interpreted by most courts, require a separate document called a "comprehensive plan" nor did they require consistency. Instead, given the alternative of invalidating almost all zoning regulations, these words were given an illogical construction in order to "save" the zoning regulations.[20]

This "quick fix" retarded the growth of land-use policy formulation and implementation through comprehensive planning and set the stage for further judicial inventions to "fix" the original fix of saving zoning by conflating it with planning. These new "fixes" through judicially created rules included "change or mistake,"[21] "appearance of fairness,"[22] and the much-discussed, but little understood, "spot zoning."[23] Because these "rules" were open-ended, they allowed judges to mask their own predilections in opaque legal language. While judges were able to create "quick fixes" as alternatives to requiring plan consistency, these "fixes" often contained neither substance nor rational explanations for the connections. Courts were thus unable to guide state or local officials in the exercise of discretion in applying the plan to regulations and actions.

In addition to the creation of "fixes" to the problem of a requirement to adhere to a comprehensive plan, courts further confused the difficulties of formulating and carrying out policy by mischaracterizing the small-tract zone change. While the standard zoning act did treat certain small tract land-use actions as administrative or "quasi-judicial" by requiring notice, hearing, and findings to justify such actions and judicial review by way of certiorari,[24] zone changes were not dealt with specifically in the standard act. There were provisions setting forth notice[25] and super-majority requirements[26]; however, a zone change was viewed as an amendment to the zoning ordinance, which itself was usually accomplished by ordinance, and was thus characterized as a "legislative act."

This characterization was especially unfortunate because it equated the formulation of policy in the adoption of the zoning ordinance with the amendment of that ordinance for a single or a few tracts of land. The legal proponents of successful changes, along with their local government colleagues, suggested that this legislative characterization of small-tract changes immunized these actions from almost all challenges, except those based on gross procedural error and constitutional violations. Judges, who were generally knowledgeable in the ways things got done at the local government level, were uneasy in attaching the legislative label to small-tract zone changes across the board, but were often trapped by the use of the word "ordinance" and the legislative procedure for adopting and amending zoning ordinances in the standard act and most other state legislation. Indeed, the reason for some of the "fixes" invented by the courts was to counteract the legislative characterization of all zone changes.

The result was chaos. The use of content-free, elastic terms, such as "spot zoning," allowed courts to achieve the result that appeared just without the inconveniences of hard rules or consistency. Such an approach allowed judges to say, on the one hand, that rezonings of which they approved were undertaken by ordinance were legislative in character, and that judges must defer to local legislative bodies; however, if the judges did not approve of the result, they could point to these rules and give them quasi-constitutional status.[27]

Just as Haar and Mandelker were prophetic in dealing with the role of the comprehensive plan, other writers suggested that not all zone changes were legislative in nature. Moreover, these writers suggested that procedures ought to be in place to limit the judicial power to second-guess local interpretations of plans.

An influential book by the late Richard A. Babcock, *The Zoning Game: Municipal Practices and Policies*,[28] was far more effective than any law review criticism of the existing legal regime. Babcock wrote from nearly 50 years of land-use advocacy experience in Chicago and the surrounding suburbs, and was eloquent in describing the corruption in the system and the intellectual laziness of those legislators, academics, and judges who would freely and without complete analysis reexamine that system. Among the reforms called out by Babcock on the basis of his considerable practical experience were comprehensive planning as the basis for regulation, regional review of needs, and procedural fairness.

Babcock was joined by Professor Mandelker once again in suggesting procedural reform,[29] as well as others who analyzed what really happened at a zoning hearing and upon judicial review.[30] The result was a simultaneous reconsideration of both the role of the plan as well as the procedural nature of the land-use regulatory process. The results of these efforts lay in the court cases[31] and legislation[32] that made the role of the plan, as well as the procedures for plan implementation, clearer.

Yet, both the cases and the legislation were not uniform in their application of mandatory implementation of the plan. There were weak adherents to the role of the plan in policy implementation, such as the "planning factor school" that gave unspecified weight to the plan, in addition to other factors, in regulatory exercises.[33] If the plan did not exist as a separate document, the regulation or action was not, by that fact, invalid.[34] Under this line of reasoning, the plan was a (nondispositive) guide in reviewing regulations or actions.

Other states viewed a statutory "consistency" standard in a negative way (i.e., that regulations or actions were consistent unless they were demonstrably inconsistent) or the consistency requirement was turned on its head so that the challenger bore the burden of proof to show inconsistency.[35] Other states, such as Oregon, place uniform limits on judicial review when considering an interpretation of a local government regulation. The relevant statute provides:

"(1) The Land Use Board of Appeals shall affirm a local government's interpretation of its comprehensive plan and land use regulations, unless the board determines that the local government's interpretation:

"(a) Is inconsistent with the express language of the comprehensive plan or land use regulation;

"(b) Is inconsistent with the purpose for the comprehensive plan or land use regulation;

"(c) Is inconsistent with the underlying policy that provides the basis for the comprehensive plan or land use regulation; or

"(d) Is contrary to a state statute, land use goal or rule that the comprehensive plan provision or land use regulation implements.

"(2) If a local government fails to interpret a provision of its comprehensive plan or land use regulations, or if such interpretation is inadequate for review, the board may make its own determination of whether the local government decision is correct."[36]

A statutory requirement of plan consistency itself involves the application of judgment as opposed to a clear answer. Because plans typically consist of one or more maps and multiple policies, a local government must make judgments as to whether a single inconsistent policy constitutes "inconsistency" so as to preclude a proposed zoning map amendment, regulation, or other action, particularly in the absence of specific statutory direction.

Even in those states that regard plans as binding standards for land-use regulations and actions, there are differences in approach. In addition to the determination of consistency as overall consistency,[37] there is the issue of action in the face of a single plan policy that does not allow the proposed action to be taken. There is some relief for decision-makers provided in the administrative or quasi-judicial characterization of rezoning amendments and the continuing like characterization of other small-tract actions, which allow the decision-maker to articulate just how it weighed competing plan policies and arrived at a reasoned decision justified by the facts and the law.

An added complication occurs in those states that require local governments to implement specific state policies. Oregon, for example, has 19 statewide planning goals,[38] some of which are applicable to plans, land-use regulations, and land-use actions.[39] The conflicts between competing goals, as well as competing plan policies, are often resolved by the process of "acknowledgement,"[40] "periodic review,"[41] and post-acknowledgment amendment[42] under which a state land-use planning agency may resolve such inconsistencies. If not objected to, the plans (and their implementing ordinances) are deemed to have complied with state policy, which normally cannot be disputed until the plan is amended or revised.[43] The resolution process, however, does not resolve competing plan policies that are not determined under the statewide planning goals.

To summarize: The greater the desire for policy consistency in the formulation and application of comprehensive plans by the local government, and deference of that interpretation by the courts unless clearly wrong, the more exacting that exercise will be. If the plan is seen as a nonrequired guide, then it will be given short shrift and subject to manipulation. If it exists at all, it is a factor and nothing more in determining the validity of a land-use regulation or action. If the burden is a showing that the regulation or action is "not inconsistent" with the plan, that burden is an easy one to bear and virtually places the burden on the opponent of the challenged regulation or action to show inconsistency. If the requirement is one of affirmative consistency, then the decision-maker is required to show plan consistency.[44] If the standard is one of plan conformity, the applicant for the regulation or action must demonstrate such consistency, usually by way of findings, and must deal with the issue of competing policies.

We now proceed to the interpretation of plans, given these various approaches.

PLAN INTERPRETATION METHODOLOGIES

Plan interpretation is somewhat akin to interpretation of statutes and ordinances. A court will attempt to divine the intent of the legislature or other policy-making body; however, the peculiar history and status of the comprehensive plan in American legal history make a pure analogy imperfect.

As noted previously, plans were not required as a separate legal document by most courts. When restored as a standard by legislative or judicial actions, the plan had to transmute itself into a binding policy document from what was often a mass of vague generalizations with which few could disagree. Thus, changing the plan policy that low- and moderate-income housing should be considered on the west side of town with "low- and moderate-income housing shall be placed in west-side neighborhoods" is bound to increase the attention of west-side residents. Similarly, the plan may no longer be conceptual but rather a binding realization of the plan policies carried out, along with a precise delineation of the limited range of uses permitted. Having an understanding of the relationship of plan policies and a land-use map in the plan is essential for administration of land-use regulations and the undertaking of land-use actions the plan is required to govern.

Drafting skills aside, there is a further reason why plans are not treated in the same way as other legislation. Plans lack the relative certainty that is given to zoning or other regulatory measures. While lawyers could generally rely upon the certainty provided by a zoning map designation, they found themselves less able to predict a future plan or zoning designation that is inconsistent with that current zoning or that required the balancing or interpretation of plan policies, or both. Because plans did not provide a consistent or fixed answer to questions relating to the future use of property, they were often seen as manipulable and subject to social and political pressure, leading to additional distrust.[45] If the plan is drafted with short-term political gratification as its purpose, it will be a very small advance over the zoning ordinance with no articulated reasoning for the development objectives of the community.

What is a Plan?

If a principle reason for a plan is to provide an outside policy basis for land-use regulations and actions, then the plan, at a minimum, must be internally consistent. Thus, a plan for future housing growth must take into consideration existing census figures and rational population projections. Similarly, plans that call for additions of commercial and industrial lands must have some idea of the amount of land planned and used for these purposes, as well as the need projections for any additional lands.

In addition to internal consistency, a plan, if it is to be useful, must have an adequate factual base. The plan cannot be internally consistent unless it has something beyond bare statements of policy. In the housing and commercial and industrial examples above, the use of existing and projected population and land-need figures presupposes that regulations and actions inconsistent with the realization of those needs and policies are inconsistent with the plan itself.[46] Further, some state statutes require internal consistency. Ca. Gov't Code § 65300.5 requires a plan to "comprise an integrated, internally consistent and compatible statement of policies."[47]

A further plan requirement for effective policy formulation and implementation is consistency with the plans of other jurisdictions affected by the plan and which are effective, in turn, by those other jurisdictions' plans. Since the 1970s, courts have been articulating—at least as part of the "general welfare" basis for land-use regulations—that the plans for suburban areas near large cities must take regional obligations to accommodate a fair share of housing needs into account.[48] If all or most local governments in a region were to up for property ratables at the expense of low- and moderate-income housing, one should not be surprised if a court steps in.

Plans, once made, are not immutable. Facts (such as population growth, land needs, and land consumption) change. So, too, does policy, such as the advent of the planned unit development and mixed land-use designations. Plans must change as well and be reviewed periodically to assure that they provide the policy desired by the community.[49] In addition to such review of the plan as a whole, changes made to parts of the plan (such as a new transportation element, the redesignation of a site for a different class of uses and that previously permitted, or a density bonus regulation) must be judged by its fidelity and consistency with the unamended portions of the plan.[50]

Plan Review for Consistency with State Policy

A fair criticism of American planning law is that courts take the easy way out by not requiring plans as a reference point for land-use regulations or actions. There is an equally fair criticism that states that do not review more than construction plans for building code compliance have not done much to encourage comprehensive planning. If a local plan has no policy expectations from the state, it is likely that land-use regulations and actions will always be found by the local governments to be consistent with their plans—much like prevailing wisdom of those courts that "saved" zoning by finding no separate plan required found the "comprehensive plan" (i.e., the overview of the zoning maps) always "in accordance" with itself.

There are two approaches for using binding state plan requirements. The first is the California model, whereby the legislature establishes those areas and those standards to which a local plan must comply, but does not provide an administrative system for review of the sufficiency of the plans.[51] It is thus left to the trial and appellate court systems to determine plan sufficiency against these (often vague) legislative standards.[52] This is a cumbersome system that may yield different results on grounds other than policy, such as the disposition of the trial court judge or the composition of the appellate court panel.

Another alternative is initial review plan sufficiency. Oregon has an established state agency, the Land Conservation and Development Commission, to adopt statewide planning standards or "goals" and review plans for sufficiency against those goals.[53] The administrative decision is subject to appellate review.[54] However, the notions of speed and consistency and inexpensive review characteristic of the administrative process[55] are present so that appellate courts have the benefit of the reasoning of the agency that formulates and applies state policy. In addition, the court has relative confidence in that decision because it has had the consideration of the specialized expertise of the agency and its staff, which has a history of applying policy in other cases. Finally, it is unlikely that this same agency will have taken much less time to decide the case than would a trial court.

A third approach comes from the State of Washington where, in 1990, it adopted its Growth Management Act, combining elements of the Urban Growth Boundary concept of the Oregon system with the concurrency requirement of the Florida program. Under the act, local governments must adopt comprehensive land-use plans to guide development consistent with the goals and then implement the plan. The Washington program provides for local administration of the consistency program subject to review on appeal by three regional, independent Growth Management Hearings Boards rather than required periodic review by a state agency.

The point of the meaningful application of the consistency requirement is that there should be a reference point outside the plan to determine the sufficiency of that plan; otherwise, planning will have changed little from the days in which the zoning ordinance doubled as the plan and courts determined whether land-use regulations and actions were valid on the basis of ad hoc rules that could justify a decision either way.

Deference

Planning law is a branch of administrative law. Plans are the exercise in rulemaking providing the policy basis for those decisions that carry out the plan. As with other areas of administrative law, the problem arises as to how much credibility, or deference, courts ought to accord plans and their interpretations by local governments. As Babcock noted, courts are mistrustful of local governments in the administration of land-use regulations and actions[56] in large part because these regulations and actions appear to be ad hoc decisions, unattached to any discernible policy base, and based solely on the iron whim of the local governing body at the time. The result of this mistrust was the bevy of rules, sometimes cloaked in quasi-constitutional language, invented to separate "good" from "bad" decisions.

A judicial or statutory requirement for land-use regulations and actions to be "in accordance with" or "consistent with" a comprehensive plan provides a court with some reference point on which to judge a land-use regulation or action. If that plan is not itself based on a separate reference point, the credibility of a plan interpretation to support a land-use regulation or action is diminished.

While local governments may increase their chances on judicial review by adopting clearer plans, the tendency of human nature is to build ambiguity into plan policies to provide "flexibility" in a future case. The worth of the plan is lessened in that event.

Additionally, a local government may increase its chances on judicial review by articulating findings and reasons that led it to the decision it made to justify the deference sought by that government. If the decision to allow a rezoning from a residential to a commercial category is challenged, the local government may be able to defend its decision by showing an oversupply of residential land compared to population projections, or a shortage of commercial land over the same planning period, and further justify its position by pointing to various plan policies, particularly those related to designation of commercial land.

If, however, the decision relating to a land-use regulation or action is based on legislatively established policy, the chance of judicial deference to the decision-maker is magnified, if only by the principle of the separation of powers. A court would certainly take into account the legislative mandate for the comprehensive plan as well as the specific policy at issue. Those chances are further enhanced if the plan policy at issue were required to be present in the plan by a state agency charged with formulation of land-use policy and the plan is a successful product of a review by that agency.

The U.S. Supreme Court reads several levels of deference into the federal Administrative Procedures Act. The most deferential of these is referred to as "Chevron deference,"[57] under which a federal agency interpretation must neither be contrary to the words of the enabling legislation nor be within the power of the agency to make.[58] The court's deference arises out of realities of the experience and specialization of the agency and the fact that it promulgates, and is generally responsible for, the policies it adopts. Additionally, it has the knowledge and expertise in addition to the ability to interpret its own policies.

Similarly, elected bodies that promulgate plans have the expertise and experience (whether of itself or its staff), the political responsibility, and the ascribed familiarity with the consequences of its actions concerning plan policies. The interpretations by local governing bodies, particularly those bodies whose plans have been found by the responsible state land-use agency to have met state policy, have a good argument for a fairly high level of deference.[59]

Conclusion

Just as there are multiple approaches to plan interpretation to comport with different requirements for plan consistency, the methods of plan interpretation vary depending upon the structure of the planning process and the role taken by the state or the courts in that process. We know that the trend is to give plans influential, if not dispositive, weight in determining the validity of zoning regulations. Judicial "fixes," such as distinguishing between legislative and quasi-judicial actions or spot zonings, are viewed as improper ways to counteract the legislative characterization of all zone changes. Clearly articulated deference standards work to respond to judicial activism concerns. It remains to discuss the ideal plan interpretation that gives appropriate weight to applicable state policy, to the level of responsibility of the local governing body, to well-constructed plans, and the articulation of the rationale given for decisions in particular cases.

IS PLAN CONSISTENCY SOMETHING TO WISH FOR?

Plan advocates have long wished for a standard, other than the zoning regulations themselves, against which land-use actions might be measured. This position is understandable, given the years in the wilderness experienced by planners who could not abide by the view that a comprehensive plan was found in the overview of the zoning ordinance or through some inexplicable power of judicial divination. Yet, there is a downside for having a reference point from which to judge land-use regulations and actions.

If American land-use law is not to repeat the mistakes of the first three-quarters of a century of its existence, planners and lawyers must step back from their satisfaction over the triumph of the comprehensive plan and come to grips with the implications of this victory. If plans remain vague and allow decision-makers to come to whatever decision they wish to reach, little will be gained. Plans must also change as policy changes and must be reviewed periodically to assure that they still meet the needs of the community. If plans are treated as constitutions or statutes for purposes of interpretation, and an accepted interpretational methodology is posited, then the law may develop as an instrument of state or local policy, or both.

While in some circumstances the courts have achieved clarity in the relationship of planning and plan implementation through "landmark cases,"[60] it was largely the courts that created the problem of the lack of clarity. It is thus more difficult for the courts to cure the problem of a long-standing, though erroneous, interpretation of statute than it would for the legislature to take action.

The better approach, therefore, appears to be to avoid the vagaries and costs of litigation in favor of legislation requiring comprehensive planning and enforcing the primacy of such planning as to local implementing regulations and actions.[61] Such a step, however bold and necessary as it may appear, is not sufficient. If such a process is undertaken to establish and enshrine policy, courts must respect that process and policy, even if the individual judges disagree with them, by deferring to local interpretations of that adopted policy when properly applied to regulations or land-use actions. This deference to policy is due if and only if the local government applies its policy through findings and a reasoned decision to justify the application of policy in its plan. If the findings make the necessarily factual determinations, and proceed to explain how policy was applied, the action at issue should normally be upheld.[62]

In the event state policy is applicable, the local government interpretation of its plan policy and its application through regulations or actions are judged on the basis of its fidelity to state policy, assuming that no statutory or constitutional "home rule" provision is applicable. In this way, overriding state law is accommodated in the context of local decision-making[63] and planning reform is realized by giving priority credence to the more important policy.

Planning reform in the 21st century will be much like that of the 20th: incremental, reflective, and governed by a standing dialogue among the professional planner and lawyer, state and local officials, landowners and developers, and others who realize that their common interest is in a planning system that works.

EDWARD J. SULLIVAN NOTES

1. See Edward J. Sullivan and Carrie Richter, *Out of the Chaos: Towards a National System of Land-Use Procedures*, 34 Urb. Law. 2 (2002).
2. New York Law, 1916, Chapter 496. As a result, the City of New York adopted the Building Zone Ordinance on July 25, 1916. That ordinance was upheld against various challenges in *Lincoln Trust Co. v. Williams Bldg. Corp.*, 229 N.Y. 313, 128 N.E. 209 (1920).
3. Standard State Zoning Enabling Act (SZEA), U.S. Department of Commerce (rev. ed.) (1926).
4. Standard City Planning Enabling Act, U.S. Department of Commerce (1928).
5. SZEA § 3.
6. Charles M. Haar, *In Accordance with a Comprehensive Plan*, 68 Harv. L. Rev. 1154 (1955).
7. Daniel R. Mandelker, *The Role of the Local Comprehensive Plan in Land Use Regulation*, 74 Mich. L. Rev. 900 (1976).
8. The impact of those works is recounted in Edward J. Sullivan and Laurence J. Kressel, *Twenty Years After; Renewed Significance of the Comprehensive Plan Requirement*, 9 Urb. Law

Ann. 33 (1975), and Edward J. Sullivan and Matthew J. Michel, *Ramapo Plus Thirty: The Changing Role of the Plan in Land Use Regulation*, 35 Urb. Law. 1 (2003).

9. Chapter 205, Hawai'i Rev. Stats.

10. See, e.g., *Baker v. City of Milwaukie*, 271 Or. 500, 533 P.2d 772 (1975); *Golden v. Planning Bd. of Town of Ramapo*, 30 N.Y.2d 359, 334 N.Y.S.2d 151-152, 285 N.E.2d 291 (1972); *Families Unafraid to Uphold Rural El Dorado County (FUTURE) v. Board of Supervisors of El Dorado County*, 62 Cal. App. 4th 1332, 1336, 74 Cal. Rptr. 2d 2-3 (3d Dist. 1998).

11. Sullivan and Kressel; Sullivan and Michel, note 8, *supra*.

12. Sullivan and Michel, note 8, *supra*, at 91.

13. Id. at 99.

14. Id. at 106.

15. Sullivan and Kressel; Sullivan and Michel, note 8, *supra*.

16. For example, if a disputed use is not specifically allowed in the zone under consideration, but is specifically allowed in another zone, the inference can be drawn that the use is not permitted in the first zone. *Clatsop County v. Morgan*, 19 Or. App. 173, 526 P.2d 173 (1974).

    A zoning ordinance must be construed reasonably with regard for the objective sought to be obtained. *Macenas v. Village of Michiana*, 433 Mich. 380, 446 N.W.2d 281 (1989).

    Courts will avoid interpreting zoning ordinances in a way that provides an "absurd or unreasonable result." *Recovery House IV v. City of Eugene*, 156 Or. App. 509, 965 P.2d 488 (1998).

    Where there are two zoning provisions—one general and designed to apply to cases generally; the other particular relating to a single subject—the particular provision must prevail and must be treated as an exception to the general provision. *Niles Imp. Ass'n. v. J. Emiol Anderson and Son*, 93 Ill. App. 2d 167, 236 N.E.2d 402 (1968); *Mallory v. Town of West Hartford*, 138 Conn. 497, 86 A.2d 668 (1952).

    The words "zones" and "districts" may be used interchangeably. *Nardi v. City of Providence*, 89 R.I. 437, 153 A.2d 136 (1959).

    Within the context of zoning, the word "shall" may be read to mean "may." *Paul v. City of Manhattan*, 212 Kan. 381, 511 P.2d 244 (1973).

17. For example, as Justice Linde explained in *Anderson v. Peden*, 284 Ore. 313, 316; 587 P.2d 59 (1978):

    > "Standing alone, the term 'conditional use' can convey quite different meanings. It could mean that the specified use is a permitted use whenever certain conditions exist or are satisfied. Or, second, it may mean that the use will be permitted subject to special conditions attached to the individual permit. Third, 'conditional use' historically has often been employed simply as a device to permit discretionary decisions on certain uses, without much attention to the meaning of 'conditional.'" See *Anderson's American Law of Zoning* (2d ed.) (Deerfield, IL: Clark Boardman Callaghan, 1968), § 18.05, 147-148.

    Norman Williams, Jr. and John M. Taylor in *American Land Planning Law: Land Use and the Police Power* (Eagan, MN: Thomson/West, 2003), § 137:1, compares the relative acceptance of special or conditional use permits, as opposed to the state-specific law of variances.

18. Sullivan and Richter, note 1, *supra*, at 451.

19. *Haines v. City of Phoenix*, 151 Ariz. 286, 727 P.2d 339 (1986). In this case, conflicting height limitations in two properly adopted comprehensive plans required the court to read the two plans together and conclude that the more limiting height restriction was only "precatory" and that the goals of the more limiting plan were still met.

20. Adherents of economic analysis of law, Marxism, or critical legal studies may speculate at length on this result-oriented jurisprudence. A simpler answer may well be that judges found it difficult to overturn desirable and accepted zoning regulations and had very little to go on with regard to legislative history.

21. The "change or mistake" rule, generally speaking, is that zone changes may only be made where there was a mistake in the original zoning, or the character of the neighborhood has changed so substantially that a rezoning is called for. Obviously, the application of the "change or mistake" rule is a matter for the judiciary to determine on the facts, making its application a quintessentially "quasi-judicial" process. If changes made pursuant to a comprehensive plan are, by contrast, entitled to deferential treatment because of the value afforded the comprehensive plan in law, then we can see that such changes are only subject to the less stringent legislative standard of review by the courts, where interference is only warranted in cases of gross error or inconsistency. See *Miller v. City of Albuquerque*, 544 P.2d 665 (N.M. 1976); *Pierrepont v. Zoning Comm'n.*, 226 A.2d 659 (Conn. 1967); *Wakefield v. Kraft*, 96 A.2d 27 (Md. 1953); *Lewis v. City of Jackson*, 184 So.2d 384 (Miss. 1966); Md. Ann. Code art. 66B, § 4.05 and Mandelker, note 7, *supra*, at 89-96 (discussing the judicially created "change and mistake rule" in Maryland and its application in Maryland, Mississippi, and other states).

22. In its essence, the "appearance of fairness" rule says that public hearings not only have to be fair, they have to look fair. RCW § 42.36.010.

23. "Spot zoning" has been described by one court as:

    "descriptive of the process of singling out a small parcel of land of a use classification different and inconsistent with the surrounding area, for the benefit of the owner of such property and to the detriment of the rights of other property owners." *Burkett v. City of Texarkana*, 500 S.W.2d 242, 244 (Tex. Civ. App. 1973).

    See also *Griswold v. City of Homer*, 925 P.2d 1015 (Ak. 1996); *Chrismon v. Guilford County*, 370 S.E.2d 579 (N.C. 1988); and *Smith v. Town of St. Johnsbury*, 554 A.2d 233 (Vt. 1988).

    "Spot zoning" can best be described by analogy to Justice Stewart's remark on pornography in *Jacobellis v. Ohio*, 378 U.S. 184, 197 (1964):

    "I shall not today attempt further to define the kinds of material I understand to be embraced . . .[b]ut I know it when I see it . . ."

24. SZEA § 7.

25. Id.

26. Id.

27. For example, the "appearance of fairness" rule resonated with procedural due process and "spot zoning" with equal protection or privileges and immunities. The "change or mistake" rule did, in fact, attempt to deal with the legislative/quasi-judicial distinction by according legislative deference to the original zoning ordinance, but treating amendments to that ordinance with skepticism, if not hostility.

28. Richard F. Babcock, *The Zoning Game: Municipal Practices and Policies* (Madison: The University of Wisconsin Press, 1966).

29. Id. at 153-154.

30. See, e.g., *Comment, Zoning Amendments: The Product of Judicial or Quasi-Judicial Action*, 33 Ohio St. L.J. 130 (1972).

31. *Golden v. Planning Bd. of Town of Ramapo*, note 10, *supra*; *Fasano v. Bd. of County Comm'rs.*, 264 Or. 574, 507 P.2d 23 (1973); *Families Unafraid to Uphold Rural El Dorado County (FUTURE) v. Bd. of Supervisors of El Dorado County*, note 10, *supra*.

32. Del. Code. Ann. Tit. 9 §§ 1301, 2651 (2004); Fla. Stat. Ann. §§ 163.2511 and 163.3194 (2004); Or. Rev. Stat. §§ 197 (state), 215 (county), and 227 (municipal) (2004); The Growth Management Act, Wash. Rev. Code. Ann. § 36.70A (2004).

33. *Enter. Partners v. County of Perkins*, 619 N.W.2d 464 (Neb. 2000); *In re Approval of Request for Amend to Frawley Planned Unit Dev.*, 638 N.W.2d 552 (S.D. 2002); *Crouthamel v. Board of Albany County Commrs.*, 951 P.2d 835 (Wyo. 1998); *S. Anchorage Concerned Coalition, Inc. v.*

Coffey, 862 P.2d 168 (Ak. 1993); *Bd. of County Commr's. of Larimer County v. Conder*, 927 P.2d 1339, 1346 (Colo. 1996); *City of Chicago Heights v. Living Word Outreach Full Gospel Church & Ministries, Inc.*, 749 N.E.2d 916 (Ill. 2001).

34. Id.

35. Despite a requirement that "municipal zoning be made in accordance with the comprehensive plan," Colorado courts have upheld zoning if it bears a reasonable relationship to the physical health, safety, and morals, without relying upon any reference to a plan. *Napio Co. v. Town of Cherry Hills Village*, 180 Co. 217, 504 P.2d 344 (1972). See also *First Harford Realty Corp. v. Planning and Zoning Comm'n. of Town of Bloomfield*, 165 Conn. 533, 338 A.2d 490 (1973), where the court held that planning was only advisory.

    The statutory requirement that the zoning commission adopt zoning regulations in accordance with a comprehensive plan refers to the zoning commissions' obligation to zone on a uniform and comprehensive basis rather than to a specific comprehensive land-use plan established by statute. *Citizens Assoc. of Georgetown, Inc. v. Zoning Com. of Dist. of Columbia*, 155 App. DC 233, 477 F.2d 402 (1973).

    In *Muchado v. Musgrave*, the court held that the party challenging a zoning action as inconsistent with the comprehensive plan must show by a preponderance of the evidence that the development is inconsistent with the plan. 519 So.2d 629 (Fla. 3rd Dis. Ct. App. 1987).

36. Or. Rev. Stats. § 197.829. This statute was originally enacted by the Oregon legislature in 1993 to codify the Oregon Supreme Court decision in *Clark v. Jackson County*, 313 Or. 508, 515, 836 P.2d 710 (1992).

37. *Rowan v. Clackamas County*, 19 Or. LUBA 163 (1990), *aff'd*. 103 Or. App. 130 (1990).

38. OAR 660-015-0000 lists the following 19 goals: (1) Citizen Involvement; (2) Land Use Planning; (3) Agricultural Lands; (4) Forest Lands; (5) Natural Resources, Scenic and Historic Areas, and Open Spaces; (6) Air, Water, and Land Resources Quality; (7) Areas Subject to Natural Hazards; (8) Recreational Needs; (9) Economy of the State; (10) Housing; (11) Public Facilities and Services; (12) Transportation; (13) Energy Conservation; (14) Urbanization; (15) Willamette Greenway; (16) Estuarine Resources; (17) Coastal Shorelands; (18) Beaches and Dunes; and (19) Ocean Resources.

39. Or. Rev. Stats. § 197.175 establishes when cities and counties must act in concert with the goals. It provides:

    "197.175 Cities' and counties' planning responsibilities; rules on incorporations; compliance with goals.

    "(1) Cities and counties shall exercise their planning and zoning responsibilities, including, but not limited to, a city or special district boundary change which shall mean the annexation of unincorporated territory by a city, the incorporation of a new city and the formation or change of organization of or annexation to any special district authorized by ORS 198.705 to 198.955, 199.410 to 199.534 or 451.010 to 451.620, in accordance with ORS chapters 195, 196 and 197 and the goals approved under ORS chapters 195, 196 and 197. The Land Conservation and Development Commission shall adopt rules clarifying how the goals apply to the incorporation of a new city. Notwithstanding the provisions of section 15, chapter 827, Oregon Laws 1983, the rules shall take effect upon adoption by the commission. The applicability of rules promulgated under this section to the incorporation of cities prior to August 9, 1983, shall be determined under the laws of this state.

    "(2) Pursuant to ORS chapters 195, 196 and 197, each city and county in this state shall:

       "(a) Prepare, adopt, amend and revise comprehensive plans in compliance with goals approved by the commission;

"(b)   Enact land use regulations to implement their comprehensive plans;

"(c)   If its comprehensive plan and land use regulations have not been acknowledged by the commission, make land use decisions and limited land use decisions in compliance with the goals;

"(d)   If its comprehensive plan and land use regulations have been acknowledged by the commission, make land use decisions and limited land use decisions in compliance with the acknowledged plan and land use regulations; and

"(e)   Make land use decisions and limited land use decisions subject to an unacknowledged amendment to a comprehensive plan or land use regulation in compliance with those land use goals applicable to the amendment.

"(3)   Notwithstanding subsection (1) of this section, the commission shall not initiate by its own action any annexation of unincorporated territory pursuant to ORS 222.111 to 222.750 or formation of and annexation of territory to any district authorized by ORS 198.510 to 198.915 or 451.010 to 451.620." (2004)

Or. Rev. Stats. § 197.180(1) provides that state agencies must similarly comply with the goals:

"Except as provided in ORS 197.277 or subsection (2) of this section or unless expressly exempted by another statute from any of the requirements of this section, state agencies shall carry out their planning duties, powers and responsibilities and take actions that are authorized by law with respect to programs affecting land use." (2004)

Or. Rev. Stats. § 197.646 requires local governments to amend their local plans and regulations anytime the goals are amended:

"(1)   A local government shall amend the comprehensive plan and land use regulations to implement new or amended statewide planning goals, Land Conservation and Development Commission administrative rules and land use statutes when such goals, rules or statutes become applicable to the jurisdiction. Any amendment to incorporate a goal, rule or statute change shall be submitted to the Department of Land Conservation and Development as set forth in ORS 197.610 to 197.625.

"(2)   The department shall notify cities and counties of newly adopted commission goals and commission rules, including the effective date, as they are adopted. The department shall notify cities and counties of newly adopted land use statutes following the legislative session when such statutes are adopted.

"(3)   When a local government does not adopt comprehensive plan or land use regulation amendments as required by subsection (1) of this section, the new or amended goal, rule or statute shall be directly applicable to the local government's land use decisions. The failure to adopt comprehensive plan and land use regulation amendments required by subsection (1) of this section may be the basis for initiation of enforcement action pursuant to ORS 197.319 to 197.335." (2004)

40.   Or. Rev. Stats. § 197.251.

41.   Or. Rev. Stats. § 197.636 to .649.

42.   Or. Rev. Stats. § 197.610 to .625.

43.   *Friends of Neabeack Hill v. City of Philomath*, 139 Or. App. 39, 46, 911 P.2d 350 (1996) and *Byrd v. Stringer*, 295 Or. 311, 666 P.2d 11 1332 (1983).

44.   *Board of County Comm'rs. v. Snyder*, 627 So.2d 469 (Fla. 1993).

45. One of the principal reasons for having a plan is to provide a reference point for zoning and other land-use regulatory measures and actions. If the plan is similarly vague or does not provide a coherent basis for these regulations and actions, little has been accomplished.

46. Thus, if there were surplus commercial land during the planning period, it would be difficult to justify the addition of further commercial lands under the plan or its implementing regulations.

47. For cases interpreting this provision, see *Concerned Citizens of Calaveras County v. Calaveras County Bd. of Supvrs.*, 212 Cal. Rptr. 273 (Cal. App. 1985).

48. See, e.g., *Southern Burlington County NAACP v. Township of Mount Laurel*, 456 A.2d 390 (N.J. 1983); *Britton v. Town of Chester*, 134 N.H. 434, 595 2d 492 (1991); *Berenson v. Town of New Castle*, 38 N.Y.2d 102, 341 N.E.2d 236 (1975).

49. A number of states require that certain comprehensive plans, which are seen as either binding or influential as to regulations and land-use actions, be reviewed on a periodic basis. See, e.g., Cal. Govt. Code § 65040.5; Ariz. Rev. Stats. § 9-461.06(k); Fla. Stats. Ann. §§ 163.3177 and 163.3191; Ga. Code § 50-8-7.1(b); Ann. Code Md. §§ 5-403(a)(2)(c) and 5-502 and -503; Minn. Stats. Ann. §§ 462.355(1)(a) and (2) and 394.232(b); N.J. Stats. Ann. §§ 52:18A-196 to 207; Vir. Code § 15.2-2230; Rev. Code Wash. § 36.70A.130; and W.V. 2004 New Laws S.B. 455 § 8A-3-11(a).

50. *South of Sunnyside Neighborhood League v. Board of Commissioners of Clackamas County*, 280 Or. 3, 21, 569 P.2d 1063 (1977).

51. Cal. Govt. Code § 65302 (2002), relating to elements required to be included in a local general plan.

52. In California, general plans (and plan amendments) may be adopted by local legislative bodies or the electorate through the initiative and referendum processes. In any event, they must be consistent with the enabling legislation, including the requirements for plan elements. That consistency is determined, however, by the superior courts of that state, subject to further judicial review. *De Vita v. County of Napa*, 38 Cal. Rptr. 2d 699, 889 P.2d 1019 (1995). If either is found to be inconsistent, the superior court may set it aside for further amendment until consistency is achieved.

53. Or. Rev. Stats. § 197.040 and 197.251.

54. Or. Rev. Stats. § 197.251(7).

55. Kenneth Culp Davis and Richard J. Pierce, Jr., *Administrative Law Treatise* (3d ed.) (Gaithersburg, MD: Aspen, 1994), at 90-91.

56. Babcock, note 28, *supra*, at 104-105.

57. *Chevron U.S.A., Inc. v. Natural Resources Defense Council, Inc.*, 467 U.S. 837 (1984).

58. At 467 U.S. 865-66, the Court explained:

> "Judges are not experts in the field, and are not part of either political branch of the Government. Courts must, in some cases, reconcile competing political interests, but not on the basis of the judges' personal policy preferences. In contrast, an agency to which Congress has delegated policymaking responsibilities may, within the limits of that delegation, properly rely upon the incumbent administration's views of wise policy to inform its judgments. While agencies are not directly accountable to the people, the Chief Executive is, and it is entirely appropriate for this political branch of

the Government to make such policy choices—resolving the competing interests which Congress itself either inadvertently did not resolve, or intentionally left to be resolved by the agency charged with the administration of the statute in light of everyday realities.

"When a challenge to an agency construction of a statutory provision, fairly conceptualized, really centers on the wisdom of the agency's policy, rather than whether it is a reasonable choice within a gap left open by Congress, the challenge must fail. In such a case, federal judges—who have no constituency—have a duty to respect legitimate policy choices made by those who do. The responsibilities for assessing the wisdom of such policy choices and resolving the struggle between competing views of the public interest are not judicial ones: 'Our Constitution vests such responsibilities in the political branches.'" *TVA v. Hill*, 437 U.S. 153, 195 (1978).

"We hold that the EPA's definition of the term 'source' is a permissible construction of the statute which seeks to accommodate progress in reducing air pollution with economic growth. 'The Regulations which the Administrator has adopted provide what the agency could allowably view as . . . [an] effective reconciliation of these twofold ends . . .'"

59. *City of Portland v. Gage*, 77 Or. App. 196; 713 P.2d 610 (1983).

60. See, e.g., *Fasano v. Bd. of County Comm'rs.*, note 31, *supra; Baker v. City of Milwaukie*, note 10, *supra; Board of County Comm'rs. v. Snyder*, note 44, *supra.*

61. See Stuart Meck, *The Legislative Requirement That Zoning and Land Use Controls Be Consistent with an Independently Adopted Comprehensive Plan*, 3 Wash. U. J.L. & Pol'y 295 (2000).

62. Or. Rev. Stats. § 227.173 sets out the reasoning process for land-use decisions by Oregon cities and states in material part:

"(1) Approval or denial of a discretionary permit application shall be based on standards and criteria, which shall be set forth in the development ordinance and which shall relate approval or denial of a discretionary permit application to the development ordinance and to the comprehensive plan for the area in which the development would occur and to the development ordinance and comprehensive plan for the city as a whole.

"(2) When an ordinance establishing approval standards is required under ORS 197.307 to provide only clear and objective standards, the standards must be clear and objective on the face of the ordinance.

"(3) Approval or denial of a permit application or expedited land division shall be based upon and accompanied by a brief statement that explains the criteria and standards considered relevant to the decision, states the facts relied upon in rendering the decision and explains the justification for the decision based on the criteria, standards and facts set forth.

"(4) Written notice of the approval or denial shall be given to all parties to the proceeding."

Oregon counties have a similar requirement under Or. Rev. Stats. § 215.416(8) to (10).

63. See note 36, *supra*, and related text.

10

The Role of the Local Comprehensive Plan as Law: Some Lessons from Florida

Thomas G. Pelham

INTRODUCTION

Perhaps the most significant modern trend in land-use planning and regulation is the elevation of the legal status of the local comprehensive plan. Historically, adoption of a separate comprehensive or master land-use plan was not a legal prerequisite to land-use regulation. If local government adopted a comprehensive plan separate from the general zoning code, it was usually treated as an advisory document and given little weight in land-use regulation. Consequently, local governments made land-use decisions on an ad hoc, piecemeal basis, constrained legally only by broad constitutional limitations and highly deferential judicial review.[1] This system led to many abuses.[2]

As the deficiencies of the traditional regulatory system became increasingly apparent, critics of the system began to advocate a greater role for planning. Professor Charles Haar and Professor Dan Mandelker were leading advocates of an enhanced role for the local comprehensive plan. Both Haar and Mandelker recommended the reform of state planning and zoning enabling acts to require adoption of a local comprehensive plan separate from the general zoning code.

For example, in his two seminal articles *In Accordance with a Comprehensive Plan*[3] and *The Master Plan: An Impermanent Constitution*,[4] Professor Haar contended that a legally binding master plan would act as a land-use "constitution" with which local land-use decisions must be consistent. This constitution would serve as a constant reminder to local governments of long-term planning goals, give certainty to landowners, counteract pressures for preferential treatment, and provide courts with a meaningful standard of review.[5] Subsequently, Professor Dan Mandelker also urged that greater weight be given to a separately adopted local plan and that the local plan be required to be consistent with state planning goals. He contended that an adopted, legally binding local plan would provide local governments with a stronger defense for their regulatory actions.[6] These proposals have been influential in reforming the local land-use decision-making process.

During the past three decades, a growing number of states have heeded this advocacy. Either through judicial decisions or the amendment of their state enabling legislation, these states have elevated the role and legal status of the local comprehensive plan. According to a recent national survey, 15 states now mandate adoption of a separate local plan with which local land-use decisions must conform, and 25 states require a comprehensive or master plan as a prerequisite to regulation and accord some weight to the plan in local land-use decision-making.[7] The former category of states, sometimes referred to as planning mandate states,[8] accord the highest legal status to the local comprehensive plan. In these states, the plan has the force of law, local land-use decisions must be consistent with the plan, and inconsistency with the plan is an independent ground for invalidation of land-use decisions.

Of the planning mandate states, Florida is arguably the strongest. Certainly, the state has the nation's most comprehensive planning enabling legislation. Enacted in 1985, and regularly amended thereafter, the Florida Local Government Comprehensive Planning and Land Development Regulation Act (hereinafter "the Florida Act")[9]:

- Directs every local government to adopt a local comprehensive plan;
- Contains detailed standards for local plans;
- Requires the local plan to be consistent with state planning standards;
- Provides for state review and approval of local plans; and
- Mandates that all local land development regulations and development orders be consistent with the adopted local plan.

To enforce the consistency requirement, the Florida Act confers broader standing on affected citizens to challenge the consistency of land development regulations and development orders with the adopted local plan.[10] Florida courts have strongly enforced the Florida Act by according the local comprehensive plan the status of a "constitution," adopting a strict interpretation of consistency, treating many land-use decisions as quasi-judicial actions, and strictly scrutinizing these decisions to determine their consistency with the adopted local plan.

There are lessons to be learned from the Florida experience. It illustrates how the planning mandate model changes and improves the local land-use regulatory process and how the original mandatory planning paradigm can be expanded to include state standards and oversight for local plans. However, it also teaches that imposition of the planning mandate model on the traditional land-use decision-making process may create issues and problems that may not be anticipated by state and local legislatures when they adopt mandatory planning legislation.

This paper acknowledges both the benefits of the Florida system and some of the unanticipated consequences that have attended its implementation. The section entitled "Achieving the Original Purposes of an 'Impermanent Constitution'" explains how the Florida system achieves the purposes of the planning mandate model as envisioned by its early advocates. The next section, "Expanding the Original Planning Mandate Paradigm," discusses how Florida has expanded the local planning mandate model through state planning standards and state review of local plans. Finally, "Anticipating the 'Unanticipated' Consequences" identifies some of the unanticipated consequences of Florida's adoption of the planning mandate model and the importance of recognizing and addressing these issues in any new planning enabling legislation.

ACHIEVING THE ORIGINAL PURPOSES OF AN "IMPERMANENT CONSTITUTION"

Florida's experience with the planning mandate model demonstrates the benefits attributed to a legally binding local comprehensive plan by the model's early advocates. Under the Florida Act, the local comprehensive plan is indeed a constitution for land use. The local comprehensive plan is recognized as the fundamental land-use regulation that has the status of law and controls all other local land-use regulations. It establishes long-term planning goals, objectives, and policies for achieving those goals, which provide meaningful standards for judicial review of local land-use decisions. Also, it is a source of authority for local regulatory initiatives and a powerful defense against challenges to local land-use planning and regulatory initiatives.

A Constitution for Land Use

Early in the history of the implementation of the Florida Act, the state's judiciary embraced Professor Haar's concept of the local comprehensive plan as a constitution for land use. For example, in *Machado v. Musgrove*,[11] the court stated that "[t]he plan is likened to a constitution for all future development within the governmental boundary" and is "a limitation on a local government's otherwise broad zoning powers."[12] Other lower appellate courts and the Florida Supreme Court followed suit.[13] The preeminent role of the local comprehensive plan has been underscored by the Florida judiciary's adoption of a strict scrutiny standard of review to determine whether local development orders are consistent with the local comprehensive plan.[14]

The Florida Act's consistency requirement provides that all local land development regulations, all local development orders, and all development must be consistent with the adopted comprehensive plan.[15] Accordingly, if a zoning or other land development regulation enacted to implement the local comprehensive plan is determined by a court to be inconsistent with the adopted plan, the adopted plan will control. The plan does not become inapplicable to a development after implementing development regulations are adopted.

For example, in *Buck Lake Alliance, Inc. v. Board of County Commissioners of Leon County*,[16] a citizens group challenged a county development order for alleged inconsistency with the local comprehensive plan. The county defended by contending that, after adoption of implementing land development regulations, the development need only be consistent with those regulations. Rejecting this argument, the court held that the local comprehensive plan is the preeminent regulatory document and, in the event of inconsistency between the comprehensive plan and the implementing regulations, the comprehensive plan controls.[17]

The preeminent local role of the local comprehensive plan was further recognized in *Pinecrest Lakes v. Schidel*.[18] The court considered a request to enter a mandatory injunction requiring demolition of a multifamily development project found to be inconsistent with the local comprehensive plan. The developer contended that issuance of the injunction was discretionary with the court and that, before granting such a drastic remedy, the court should balance the equities by weighing the loss suffered by the developer if demolition were ordered and the loss suffered by the adjacent neighbors as a result of the development.[19] Citing the Florida Act's mandatory consistency requirement and the legislative provision for injunctive relief to enforce the consistency requirement,[20] the court rejected both arguments. In explaining its decision, the court expounded on the legal status of the adopted local comprehensive plan as follows:

> "The real countervailing equity to any monetary loss of the developer is in the flouting of the legal requirement of the comprehensive plan. Every citizen in the community is intangibly harmed by failure to comply with a comprehensive plan, even those whose properties may have not been directly diminished in value."[21]

Further, in one of the strongest judicial pronouncements ever made about the importance of complying with a legally binding comprehensive plan, the court stated:

> "A society of law must respect law, not its evasion. If the rule of law requires land uses to meet specific standards, then allowing those who develop land to escape its requirements by spending a project out of compliance would make the standards of growth management of little real consequence. It would allow developers such as this one to build in defiance of the limits and then escape compliance by making

the cost of correction too high. That would render [the statute] meaningless and effectual."[22]

Accordingly, the court proclaimed that "respect for law, in this case the Comprehensive Plan, trumps any 'inequity' of financial loss arising from demolition."[23]

Finally, in granting the injunction, the court based its decision squarely on the legal status of the local comprehensive plan and the consistency requirement:

> "The statutory rule is that if you build it, and in court it later proves inconsistent, it will have to come down. The court's injunction enforces the statutory scheme as written. The County has been ordered to comply with its own comprehensive plan and restrained from allowing inconsistent development; and the developer has been found to have built an inconsistent land use and has been ordered to remove it. **The rule of law has prevailed.**"[24]

Planning Standards for Land-Use Decisions

As envisioned by the Florida Act, the local comprehensive plan is a blueprint for the future development of the community. It must include "principles, guidelines, and standards for the orderly and balanced future economic, social, physical, environmental, and fiscal development" within each local government's jurisdictional area.[25]

At a minimum, the local plan must include:
- Elements covering future land use;
- Capital improvements generally and sanitary sewer, solid waste, drainage, potable water, and natural groundwater aquifer protection specifically;
- Conservation;
- Recreation and open space;
- Housing;
- Traffic circulation;
- Intergovernmental coordination; and
- For certain local governments, coastal management and mass transit.[26]

A local government may elect to include other elements such as community design, safety, economic development, and public school facilities.[27] The elements of the plan must be internally consistent and coordinated with each other[28] and must be based on relevant and appropriate data and analyses.[29]

Each element of the local plan must include goals, objectives, and policies:[30]
- A goal is "the long-term end towards which programs or activities are ultimately directed."[31]
- An objective is "a specific, measurable, intermediate end that is achievable and marks progress toward a goal."[32]
- A policy is "the way in which programs and activities are conducted to achieve an identifiable goal."[33]

The goals, objectives, and policies are the planning standards with which local land development regulations and development orders must be consistent.

Consistency with the Adopted Planning Standards

Under the Florida Act, land-use decisions must be made in accordance with the goals, objectives, and policies of the adopted local plan. The statutory consistency requirement creates the linkage between the plan's provisions and implementing land development regulations and approvals. The Florida Act expressly requires that all local land development regulations, all local development orders, and all development approved and undertaken by a local government "shall be consistent with the adopted comprehensive plan."[34]

As generally defined by statute, consistency means that development or a development order or land development regulation is "compatible with and furthers the objectives, policies, land uses, and densities or intensities in the comprehensive plan and if it meets all other criteria enumerated by the local government."[35] As discussed below, the interpretation and application of this general definition can have important consequences for the land-use decision-making process.

Meaningful Standards for Judicial Review

Land-use decisions frequently involve a clash between the interests of government, landowners/developers, and third parties such as neighborhood and environmental groups. These conflicts generate litigation when either a landowner/developer applicant or an affected third party challenges the local government's decision.

Various Florida court decisions illustrate how an adopted local comprehensive plan provides meaningful standards by which the judiciary can review and evaluate the appropriateness of the local decision. As the discussion of the following cases indicates, the local plan's standards and criteria may protect the interest of the local government, the landowner/developer, or other affected citizens, depending on the circumstances of the particular case.

Southwest Ranches Homeowner's Association, Inc. v. County of Broward[36] is an example of how a comprehensive plan can provide the local government with adequate justification for approving an unpopular land use over citizen opposition. Broward County adopted two rezoning ordinances for the purpose of allowing a county-owned sanitary landfill and resource recovery facility in an area designated as agricultural in the county's comprehensive plan. One ordinance changed the existing zoning district to a more intensive agricultural zoning district; the other ordinance amended the zoning district text to permit the landfill and resource recovery facility. An association of rural homeowners challenged the rezoning ordinances on the basis that they were inconsistent with the county's comprehensive plan.[37]

Observing "that zoning decisions should be made on the basis of rational planning goals and not political pressure"[38] and that the rezonings "should not only meet the traditional fairly debatable standard, but should also be consistent with the comprehensive plan,"[39] the court proceeded to strictly scrutinize the relevant provisions of the county comprehensive plan. After carefully reviewing and analyzing the relevant provisions of the future land-use element, the conservation element, and the potable water element, the court concluded that the rezoning ordinances were not inconsistent with the county's plan.[40]

In other cases, the local government may yield to pressures from the land developer applicant and approve development orders that are contrary to the standards and criteria in the local comprehensive plan. For example, in *Dixon v. City of Jacksonville,*[41] the city rezoned property from "commercial office" to "planned urban development" to permit construction of a hotel. Surrounding homeowners objected to the rezoning on the grounds that it was inconsistent with the city's comprehensive plan. The city plan designated the property as residential/professional/institutional (RPI), but the RPI land-use classification did not mention hotels as a permissible primary or secondary use. After concluding that the RPI land-use classification made no express mention of hotels, the court then strictly scrutinized other related comprehensive plan provisions to see if they contained any support for the city's interpretation allowing hotels in the RPI classification.[42] Based on this careful examination of the plan's provisions, the court concluded that hotels were not a permissible use within the RPI land-use classification and directed the trial court to enjoin the city from implementing the rezoning ordinance.[43]

Similarly, in *Pinecrest Lakes, Inc. v. Shidel,*[44] Martin County granted a development order for a multistory, multifamily apartment complex immediately adjacent to a single-family subdivision over the strenuous objections of the neighboring homeowners. The homeowners then challenged the development order for inconsistency with the comprehensive plan. Specifically, the neighbors claimed that approval of the apartments directly adjacent to one-story, single-family homes violated a provision of the comprehensive plan requiring a transition zone in the "first tier" of new development adjacent to existing development.[45]

The purpose of the transition zone was to ensure compatibility of new development with existing development. After strictly scrutinizing the various relevant provisions of the county's comprehensive plan, the court concluded that the development order was inconsistent with the plain language of the comprehensive plan.[46] Accordingly, as discussed in the section entitled "Achieving the Original Purposes of an 'Impermanent Constitution,'" the appellate court affirmed the trial court's order directing demolition of the apartment complex, which had been constructed during the pendency of the litigation.[47]

A local comprehensive plan can also protect a landowner/developer from arbitrary action and neighborhood pressures. In *ABG Real Estate Development Company v. St. Johns County*,[48] the developer applied for a development order authorizing a fast-food restaurant in a shopping center. Although the local planning department found that the proposed use was consistent with the county's comprehensive plan, local residents opposed it because of generalized concerns about traffic and aesthetics.[49] The local governing body then denied the application based on vague and unspecified public health, safety, and welfare concerns.[50] Finding that the application's consistency with the comprehensive plan was undisputed in the record, the court quashed the board's denial of the development order.[51]

Providing a More Defensible Basis for Local Planning and Regulatory Actions

Advocates of a mandatory local comprehensive plan have long contended that an adopted plan will provide local governments with a stronger defense if their land-use regulatory actions are challenged. Support for this contention can be found in numerous federal and state judicial decisions.

For example, in *Penn Central Transp. Co. v. New York City*,[52] the United States Supreme Court, in upholding New York City's Historical Landmarks Preservation Law, emphasized that the regulation "embodies a comprehensive plan to preserve structures of historic or esthetic interest where ever they might be found in the City."[53] Similarly, the adoption of a comprehensive plan was critical to the judicial validation of timed and sequential zoning controls in *Golden v. Town of Ramapo*.[54] The Ramapo comprehensive plan linked the approval of subdivision approvals to the availability of adequate public facilities as provided in accordance with the plan. In upholding Ramapo's innovative growth management system, the New York high court noted that the regulations were based on and were supported by the town's adopted comprehensive plan.[55]

The Florida experience provides further support for the proposition that an adopted comprehensive plan strengthens local government's regulatory hand. For example, *Martin County v. Section 28 Partnership, Ltd.*[56] illustrates how the adopted local plan may provide a formidable defense against landowner/developer challenges to local land-use decisions. In *Section 28 Partnership*, a landowner challenged the county's denial of a comprehensive plan amendment to redesignate property from a rural and agricultural use classification to a planned unit development containing a mix of residential, recreational, retail, and office uses and to create a new, special, urban service district for the property. The county's defense relied heavily on its adopted comprehensive plan.

In upholding the county's action, the court in *Section 28 Partnership* noted the testimony of planning experts who testified that the county's comprehensive plan provided for urban services only in existing urban service areas in order to prevent urban sprawl and protect natural resources. Further, the court pointed to testimony that the county's comprehensive plan was based on rational and sound planning principles, which were designed to prevent urban sprawl and protect agricultural lands and other natural resources, and that the adopted plan and its current land-use designation of the Section 28 property were "reasonable from a planning, economic, environmental, and fiscal responsibility standpoint."[57] The court concluded that the record contained abundant evidence that the county's denial of the requested plan amendment accomplished the adopted plan's growth management goals for both the Section 28 property and the county as a whole.[58]

Florida also provides perhaps the most dramatic example of how an adopted local plan can overcome legal barriers to the achievement of important planning goals. The example involves the problem of preserving and protecting future transportation corridors with which many states and local governments have wrestled for years.

In 1987, the Florida legislature addressed this issue by enacting legislation that authorized the state's Department of Transportation (DOT) to record maps of reservation to protect rights-of-way for future new or expanded roads. After the DOT recorded a map of reservation in a county's public records, local governments were prohibited from issuing permits for any development, with a few exceptions, within the reserved area for a five-year period, which could be extended for an additional five years by recording another map. The state was not required to purchase the reserved property at any time during the reservation period.[59]

In *Joint Ventures, Inc. v. Department of Transportation*,[60] the Florida Supreme Court declared the map of reservation legislation facially unconstitutional as a violation of due process. The court was especially troubled by the DOT's acknowledgment that the legislation's purpose was the freezing or holding down of the value of privately owned property that might later be condemned for roadway purposes, and the fact that the statute imposed a moratorium on development for the length of the reservation, which might be as long as 10 years. Accordingly, the court described the regulatory scheme "as a thinly veiled attempt to 'acquire' land" by circumventing the protections of Florida's eminent domain statutes.[61]

Although the *Joint Ventures* decision appeared to doom any effort to preserve and protect future transportation corridors in the state, the Florida Act provided a solution. The act requires each local comprehensive plan to include a transportation or traffic circulation element. This element must contain a thoroughfare map that designates the generalized location of transportation corridors, which will be needed to serve the local government during the course of its 10- or 20-year planning period.[62]

Pursuant to this statutory mandate, Palm Beach County adopted a comprehensive plan containing the required thoroughfare map. This map designated protected transportation corridors for the construction or expansion of roadways. The land-use element of the county's comprehensive plan prohibited any land-use activities within any designated corridor that would interfere with future roadway construction.[63] After lower courts declared these provisions unconstitutional based on the *Joint Ventures* decision, the Florida Supreme Court was asked to consider the following question of great public importance:

> "Is a county thoroughfare map designating corridors for future roadways, and which forbids land use activity that would impede future construction of a roadway, adopted incident to a comprehensive county land use plan enacted under the local government comprehensive planning and land development regulation act, facially unconstitutional under *Joint Ventures, Inc. v. Dept. of Transportation*, 563 So.2d 622 (Fla. 1990)?"[64]

The Florida Supreme Court, in *Palm Beach County v. Wright*,[65] determined that the corridor protection provisions in the Palm Beach County comprehensive plan were not facially unconstitutional. The court distinguished the state's map of reservation statutes at issue in *Joint Ventures* from corridor protection provisions in adopted local comprehensive plan in various ways.

For purposes of this discussion, the most important distinction cited by the court was the fact that the Palm Beach County corridor protection provisions were part of a local comprehensive plan adopted pursuant to the Florida Act. The court expressly endorsed comprehensive planning for future road development, noting that "planning for future growth must include designations of the areas where roads are likely to be widened and future roads are to be built" and recognizing the "many public benefits to be achieved through comprehensive planning of future road development."[66] The court characterized the Palm Beach County corridor protection provisions, in particular the thoroughfare map, as an invaluable tool to accomplish the various purposes of comprehensive planning, and stated that "[t]he County's ability to plan for future growth would be seriously impeded without the thoroughfare map."[67]

EXPANDING THE ORIGINAL PLANNING MANDATE PARADIGM

Some states, most notably Florida and Oregon, have moved beyond the original planning mandate model by providing for a significant state role in the planning process. In Florida, the legislature has decreed that planning must be a continuous process in which local plans are regularly amended and updated in accordance with substantive statutory standards and subject to state supervision. As a result, the local constitution for land use also serves as a vehicle for implementing state planning policy.

Planning as a Continuous Process

Under the Florida Act, the local comprehensive plan is neither a fixed, end-state-type master plan nor a static planning policy document. The adoption of a local comprehensive plan does not conclude the planning process; rather, the preparation and adoption of the plan is only the beginning of an ongoing process. The act requires that planning "be a continuous and ongoing process."[68] Accordingly, the Florida Act not only anticipates the necessity for changing the local plan on an annual basis, but it requires each local government to evaluate comprehensively its plan and update it on a periodic basis.

The Florida Act establishes the exclusive procedures for amending adopted local plans. Significantly, with some exceptions, comprehensive plan amendments may not be adopted "more than two times during any calendar year."[69] This limitation ensures a degree of plan stability and enables the local government to consider the cumulative effects of all plan amendments considered during each biennial plan amendment cycle.

Every seven years, each local government is required to undertake a comprehensive evaluation of its adopted local plan by preparing and adopting an evaluation and appraisal report (EAR) in accordance with statutory requirements. The Florida Act contains a list of issues that must be addressed in the EAR.[70] The purpose of the EAR is three-fold:

1.   To respond to changes in state, regional, and local planning policies and other changing conditions;

2.   To evaluate the current comprehensive plan and its effectiveness; and

3.   To identify and analyze major planning issues and recommend comprehensive plan amendments to address those issues.[71]

The importance of the plan evaluation and update process is underscored by the requirement for state review of the EAR. After adopting its EAR, the local government must submit it to the state land planning agency for a sufficiency review.[72] Once the EAR is determined to be sufficient, the local government is required to amend its comprehensive plan based on the recommendations in the EAR within 18 months, unless extensions are granted for good cause.[73]

The Local Comprehensive Plan as a Vehicle for Implementing State Planning Policy

The Florida planning system utilizes the local comprehensive plan as a vehicle for the application of state and regional planning policies at the local governmental level. The local plan is required to be consistent with the Florida Act's substantive planning requirements, the state's administrative minimum criteria rule for local comprehensive plans, the state comprehensive plan, and the appropriate strategic regional policy plan.[74] In formulating its local comprehensive plan, each local government must address local issues and problems with planning policies that are consistent with state and regional policies.

The state planning statutes contain a wide range of substantive planning policies with which local plans must be consistent. For example, the Florida Act contains policies and standards addressing such issues as adequate public facilities,[75] the discouragement of urban sprawl,[76] low- and moderate-income housing,[77] and environmental and natural resource conservation and protection.[78] Also, the state comprehensive plan, embodied in a separate statute, contains 25 planning goals and accompanying policies that cover such subjects as housing, water resources, urban and downtown revitalization, transportation, and agriculture.[79] Each local comprehensive plan must address "the [state comprehensive plan] goals and policies which are relevant to the circumstances or conditions in its jurisdiction."[80] Finally, the strategic regional policy plan contains policies addressing regional issues in a manner consistent with the state comprehensive plan.[81]

The Florida planning framework is an effective vehicle for addressing new planning issues of statewide concern at the local level. As new planning issues and problems develop, the Florida legislature may amend the Florida Act to require local governments to address these issues in their local comprehensive plans consistent with state standards and policies. Local governments, in turn, must then amend their local comprehensive plans to comply with the new statutory requirements.

To illustrate, in recent years, water supply and public school capacity have become critical issues in many parts of Florida. The Florida legislature responded to the water issue by first requiring the state's water management districts to adopt regional water supply plans.[82] Next, the legislature amended the Florida Act to require local comprehensive plans to consider the regional water supply plan and to include a work plan for building the water supply facilities necessary to serve existing and new development within the local jurisdiction.[83]

Similarly, to address the adequate school facilities issue, in 2002 the legislature amended the Florida Act to authorize each county, in conjunction with its municipalities, to adopt an optional public educational facilities element in cooperation with the applicable school district. In order to adopt such an element, the Florida Act provides that the county and each municipality, with certain exceptions, must enter into an interlocal agreement regarding school concurrency and adopt a consistent public educational facilities element in accordance with statutory criteria.[84]

State Review and Approval of Local Comprehensive Plans and Plan Amendments

To ensure that local comprehensive plans comply with state planning requirements, the Florida Act provides that all local comprehensive plans and plan amendments must be reviewed by the Department of Community Affairs, the state land planning agency, for compliance with state requirements.[85] A proposed local plan or plan amendment, with few exceptions, must be submitted to the department for its review and comment. After the department issues to the local government its objections, comments, and recommendations, the local government may then adopt the plan or plan amendment. The adopted plan or plan amendment must then be transmitted back to the department, which then determines whether the plan or plan amendment is in compliance with state requirements.[86]

After the department makes its compliance decision, either the local government or an affected person may challenge the state agency's determination in a state administrative proceeding.[87] The State Administration Commission (the governor and cabinet) makes the final administrative decision as to whether a plan or plan amendment is in compliance. If the commission determines that the plan amendment is not in compliance, it is required to specify remedial actions and may impose financial sanctions if the local government decides to implement a plan amendment that has been determined not to be in compliance with state law.[88] A local comprehensive plan amendment cannot become legally effective until the commission makes its compliance determination.[89]

ANTICIPATING THE "UNANTICIPATED" CONSEQUENCES

Mandating the adoption of a legally binding local comprehensive plan with which rezonings and other land-use decisions must be consistent can have profound consequences for the local land-use decision-making process. Application of a plan consistency requirement may transform land-use decisions from legislative into quasi-judicial action. In turn, this transformation affects the procedures by which the decisions must be made, the role of the local officials in making land-use decisions, and the rules by which their land-use decisions are reviewed by the judiciary. The imposition of state substantive planning policies and state review of local plans may create state/local conflicts that further complicate the new planning process. State and local legislatures should anticipate and carefully consider these potential issues and problems when drafting legislation conferring legal binding status on the local comprehensive plan.

The Judicialization of the Local Land-Use Decision-Making Process

Traditionally, and in the great majority of states today, rezoning decisions are considered legislative actions that are entitled to great deference by the courts. However, the requirement that a rezoning application be consistent with the policies and standards in the adopted local comprehensive plan arguably transforms the rezoning decision from a legislative to a quasi-judicial action.

For example, in 1973 the Oregon Supreme Court, in *Fasano v. Board of County Commissioners of Washington County*,[90] held that rezoning should be treated as quasi-judicial acts, in part, because of Oregon's state statutory requirement that zoning actions must be consistent with an adopted comprehensive plan.

Nevertheless, when it enacted the Florida Act in 1985, the state legislature did not anticipate this development or adequately provide for it in the state legislation. As a result, the state's local governments were not prepared for Florida's version of *Fasano*, which was issued by the Florida Supreme Court in 1993 in *Board of County Commissioners of Brevard County v. Snyder.*[91]

Snyder revolutionized the local rezoning process in Florida. It partially reversed the state's long-standing rule that rezoning actions are legislative acts subject to the highly deferential fairly debatable rule. Based on the new statutory requirement that all development orders, including rezonings, must be consistent with the adopted local comprehensive plan, the Supreme Court reasoned that application of comprehensive plan policies to requests for site-specific rezonings affecting limited parties and interests constitutes quasi-judicial and not legislative actions.[92] Consequently, according to the court, the fairly debatable rule no longer applies to such rezonings, which will be strictly scrutinized to determine their consistency with the comprehensive plan. Further, because these rezoning decisions are quasi-judicial in nature, they must be supported by competent substantial evidence in a record compiled at the rezoning hearing.[93]

Many local governments were not prepared for this dramatic change in the local zoning process. They were not accustomed to conducting quasi-judicial-type hearings and did not have established procedures for conducting such hearings. The *Snyder* decision did not fully explain the extent to which procedural due process protections, such as the swearing in and cross-examination of witnesses, must be afforded in local quasi-judicial hearings, and Florida's initial legislation provided no guidance. As a result, in the years immediately following the *Snyder* decision, a great deal of confusion reigned throughout the state as to the manner in which local quasi-judicial hearings should be conducted.

The controversy was exacerbated by another Florida court decision, *Jennings v. Dade County,*[94] which held that ex parte communications with local officials in quasi-judicial-type proceedings were presumed prejudicial and a violation of state constitutional procedural due process. Suddenly, local elected officials who make rezoning decisions were being advised that they could no longer communicate with their constituents about rezoning cases. This led to the enactment of constitutionally suspect state legislation declaring that such ex parte contacts are not presumed prejudicial and that local officials have a right to communicate with their constituents.[95]

Much of the controversy and confusion about the quasi-judicial hearing process could have been avoided if the Florida legislature had anticipated these issues and addressed them in the state's 1985 local planning legislation. For example, the legislation could have included minimum procedural requirements for local quasi-judicial hearings involving plan consistency issues. Unfortunately, the Florida legislature did not adopt minimum quasi-judicial hearing procedures for local governments until 2002, almost a decade after the *Snyder* decision. These procedures are optional[96] and the author is unaware of any local government that has elected to adopt them.

The Changing Role of the Local Legislator

The judicialization of local land-use hearings has important ramifications for local legislatures. Traditionally, at the local level, municipal councils and county commissions have made rezoning and other land-use decisions. Many of these decisions, particularly rezonings, have been treated as legislative decisions. In making these decisions, elected local officials have acted as typical legislators: they preside over legislative-type hearings; are politically sensitive to constituent voters; and exercise great discretion, constrained only by the most minimal procedural due process requirements.

Recharacterizing land-use decisions as quasi-judicial acts requires the elected local legislator to assume the role of judge. Many elected officials do not wear this judicial hat comfortably. Unlike legislators, quasi-judicial officials are asked to act like neutral arbiters, presiding fairly and impartially over more formal hearings with some of the due process trappings of a courtroom proceeding, and giving little or no weight to the preferences of citizens and neighbors. In other words, elected legislators are asked to perform the unnatural act of being judge-like. The demands on the legislator are intensified by the fact that quasi-judicial-type hearings can be far more time consuming than the ordinary legislative-type zoning hearing.

In Florida, following the *Snyder* decision, local legislators have had to make a difficult choice. Do they retain full responsibility for quasi-judicial land-use proceedings or do they delegate at least some part of the process to other entities? A growing number of Florida local governments are utilizing hearing officers to conduct quasi-judicial hearings and make findings of fact and recommendations to the local governing body. Although delegation of these responsibilities to hearing officers provides some relief to elected officials, it also raises significant governance and budgetary issues.

The Meaning of Consistency

What is the substantive effect of requiring land-use decisions to be "consistent" with an adopted local comprehensive plan? The answer depends on the definition of consistency and how that definition is construed and applied by local land-use planners and decision-makers and, in the final analysis, by the courts. Accordingly, when considering adoption of a plan consistency requirement, state and local legislatures should pay close attention to this critical definitional issue. As the Florida experience illustrates, a general statutory definition can acquire surprising specificity and bite when construed by the courts.

As defined by the Florida Act, consistency means that the aspects of development must be:

"... *compatible with and further* the objectives, policies, land uses, and densities or intensities in the comprehensive plan and if it meets all other criteria enumerated by the local government."[97]

The key words in this statutory definition are "compatible with and further"; however, the statute does not specify what degree of compatibility is required or to what extent the plan's provisions must be furthered. Additionally, it does not address whether a development order or regulation must be consistent with each provision of the plan or only with the plan as a whole.

This imprecise statutory language lends itself to a range of interpretations regarding the requisite degree of conformity with the plan. Must the consistency be reasonable, substantial, or strict? The task of fleshing out the statutory definition was left to the Florida judiciary.

Florida courts have generally taken a strong approach to the consistency requirement. An early decision, *Machado v. Musgrove*,[98] approved of the following "working definition" of consistency:

"The word 'consistent' implies the idea or existence of some type or form of model, standard, guideline, point, mark or measure as a norm and a comparison of items or actions against that norm. Consistency is the fundamental relation between the norm and the compared item. If the compared item is in accordance with, or in agreement with, or within the parameters specified, or exemplified, by the norm, it is 'consistent' with it but if the compared item deviates or departs in any direction or degree from the parameters of the norm, the compared item or action is not 'consistent' with the norm."[99]

Equally important, the *Machado* court ruled that the issue of whether a zoning decision conforms to each element and the objectives of the local plan is subject to strict judicial scrutiny.[100] According to the court, "strict implies rigid exactness, ... A thing scrutinized has been subjected to minute investigation."[101] Thus, the court explained, "[s]trict scrutiny is ... the process whereby a court makes a detailed examination of a statute, rule or order of a tribunal for exact compliance with, or adherence to, a standard or norm."[102]

Subsequently, in the *Snyder* decision, the Florida Supreme Court endorsed the strict scrutiny standard of review and cited with approval the *Machado* analysis. The court noted that strict scrutiny "arises from the necessity of strict compliance with a comprehensive plan."[103]

Some other jurisdictions have adopted a more lenient approach to the consistency doctrine. For example, in *Willapa Grays Harbor Oyster Growers Ass'n v. Moby Dick Corp.*,[104] the Washington court rejected the strict scrutiny standard in favor of a "general conformance" standard.[105] As explained by the court, under Washington law, "strict adherence is not required" because the local comprehensive plan is only a general planning guide and not "a land use decision-making tool."[106]

Interpretation of the Local Comprehensive Plan

Requiring consistency with a legally binding local comprehensive plan has important implications for the interpretation and application of the local plan. Obviously, the determination of whether a land-use decision is consistent with the local plan requires interpretation of the plan's provisions. When given the status of law, the local plan is a legal as well as a planning document. Interpretation of a legal document is within the province of the courts, which have devised rules of statutory construction to aid in this endeavor. Consequently, in the event of a judicial challenge to a local land-use decision for inconsistency with the local comprehensive plan, the meaning of the local plan will ultimately be determined by the courts and not by local planners and officials.

How much deference should be given by the courts to a local government's interpretation of its adopted plan? This issue, which is the subject of vigorous debate in Florida, has been addressed by the state's lower appellate courts. To the chagrin of some local government planners and officials, the judiciary is giving little or no deference to local interpretation.

For example, in *Dixon v. City of Jacksonville*,[107] the court rejected "the City's argument that deference should be given to the City's interpretation of [the comprehensive plan] which it administers."[108] Instead, the court ruled that the interpretation of the plan "is a question of law reviewable *de novo*"[109] by the court, unless the meaning of the plan is ambiguous. Therefore, the court was "not constrained by more deferential standards from substituting [its] judgment for that of the lower tribunal."[110] According to the court, if a deferential standard were applied,

> "... the ultimate determination of a planned development would be placed within the discretion of whoever composes the membership of the governmental body's planning department at any given time, and the goal of certainty and order in future land-use decision-making would be circumvented."[111]

The court then proceeded to carefully examine the language of the plan provision in question and rejected the local government's interpretation.

The court in *Pinecrest Lakes, Ltd. v. Martin County*[112] offered a further rationale for the no-deference rule. As interpreted by the *Pinecrest Lakes* court, the structure and provisions of the Florida Act reflect that no deference is to be given to the local government's interpretation. First, in plan consistency cases, the act requires the court to determine the consistency of a local development order and, therefore, it should not be assumed that deference must be given to the local officials whose action is being judged.[113] Second, because the act "is utterly silent on the notion of deference," it is presumed that the legislature intended that none be given.[114] Third, because the act requires local governments to act consistently with their plans, the courts should not defer to their decisions regarding consistency in the absence of a contrary statutory provision.[115]

This rationale is persuasive. Nevertheless, some jurisdictions may be concerned that the judiciary, and not locally elected officials and planners, will determine planning policy. Therefore, any jurisdiction contemplating legislative adoption of a comprehensive plan consistency requirement may want to address the issue of plan interpretation. For example, Oregon has adopted legislative standards regarding the interpretation of local comprehensive plans by the State Land Use Appeals Board.[116]

Polarization of State-Local Relations

The state's assumption of a larger role in land-use regulation—an area traditionally delegated to local governments—will have implications for future state-local governmental relations. Even if the state role is limited to adopting enabling legislation, which prescribes substantive state planning standards for local comprehensive plans, local governments are likely to resent this perceived intrusion into their "home rule" prerogatives.

Further, if the state assumes an even larger role, as in the Florida system, by requiring local governments to engage in a continuous and ongoing planning process, with periodic comprehensive plan evaluations and updates and every local comprehensive plan amendment subject to state review and approval, substantial budgetary and governance issues will arise. Unless these issues are treated with sensitivity, local governmental resentment may quickly turn into open hostility and resistance to the planning process.

The imposition of a mandatory planning requirement, especially one that is attended by a strong state oversight rule, can have serious budgetary implications for the local government. Compliance with new planning mandates may involve substantial additional costs. For example, in Florida, many local governments had to either create or increase the size of their local planning departments or hire outside planning consultants to prepare comprehensive plans in accordance with state requirements. Given the statutory requirement to conduct a periodic, comprehensive evaluation and update of the local plan, the impact on the local budget is not temporary.

If implementation of state planning mandates through the local comprehensive planning system also requires significant funding, the pressures on the local government's budget will be even greater. For example, under the Florida system, local governments must prepare a financially feasible capital improvements element that ensures compliance with the state's mandatory concurrency requirements for public facilities. If the state imposes such mandatory planning requirements on local governments without granting financial assistance or providing adequate revenue sources, these mandates may poison state-local governmental relations and undermine implementation of the planning process.

A strong state role in the planning process may also raise significant governance issues. State oversight through the review and approval of local comprehensive plans and plan amendments can lead to an adversarial relationship between the two levels of government. Local governments do not react well to the rejection of their plans by state officials, particularly if the state officials are appointed rather than elected. For this reason, in Florida, final state administrative decisions about local plans are made by the elected governor and cabinet. If the state reviews every plan amendment, regardless of its scope and nature, and if disputes over plan amendments are resolved through administrative litigation, the potential for conflict between the state and local governments is substantial.

Almost 20 years after enactment of the state's mandatory planning legislation, these issues are still being debated in Florida:

• How are local governments going to pay for implementation of their comprehensive plans? Is the state providing adequate financial support?

• Should the state be reviewing all local comprehensive plan amendments?

• Should the state review local plans and plan amendments only to the extent that they affect state interests?

• Are the state's administrative minimum criteria rules for local comprehensive plan compliance too rigid and inflexible?

• Should disputes between the state and local governments over plan compliance be resolved through alternative dispute resolution processes rather than litigation?

• Should the state establish a special land-use court or administrative body, such as Oregon's Land Use Appeals Board, to resolve planning disputes between state and local governments?

The failure to carefully consider and address many of these issues when the Florida Act was adopted in 1985 has complicated the implementation of the state's comprehensive planning laws. Debates over these issues have detracted from the primary mission of the mandatory planning program and has generated continuing efforts to weaken or repeal significant portions of the Florida Act. Any state that considers adoption of the planning mandate model, particularly one involving an expanded state role, should carefully evaluate the potential impacts on local government budgets and on state-local relations.

CONCLUSION

The Florida experience demonstrates the wisdom of the early advocates of the planning mandate model. The adoption of a local comprehensive plan with which land-use decisions must be consistent can improve the land-use regulatory process in several important respects.

First, as a constitution for land use, the local plan sets forth the policies and standards that the local government will follow in making land-use decisions. The "constitution" protects against arbitrary and capricious decisions by government and provides a greater degree of certainty in land-use decision-making by giving all affected parties advance notice of the standards that will be applied by the government.

Additionally, a local comprehensive plan establishes meaningful criteria for judicial review of local land-use decisions. Instead of deferring to local government under the traditional fairly debatable rule, a court may now more closely review local decisions for compliance with the substantive standards contained in the local comprehensive plan. The combination of legislatively adopted standards of general applicability and more effective judicial review rationalizes the decision-making process and reduces the influence of rank political pressure and influence. As long as the local government adheres to its adopted plan, landowners and other affected persons will find it difficult to invalidate the local government's land-use decisions.

Finally, the Florida experience illustrates that adoption of a legally binding local plan provides a more defensible basis for innovative planning and regulatory initiatives and can enable a local government to accomplish various planning goals that might otherwise be difficult to achieve.

Although the planning mandate model has much to recommend it, its adoption and implementation can have unintended or unanticipated consequences. The adoption of a comprehensive plan consistency requirement will change the way local governments deal with land-use issues. Inevitably, the judiciary will rule that adoption of such a requirement transforms land-use decisions from legislative to quasi-judicial actions. This transformation has significant implications for both the local decision-making process and judicial review.

The nature of the local hearing process and the role of local legislators will be significantly impacted. Also, the assertion of a stronger state role in the local land-use decision-making process will generate governance and budgetary issues that can further complicate the transition to a new regulatory system. The transition will be much smoother if these issues and problems are anticipated and addressed at the time the mandatory planning requirement is adopted. Accordingly, other jurisdictions should carefully consider the Florida experience before enacting legislation that mandates the adoption of a legally binding comprehensive plan with which land-use decisions must be consistent.

THOMAS G. PELHAM NOTES

1. For a discussion of the traditional role of planning, see D. Mandelker, *The Role of the Local Comprehensive Plan in Land Use Regulation,* 74 Mich. L. Rev. 899 (1976).

2. See Richard F. Babcock, *The Zoning Game: Municipal Practices and Policies* (Madison: The University of Wisconsin Press, 1966), for a classic indictment of the traditional, local, land-use regulatory system.

3. Charles Haar, *In Accordance with a Comprehensive Plan*, 68 Harv. L. Rev. 1154, 1174 (1955).
4. Charles Haar, *The Master Plan: An Impermanent Constitution*, 20 Law & Contemp. Probs. 353 (1955).
5. Haar, note 3, *supra*, at 1174.
6. Mandelker, note 1, *supra*.
7. E. Sullivan and M. Michel, *Ramapo Plus 30: The Changing Role of the Plan and Land Use Regulation*, 35 Urb. Law. 75, 76, n. 7 (2003).
8. Id. at 78.
9. Chapter 163, Part II, Florida Statutes (2004) (hereinafter "the Florida Act").
10. For an overview and analysis of the Florida Act, see T. Pelham, W. Hyde, and R. Banks, *Managing Florida's Growth: Toward an Integrated State, Regional, and Local Comprehensive Planning Process*, 13 Fla. St. U. L. Rev. 515 (1985); T. Pelham, *Adequate Public Facilities Requirements: Reflections on Florida's Concurrency System for Managing Growth*, 19 Fla. St. U. L. Rev. 974-1011 (1992).
11. 519 So.2d 629 (Fla. 3d DCA 1987).
12. Id. at 632.
13. See, e.g., *Gardens Country Club, Inc. v. Palm Beach County*, 590 So.2d 488. (Fla. 4th DCA 1991); *Lee County v. Sunbelt Equities, II, Ltd. Partnership*, 619 So.2d 996 (Fla. 2d DCA 1991); *Martin County v. Yusem*, 690 So.2d 1288 (Fla. 1997).
14. See *Board of County Commissioners of Brevard County v. Snyder*, 627 So.2d 469 (Fla. 1993). For a discussion of this decision, see T. Pelham, *Quasi-Judicial Rezonings: A Commentary on the Snyder Decision and The Consistency Requirement*, 9 J. Land Use & Envtl. L. 243 (1994).
15. Fla. Stat. § 163.3194(3)(a) and (b).
16. 765 So.2d 124 (Fla. 1st DCA 2000).
17. Id. at 127.
18. 795 So.2d 191 (Fla. 4th DCA 2001).
19. Id. at 207-208.
20. Id. at 106-107.
21. Id. at 209.
22. Id. at 208.
23. Id. at 209.
24. Id. [Emphasis added.]
25. Fla. Stat. § 163.3177(1).
26. Id. § 163.3177(6).
27. Id. § 163.3177(7).
28. Id. § 163.3177(2).
29. Id. § 163.3177(8); Fla. Admin. Code Ann. R. 9J-5.005(2).
30. Fla. Admin. Code Ann. R. 9J-5.001(8); 9J-5.005(1)(c)1.
31. Id. R. 9J-5.003(51).
32. Id. R. 9J-5.003(81).
33. Id. R. 9J-5.003(89).
34. Fla. Stat. § 163.3194(1)(a) and (b).
35. Id. § 163.3194(3)(a) and (b).
36. 502 So.2d 931 (Fla. 4th DCA 1987).
37. Id. at 933, 937.
38. Id. at 939.
39. Id. at 936.
40. Id. at 936-940.
41. 774 So.2d 763 (Fla. 1st DCA 2000).
42. Id. at 766-767.
43. Id.

44. 795 So.2d 191 (Fla. 4th DCA 2001).
45. Id. at 2003.
46. Id. at 2003-204.
47. Id. at 209.
48. 608 So.2d 59 (Fla. 5th DCA 1992).
49. Id. at 61-62.
50. Id. at 63.
51. Id. at 63-64.
52. 438 U.S. 104 (1978).
53. Id. at 132.
54. 285 N.E. 2d 291 (1972), *appeal dismissed,* 409 U.S. 1003 (1972).
55. Id. at 294-95, 302-304.
56. 772 So.2d 616 (Fla. 4th DCA 2000).
57. Id. at 620.
58. Id. at 621.
59. Fla. Stat. § 337.241(2)-(3) (1987).
60. 563 So.2d 622 (Fla. 1990).
61. Id. at 625-26, 627, n. 13.
62. Fla. Stat. § 163.3177(6)(b).
63. *Palm Beach County v. Wright*, 641 So.2d 50, 51 (Fla. 1994).
64. Id.
65. Id.
66. Id. at 53.
67. Id. at 54.
68. Fla. Stat. § 163.3191(1).
69. Id. § 163.3187(1).
70. Id. § 163.3191(2).
71. Id. § 163.3191(1).
72. Id. § 163.3191(6).
73. Id. § 163.3191(2).
74. Id. § 163.3184(1)(b).
75. Id. § 163.3180.
76. Fla. Admin. Code R. 9J-5.006(5).
77. Fla. Stat. § 163.3177(6)(f).
78. Id. § 163.3177(6)(d).
79. Chapter 187, Fla. Stat. (2004).
80. Fla. Stat. § 163.3177(10)(b).
81. Chapter 186, Fla. Stat. (2004).
82. Fla. Stat. § 373.0361.
83. Fla. Stat. § 163.3177(6)(c).
84. Id. § 163.3177 (6)(h); 163.31776; 163.3180(13).
85. Id. § 163.3184.
86. Id.
87. Id. §163.3184(9) & (10).
88. Id. § (11); 163.3189(2)(b).
89. Id. § 163.3189(2)(a).
90. 507 P. 2d 23 (Ore. 1973).
91. 627 So.2d 469 (Fla. 1993).
92. Id. at 474.
93. Id. at 475-76.
94. 589 So.2d 1337 (Fla. 3d DCA 1991).

95. Fla. Stat. § 286.0115.

96. Fla. Stat. § 163.3215(4).

97. Id. § 163.3194(3)(a) and (b).

98. 519 So.2d 629 (Fla. 3d DCA 1978).

99. Id. at 633-34.

100. Id. at 632.

101. Id.

102. Id.

103. 627 So.2d at 475.

104. 62 P. 3d 912 (Wash. Ct. App. 2003).

105. Id. at 918.

106. Id.

107. 774 So.2d 763 (Fla. 1st DCA 2000).

108. Id. at 765.

109. Id.

110. Id.

111. Id.

112. 795 So.2d 191 (Fla. 4th DCA 2001).

113. Id. at 197.

114. Id. at 198.

115. Id.

116. Ore. Rev. Stat. § 197.829.

11

Commentary: The Role of the Comprehensive Plan

Nancy E. Stroud

I would like to make a few comments on the observations that Mr. Sullivan (Chapter 9) and Mr. Pelham (Chapter 10) have so cogently made about comprehensive planning in the mandatory state-planning systems of states such as Florida and Oregon. I also have some remarks on the reforms that are currently being proposed to the Florida comprehensive planning act. First, however, I would like to join the others here and thank Dan Mandelker for the rare opportunity to participate with the "brain trust" at this conference and to talk and think about planning reform for the new century.

Mr. Sullivan and Mr. Pelham seem to agree that our prayers for comprehensive planning, indeed, have been answered, at least in part in those states that require comprehensive plans, as well as in many states that do not require comprehensive plans. "In accordance with the comprehensive plan" has grown to mean, in a substantial number of states even where not mandated, that plans must be given an influential role in the land development and regulation process.

This has had the beneficial effect of holding local governments and the judiciary to a more honest evaluation of local land development decisions. It is particularly the case where local decisions are made pursuant to a quasi-judicial process, which requires adequate findings and analysis of the proposed land development. The comprehensive plan has also gained significance where the plan is required to have specificity and internal consistency.

Mr. Sullivan particularly in his paper speaks of how the language of the plan is important and how plans must be carefully drafted so that they can have legal meaning and effect that is sensible and understandable. We also see in the papers that both gentlemen agree that comprehensive plans are more meaningful when they carry forward important state policies, as in Oregon and Florida.

Both papers refer to the prophetic works of 40 to 50 years ago by both Richard Babcock and Dan Mandelker, and by others, who argued that comprehensive planning should be a basis of land development regulation, that regional and state needs should be considered in comprehensive plans, and that, where comprehensive planning is a basis for land regulations, there is more likely to be procedural fairness in the entire land development process. Procedural fairness, I agree with Mr. Pelham, in itself is an important result even if comprehensive plans do not solve every land development problem that might occur.

I have spent my career working within the Florida comprehensive planning system and I am particularly convinced that it is an effective and very workable system that carries forward the planning reform advocated in the last century. Over the 20 years since the adoption of Florida's most meaningful comprehensive planning act, the legislation has been frequently amended and is subject to considerable criticism for its failures; however, I remain convinced that it is fundamentally an important and ground-breaking planning system and continues to provide an example of reform that is worthwhile pursuing in this century.

What is it about the Florida system that establishes the comprehensive plan as more than just a paper exercise? I can offer a number of reasons. First, because of the way the system has unfolded in Florida, local governments and citizens have gained the perception that the state process is actually more powerful than it is, and that the state Department of Community Affairs has more influence and more strength to make plans better than perhaps it really does—and frankly that may not be a bad thing.

One hears from planners and local government officials that having a state presence in the process, as it is in Florida, is a convenient excuse to do good comprehensive planning. Perhaps that in itself is a good reason to have a system like Florida's. The perception that the state is stronger than it is makes local governments and all parties in the process reluctant to take on a fight with the state, especially if they have completed a local process that often is, if not tedious, contentious and painful. Once a local government through this process has adopted its plan and is fairly satisfied with the result, no one wants to then take on the state. If the state makes suggestions for improvements to the plan during the compliance review process, local governments will often make the improvements without too much of a fight.

Second, in Florida, the judiciary has played a very important role in keeping the comprehensive plan meaningful. This is in part because the language of the statute is very strong and thus can reasonably be interpreted the way that the judiciary has interpreted it, to require strict scrutiny of land development actions that must be consistent with the plan. This standard of review is not a constitutional standard of "strict scrutiny" but rather a more moderate standard, and Mr. Pelham has described this in his paper.

The fact that Florida local governments are not given deference by the courts in the interpretation of their comprehensive plan means that the courts have a strong role in the comprehensive planning system. This judicial interpretation of the Florida planning statute may also be in part a political legacy from the fact that many of the state's appellate judges were appointed in the 1970s and 1980s—a time of progressive change in Florida government—so that the judiciary in some part still reflects that progressive viewpoint.

Third, the processes set up in the comprehensive planning act help to ensure that the comprehensive plan is present in the thoughts of planners and local government participants when reviewing land development decisions. Even if local decision-makers rarely read the plan, they know as a result of certain processes that the plan is important and, if it is mentioned, they need to pay attention.

Let me point out a few ways in which this occurs. In the Florida system, every local government must have a "local planning agency"; once established, the local planning agency must review all land development regulations for consistency with the plan. In many circumstances, the local planning agency is the city council or the county commission itself. When reviewing and adopting land development regulations, the decision-making body is continually reminded of the requirement to be consistent with the comprehensive plan.

Additionally, the comprehensive plan must go through periodic review, which is another opportunity for it to come before the local decision-makers in a public process. Any amendments to a comprehensive plan undergo regional and state reviews, so local decision-makers know that not only are local citizens watching the process, but other parties (e.g., the adjacent local governments, the regional agencies, and the state agencies) will be able to review their actions regarding the local plan.

Finally, the threat of third-party litigation keeps the comprehensive plan meaningful. In Florida, by statute, third-party challengers have liberal standing to challenge decisions that are inconsistent with the plan. One of the decisions that Mr. Pelham discusses in his paper, the *Pinecrest Lakes* case,[1] made it very clear that local government decisions that are inconsistent with the plan can have severe consequences. *Pinecrest Lakes* held that a development that is approved and built, but which is inconsistent with the plan, can be required to be torn down. The decision in fact says that the judiciary has no discretion if asked but to require that it be torn down.[2]

Additionally, the Florida courts, starting with the *Snyder* case,[3] have required that land development decisions such as rezonings be conducted pursuant to quasi-judicial procedures. During the quasi-judicial proceeding, evidence is taken, the evidence has to be evaluated according to criteria, and an important criterion for approval is consistency with the comprehensive plan. This process emphasizes the importance of the comprehensive plan. The process also helps to make the system of land development regulation more transparent and honest, which is contrary to the excesses of the "zoning game" that we learned about from Richard Babcock's renowned and admired book.[4]

The Florida system has been subject to criticism and change over the years and this year is no exception. The new secretary of the Department of Community Affairs has proposed a comprehensive set of changes that is being seriously reviewed by state legislative committees and planning professionals.[5]

One interesting and important proposal is to devolve the state review and approval of comprehensive plan amendments to the regions, giving regions more responsibility to ensure the adequacy of plans. Notably, the proposal mentions the possibility of addressing "regional concurrency," possibly suggesting a greater importance to regional affordable housing problems. The proposal seeks to reduce and at the same time focus the state role for comprehensive planning on certain state policy areas, such as transportation, natural disasters, environmental protection, and affordable housing. The state role is anticipated in the long term to be further reduced by a certification of local plans that would make unnecessary the state and regional review of those plans. The state would then play a greater role in technical assistance and monitoring of plans through the use of planning "indicators."

The proposal, if successfully implemented, would make critical changes to the system and hopefully those changes are for the good. However, the changes need to be carefully made because, if the system devolves to the regional level, it is only going to be as effective as the regional agencies given responsibility for it. Many fear that the devolution is actually a way for the state to back away from its commitment to comprehensive planning, where a failure of the system can be blamed on the regions while not having first established and supported an effective regional governance system.

When one considers the popular currents apparent, for example, in the adoption of Oregon's Measure 37, one might lose confidence in the ability of a meaningful comprehensive planning system to survive much less undergo significant reform. Perhaps on the other hand, as Mr. Sullivan has suggested in his comments here, the Oregon referendum measure is so complicated and so fraught with potential problems that it might just implode on itself.

Certainly Florida is not immune to such currents. Comprehensive planning in Florida has a good track record as an effective and meaningful tool—one that brings transparency to the land development process and thus integrity to that process. Because of the strength of the system, I continue to hope that it functions well into this new century.

NANCY E. STROUD NOTES

1. *Pinecrest Lakes, Inc. v. Shidel,* 795 So.2d 191 (Fla. 4th DCA 2001).
2. Id.
3. *Board of County Commissioners of Brevard County v. Snyder,* 627 So.2d 469 (Fla. 1993).
4. Richard F. Babcock, *The Zoning Game: Municipal Practices and Policies* (Madison: The University of Wisconsin Press, 1966).
5. The 2005 Florida legislature adjourned prior to the publication of this commentary without adopting significant changes to the comprehensive planning law.

Housing and Regulatory Streamlining

CHAPTER

12

Trying to Remove Regulatory Barriers to Affordable Housing

Anthony Downs

INTRODUCTION

Concerning any well-known subject, there are some things that supposedly "everyone knows." When it comes to affordable housing, everyone knows that complex and time-consuming local government regulations are an important cause of why housing costs so much in America and therefore why so many people find housing "unaffordable." I believe the key issues about regulatory barriers to affordability are not "What is the impact of local regulations on housing?" or "Which regulatory barriers impede affordable housing the most?" Rather, they are "Why do communities adopt such barriers?" and "What can we do about it?" Therefore, this paper will discuss these last two issues.

My qualifications to discuss these subjects are that:

- I have been on two federal commissions focused on them;
- I have written or edited several books on them; and
- I submitted a paper to the Millennial Housing Commission on them (which, I must admit, it completely ignored).

However, my approach to this subject differs from the approaches of most others. Moreover, my views on this subject are considered by many elected officials too radical to be used as the basis for public policy. I will start with my basic conclusion.

THE POLITICAL CAUSE OF COST-RAISING
LOCAL GOVERNMENT REGULATIONS

In my opinion, many suburban governments in the United States deliberately pass local regulations aimed at maintaining or raising housing prices within their jurisdictions. They do so because they are politically dominated by homeowners, who form a majority of the residents in most suburbs. Those homeowners want to maximize the market values of their homes. This view has been well stated by William Fischel in his book *The Homevoter Hypothesis.*[1] Such homeowners believe that any less costly housing in their neighborhoods might threaten their ability to maximize the market values of their own homes. Since their homes are their major financial assets, they pressure their governments to oppose cost-reducing changes in regulation such as permitting apartments or other lower-cost housing nearby. Therefore, *as long as we leave full regulatory power over housing planning and construction in the hands of local governments, there is no realistic chance that housing costs can be reduced by changing regulations that increase those costs.*

This *economic* motivation to maintain high housing costs is reinforced by two widespread *social desires* among Americans. One is to live in neighborhoods occupied by others who are at least as well off economically as they are, and surely not worse off. The other is found among most whites, who do not want to live in neighborhoods where African Americans comprise more than about 25 to 33 percent of the residents. Both these social goals are also served by keeping housing prices high.

Thus, *merely urging local governments to change their regulations in recognition that society needs more affordable suburban housing is a waste of time.* The elected officials who run those governments have no incentives to change the policies their voters want, yet such exhortation is the main action carried out by every past federal housing commission—with no perceptible results whatever. Those who seriously consider this subject agree with me privately, but almost no one in authority has the guts to come out and say it, because local "sovereignty" over housing policies is a sacred cow that few are willing to challenge.

THE FUNDAMENTAL HOUSING AFFORDABILITY PROBLEM

The U.S. Department of Housing and Urban Development (HUD) has declared that any low-income household that spends more than 30 percent of its income on housing has a "housing affordability" problem.[2] HUD further defines that any household with an income lower than 80 percent of its region-wide median income can be considered to have a "low income."[3] Also, any household with an income below 50 percent of its region-wide median income has a "very low income."[4] Thirty percent of income was presumably chosen because HUD concluded that any low-income household spending more than that share on housing would be quite likely to be unable to afford other basic necessities of life such as food, medical care, and transportation.

By using HUD's definition of housing affordability problems, this concludes that a very large proportion of all American households have such problems (see Table 12-1).

There were 105.5 million American households in 2000. The 2000 census revealed that about 39.4 percent of them (41.6 million households) had incomes roughly below 80 percent of the national median income. One-third of all households (35.7 million) were renters, of whom 21.9 million had low incomes; 13.2 million of those low-income renters spent more than 30 percent of their incomes on housing in 1999. Another two-thirds (69.8 million households) were owner-occupants, of whom 19.7 million had low incomes; 9.0 million of those were spending 30 percent or more on housing. Thus, 22.3 million American households (21.1 percent of all American households and 53.6 percent of all those with incomes below 80 percent of the national median) had problems in 1999 by this definition.

Since then, housing costs have risen much more sharply than household incomes. According to the National Association of Realtors, the median sales price of single-family homes sold (in current dollars) rose from $133,300 in 1999 to $191,000 in June 2004, a gain of 43.2 percent in five years.[5] (In California, median home prices rose 123.4 percent in that same period.[6]) However, U.S. median household incomes rose only slightly in the same five-year period, so a lot more households are having "housing affordability problems" today than they did just five years ago.

One possible reaction to the high numbers of households considered to have housing affordability problems by HUD's definitions is to adopt some other set of definitions that produces lower numbers. This is the tactic adopted by the State of New Jersey's Council on Affordable Housing (COAH).[7] Its analysts thought that using HUD's definitions would designate so many households as in need of assistance that no reasonable government would ever be able to aid all or even most of them—especially through programs involving new housing construction.

Therefore, COAH adopted another method of counting the number of households "needing assistance." COAH counts all those existing housing units that are seriously deficient because they lack plumbing or kitchens as one part of its definition. Then it adds an estimate of the number of future low-income households that will not be adequately served by older units "filtering" downward in the inventory or by new construction.

COAH's method produces much smaller estimates of the number of affordable housing units that New Jersey needs to create in the future than would the use of HUD's definitions. However, though I have great respect for Professor Robert Burchell of Rutgers and his colleagues, who have developed this method, I confess I cannot understand how it works—even after reading

Table 12-1. U.S. Households' Spending on Housing in 2000

	Total American Households	Percent	Owners	Percent	Renters	Percent
	105,480,101	**100.00**	69,816,513	**66.19**	35,663,588	**33.81**
Median income = $41,994						
Incomes below 80% of median	41,605,404	**39.44**	19,735,660	**28.27**	21,869,743	**61.32**
Low incomes, spending 30% or more =	22,283,582	**21.13**	9,020,293	**12.92**	13,263,288	**37.19**
All incomes, spending 30% or more =	29,564,591	**28.03**	15,352,651	**21.99**	14,211,940	**39.85**
INCOME IN 1999	Low income groups in boldface					
Less than $10,000:	**9,586,419**	9.09	**3,225,466**	4.62	**6,360,953**	17.84
$10,000 to $19,999:	**12,525,452**	11.87	**5,751,910**	8.24	**6,773,542**	18.99
$20,000 to $34,999:	**19,493,533**	18.48	**10,758,285**	15.41	**8,735,248**	24.49
$35,000 to $49,999:	17,127,559	16.24	11,357,763	16.27	5,769,796	16.18
$50,000 to $74,999:	21,133,960	20.04	16,356,946	23.43	4,777,015	13.39
$75,000 to $99,999:	11,558,521	10.96	9,824,035	14.07	1,734,486	4.86
$100,000 to $149,999:	9,382,193	8.89	7,869,644	11.27	1,512,549	4.24
$150,000 or more:	4,672,465	4.43	4,672,465	6.69		
Totals	105,480,101	100	69,816,513	100	35,663,588	100

Table 12-1. U.S. Households' Spending on Housing in 2000 (continued)

Total Households	105,539,122
Less than $10,000	10,067,027
$10,000 to $14,999	6,657,228
$15,000 to $19,999	6,601,020
$20,000 to $24,999	6,935,945
$25,000 to $29,999	6,801,010
$30,000 to $34,999	6,718,232
$35,000 to $39,999	6,236,192
$40,000 to $44,999	5,965,869
$45,000 to $49,999	5,244,211
$50,000 to $59,999	9,537,175
$60,000 to $74,999	11,003,429
$75,000 to $99,999	10,799,245
$100,000 to $124,999	5,491,526
$125,000 to $149,999	2,656,300
$150,000 to $199,999	2,322,038
$200,000 or more	2,502,675
Total	105,539,122

Source: U.S. Census Bureau, American Factfinder, Data Sets, Census 2000 Summary File 4, Detailed Tables on the Census Bureau (http://factfinder.census.gov/servlet/ DTGeoSearchByListServlet? ds_name=DEC_2000_ SF4_U&_lang=en&_ts=132738076687), 2002.

their detailed description of it.[8] Yet I believe that pursuing alternative definitions of how many households suffer from housing affordability problems
may be a fruitful path to follow.

Such "housing affordability problems" arise because millions of American
households cannot afford to buy or rent shelter that meets prevailing middle-
class standards of "decent quality" without spending more than 30 percent of
their incomes for housing. This situation occurs because many households
have low incomes, and because "decent" homes—especially new units—cost
too much due mainly to the high building standards we require. Those standards have little to do with health and safety; they are effectively exclusionary.

HOW HOUSING AFFORDABILITY PROBLEMS
MANIFEST THEMSELVES IN AMERICA

In practice, American housing affordability problems have five different manifestations. The first is *the simple "gap" between the incomes of the very poor and
minimum costs of reasonably adequate shelter.* Our economy needs many low-
wage workers who do not earn enough to close this "gap" but who need to
live somewhere near their jobs. This aspect is found in all metropolitan areas
and relates to the next one.

The second manifestation is *the absence of affordable housing in new-growth
areas, especially affluent suburbs.* These are the areas where most new jobs are
being created; hence, low-wage workers need to live in or near such areas.
However, such areas often adopt building codes that prevent construction of
low-cost housing. This causes many poor people—especially minorities—to
become concentrated in older, inner-city neighborhoods with highly undesirable consequences.

The third manifestation is regional. *Housing costs vary immensely among specific metropolitan areas.* Median home sales prices are over six times as high in
the most costly area (the San Francisco Bay Area) than in the least costly region
(Ocala, Florida). Income variations among metro areas are much less
extreme—only about 2.5 to 1.[9] Regressions show that the most powerful factor
underlying high prices in 2000 was high prices in 1990. Removing that factor,
the most significant positive factors are increases in regional jobs and income,
warm winter climate, share of apartments in the central city, and percentage of
old housing therein. The presence of central city decline is a strong negative
factor. Thus, housing affordability problems also affect middle-income people
in high-cost regions. Those regions include California, Boston, New York, Seattle, and Washington.

The fourth manifestation concerns revitalization of older, in-city neighborhoods through *the process of gentrification*, which causes housing prices to rise.
This may lead poorer residents there to be displaced or to experience hard-
ships due to rising rents. This problem is inherent in any upgrading of older
areas, so it cannot be eliminated.

The last manifestation arises from *the immigration of very poor people from abroad*, many of whom arrive in this nation annually with almost no money, often illegally. At first, they cannot afford "decent" accommodations and do not qualify for subsidies. Hence, they must live overcrowded in older quarters until they amass enough money to move into "decent" shelter. Their occupancy of slum dwellings is usually temporary, but when they move out, other newcomers move in.

This problem is essentially unavoidable. We cannot stop this constant inflow of poor immigrants because:

- Our wages are much higher than the wages in their home nations; and
- We are unwilling to adopt the draconian and brutal border policy of killing anyone who attempts to enter the nation illegally, as the Soviets did to people trying to leave the Iron Curtain.

To accommodate these poor newcomers, the nation needs a sizable supply of low-cost, substandard housing that becomes overcrowded without being dangerous. In short, *we rely on such slum housing to accommodate this ever-changing group of very poor people and some poor households who have permanently low incomes.*

HOW TWO SETS OF FORCES HAVE RECENTLY CAUSED HOUSING MARKETS TO BECOME LESS ACCEPTING OF AFFORDABLE HOUSING

Two sets of forces have recently influenced housing markets to be more hostile to affordable housing: *structural conditions* and *dynamic forces*.

Structural Conditions

A key structural condition is *a greater increase in citizen participation* in land-use decisions over the years. Housing development was once politically dominated by homebuilders, but their influence has been overshadowed. Local citizens have become more informed and better organized to fight neighborhood changes, and planning laws require more citizen participation. Also, new environmental laws require countless studies before developments can be approved. Each step is an opportunity for a lawsuit aimed at stopping new construction or causing long delays, which are costly to the developers involved.

A second structural condition is *the homeownership bias in federal housing policy*. Owners receive large-scale tax benefits that encourage investment in bigger dwellings. Low-income renters comprise the vast majority of people with serious housing problems, but the value of subsidies they receive is small compared to benefits enjoyed by homeowners—especially wealthy ones. This bias strengthens the political clout that homevoters exercise over local governments. The bias is justified by beliefs that homeowners are better citizens. The claim that homeownership helps build household wealth is sounder, but those who need help most are poor renters. Ironically, the more public policy emphasizes homeownership, the more it leads to NIMBY (Not In My Back Yard) resistance to affordable housing by suburban homeowner majorities.

The third structural condition is the *fragmented control over land-use decisions* built into local governments in America. This control results in parochial attitudes by local officials, who adopt policies designed to benefit only their voting constituents and push off costs onto other jurisdictions. Nobody is motivated to serve the interests of the whole region, yet few elected officials are willing to challenge local control over housing policy because most American homeowners want to be able to influence who lives near them, for the reasons I have explained. Therefore, localities adopt laws concerning lot size, setbacks, building materials, rejection of multifamily units, and others that are by no means required for health and safety but are purely exclusionary in nature.

Dynamic Forces

Several dynamic forces operating within those structural conditions have produced a rising tide of resistance towards affordable housing, expressed in higher regulatory barriers.

The most important dynamic factor is *inescapable regional population growth.* Many metropolitan areas are going to grow fast whether their residents want such growth or not. The causes of growth are both a natural increase and immigration from outside. Our nation's compound annual growth rate of total population in the 1990s was about 1.24 percent per year.[10] We cannot stop immigration from abroad, so we are surely going to keep growing, especially in certain attractive regions, even if existing residents there do not want growth.

In fact, no specific region can control its own growth rate. That rate is determined by the region's basic traits such as location, climate, topography, demography, and past investments in businesses and institutions. The most attractive big regions grow much faster than the nation (e.g., five grew at rates above 3 percent per year, and nine more grew from 2 to 3 percent per year in the 1990s).[11] Attempts by local governments to limit their own growth just push the region's growth to other parts of the region—usually farther out—aggravating sprawl. Because local governments are parochial, most care only about their own growth rates, ignoring the effects that local policies have on regional growth.

The second dynamic factor consists of the *problems that accompany fast growth*, especially rising traffic congestion. However, congestion would get worse even with no growth, since Americans keep driving more vehicles farther per capita each year.[12] These problems irritate millions of citizens who conclude that slower growth would help. Growth does produce more problems, which might be mitigated if it stopped, but no region can stop its own growth via local policies. Also, growth produces many important benefits such as providing more young workers to support our aging population and add to rising output.

The third dynamic factor is *the smart growth movement*. Its advocates support three axioms hostile to affordable housing:

1. Strong citizen participation;
2. Support for fragmented local control over land-use policies; and
3. An implicit axiom that local governments should never adopt policies that might inhibit increases in home values.

This hostility is disguised as fiscal responsibility under the theory of *fiscal zoning*. That theory declares that no *new* local uses should be permitted if they add more to spending than to tax revenues. Multifamily housing is considered a fiscal loser, although it generates fewer children per unit than most single-family housing—except the costliest. In fact, fiscal zoning denies local shelter for all low-wage workers, even though local and regional economies need such workers to function. For this reason, universal use of local fiscal zoning by all or most communities within a region is a disaster for that region as a whole, yet many areas use it because each local government looks only at its own residents' welfare.

IMPACTS OF THE WEALTH EFFECT FROM RISING HOME PRICES

Another critical factor supporting local government hostility to more affordable housing is *the immense increase in homeowner wealth caused by a sizable rise in home prices* across the nation—and much of the world—in the past decade. The median price of housing in the United States as a whole measured in current dollars increased by 51.0 percent from 1990 to 2000, and by another 37.4 percent from 2000 to June 2004, according to the National Association of Realtors.[13] That was a surge of 107.6 percent in 13.5 years, or a compound annual growth rate of 5.6 percent per year—more than double the 2.5 percent compound annual growth rate of inflation in the same period.

Inflation was kept low during this period mainly because of the entry of millions of low-wage Chinese and some Indian workers into the world's industrialized labor force in this same period. Their entry comprised almost a 29 percent increase in the world's supply of industrialized labor—all at low wages.[14] This immense change kept manufacturing firms around the developed world from being able to raise prices, thereby holding inflation at low levels. Those low levels of inflation inspired central banks throughout the developed world to reduce interest rates, which in turn stimulated an upward movement in housing prices. Millions of former renters were able to buy homes under these conditions, pushing up the demand for ownership housing. At the same time, a worldwide collapse in stock prices in 2000 caused many investors to shift capital from stocks into real estate—including ownership housing—thereby further increasing upward pressures on housing prices.

Thus, ironically, the supposed loss of U.S. manufacturing jobs to China and India bemoaned by John Kerry in the 2004 election campaign was a central cause of a huge enrichment of American homeowners of all economic classes. Contrary to popular opinion, most of the loss of U.S. manufacturing jobs, which began in 1979 and has continued steadily since then, was caused by rising productivity within American factories. Though some U.S. jobs were lost to foreign firms, the main impact of foreign, low-wage workers was to check inflation worldwide.

This linkage of rising home prices in America—and all over the developed world—to increasing numbers of low-wage Chinese and other foreign workers in modern industries may seem a far-fetched argument, but it is not. Trillions of dollars of additional equity were added to the balance sheets of American households by rising home prices, thereby stimulating higher retail sales to those households as well, and sustaining developed economies worldwide through the mild recession of 2000 to 2002. The most spectacular results occurred in California, where housing prices in current dollars soared by 123 percent in the five years from 1999 to 2004.[15] In fact, after subtracting mortgage debt from higher home prices, and converting current dollars to constant 2004 dollars, I calculated that California homeowners as a group gained a much bigger total increase in net housing equity from 1999 to 2004 than all other homeowners in all 49 other states combined!

What does all this have to do with regulatory barriers to housing? Plenty! Homeowners who have gained huge increases in their net worth from rising home prices become zealots against any factors likely to threaten those equity gains. Further, they believe that permitting lower-cost housing anywhere near their own homes might slow down or reverse the price gains from which they have benefited.

The resulting implicit homeowner conspiracy to avoid jeopardizing rising home values is tacitly supported by homebuilders, realtors, local government officials coveting property taxes, retailers, and the entire mortgage finance industry, which has trillions of dollars in home loans at stake. *This politically powerful group of economic interests strongly opposes any policies that might raise overall housing supplies enough to stop or slow rising home prices.* Yet any general increase in housing affordability requires a significant decline in housing prices across the board. So the simple reason America does not have more affordable housing is because two-thirds of American households—home-owners—and the entire housing finance industry and all those other interests mentioned above do not want it. No elected officials at any level of government are going to act against the combined wishes of those powerful groups.

WHERE HOUSING AFFORDABILITY APPEARS TO BE WORST

Since incomes do not vary nearly as much from region to region as housing prices, there are two ways to estimate which regions have the worst housing affordability problems. One way is by the *absolute level of home sales prices*; the higher the prices are in a region, the less affordable the housing is there. By this measure (using 2004 National Association of Realtors home sales price data), both California and coastal parts of the northeast seem to have the least affordable housing (see Table 12-2). It contains median home sales prices for the 50 highest-priced metropolitan areas as of the first quarter of 2004, ranked from highest to lowest.

The second way to estimate which regions may have serious housing affordability problems is by *recent percentage increases on housing prices*; the greater those increases are, the less affordable housing may have become for many residents there. By this measure (also using National Association of Realtors home sales price data), regions that may have serious housing affordability problems are both concentrated in Florida and scattered around the nation (see Table 12-3). It contains regions with the 50 largest percentage increases in median home sales prices from the second quarter of 1990 to the first quarter of 2004. Because California had declining home prices in the 1990s, its regions do not dominate this table, but many Florida regions had sharp home price increases in this period; in six of those regions, prices rose over 100 percent.

The data in these tables suggest that housing affordability problems probably exist in a great many American metropolitan areas in all parts of the nation, but especially in California, the coastal northeast, and Florida. However, since low-income households reside in nearly every metropolitan region, such problems are most likely found almost everywhere.

This conclusion is confirmed by the report, *State of the Nation's Housing: 2004*, published by the Joint Center for Housing Studies of Harvard University, which states:

> "Although the overwhelming majority of Americans are well housed, nearly a third of all households spend 30 percent or more of their incomes on housing and 13 percent spend 50 percent or more. In addition . . . crowding is on the increase, some 2.5 to 3.5 million people are homeless at some point in a given year, and nearly 2 million households still live in severely inadequate units. . . . Fully half of lowest-income households spend at least 50 percent of their incomes on housing."[16]

Although the nation's overall housing supply has grown remarkably in the past decade, the supply of low-cost units affordable to low-income households continues to decline.

THE RESULTING FOREST OF REGULATORY OBSTACLES TO CREATION OF MORE AFFORDABLE HOUSING

The result of all these factors is that we are increasingly refusing to create additional housing affordable to the lower strata of our income groups. This

Table 12-2. Regions with the Highest Median Home Sales Prices in Q1, 2004

Rank	Metropolitan Area	Median Price in 2004: Q1	Rank	Metropolitan Area	Median Price in 2004: Q1
1	San Francisco Bay Area, CA	597.30	26	New Haven/Meriden, CT	225.00
2	San Diego, CA	483.00	27	Las Vegas, NV	224.90
3	Honolulu, HI	420.00	28	Baltimore, MD	220.10
4	Los Angeles Area, CA	387.70	29	Portland, ME	218.10
5	Nassau/Suffolk, NY	384.00	30	Hartford, CT	212.30
6	Bergen/Passaic, NJ	379.40	31	Trenton, NJ	208.80
7	New York/N. New Jersey/Long Island, NY/NJ/CT	369.70	32	Minneapolis/St. Paul, MN/WI	205.00
8	Boston, MA	347.10	33	Madison, WI	195.20
9	Newark, NJ	334.30	34	Portland, OR	195.10
10	Middlesex/Somerset/Hunterdon, NJ	322.70	35	Bradenton, FL	188.90
11	Washington, DC/MD/VA	300.70	36	Tacoma, WA	185.90
12	Monmouth/Ocean, NJ	298.00	37	Milwaukee, WI	182.30
13	Seattle, WA	282.50	38	Colorado Springs, CO	181.40
14	Sacramento, CA	277.90	39	Charleston, SC	177.10
15	W. Palm Beach/Boca Raton/Delray Beach, FL	267.00	40	Raleigh/Durham, NC	174.60
16	Riverside/San Bernardino, CA	258.90	41	Ft. Myers/Cape Coral, FL	171.80
17	Worcester, MA	256.40	42	Wilmington, DE/NJ/MD	169.70
18	Miami/Hialeah, FL	245.90	43	Tucson, AZ	164.30
19	Ft. Lauderdale/Hollywood/Pompano Beach, FL	243.40	44	Philadelphia, PA/NJ	162.10
20	Lake County, IL	242.00	45	Phoenix, AZ	155.80
21	Providence, RI	239.90	46	Eugene/Springfield, OR	155.10
22	Sarasota, FL	239.90	47	Richmond/Petersburg, VA	153.00
23	Denver, CO	231.80	48	Orlando, FL	151.10
24	Chicago, IL	228.10	49	Tampa/St. Petersburg/Clearwater, FL	149.30
25	Reno, NV	227.50	50	Salt Lake City/Ogden, UT	148.00

Source: National Association of Realtors, *Real Estate Outlook: Market Trends and Insights,* September 1990 and June 2004.

**Table 12-3. Regions with the Largest Percentage Gains
in Median Home Sales Prices from 1990 to 2004**

Rank	Metropolitan Area	1990 Q2 Price	2004 Q1 Price	% Gain
1	Miami/Hialeah, FL	89.00	245.90	176.3
2	Denver, CO	87.00	231.80	166.4
3	Ft. Lauderdale/Hollywood/Pompano Beach, FL	92.20	243.40	164.0
4	San Diego, CA	183.70	483.00	162.9
5	W. Palm Beach/Boca Raton/Delray Beach, FL	108.20	267.00	146.8
6	Ft. Myers/Cape Coral, FL	69.90	171.80	145.8
7	Portland, OR	79.70	195.10	144.8
8	Madison, WI	80.00	195.20	144.0
9	Las Vegas, NV	93.30	224.90	141.1
10	Nassau/Suffolk, NY	161.90	384.00	137.2
11	Des Moines, IA	58.10	133.30	129.4
12	Charleston, SC	77.20	177.10	129.4
13	Minneapolis/St. Paul, MN/WI	90.30	205.00	127.0
14	San Francisco Bay Area, CA	263.60	597.30	126.6
15	Daytona Beach, FL	63.80	142.90	124.0
16	Baltimore, MD	100.90	220.10	118.1
17	Salt Lake City/Ogden, UT	69.20	148.00	113.9
18	Omaha, NE/IA	61.40	130.80	113.0
19	Spokane, WA	55.30	117.40	112.3
20	Tampa/St. Petersburg/Clearwater, FL	70.40	149.30	112.1
21	New York/N. New Jersey/Long Island, NY/NJ/CT	175.40	369.70	110.8
22	Milwaukee, WI	86.60	182.30	110.5
23	Reno, NV	109.00	227.50	108.7
24	Lincoln, NE	61.90	127.70	106.3
25	Middlesex/Somerset/Hunterdon, NJ	157.00	322.70	105.5
26	Seattle, WA	139.60	282.50	102.4
27	Lansing/East Lansing, MI	64.10	128.20	100.0
28	Melbourne/Titusville/Palm Bay, FL	71.30	142.30	99.6
29	Washington, DC/MD/VA	150.90	300.70	99.3
30	Sacramento, CA	140.20	277.90	98.2
31	Boston, MA	176.20	347.10	97.0
32	Jacksonville, FL	73.00	143.60	96.7

**Table 12-3. Regions with the Largest Percentage Gains
in Median Home Sales Prices from 1990 to 2004 (continued)**

Rank	Metropolitan Area	1990 Q2 Price	2004 Q1 Price	% Gain
33	Bergen/Passaic, NJ	193.60	379.40	96.0
34	Chicago, IL	116.60	228.10	95.6
35	Kansas City, MO/KS	73.20	142.30	94.4
36	Riverside/San Bernardino, CA	133.20	258.90	94.4
37	New Orleans, LA	66.50	127.30	91.4
38	Worcester, MA	134.80	256.40	90.2
39	Grand Rapids, MI	68.60	130.40	90.1
40	Oklahoma City, OK	54.10	100.90	86.5
41	Kalamazoo, MI	61.20	113.90	86.1
42	Phoenix, AZ	84.00	155.80	85.5
43	Providence, RI	130.50	239.90	83.8
44	Baton Rouge, LA	66.50	122.00	83.5
45	Houston, TX	71.40	130.70	83.1
46	Orlando, FL	83.30	151.10	81.4
47	San Antonio, TX	62.80	113.80	81.2
48	Los Angeles Area, CA	216.90	387.70	78.7
49	Richmond/Petersburg, VA	87.50	153.00	74.9
50	Lexington/Fayette, KY	76.60	129.70	69.3

Source: National Association of Realtors, *Real Estate Outlook: Market Trends and Insights,* various issues.

refusal is accomplished mainly by local governments adopting myriad regulations that make building any housing—especially low-cost housing—extremely difficult and time-consuming, yet we are reducing existing supplies of low-cost units through demolitions, renovations, and higher rents. We constantly set aside more and more land well located for housing as open space reserves, or environmentally fragile areas, or high productivity farmland, or habitats for endangered species. Furthermore, we continuously receive more low-income people into America.

As a result, in many regions, there are far fewer housing units that are affordable to low-income households than there are such households who need those units. Yet we have no effective policies to remedy this situation because a majority of Americans are strongly opposed to such policies. Moreover, the rising price levels of existing housing make subsidizing occupancy for low-income households ever more costly, thereby increasing resistance to any widespread use of such subsidies. Therefore, we must resort to more overcrowding in older neighborhoods to house our poorest households (i.e., *slum housing*).

In reality, America has always depended upon overcrowded and often deteriorated slums to accommodate its poorest urban dwellers . . . and we still do . . . but we do not like to admit it, so we pretend that the word "slum" is obsolete. We do not want to confront the practices we must adopt as a result (e.g., differentially enforced housing codes, which we must loosely enforce in poor parts of big cities to avoid throwing thousands of low-income households out onto the streets).

Faster population growth, including many poor immigrants, plus rising hostility to housing production in certain regions—especially California—has accelerated our reliance upon *overcrowded slum housing* and *far outlying sprawl* to provide shelter. This is worsening the quality of life even for many middle-class households.

True, some smart growth advocates strongly support affordable housing. They promote a diversity of housing types including units for low-wage households all over a region, but that attitude is exceptional. The strongest smart growth advocates are so focused on preserving open space and stopping sprawl that they give little emphasis to housing for the poor. One reason is that the subsidies needed would be very costly if we maintain high standards; a stronger reason is the potential loss of homevoter support if they adopt that view.

SOME POSSIBLE PUBLIC POLICIES TO CHANGE THIS SITUATION

In theory, there are two basic ways to "solve" housing affordability problems (i.e., to eliminate them for those households experiencing them):

1. Raise the incomes of poor households, or provide them with subsidies, so they can pay the high prices required to obtain decent shelter.

2. Reduce the cost of decent units by, for example, reducing the minimum quality standards we demand, improving the terms of ownership, reducing various regulatory barriers erected by local and other governments, and expanding the supply of housing enough through massive new production to drive down the prices of existing units.

Unfortunately, both of these basic approaches are strongly opposed by most American households. The first approach (adequate subsidies for all low-income households) has long been considered too costly by the U.S. Congress and federal administrations. In 1949, Congress declared that providing "every American household with a decent dwelling unit in a suitable neighborhood" was a national goal,[17] but Congress has never provided enough money to come close to achieving that goal. For decades, the federal government has provided only enough money to aid less than half of the households that its own agency—HUD—declares need housing assistance. The reluctance of both of these branches of the federal government to "cure" housing problems through adequate subsidies is presumably based on their belief that the American public does not want to pay that sizable cost through redistributive policies.

The second approach (reducing the cost of existing and new housing units) is a political anathema to powerful groups in America, as explained earlier. Hence, almost no one in America with any influence publicly espouses this policy on an across-the-board basis.

This leaves only a few alternative tactics available to attacking housing affordability problems effectively. They are discussed in turn below.

• *The first approach is reducing homeowners' fears that affordable housing nearby will reduce the market values of their own homes.* The widespread belief that home values would decline if lower-cost housing is built nearby can be addressed through conducting many more studies of the impacts of lower-cost housing on values and then publicizing the results. In most past studies, those results do not show adverse effects,[18] but homeowners are hard to convince.

A more novel but untested approach suggested by William Fischel[19] is home-value insurance that guarantees that the values of homes near affordable units will not decline, or will rise at some minimal rate, when the existing homeowners sell their homes. The insurance premiums could be paid for by the developers of the affordable housing, or by the locality as a whole.

• *A second approach is to make it legal to build smaller, less costly housing units.* One tactic is to remove zoning obstacles to manufactured housing, which is far less costly than new traditional units. In the past 50 years, over 12 million manufactured housing units have been shipped (one out of every 7.2 new units built),[20] so this is nothing new. A standard, single-wide home contains only 360 square feet.

Another tactic is legalizing accessory housing units added to relatively large, single-family units as a matter of right to the owners of such large units. This could produce thousands of new, low-rent units at no public costs to taxpayers. However, most suburban governments are opposed to such units for fear that they would reduce the market values of nearby homes. There is little clear evidence supporting this view, but it corresponds to the desire of many homeowners to prevent any lower-income households from living near them.

A third tactic is legalizing very small, new, conventionally built homes. I have recently visited large cities and small towns in which thousands of tiny housing units were built in the 1950s and some new ones are being built now. These units often contain less than 500 square feet but have the basic amenities that a family needs. They are better than crowding four families into a 1,000-square-foot unit and they help many low-income households own their own homes.

• *A third approach is a concerted political reaction by powerful groups.* We will react to shortages of affordable housing only when they start to injure two groups with real political clout: (1) employers who cannot find low-wage workers nearby; and (2) middle-class households, especially public workers, who cannot afford decent housing without overly long commutes. Until these groups suffer enough to insist upon mandatory statewide action, remedies are unlikely, thanks to the dominance of local policies by anti-affordability home-owners, and the greater political strength in our national electorate of subur-ban homeowners plus financial institutions. These two groups are suffering the worst problems in California, where the median sales price of ownership housing in June 2004 was $486,020—2.5 times as high as the median for the entire U.S.[21] Yet, even there, political support for decisive action has not yet become strong enough to overcome widespread local government resistance.

USING INCLUSIONARY ZONING TO PROVIDE LOW-INCOME HOUSEHOLDS WITH AFFORDABLE SHELTER

Another approach is using *inclusionary housing or zoning* laws. They require developers of any new units to create from 10 to 20 percent affordable units in exchange for gaining higher density for their market-rate units and other bene-fits. If adopted on a mandatory basis nationwide, this policy could substan-tially add to the affordable housing supply, especially in fast-growing regions. Regulations must require that such units be kept affordable for at least a certain minimum number of years.[22] Such laws are opposed by most homebuilders. They argue that inclusionary zoning imposes the costs of achieving a public policy goal (aiding low-income households) upon private groups (homebuild-ers and landowners) in order to avoid having taxpayers bear those costs.

I believe their argument is essentially correct. Therefore, inclusionary zon-ing laws are legitimate only if two conditions are met:

1. If housing prices are rising fast enough to provide large profits to homebuilders and landowners at the same time they make attaining shelter more difficult for many low-income households; and

2. If the laws are designed both to minimize the extra costs placed upon homebuilders and to provide them with offsetting benefits.

Examples of how homebuilder costs could be minimized include allowing builders to:

• Create affordable units that are smaller and less luxurious than the mar-ket-rate units they build.

• Locate the affordable units they create on sites different from where they build market-rate units.

• Use rental units to act as affordable offsets to market-rate sales units.

• Use accessory apartments to act as affordable units in some cases.

• Benefit from density bonuses and waivers of impact fees, development fees, and local property taxes.

Other offsetting benefits are also conceivable. For example, builders of non-residential structures can also be required to make financial contributions to the creation of affordable housing through "linkage fees." Such fees should vary depending upon the type of structures involved and the number of workers in each type who would probably have low incomes. As for landowners, I believe the costs imposed on them are part of the risks of investing in land, just as the benefits they derive from rising housing prices are part of the rewards from such investments.

I also believe that inclusionary zoning should be applied primarily on a mandatory statewide basis, using the same rules (as described above) in all communities. This will eliminate the ability of individual communities to adopt rules that are ineffective or unfair to homebuilders, or to avoid any policies designed to help low-income households. Also, if every community must add new, affordable housing units, they will become more acceptable in general over time.

A major problem with inclusionary zoning is that it almost certainly could not create enough affordable housing to serve a large percentage of all the households who need housing assistance. As noted earlier, at least 22 million American households both had low incomes and spent over 30 percent of their incomes on housing in 1999.[23] From 1990 to 2003, the average number of housing units started in the United States was 1.459 million.[24]

If that number persisted in the future, and 20 percent were affordable units, that would be 291,800 per year; at 10 percent, it would be 145,900 per year. To provide 22 million households with affordable units at those rates would take 75 years at the 20 percent rate, or 151 years at the 10 percent rate. Of course, by the time those periods had elapsed, the number of households needing aid might be much larger, and many existing housing units would no longer be usable. In any case, *it is clear that inclusionary zoning—even if made mandatory nationwide—cannot "solve" the problem of housing affordability in any complete sense within any reasonable time period.* Rather, inclusionary zoning is what might be termed a "second-best" policy.

However, using "second-best" policies to attack housing problems is nothing new. As noted earlier, Congress has never provided enough money to come close to achieving the national housing goal its own members passed in 1949. For decades, the federal government has provided only enough money to aid less than half of the households that HUD declares need housing assistance.[25] Hence, "second-best" housing policies have long been the basic approach of our entire nation to housing needs.

THE CRUCIAL ROLE OF STATE GOVERNMENT LEADERSHIP IN TACKLING HOUSING PROBLEMS

The Millennial Housing Commission recommended a new subsidized rental housing construction program to expand the supply of affordable units.[26] That is a good idea, but it cannot work well if suburbs continue to prohibit low-cost housing within their borders. *I believe that, in the long run, we will be unable to build or otherwise create sufficient affordable housing—especially in the suburbs where it is most needed—as long as full control over where all housing is located is left entirely up to local governments.* Then, too many such governments will remain dominated by the narrow parochial desires of their homeowning residents (usually a majority of local voters) to protect the values of their homes by excluding any meaningful local construction of affordable housing from their communities.

However, moderating the full control of local governments over housing can only happen if state governments assume a leadership role in grappling with housing problems. Only state governments have the constitutional power to alter the rules controlling what powers local governments can exercise. Recognizing this fact, several states[27] have already passed laws requiring all their localities to adopt specific planning procedures and planning goals concerning their future development. These laws usually set forth certain statewide goals that the governor and state legislators believe should permeate all future growth in their territory. This movement began as a means of protecting delicate physical environments, but it has spread to many other aspects of planning future growth and development. However, some states have been reluctant to include specific housing procedures in these goals for fear of treading upon "local sovereignty" or "home rule." Only the government of the entire state has the breadth of perspective to include the welfare of all those households with low incomes who are besieged by housing affordability problems arising from high housing prices and pervasive regulatory barriers to affordable housing

Experience across the nation shows that significant progress has been made only where the state government has assumed a leadership role in coping with housing problems (e.g., Oregon, Washington, Maryland, New Jersey, California, Georgia, and Florida). Moreover, states are most effective in this subject area if the governor assumes the key leadership role, because the governor can influence all the executive departments and the legislature to do something about such problems. The governor also has the best chance of influencing public opinion in the state as a whole to recognize the importance and seriousness of housing problems.

What should states do? I believe the answer involves the following elements:

- *Set general housing goals* that every municipality, village, and locality must incorporate into their comprehensive plans. Such goals should include acting to improve the welfare of low-income households suffering from housing affordability problems caused by high housing prices. Oregon and Washington provide excellent examples of this step.
- *Set forth specific planning procedures* that every municipality, village, and locality must carry out as part of its planning process. These include:
  - Inventorying all vacant land that might be suitable for future development with housing;
  - Estimating how many additional households will be added to the community through natural increase and immigration and how many jobs will be added through economic development;

o   Relating those added households and added jobs to housing needs for the workers concerned at different income levels;

o   Establishing quantitative zoning needs for future housing development at different price levels over a period of 10 to 20 years into the future; and

o   Tentatively establishing locations for different types of housing zoning needed over those 10 to 20 years as guidelines to homebuilders.

Several states[28] have already established such procedures for their localities. California's mandatory housing element in its municipal planning process requires many of these procedures.

• *Provide for a systematic process of having a state or regional agency review the local plans of every community in the state at least every three years.* This agency should have the power to suggest changes in the community's plans to make them consistent with statewide goals and procedures. Only after communities have satisfied this agency's scrutiny and adapted their plans to its suggestions should the agency approve those plans.

• *Set up a state agency to review the regulatory rules concerning housing of every community in the state over a period of three years,* with this agency having the power to require communities to change their rules if they are excessively exclusionary or cost-increasing. This agency should be staffed by a group of housing experts, housing advocates, homebuilders, and experienced local officials. Any locality that fails to adjust its regulations along the lines suggested by this agency should have its zoning powers suspended until changes are made.

• *Consider having that same state agency set annual "affordable housing targets"* for the state as a whole and for specific subregions of the state. Regional planning bodies in each such region should have the assignment of allocating those "targets" to specific communities. These "targets" need *not* be based on the entire group of households who are considered to have "housing affordability problems" by HUD's definitions, since that might lead to unrealistically high goals that cannot be attained. Instead, the agency should devise its own method of setting "targets" as New Jersey's COAH has done,[29] although I believe its methods are far too complex to be practical.

• *Consider establishing significant financial incentives* to reward those communities that succeed in developing approved plans *and* meeting their affordable housing "targets." These incentives could include infrastructure assistance, school construction assistance, and direct monetary fines for failing to have plans approved or to meet "targets."

• *Pass laws empowering private developers seeking to build affordable housing to sue communities that prevent their doing so if those communities do not have housing plans approved by the state agency mentioned above.* New Jersey has done this.[30]

This may require special courts. Massachusetts has tried this approach with limited success.[31]

• *Investigate the desirability of establishing a mandatory, statewide, inclusionary zoning program* along the lines described earlier in this paper. Such a program would be advisable mainly in those states where housing prices have risen very rapidly to very high levels that are creating serious housing affordability problems for many low- and moderate-income households. California is the outstanding example since, as of 2004, it had the highest and fastest-rising housing prices in the nation.[32]

These are complicated steps not easy to carry out effectively but, unless a state government takes the initiative in doing so, little progress toward making even small, positive steps in attacking housing affordability problems will appear. The parochial desire of local homeowners to protect their home values through exclusionary zoning and other regulations will perpetuate the difficulty of coping with such problems. Up to now, almost no elected officials have been willing to face this situation realistically; they fear the wrath of the suburban homeowning majority and mortgage finance institutions.

CONCLUSION

One of the lessons learned from September 11, 2001, should be the central importance of refocusing the priorities in our daily lives to do those things that are really meaningful. One such thing is providing decent shelter for the low-income households whose contributions to all our lives are crucial, both personally and socially. However, doing that will require the political courage to call for changes in the locus of authority over at least some housing regulations.

ANTHONY DOWNS NOTES

1. William A. Fischel, *The Homevoter Hypothesis* (Cambridge, MA: Harvard University Press, 2001).

2. "The generally accepted definition of affordability is for a household to pay no more than 30 percent of its annual income on housing. Families who pay more than 30 percent of their income for housing are considered cost burdened and may have difficulty affording necessities such as food, clothing, transportation and medical care. An estimated 12 million renter and homeowner households now pay more then 50 percent of their annual incomes for housing, and a family with one full-time worker earning the minimum wage cannot afford the local fair-market rent for a two-bedroom apartment anywhere in the United States. The lack of affordable housing is a significant hardship for low-income households preventing them from meeting their other basic needs, such as nutrition and healthcare, or saving for their future and that of their families." Taken from the Community Development Web site of the U.S. Department of Housing and Urban Development (http://www.hud.gov/offices/cpd/ affordablehousing/index.cfm) (visited April 27, 2005).

3. Department of Housing and Urban Development, HUD User, Income Limits (http://www.huduser.org/datasets/il.html) (visited April 27, 2005). The specific income limits set forth for each community indicate that "very low income" is normally 50 percent of regional median income, and "low income" is 80 percent of regional median income.

4. Id.

5. National Association of Realtors, *Real Estate Outlook: Market Trends and Insights*, Vol. 11, Issue 7 (July 2004), 15, and other earlier issues.

6. California Association of Realtors, *Trends* (June 2004 and February 2000).

7. New Jersey, Council on Affordable Housing, *Guide to Affordable Housing in New Jersey, 2004 Edition* (http://www.state.nj.us/dca/codes/affdhsgguide/index.shtml) (visited April 27, 2005).

8. Id.

9. Note 5, *supra*, Vol. 11, Issue 3 (March 2004), 18-19.

10. U.S. Census Bureau, *Statistical Abstract of the United States: 2004-2005, 124th Edition* (Washington, DC: U.S. Census Bureau, 2004), 7.

11. Id., 26-28.

12. For a comprehensive analysis of traffic congestion, see Anthony Downs, *Still Stuck In Traffic* (Washington, DC: The Brookings Institution, 2004).

13. Note 5, *supra* (various volumes and monthly issues, 1990 through 2004).

14. This estimate was stated by Lael Brainard, Senior Fellow in the Foreign Policy Studies Department of the Brookings Institution, at a briefing at Brookings (Spring 2004).

15. Note 6, *supra* (issues in 2000 and June 2004).

16. Joint Center for Housing Studies, Harvard University, *State of the Nation's Housing: 2004* (Cambridge: Joint Center for Housing Studies, 2004), 4.

17. U.S. Congress, Housing Act of 1949, Title 12, § 1701e.

18. For a discussion of the relation between low-cost housing and the values of nearby homes, see George C. Galster, "The Effects of Multi-Family and Affordable Housing on Market Values of Nearby Homes," in Anthony Downs, *Growth Management and Affordable Housing: Do They Conflict?* (Washington, DC: The Brookings Institution, 2004), 176-211.

19. Note 1, *supra*, 75-281.

20. Manufactured Housing Institute, *Monthly Manufactured Housing Shipments (1959-2005)* (http://www.manufacturedhousing.org/admin/template/subbrochures/387temp.pdf) (visited April 27, 2005).

21. Note 5, *supra* (August 2004) and note 6, *supra* (August 2004).

22. For an in-depth analysis of inclusionary zoning, see Douglas R. Porter, "The Promise and Practice of Inclusionary Zoning," in Anthony Downs, *Growth Management and Affordable Housing: Do They Conflict?* (Washington, DC: The Brookings Institution, 2004), 212-263.

23. See Table 12-2.

24. Note 10, *supra*, 599.

25. Millennial Housing Commission, Table 4, "Project vs. Tenant Based (Subsidized) Units" (http://www.mhc.gov/tables.xls) (visited April 27, 2005).

26. See generally note 25, *supra*.

27. These include California, Florida, Washington, and Oregon.

28. Id.

29. See note 7, *supra*.

30. Id.

31. Massachusetts Department of Housing and Community Development, "Procedural Regulations of the Housing Appeals Committee" (760 CMR 30) and "Housing Appeals Committee: Criteria for Decisions" (760 CMR 31) (http://www.mass.gov/dhcd/components/hac/hacindex.htm) (visited April 28, 2005).

32. Note 5, *supra* (January and February 2005).

13

Intersections, Roadblocks, and Dead Ends— Sketching a Housing Social Efficiency Analysis

Charles E. Daye

INTRODUCTION

"There is . . . an overwhelming irony that the 'better life' has always eluded the poor and the black, as masses. When they predominated in rural areas, the good life was 'The City.' When they got there, the good life was 'The Suburb.' To that place neither poor nor black may go. Either there are no homes they can afford, or they are barred in other ingenious and devious ways through use of various sorts of local land use controls."[1]

Much has changed in a quarter century since I made this observation. We have changed our ways of describing housing problems. We have changed the tools we use to regulate the building, spatial settings, type, and quality of housing. We have changed some roles of governmental and private actors. We speak of "comprehensive planning," "smart growth," "new urbanism," "affordable housing," "regionalism" and even "new regionalism," "poverty concentrations," "racial segregation" and even "hyper segregation," and "sustainable development," to mention a few rather modern terms.

What we have not changed is one reality: No matter how we assess our nation's progress, and there has been much, our prospect to become "one nation" is not at hand and our problems with issues that touch on race, class, and housing are nowhere near "solved." I placed "solved" in quotes to suggest that I am not sure we even have a common perception of what the solution is that we might be trying to achieve; not to mention that, I am reasonably certain, we have no consensus on the specific dimensions that a solution would entail. As to race, our metropolitan areas and suburbs are still largely segregated by race.[2] As to class, affordable housing is still a limited commodity and is excluded in many ways from many settings due to parochialism and "NIMBY-ism" that dominate local actions on land-use and developmental controls.[3] As to housing, affordability is problematic for a large segment of families and households that cannot afford a unit at all, are homeless, or can only secure housing at a price that consumes a disproportionate share of resources.[4]

After studying and working on the race, class, and housing conundrum for a quarter century, in addition to growing old, I am growing cynical. We have not solved the conundrum for lack of analysis. Articles have been published on every conceivable aspect of race, class, and housing.[5] Well-attended symposia and conferences have been organized.[6] Groups of all varieties have issued well-documented reports and studies.[7] Laws have been enacted at every level dealing with planning, zoning, and fair housing.[8] Programs have come, and sometimes gone, that demonstrate an almost unclassifiable array of mechanisms designed, in some way, to make housing more affordable and available by increasing production, offering incentives to players at every level of the housing delivery system, or subsidizing units and tenants.[9]

All of these measures have not been for naught, but all of these measures have not "succeeded" at causing housing for all citizens to be much more racially integrated, locating housing in highly desirable places to live and prosper, or making good housing available at prices all citizens can afford.

IS IT REALLY A "HOUSING" PROBLEM?

One question that might be worth asking and perhaps reviewing is: When we work on "housing" as to integration, spatial placement, or affordability, are we working on the "right" problem?

Generally speaking, housing has multiple dimensions—and no one reading this paper needs to be informed about that. Nevertheless, I mention these aspects of housing as a way of providing a theoretical framework for later comments. Housing is shelter, a home, part of a neighborhood, an investment, and a capital resource.[10]

Housing as "shelter" represents, perhaps, its prime and foremost function in any society, as a refuge from the outdoors and the elements of nature. We all know that on this front we have made many strides over the last years, although we are not entirely there. We still have housing that does not pass the shelter adequacy test.[11]

Housing also embodies the broader concept of "home." The concept of home includes shelter adequacy, but it means more than shelter. The "home" concept encompasses a "bundle of rights"[12] and statuses.[13] It means that housing must have design characteristics suitable for the uses the occupants desire to make of it. "Home" implies a level of shelter that makes the occupants comfortable, provides a zone of privacy both internally (e.g., a separate bedroom and private bath facilities) and externally (e.g., police, landlords, or housing inspectors cannot enter ordinarily except upon advance notice without a warrant), offers a sense of security, and gives a right of exclusive possession. "Home" means that the structure has amenities that suit the uses being made of the structure, that are suitable for the climate in which it is located, that fits the cultural needs of the occupants, and that has the esthetics that bring satisfaction and pride to the occupants.[14] In sum, a "home" can bring not only the elemental aspects mentioned but, in its qualities and characteristics, can reflect or even augment one's status and social position in the sight of others.[15] In this respect, "home" may be regarded as a sociolegal construct.

However, no matter how adequate housing is as structure for shelter and the many aspects of satisfaction it brings with its "home" attributes in isolation from its surroundings, a home is not an island unto itself any more than a person is.[16] A home is part of and partakes of the *neighborhood* or *community* in which it is situated. Neighborhoods and communities have characteristics and features in which shelter and home derive meaning and context. Neighborhoods and communities may be appealing or attractive because there may be family members or places of cultural or religious significance nearby. They may offer access to high-performing and safe schools, shopping facilities, and organizations; have streets, traffic patterns, and controls with thoughtful configurations that are attractive and safe; have high levels of positive factors (e.g., good interactions with members of the community individually and in groups, such as through clubs and other associations); and have low levels of negative factors (e.g., crime and forces that engender insecurities). Appealing and desirable neighborhoods and communities have proximity or good access to available public resources (e.g., libraries and parks) and offer ready access to transportation routes and services for getting to jobs, businesses, and entertainment venues.[17]

As we all know, housing—for about 65 percent of the population that owns a home[18]—is most families' largest capital *investment*. It is a highly desirable investment because a home is one of the few investment vehicles that one gets to actually use and enjoy while it is appreciating.[19] Under our national policy, homeownership gets special tax treatment compared to nonownership housing or other investment vehicles. We can lower our effective tax bills, asserting our entitlement to deduct our local real property taxes and mortgage interest paid, and then, when and if we sell the home, our capital gain from appreciation is not taxed.[20]

Housing is also a *capital resource* in two respects: (1) from the *microeconomic perspective* of individuals and families; and (2) from the *macroeconomic perspective* of the patterns of production and consumption of the nation. From a micro perspective, we are concerned with the individual's access to housing and the way exchanges are manifested in the purchase and sale of housing and related goods and services. We study how pursuit of individual wishes and desires can be manifested and effective in the marketplace. We examine prices of housing from sellers and providers, and scrutinize incomes of consumers and buyers to determine the impacts and effects of price on the capacities of families and individuals to make effective demands.[21]

Shifting to the macro perspective, we focus on general patterns of production and consumption of housing. We scrutinize the role of housing in the national economy and its contribution to total production. We examine housing's contribution to gross domestic production and analyze the effects of governmental monetary and fiscal policy on housing and of housing policies on the overall fiscal well-being of the nation.[22] We analyze the interrelations and mutual effects of housing markets, financial institutions, the building industry, the patterns of wealth accumulation in the nation, and the distribution of income and wealth.[23] We analyze the multiplier effect of housing on purchases of related goods and services. We monitor the way housing is used as a financial resource to spur economic activities through second mortgages that not only get special tax treatment but the use of proceeds to make consumer purchases of other goods and services to sustain the consumption levels of the economy. We examine consumer cash-outs of equity by refinancing when interest rates fall, and we scrutinize the impact of interest rates on housing production and sales activities in both the new and existing housing markets.[24]

INTERSECTIONS ON THE ROAD TO HOUSING

From these perspectives, one might ask, "What has this got to do with the race, class, and housing conundrum?" Perhaps we need a broader focus than housing. Would solving some other problem solve the housing problem? If we move away from housing issues, where would we go? We could focus on education. We could examine employment issues. We could focus on social and economic welfare. We could focus on more broadly defined distributive justice for America's poor. We could focus on barriers that exclude racial and ethnic minorities from a higher level of well-being. We could focus on political empowerment.

Yet, even if we focus on these dimensions, we will frequently come back to the central role housing plays in any dimension from which we approach the problem of social justice in America.[25] Thus, housing is at the intersection where we encounter housing-related issues when we look at the social problems we face in virtually any domain toward which we travel. While I make no claim that solving some other problem would not make a measurable contribution to solving housing problems, I do suggest that one is not likely to find much of a solution to any other social problem that does not at some point intersect with housing. Conversely, solving—*really* solving—housing problems very likely cannot be accomplished without working to solve virtually any other social problem we might seek to address. If housing solutions encounter roadblocks, not to mention dead ends, we may be trapped in the equivalent of gridlock on any route we wish to take toward solving almost any social problem we tackle.

ROADBLOCKS AND DEAD ENDS ON THE ROAD TO HOUSING

I have taught a housing course for more than 30 years. I use a problem to try to examine the question of why it is so hard to get and hold a strong consensus for solving housing problems. A slightly modified version of that problem is set forth below:

> *You are employed as an assistant to Representative Jones, a recently elected member of the U.S. House of Representatives. Representative Jones will serve on the subcommittee that will consider any housing legislation before it is passed on to the full committee and, perhaps, the House floor.*

> *If Representative Jones were to support housing legislation, please advise Representative Jones on how she should respond to the following assertions:*

> 1. "Some liberals argue that the private market has not provided and cannot provide decent housing for all citizens, but every time the government intervenes in any form in housing matters, it always involves one or both of:
>   a. some restriction on a citizen's use of private property like so-called civil rights acts, or
>   b. some kind of taxation and program of resource transfers (such as housing subsidies) to so-called poor people from the rest of us."
> 2. A local newspaper—known for its conservative editorial views—once advised Representative Jones that she should not support federal funding for housing programs to serve people who could not be reached by the private market. The editorial asked:
>   "In a country largely characterized by democratic capitalism, what basis can there be for all of this liberal-think that supports the notion of taking from 'them that's got, to give to them that don't,' when everybody in this country is free to pursue their prosperity through whatever talents and drive they have?"

When it comes to housing—virtually any form of the housing problems we might like to eliminate—we immediately come to roadblocks and even dead ends. That seems to be true for almost any aspect of housing problem we address in attacking the race, class, and housing conundrum. So if we want to work on integration of housing, the race dimension we encounter for any number of difficulties is recounted over and over,[26] and we are not there yet. The recent *Report of the Bipartisan Millennial Housing Commission*, with the exception of noting a homeownership rate gap between whites and minorities even with comparable incomes,[27] paid scant attention to any dimension of the housing problem touching on race (such as racial concentration, racial segregation, or discrimination in affairs affecting housing). Similarly, the report entitled *Planning Communities for the 21st Century*, apart from references to "affordable housing," makes no mention that planning might need to take into account the impact on planning activities that racial concentration, racial segregation, or racial discrimination might have on the efficacy that any proposed planning might have.[28]

With respect to class issues, the commission did discuss the need for more units in the affordable range, the lack of funding for the two-thirds of eligible households for which no funding is available,[29] and the more than 41 million renter- and owner-occupied households spending over 30 percent of income in housing costs.[30] However, there is no social or political consensus that subsidies should be increased or that funding should match needs for subsidies. In a time of budget crunches and record deficits at the federal level, it would be true to say that even funding presently available for such things as Section 8 faces challenges and cutbacks.[31]

With respect to subsidies to improve housing quality and boost production, we find a mishmash of activity from HOPE VI for public housing,[32] to Low Income Housing Tax Credits for new production,[33] to Home Program Assistance.[34] There is the loss or potential loss of affordable units under mortgages that are reaching maturity,[35] but there is no great thrust to increase activities or programs that would boost production or improve quality of existing units.

It would not be an exaggeration to say that the consensus—social, political, and economic—is not there for the kind of thrusts that it would require to affect a broader measure of social justice.[36]

A FRAMEWORK FOR THINKING ABOUT "SOCIAL EFFICIENCY"

Before going further, I must point out by way of caveat that I am not an expert in economic analysis. Indeed, I may have acquired just enough vocabulary to be really dangerous and to make fundamental errors. To the extent that these comments do have validity, the analysis I make is more in the nature of a call for research on the ideas sketched here and advocacy with a new premise, but should in no way be regarded as a complete or fully developed analysis. I am proposing a framework for thinking and rethinking about our "ongoing social dialogue"[37] about race, class, and housing with a vocabulary and focus that might be more fruitful at generating consensus, or at least forestalling some of the virulent opposition that our current approaches frequently engender.

I advance the following ideas in the belief that I am proposing and with a purpose to propose more than merely a semantic shift, probably not a paradigm shift, but a new synthesis for a new dialogue that might point us to routes through roadblocks and around dead ends on the road to reaching a possible solution to the race, class, and housing conundrum.

The proposal I make here is *not* that we should make either a micro or macro analysis of the housing market *for the purpose* of determining causes or effects of particular behaviors on housing market outcomes. The burden here is *not* to explain the dynamics of the housing market, or submarkets, nor to model the behavior of housing suppliers or housing consumers. These kinds of analyses have been going on for years.[38] What I want to focus on is whether concepts of economic analysis can more fully illuminate the ways by which we *all benefit* as a justification for the costs we think we need to incur to provide desegregated housing, spatial placement of housing that does not exclude by race or class, and affordable housing. In many senses, even this notion has historical antecedents.

In his work on government and slum housing, Professor Lawrence Friedman pointed out that there were two ways of analyzing the problem of slum housing. These, he said, were a "social cost approach" that considers the costs imposed by the slums on society at large and a "welfare approach" that considers the costs imposed by the slums on the people who live in them.[39] I think he was using "cost" as more than dollars and cents. The social cost approach he outlined focused on the "negative externalities" of poor housing. While that is a useful perspective for assessing the matter, it does not intuitively resonate with what I will call, hypothetically, the "suburban homeowner" to justify why he or she should spend money or devote other things that have value to an effort to avoid a cost imposed by a condition for which that person feels no causal responsibility. However, would a focus on what one might call a "social benefit approach" be any more successful if one could establish a basis in economics to calculate and demonstrate the benefit the suburban homeowner can derive if we worked to solve housing problems?

My goal would be to approach the question from the opposite angle to the costs imposed on the person in the suburban home by our failure to "solve" the race, class, and housing conundrum. I want to emphasize not the costs imposed but *the benefits to be derived* by suburban homeowners for the purpose of determining what the benefits are, and of examining whether the benefits will exceed the costs to be incurred in working to solve the race, class, and housing conundrum. So the task is to determine the elements of benefit the suburban homeowner can expect for our efforts at solving housing problems and to weigh the associated costs. Put in the language of economic analysis, this proposal asks us to analyze the "positive externalities" we may expect from solving race, class, and housing problems.

PRELIMINARY SKETCH OF A "SOCIAL EFFICIENCY" HOUSING ANALYSIS

An economist might define "efficiency" as addressing the relationship of the aggregate benefits of something and the aggregate costs of that something.[40] Applying "Kaldor-Hicks" terms, one would posit that the *efficient* outcome is produced when the monetary value of society's resources is maximized.[41] In general terms, efficiency measures are deployed to examine how we are allocating scarce resources to meet the needs and wants of consumers.[42] "Pareto efficiency" is said to exist when no one could be made better off without making someone else worse off.[43]

The concept of efficiency expresses a relationship between ends and means.[44] One economist points out that, "When we call a situation inefficient, we are claiming that we could achieve the desired ends with less means, or that the means employed could produce more of the ends desired. *Less* and *more* in this context necessarily refer to less and more value."[45] "Thus, economic efficiency is measured not by the relationship between the physical quantities of ends and means, but by the relationship between the *value* of the ends and the *value* of the means."[46]

One source speaks of social efficiency as follows: The "socially efficient" level of output and/or consumption occurs when "social marginal benefit" equals "social marginal cost."[47] The author goes on to posit that when we achieve *social efficiency* we will have reached the "point [at which] we maximise social economic welfare."[48] The author then tellingly makes what I regard, or at least interpret in a nonexpert's way, as a point most relevant to the topic of housing: "The presence of externalities means that the *private* optimum level of consumption/production often differs from the *social* optimum."[49]

THE HOUSING CONTEXT OF THE "SOCIAL EFFICIENCY" CALCULUS

One of the problems of adapting economic theory to housing issues such as those raised by the race, class, and housing conundrum is that several of the prime considerations or dimensions require an accounting that cannot be reckoned in dollars, although at some level anything can be given a "price," a "cost," or a "value." However, doing that for the matters we must address raises enormous difficulties because of ferocious complexities. What we deal with is so much more than "economics"; dollars are important, but we must be prepared to do more than tally up the dollars.

What one ought to connect to housing is problematic given the various dimensions of housing set forth above.[50] Recall that we discussed shelter, home, neighborhood, investment, and capital resource. Using these items as a framework, I believe john powell has set forth a comprehensive and complex set of connections between housing and "opportunity structures"[51] that is succinct enough to fit within the framework of housing proposed here. The list thus has two key virtues that commend itself to this essay: comprehensiveness and succinctness. These connections are in no sense isolated, discrete, or exhaustive. Indeed, it is in some senses impossible to singularly reckon these interconnected attributes of housing, even for analytical purposes. Therefore, with the caveat that housing dimensions cannot be separated except in the most artificial way, I think it would help to set forth how powell's connections can be analyzed as affecting one or more of the dimensions of housing I have previously discussed.

Housing as Shelter

The existence of shelter is the minimum requirement of housing.[52] Without shelter, there is no stability. Accordingly, both homelessness and exposure within a dwelling to the elements represent failures of shelter. The lack of shelter and poor shelter represent the abject failure of housing to offer any other attribute that might be associated with housing. Thus, no positive externalities can be contemplated from this condition. Conversely, solving the problem of actually having some kind of shelter and the adequacy-of-shelter problem cannot be seen as distinct from solving any other aspect of a housing problem because shelter represents the minimum essential condition. Thus we might think of every other attribute of housing we can examine as a variable that is dependent on shelter availability and adequacy.

It is not clear how we ought to reckon the impact of what has been called a "housing crisis" in which there is a pressing lack of affordable housing.[53] Housing is not affordable when, in order to acquire minimally adequate housing as shelter, one must devote a disproportionate share of family income to procure that housing.[54] In one sense, if a family must devote, for example, 50 percent of income to acquire shelter, we all know that is a housing problem. However, do we count it as inadequate shelter, as diminishing the concept of "home," or as comprising an inadequate investment? One might debate that. I will temporarily identify excessive cost as a part of the problem I identify as a "shelter problem." I do so not because the structure is physically deficient but because, when it comes to providing adequate shelter, the housing's *financial structure* is "deficient." The family seeking a physically adequate structure cannot demand it except at an "excessive" share of family resources.

I think the lack of affordability—because cost exceeds a reasonable share of income (i.e., a deficient financial structure)—can be analyzed as a shelter problem in many respects. It is a problem that imposes limitations that effectively undercut the housing's ability to meet the other aspects of housing that we have identified. If the family does not have resources left after paying for shelter to cover the costs of healthcare, decent clothing, educational expenses, participation in community functions, and funds needed for family members to participate in activities in the area, then aspects of "home" and neighborhood will be diminished. Similarly, investment dimensions will be adversely affected because the family may not be able to maintain the housing in a good repair and in attractive upkeep, thus diminishing resale value—one of the attributes of housing as an investment. Neighborhoods with families experiencing such difficulties are more likely to suffer decline, which undercuts housing as both a micro and a macro capital resource. Similarly, powell points out that gentrification can make housing unaffordable or unavailable by causing raises in rents and taxes or other measures in which families are priced out.[55]

Of course, if we are to apply social efficiency measures to housing as shelter, we must, of course, begin to think about how helping members of society acquire shelter that is adequate along these dimensions will benefit the person in the suburban home by showing that, if society fosters adequate shelter, it will promote a "socially efficient outcome" on a criterion that requires that the aggregate benefits of improving shelter for others must exceed the suburban homeowners' aggregate costs of doing that. I hope it is not pushing the concept beyond its recognizable limits to say that the goal would be to achieve "Pareto efficiency," thus creating a situation in which families assisted to acquire adequate shelter would be better off, but that result would be accomplished without making the suburban homeowner worse off. Indeed, the burden posited for this essay is to demonstrate that the suburban homeowner will not only not be worse off but will actually be *better* off *economically* and in other ways that the suburban homeowner *values*.

Housing as "Home"

To be adequate from a nonphysical perspective, housing must offer attributes that are derived from the sociolegal construct that I called "home." As a "home," housing must be able to provide the occupants with a number of well-known satisfactions and statuses, frequently identified as a "bundle of rights," if we are to regard that housing as a "home."

If one is subject to involuntary dislocation without justification from his or her housing, adverse influences of crime, the social effects of poverty, or excessive police activity or violence, no amount of adequacy as shelter will be sufficient as a home. If the shelter does not have adequate space for the occupants or does not meet the needs of the occupants as to layout or design, the shelter will diminish the concept of the shelter as a home.

If the shelter does not have adequate heat or air conditioning for the climate, it is not adequate as a home. If the shelter leads to excessive density of residences for the available services in the community, such as parks and recreational services, it will be lacking attributes of home, although these dimensions begin to shade over into the neighborhood dimension. It seems clear that housing that fails in these dimensions will not provide the satisfactions, statuses, and "bundle of rights."

Opportunity housing, as powell demonstrates, connects to other key "opportunity structures."[56] Here again, we need to demonstrate why providing assistance to families to assure that housing does not fail in its dimension of home will withstand a social efficiency analysis.

Housing as Neighborhood

Many of john powell's connections for "opportunity housing" can be seen as directly related to the concept of neighborhood or community. Racially isolated neighborhoods and those with concentrated poverty have enormous impact on housing, as powell demonstrates.[57] Whether a neighborhood is convenient for residents to reach their employment has an impact not only on the residents of the neighborhood[58] but on the neighborhood itself in all the obvious ways. Availability of transportation to reach jobs affects the employment prospects of neighborhood residents.[59] The analytical model powell proposes for opportunity housing recognizes that the availability of childcare will affect the employment of parents and their ability and capacity to seek and sustain employment.

Housing has a direct impact on education. It has been well documented, as powell sets forth, that segregated housing patterns lead to segregated schools and to the need for extraordinary measures to achieve any measure of integrated education. In many places, schools are supported in major part by property tax revenues with the consequence that low-wealth communities cannot support their schools and are more likely to have poorly performing schools.[60] The model for analysis that powell proposes posits that students from racially and economically segregated schools get substandard educations. Parents in poor, segregated communities do not have the economic wherewithal to provide home environments that nurture learning; do not have the skills to assist their children with homework; and may lack the skill, time, or capacity to monitor what teachers and schools are doing.

Health effects of poor housing are set forth in powell's discussion. He notes the multiple effects poor and minority neighborhoods suffer that have health implications, including pollution of various sorts from hazardous waste facilities to sewer plants, and exploitation by stores that mark up unhealthy food products and sell them to residents at inflated prices due to residents' lack of accessible food stores with higher quality and fresher foods at lower costs.[61]

The effects of housing in neighborhoods are compounded or isolated because of what john powell calls "jurisdictional fragmentation."[62] Here the affected families who need relief from the ill effects of the race, class, and housing conundrum are not able to influence the political decision-makers across political jurisdictional boundaries. Thus, these jurisdictions can engage and do engage in exclusion, which forces isolation of affordable housing and housing occupied by minorities to municipalities that are attempting to deal with the conundrum but are likely to have losses of population, a demographic profile of poorer citizens, and lower tax bases.

Housing as Investment

All of the foregoing housing problems will adversely affect the investment a family can make in and derive from its housing. To the extent that it is paying a disproportionate share of income in rental housing due to the crisis of affordable rents, the family consumes its income for present shelter and thus is further disabled from accumulating a down payment. It might even be suggested that the burden of renting takes away the family's incentive or even desire for homeownership because it cannot imagine becoming a homeowner. Thus, rental families are excluded from all of the benefits families derive from homeownership, including the acquisition of shelter that may be physically more adequate, the tax benefits of homeownership, the ability to earn appreciation, the inability to take advantage of lower interest rates, the capacity to cash out equity to make other purchases or to finance education, as well as the satisfactions and stability of being a homeowner. Housing, therefore, contributes to wealth accumulation and is well documented in powell's presentation.[63]

Because housing is intricately tied to its neighborhood, and because sound and high-quality housing both contributes to and derives value from the neighborhood, in some respects an investment in one's housing is an investment in one's community or neighborhood. Conversely, municipalities that do not perceive the connection do not, or who lack resources cannot, make neighborhood investments that increase the investment potential of units within their political boundaries. They thus undercut the value of investment interests for homeowners and their own potential higher taxes to be derived from increasing home values.

Housing as Capital Resource

All of the dimensions discussed are important to housing as a capital resource to individuals (the micro perspective) and to the economic well-being of the nation (the macro perspective). The capital resource aspect of housing is particularly dependent on all of the other aspects of housing we have already identified.

The list powell provides includes a connection to democratic participation.[64] This dimension also cross-cuts virtually all of the other dimensions. However, as powell points out, housing—especially homeownership—gives people a stake in the nation.[65] It gives them upward mobility and can provide an outlook of participation and belonging that will engender a higher incentive to vote and take interest in civic and political affairs. People who are abjectly downtrodden can understandably perceive that the political process is rigged against them, that voting is futile, that politicians are not interested in the downtrodden, and that things are not going to get better. Political defeatism saps the vigor that one might have had to devote to political matters. Accordingly, many of these people disengage in the political process and further relieve politicians from any obligation to support policies and programs that would benefit the downtrodden.

This kind of defeatism is not only destructive to the legitimacy or perceived legitimacy of the political process, but it is destructive of motivation to strive for a better tomorrow because of the belief that what one does will not change the fortunes one will experience in the future.

APPLYING "SOCIAL EFFICIENCY" ANALYSIS

In order to use the insights of economic analysis, I think it is reasonable to examine the nature of the costs and benefits that might, or perhaps must, be examined. In the housing context, as already discussed, some costs and some benefits are tangible, such as a physically adequate shelter. Other costs and benefits are intangible, such as many of the factors we examined in the concept of "home." That intangibility, it seems, calls (like tangible items) for an attempt to assign value and assess the costs one would incur to produce or procure a better housing outcome.

Housing as neighborhood presents dimensions that are both tangible (e.g., physical condition of streets and parks) and intangible (e.g., the status and prestige of a neighborhood that arise out of perceptions about its qualities). Investment is tied most directly to tangible factors and can be reckoned to have a value determined at the marketplace. However, to the extent that inherently subjective and even idiosyncratic factors about the adequacy of the housing as shelter, home, and neighborhood influence value in the marketplace, one cannot disentangle tangible from intangible factors.

It would probably be useful to emphasize once again that the costs we would be examining are *not* the *costs imposed* as externalities of bad housing conditions. Rather, while we would not ignore those costs as part of the equation, we will be scrutinizing the costs *one would incur* to produce or acquire the housing that would provide the *benefit* we will count to reckon the efficiency of the effort. In this light, to have an efficient "transaction," the benefit to be derived must exceed the costs of acquiring that benefit. The outcome is efficient only when costs are less than benefits.

In assessing costs and assigning value to benefits, a strict market approach probably will not be sufficient. First, some elements of both costs and benefits have no "true marketplace." Second, some costs and benefits have value but cannot be really reckoned as "market value." Third, some costs and benefits will present daunting calculation challenges.

On the "cost side," the suburban homeowner would pay taxes to multiple levels of government to support the housing programs and activities. Achieving accuracy as to these costs would be a difficult but not insurmountable task. Certainly there are models and methodologies for analyzing and at the very least making rough estimates of such things.

There undoubtedly could be other "costs," such as loss of some level of autonomy at the marketplace by vigorous enforcement of antidiscrimination laws. At some level, one might even suppose that "associational freedoms" would be affected to the extent that local communities relinquished some control over land-use decisions and related issues. More likely, local controls would have to be required to be relinquished by legislation or regulations at the municipal, county-wide, regional, state, or federal levels. Also, it may be that there will be a delay of greater or lesser length between the expenditure of funds (the costs) and the putative benefit to be derived by actions to remove some roadblock or impediment that is helping to create race, class, and/or housing problems. Governmental funds would, of course, be raised by taxes at some level. This, too, is a cost—a cost paid in present-value dollars against the discounted value of the benefit to be derived in the future.

Many housing programs involve a combination of public and private efforts. This factor also makes accounting for costs difficult, but not preclusive, at least to some thinking about the social efficiency analysis. The funds might be raised by some form of "exaction" of fees to fund a housing benefit or to require a housing benefit, such as an "affordable housing" set aside. These are all costs that can be counted or at least estimated.

The more difficult challenge may be in determining how to account for benefits. I assume that all aspects of housing that I previously set forth must be analyzed. The concepts of shelter, home, neighborhood, investment, and capital resource loom large. The essential burden of the social efficiency analysis is to make the argument that not only will "society in general" be better off in a macro sense, for example, but to translate and demonstrate that the individual suburban homeowner, at the micro level, will benefit. Is this possible?

Let me set out what I shall call six "social efficiency interests."[66] I think we can sketch (and reasonably assume) that every suburban homeowner is motivated to maximize and sustain the:

1. Economic value of the home purchase (*Home Value interest*);

2. Social value derived from the suburban home setting (*Social Value interest*);

3. Satisfactions from homeownership that the homeowner values (*Satisfactions of Homeownership interest*);

4. Good citizenship image derived from joining with neighbors to improve general well-being that will enhance the value of other interests (*Good Citizenship interest*);

5. Beneficial effects of general national economic well-being (*National Economic Well-Being interest*); and

6. Competitive success of the United States in international exchanges and relations with the rest of the world (*U.S. Competitive Success interest*).

With these social efficiency interests or constructs in focus, I now turn to a further sketch of these interests in the framework already discussed for thinking about the various aspects of housing.

Home Value Interest

It is reasonable to believe that suburban homeowners support regulatory restrictions in an effort to maximize the economic value of their homes. Zoning is designed for this purpose. The suburban homeowner can exert maximum influence in small, localized entities and so resists all of the approaches to regionalism that have been offered, theorized, and proposed. However, planners without a constituency cannot implement their plans even if they would be beneficial at helping to solve the race, class, and housing conundrum.

Would it matter to the suburban homeowner if one could demonstrate that the health of a region contributes something to home values in the suburbs of those regions? Is this in fact true? I think so. If urban centers decay and become dysfunctional, entire regions of which they are a part lose vitality and, at some level, homes in the region do not maintain their value as well or do not appreciate at the optimal rate because they become less attractive due to problems (real or perceived) in a region that is suffering decay. Conversely, if the urban center or centers within the region of the suburban homeowner's community are vibrant and attractive, and if the region is organized functionally to cope with controlling undesirable outcomes and to promote positive ones, the entire region gains vitality and, at some level, homes in the region will show greater appreciation than they otherwise would due to increased demand in that region, including the region's suburbs.

• *Research Agenda Item #1 for Social Efficiency Analysis: Measuring Economic Benefits.* This question will require establishing the validity and the contours of the suburban homeowner's motivation to increase the economic value of the home purchased, and quantifying the benefits to suburban homeowners including the extent to which the motivation to maximize the economic value of the home purchase is furthered by helping to solve the race, class, and housing conundrum.

Social Value Interest

The social values that suburban homeowners would associate with housing seem to include virtually all of the aspects, considered together, of shelter, "home," and neighborhood previously identified. These include the "bundle of rights" sociolegal construct; safety and security; the interest in permanence and stability; the right configuration and density; spatial placement in proximity to jobs, schools, public and private community resources; and the living environment for children and a healthy family life. How will working to solve aspects of the race, class, and housing conundrum benefit these interests of the suburban homeowner?

Healthy urban areas in which the urban crisis, the affordability crisis, and the housing crisis do not exist will contribute to the desirability of the home in its suburban milieu by enhancing the market value of the homes. Living in proximity to vibrant, safe urban centers will promote social interactions in the neighborhoods as people will feel safe moving about at night and alone. This will enhance social interchange. Children and young family members will have improved and multiplied outlets for excursions, recreation, schools, and opportunities for work and other activities. In many ways, the lives of suburbanites will be socially richer if the urban regions in which their homes are located can solve issues that sustain the race, class, and housing conundrum.

Any difficulty we encounter in *identifying* what the relevant social value interests may be pales in comparison to the task of finding a model or methodology to begin to sketch both the valuation of each of the discrete interests and the assessment of how and the degree to which some aspect of the suburban homeowners' social value interest is improved by housing-related costs the suburban homeowner would be asked to bear. Is this analysis something that can be done?

• *Research Agenda Item #2 for Social Efficiency Analysis: Measuring Social Benefits.* This question will require establishing that suburban homeowners do derive and place value on social benefits of housing, examining how to assign values to the social benefits suburban homeowners are motivated to maximize, and quantifying the benefits that suburban homeowners can expect to get by paying the costs (monetary and other) imposed to help solve the race, class, and housing conundrum.

Satisfactions of Homeownership Interest

The satisfactions derived from housing include all of the aspects of housing already set forth. Yet, after we consider housing as shelter, "home," and neighborhood, I think we may not have accounted for additional considerations that may motivate the urge to move to suburbia and the urge to build walls of local land-use and other regulations and practices that exclude along lines of race, class, and housing.

How do we account for the widespread resistance to open housing or the remarkable robustness of racial exclusion even when the other race is of the same economic class? There must be some satisfactions suburban homeowners derive that propel these drives. Similarly, consider how quickly the building of multifamily housing in neighborhoods of single-family homes will generate resistance about the feared lowering of home values, about the "they are different from us" theory, or about apartment dwellers being too transient to be invested in the long-term life of the neighborhood. Combine race and class with integrated apartment structures and one is proposing a course of action to likely provoke something with the earmarks of a civic insurrection. Do not think about making the units affordable, as in "low priced" or governmentally assisted or modular construction; the problem will be compounded now by revolutionary-zeal resistance to "that" kind of housing, thus illustrating the intractable quality of the race, class, and housing problem.

Could a suburban homeowner be persuaded that any program attacking the race, class, and housing problem would benefit any interest in the satisfaction of homeownership? I think so. If the regional approach were taken, and if the fair share plans both prevented "over concentration" of nonsuburban style housing at any location (especially the homeowners' particular area) and assured that all communities in the region would bear the "costs" of a share of affordable kinds of housing, a suburban homeowner might derive satisfaction from that knowledge. Also, the homeowner would benefit from not having to fear intractable litigation on fair housing grounds, and from not having to endure the destabilizing risk of losing an exclusion fight at some level of the legislative or judicial process. A homeowner might think that these considerations had some value worthy of being taken into account.

This discussion does not assume that every suburbanite is against trying to solve some of our race, class, and housing issues. Some number of suburban homeowners might derive satisfaction from the thought that they are contributing to a solution rather than being part of the problem, although this begins to shade into the Good Citizenship interest.

Additionally, there might be value in many communities that homeowners would derive from having a broad economic mix of families. Service workers, childcare providers, in-home workers, and the like might be more readily available for employment if there were available and affordable housing in the community. It would enable such persons to reach jobs more expeditiously and reliably to the benefit of the suburban homeowner who wanted to employ them.

- *Research Agenda Item #3 for Social Efficiency Analysis: Measuring Satisfactions Benefits.* This area might prove to be the most challenging to set forth with clarity and to develop a way to capture and estimate benefits along monetary lines. I doubt that it is impossible. How to evaluate "pride" of homeownership and cost out intangible satisfactions might prove to be challenging, but is it impossible?

Good Citizenship Interest

It may well be a fact, and I think it is, that many citizens have a public spiritedness about them. They may not be motivated to make great sacrifices to demonstrate it, but suburban homeowners, like all other classes of people, contribute money, time, support, and interest to any number of causes great or small and well known or virtually unknown.

It would be reasonable to assume that, by and large, all or certainly most of us, including suburban homeowners, desire a society that is peaceful and prosperous enough to allow all people to make some efforts in the pursuit of happiness. Suburban homeowners, I believe, would make some sacrifice to produce an outcome that furthers these ends.

At the very least, some homeowners in the suburbs, like the rest of us, desire a nation that strives to solve its most intractable problems. They want to contribute to that solution as long as the costs are not too dear or the solutions too intrusive. They may be persuaded to do so if they believe the solution will be advanced in an efficient way by whatever costs they are asked to incur and so long as the solutions do not undercut other social efficiency interests they have, such as their Home Value interest, Social Value interest, and Satisfactions of Homeownership interest.

Although we are not analyzing the externalities that housing problems impose on suburban homeowners, it might be worth mentioning that the

Good Citizenship interest can be furthered if a benefit of that effort is that it reduces the costs society, and even suburban homeowners, must pay because other citizens are trapped in the web of race, class, and housing ill effects or are dispirited and antisocial, quite apart from the lost potential such persons might have had in better circumstances. From another perspective, it becomes a matter of the suburban homeowners' self-interest to promote what john powell has identified as the "opportunity structures" of housing.

A major problem will be identifying all of these benefits and, once that is accomplished, to determine the value of these benefits—not merely in the aggregate, but at the individual suburban homeowners' micro level. Can that be done?

• *Research Agenda Item #4 for Social Efficiency Analysis: Measuring Good Citizenship Benefits.* This task will require establishing that suburban homeowners do derive and place value on good citizenship matters; identifying how the Good Citizenship interest is advanced by any costs incurred toward helping to solve the race, class, and housing problems; and determining a valuation scheme to assess the benefits suburban homeowners derive.

National Economic Well-Being Interest

This interest of suburban homeowners aligns rather nicely with the capital resource aspects of housing observed previously, especially from the suburban homeowners' macroeconomic interests in housing. In addition, this interest incorporates some, perhaps many, micro interests as well. We will recall that, from a macro perspective, general patterns of production and consumption of housing become important. We recognize that housing production and consumption, at all levels, contribute to, stimulate, and in many respects help sustain a healthy national economy. Housing contributes to the total gross domestic product, to overall national fiscal well-being,[67] and to homeowners' abilities to accumulate wealth.[68]

Recall that housing also has a multiplier effect on related goods and services and is a source of jobs for workers—from factories, which produce furniture and appliances at sites distances from the housing being constructed, to carpenters and brick masons in the local area. A healthy housing market therefore can even cause a higher level of economic activity through second mortgages.[69] As noted earlier, from a micro perspective, we are concerned with the individuals' access to housing and the way exchanges are manifested in the purchase and sale of housing and housing-related goods and services. We study how pursuit of individual wishes and desires can be manifested and prove effective in the marketplace. We examine prices of housing from sellers and providers, and incomes of consumers and buyers, to determine the impacts and effects of price on families and individuals.

All of these dimensions of housing can be shown to be of direct benefit to suburban homeowners. However, there are additional ways a healthy economy enables increased revenue to local, state, and federal governments, which enables them to provide and maintain infrastructure, streets and highways, facilities, services, programs, and activities that directly benefit suburban homeowners. Thus, it appears clear that a strong demonstration can be made that many of the costs to solve intractable issues of race, class, and housing contribute a measurable benefit to suburban homeowners in ways that might give them incentives to bear some of the costs of helping to solve some of the housing problems our nation faces.

- *Research Agenda Item #5 for Social Efficiency Analysis: Measuring National Economic Benefits.* Given that these are matters of current study and analysis, this task should find ready analytical tools and models to discover, value, and connect the benefits suburban homeowners will derive from helping to solve housing problems.

U.S. Competitive Success Interest

All of us recognize that the United States competes in the international arena on many levels—economically, through trade and commerce, and in the global competition for materials, markets, labor, innovation, and even democratic governmental ideas and ideals. There is nothing novel in this observation.

The impact of trade policies and trade treaties can have international and, for our discussion, important local impacts. Jobs can be lost as corporations go overseas, plants can move and take production offshore, and prices can be affected for imported and exported goods by the value of the dollar on international money markets. Moreover, a downturn in our economy (or a tax cut) can require reduction in governmental services or borrowing on the international market to finance our deficits. Borrowing on the international market, in turn, can put excessive dollars in the international market with direct impacts on local areas caused by the dollar's loss of value against other currencies.[70]

There are ample models for analyzing these effects globally and nationally. One might require more tools or new models to assess and value the benefits that a suburban homeowner derives. However, I think there are certainly demonstrable benefits to be identified and valued. Some of these benefits are monetary, direct, and tangible. Other benefits are nonmonetary, indirect, and highly intangible, such as an interest in "national pride" or an interest in a "good" or "positive" international "image." Suburban homeowners' benefits such as these are nevertheless important, and real, and can give motivation to a homeowner to incur some costs to produce and derive the benefit, assuming the homeowners can be convinced that the costs will have a real tendency to produce the benefit identified.

- *Research Agenda Item #6 for Social Efficiency Analysis: Measuring U.S. Competitive Success Benefits.* The tangible aspects of international competitiveness interests should not prove difficult to demonstrate. The intangible aspects may prove challenging, but I think they are not beyond skilled analysts' tools.

TENTATIVE CONCLUSION

How far a social efficiency analysis can change the dialogue or make a difference is imponderable. What I do know is this: So far, nothing has worked to really solve the race, class, and housing dilemma. Even for someone who has become rather cynical as to whether the nation has the will to try to get over its race, class, and housing problems, I think it might be worth trying new approaches.

The social efficiency analysis sketched in this paper proceeds from the premise that people, such as suburban homeowners, will be most motivated to pursue their own "enlightened self-interest"[71] and social efficiency analysis attempts to speak the language of economic concerns based on the assumption that everything can be analyzed for its contribution to tangible well-being. The goal is to demonstrate that solving race, class, and housing problems support that self-interest.

There are possibly many issues one might find to critique in this report. There is one critique that I want to anticipate: Much of this paper is pitched at a simple level and is not a sophisticated or intellectually complex analysis. It does not have a lot of graphs and charts or depth of economic principles. There are two reasons for this simplicity. One reason is the limitation of the author. The other reason is that the presentation ultimately must be addressed to non-experts in a lay audience—the hypothetical suburban homeowner—in order to attempt to persuade them to support the efforts and measures we need to take in the housing arena. We cannot reduce all of these considerations to a "20-second sound bite," but the argument cannot be prolix or complex if it is to gain any practical audience.

CHARLES E. DAYE NOTES

1. Charles E. Daye, *The Race, Class and Housing Conundrum: A Rationale and Proposal for a Legislative Policy of Suburban Inclusion*, 9 N.C. Cent. L.J. 37, 39 (1977). [Footnotes omitted.]

2. See generally William H. Frey and Dowell Myers, *Neighborhood Segregation in Single-Race and Multirace America: A Census 2000 Study of Cities and Metropolitan Areas*, Fannie Mae Foundation (2002) (working paper) (examining segregation patterns and variation across different types of metropolitan and submetropolitan areas using data from the 2000 census). See also Nancy A. Denton, *Half Empty or Half Full: Segregation and Segregated Neighborhoods 30 Years After the Fair Housing Act*, 4 Cityscape 107 (1999) (describing the progress made in desegregation over three decades, while simultaneously illustrating that there is a long way to go).

3. "NIMBY" is a popular acronym for "Not In My Back Yard." See, e.g., Richard Schragger, *The Homevoter Hypothesis: How Home Values Influence Local Government Taxation, School Finance, and Land Use Policies*, 101 Mich. L. Rev. 1824 (2003) (book review) (describing that homeowners will consistently act in such ways as to maximize the value of their homes, including their voting record); see also Jonathan D. Weiss, *Preface: Smart Growth and Affordable Housing*, 12 J. Affordable Housing & Commun. Dev. L. 165, at 169 (2003) (discussing the practice of fiscal zoning by municipalities), and Jeffrey M. Lehman, *Reversing Judicial Deference Toward Exclusionary Zoning: A Suggested Approach*, 12 J. Affordable Housing & Commun. Dev. L. 229 (2003). (Municipal competition, though

encouraged by contemporary land-use jurisprudence, is fundamentally unjust when held up against the history of racial and economic segregation, and moreover will serve to self-propagate and further polarize in the absence of legislative measures to counter these effects.)

4. See *Report of the Bipartisan Millennial Housing Commission Appointed by the Congress of the United States,* completed pursuant to PL106-74, § 206(b), at 14 (May 30, 2002) [hereinafter "Bipartisan report" with page reference] (outlining generally, though without significant attention to race as a variable, the state of the current housing affordability problem); Paulette J. Williams, *The Continuing Crisis in Affordable Housing: Systemic Issues Requiring Systemic Solutions,* 31 Fordham Urb. L.J. 413 (2004).

5. See generally Robert D. Bullard, Glenn S. Johnson, and Angel O. Torres, *Race, Equity, and Smart Growth: Why People of Color Must Speak for Themselves,* from the Environmental Justice Resource Center (http://www.ejrc.cau.edu/raceequitysmartgrowth.htm) [hereinafter "Bullard/Johnson/Torres"] (compiling a massive volume of statistics and facts gathered in previous studies); Dolores Acevedo-Garcia, Theresa L. Osypuk, Rebecca E. Werbel, Ellen R. Meara, David M. Cutler, and Lisa F. Berkman, *Does Housing Mobility Policy Improve Health,* Housing Policy Debate 15:1 (2004); Greg J. Duncan and Jens Ludwig, "Can Housing Vouchers Help Poor Children?," The Brookings Institution Children's Roundtable No. 3 (July 2000); Lance Freeman and Hilary Botein, *Subsidized Housing and Neighborhood Impacts: A Theoretical Discussion and Review of the Evidence,* J. Plng. Lit. 16:3 (2002), 359-378; John Goering, Judith D. Feins, and Todd M. Richardson, *A Cross-Site Analysis of Initial Moving to Opportunity Demonstration Results,* J. Hous. Res. 13:1 (2002), 1-30. See compilation of bibliographic references at http://www.prrac.org/mobility (visited Jan. 7, 2004).

6. A cursory examination of the American Planning Association conference schedule, for example, representing only one of many organizations dedicated to the study of planning and development, gives some indication of the level of discussion within the planning profession; see also Third National Conference on Housing Mobility, "Keeping the Promise," at the Urban Institute, Washington, DC, Dec. 3 and 4, 2004 (http://www.prrac.org/mobility/agenda.htm) (visited Jan. 7, 2004).

7. E.g., Lisa Robinson and Andrew Grant-Thomas, *Race, Place, and Home: A Civil Rights and Metropolitan Opportunity Agenda,* the Harvard Civil Rights Project (Sept. 2004) (report), containing a comprehensive bibliography at 94-105 (http://www.civilrightsproject.harvard.edu/research/metro/Race_Place_Home.pdf) (visited Nov. 2004); see also Zhong Yi Tong, *Special Report—Homeownership Affordability in Urban America: Past and Future,* Fannie Mae Foundation, Washington, DC (April 2004), copyright © 2004 Fannie Mae Foundation.

8. See, e.g., Bipartisan report, at 106 (describing federal housing programs as of 2002); *Planning Communities for the 21st Century,* A Special Report of the American Planning Association's Growing Smart[SM] Project (2000) (describing planning initiatives on the state level); Justin Phillips and Eban Goodstein, *Growth Management and Housing Prices: The Case of Portland, Oregon,* Contemporary Economic Policy (July 2000) at 334 (describing planning initiatives taken at the regional metropolitan level in Portland, Oregon). "Fair Housing" is the goal of the Fair Housing Act of 1968 as amended, 42 U.S.C. § 3601-3617 (2004), and the host of state laws and local laws encouraged by "substantially equivalent" provisions for deferral of most fair housing actions to state and local agencies operating under "substantially equivalent" statutes and ordinances.

9. See, e.g., Bipartisan report, at 106 (listing currently funded and no longer funded federally funded housing initiatives).

10. Wallace F. Smith, *Housing: the Social and Economic Elements* (Berkeley, CA: University of California Press, 1970), 7-9, 223-31. Reprinted in Roger Montgomery and Daniel R.

Mandelker, *Housing in America: Problems and Perspectives* (2d ed.) (Indianapolis: Bobbs-Merrill, 1979), Chapter 1, "What is Housing?," 3-38.

11. Bullard/Johnson/Torres (describing frequency of environmental shortcomings in housing); Susan J. Popkin, Dianne K. Levy, Laura E. Harris, Jennifer Comey, and Mary K. Cunningham, *The HOPE VI Program: What about the Residents?*, 15 Housing Policy Debate 385, at 400 (2004) (describing the failures of even governmentally maintained public housing to provide an adequate shelter environment).

12. E.g., Lynn E. Cunningham, *A Structural Analysis of Housing Subsidy Delivery Systems: Public Housing Authorities' Part in Solving The Housing Crisis,* 13 J. Affordable Housing & Commun. Dev. L. 95 (Fall 2003).

13. Michelle Adams, *Knowing Your Place: Theorizing Sexual Harassment at Home,* 40 Ariz. L. Rev. 17, 50 (1998) (speaking, in the context of sexual harassment at home, of a need to understand "the full spectrum of the symbolic and emotional weight of the concept of home"); Paul Sullivan, note, *Security of Tenure For The Residential Tenant: An Analysis and Recommendations,* 21 Vt. L. Rev. 1015, 1040 (1997); Deborah Hodges Bell, *Providing Security of Tenure for Residential Tenants: Good Faith as a Limitation on the Landlord's Right to Terminate,* 19 Ga. L. Rev. 483, 541 (1985). ("In a society in which many individuals cannot realistically expect to become homeowners, providing some security of tenure in rental housing is an important step toward encouraging *the sense of autonomy and stability associated with the concept of home.*") [Emphasis added.]

14. E.g., Bonnie Lindstrom, *A Sense of Place: Housing Selection on Chicago's North Shore*, The Sociological Quarterly, Winter 1997, at 19 (suggesting that "individuals purposively use the externally shared meanings of housing and community in American society" as a mechanism for projecting and maintaining social status).

15. Id.

16. See John Donne, *Meditation 17, Devotions Upon Emergent Occasions* (London, 1624) ("No man is an island . . .").

17. See Emily Talen, *The Social Goals of New Urbanism,* 13 Housing Policy Debate 165, at 178 (2002) (describing the positive effects of accessible environmental amenities on neighborhood residents).

18. "New Homeownership Record," Housing Affairs Letter 04-43, Oct. 29, 2004, 3.

19. A home can be used and enjoyed up to a point of obsolescence, which can be forestalled for many decades, assuming proper use and good maintenance.

20. This is again within certain limits that apparently do not apply to most homebuyers and sellers. The effect of the tax policy is to generally grant benefits inversely proportioned to need: the bigger one's home, the bigger one's mortgage is likely to be. In general, the bigger the mortgage, the greater the interest one pays and gets to deduct. See generally Internal Revenue Code § 163, 26 U.S.C.A. § 163 (2003) (interest deduction). Again, in general, the more valuable one's home, the more taxes one pays and gets to deduct. See generally Internal Revenue Code § 164, 26 U.S.C.A. § 164 (2003) (property tax deduction); and id., § 121, 26 U.S.C.A. § 121 (2003) (exclusion of gain on sale of principal residence). In order to pay these bigger mortgages, one must have a higher income level. Within limits, the higher one's income is the higher one's marginal tax bracket. The higher marginal tax bracket in turn increases the value of each dollar that is deducted. Moreover, these deductions are *entitlements* that are not limited to amounts annually appropriated and not subject to scrutiny, such as housing vouchers are, as to misuse or improper use.

21. See generally Richard G. Lipsey et al., *Microeconomics* (12th ed.) (Reading, MA: Addison-Wesley, 1999), 254, and Joseph E. Stiglitz and Carl E. Walsh, *Principles of Microeconomics* (3d ed.) (New York: W. W. Norton & Co., Inc., 2002), 251.

22. See, e.g., Robert J. Samuelson, "Housing's Last Hurrah?" *Washington Post*, Apr. 9, 2003, A21.

23. See generally Karl E. Case and Ray C. Fair, *Principles of Macroeconomics* (4th ed.) (Upper Saddle River, NJ: Prentice Hall, 1996).

24. See, e.g., Sam Berry, "Housing Slowdown Predicted," *Architecture,* Aug. 2000, at 150 (reporting the prediction by economists that interest rate increases will slow housing production).

25. See, e.g., Chester Hartman, *The Case for a Right to Housing,* 9 Housing Policy Debate 223 (1998); Tim Iglesias, *Housing Impact Assessments: Opening New Doors for State Housing Regulation While Localism Persists,* 82 Or. L. Rev. 433 (2003).

26. See, e.g., Charles E. Daye, *Whither "Fair" Housing: Meditations on Wrong Paradigms, Ambivalent Answers, and a Legislative Proposal,* 3 Wash. U. J.L. & Pol'y 241 (2000); Bullard/ Johnson/Torres (offering statistical description of current housing inadequacies for persons of color).

27. See Bipartisan report, at 14.

28. See *Planning Communities for the 21st Century,* A Special Report of the American Planning Association's Growing Smart[SM] Project, 18-19, and subsequent discussions of individual state requirements for affordable housing, 34 (Maryland), 46 (New Jersey), 57 (Oregon), 67 (Rhode Island), 75 (Tennessee), and 83-84 (Washington).

29. See Bipartisan report, at 14.

30. See Bipartisan report, at 15 (noting that 30 percent figure may understate the problem of affordability as the average American household spent only 20 percent of its income for housing).

31. See "The War on Affordable Housing," *The New York Times,* Oct. 16, 2004, editorial page (discussing the Bush administration's attack on Section 8 funding).

32. Bipartisan report, at 106. "HOPE" stands for "Home Ownership and Opportunity for People Everywhere."

33. Internal Revenue Code § 42, 26 U.S.C.A. § 42 (2004).

34. 42 U.S.C.A. § 12721 (2003).

35. James R. Barth and Robert Litan, "The Housing Disaster That's Not Being Fixed," Policy Brief #1 (1996), The Brookings Institution (http://www.brook.edu/comm/policybriefs/pb01.htm):

> "Over the next seven years, subsidy contracts will expire on more than 700,000 units in apartment buildings (housing more than 1 million tenants) located throughout the nation that receive rental assistance under HUD's [Housing and Urban Development] 'Section 8' (and predecessor) programs. . . . In today's tight budgetary environment, however, there is no prospect that these contracts will be renewed at their current subsidy levels."

36. There is no consensus in any other area either: income gaps have widened; enforcement has lagged; and resistance to "affirmative action" is under attack everywhere by well-funded, determined, "no-holds-barred," willful partisans. For a self-accounting of one such entity, see The Center for Individual Rights (http://www.cir-usa.org/history.html).

37. Roger Montgomery and Martin Gellen, "Emerging Issues in American Housing Policy," in Donald Phares, ed., *A Decent Home and Environment: Housing Urban America* (Cambridge, MA: Ballinger Publishing Company, 1977), 157-58.

38. See generally, e.g., Roger Montgomery and Daniel R. Mandelker, *Housing in America: Problems and Perspectives* (2d ed.) (Indianapolis: Bobbs-Merrill, 1979), Chapter 2, "The Housing Economy," 39-79.

39. Lawrence M. Friedman, *Government and Slum Housing* (Chicago: Rand-McNally, 1968), 3-4.

40. A. Mitchell Polinsky, *An Introduction to Law and Economics* (Boston: Little, Brown and Company, 1983), 7; see also Jules Coleman, *The Normative Basis of Economic Analysis:*

A Critical Review of Richard Posner's The Economics of Justice (book review), 34 Stan. L. Rev. 1105 (1982).

41. One source describes Kaldor-Hicks efficiency as "A type of efficiency that results if the monetary value of society's resources are [sic] maximized" (http://www.amosweb.com/cgi-bin/gls.pl?fcd=dsp&key=Kaldor-Hicks+efficiency) (visited Jan. 8, 2005).

42. See generally Lars Werin, *Economic Behavior and Legal Institutions* (Singapore: World Scientific, 2003), Chapter 3.

43. A. Mitchell Polinsky, *An Introduction to Law and Economics* (Boston: Little, Brown and Company, 1983), 7.

44. Paul Heyne, "Efficiency," *The Concise Encyclopedia of Economics,* The Library of Economics and Liberty (http://www.econlib.org/library/Enc/Efficiency.html) (visited Oct. 16, 2004).

45. Id. [Emphasis in original.]

46. Id. [Emphasis added.]

47. tutor2u™ (http://www.tutor2u.net/economics/content/topics/competition/efficiency.htm) (visited Oct. 16, 2004).

48. Id.

49. Id. [Emphasis added.]

50. See text accompanying notes 11-25, *supra.*

51. john a. powell, *Opportunity-Based Housing*, 12 J. Affordable Housing & Commun. Dev. L. 188-228 (2003) [hereinafter "powell" with page reference].

52. powell, 190.

53. powell, 193; Paulette J. Williams, *The Continuing Crisis in Affordable Housing: Systemic Issues Requiring Systemic Solutions,* 31 Fordham Urb. L.J. 413 (2004).

54. Today's standard is generally referred to as 30 percent of income to be devoted to housing, because that is the standard adopted by federal housing programs; see, e.g., 42 U.S.C.A. § 1437a(a) (1) (A) (2000) (the standard for public housing) and 42 U.S.C.A. § 1437f(o)(3). The current standard was increased to 30 percent from the 25 percent standard during the Reagan administration.

55. powell, 194.

56. powell, 195.

57. powell, 193.

58. "Homeownership, Home Buyers Favor Short Commutes," Housing Affairs Letter 04-43, Oct. 29, 2004, 2.

59. "Affordable Housing, Work Force Housing Regional Concern," Housing Affairs Letter 04-43, Oct. 29, 2004, 4, citing http://www.chicagometropolis2020.org (Chicago Metropolis 2020) (visited Nov. 6, 2004), pointing out that "Policies as simple as synchronizing traffic

lights from town to town, or *as complex as ensuring that workers in our region can find housing near their jobs*, require more than 272 municipalities acting independently. A strong region requires that communities work together on issues that transcend local political boundaries. Local governments can give up a little in order to gain much more: a region that is attractive and prosperous." [Emphasis added.]

60. powell, 198.
61. powell, 200.
62. powell, 193.
63. powell, 195-96.
64. powell, 200-201; Professor Craig-Taylor has made a thorough analysis and argument about the essentials of participating in "productive property" and citizenship. Phyliss Craig-Taylor, *To Be Free: Liberty, Citizenship, Property and Race,* 14 Harv. BlackLetter L.J. 45 (1998) (detailing "the history of the social and legal constructions of a system of property ownership and access to credit which has discriminated against African Americans" and noting that this "system ensured their exclusion from the rights and opportunities of republican citizenship and its neo-republican synthesis").
65. powell, 201, n. 95, quoting Michael Schubert, "More than Bricks and Mortar: Housing That Builds Community" (Charlottesville, VA: Pew Partnership for Civic Change, 1999).
66. I do not suggest that these interests are exhaustive or exclusive. There may indeed be other interests to add or substitute for this to be identified as a beginning point.
67. See, e.g., Robert J. Samuelson, "Housing's Last Hurrah?" *Washington Post,* Apr. 9, 2003, A21.
68. See, e.g., Sean Zielenbach, *A Critical Analysis of Low-Income Homeownership Strategies,* 13 J. Affordable Housing & Commun. Dev. L. 446 (2004).
69. See, e.g., Sam Berry, "Housing Slowdown Predicted," *Architecture,* Aug. 2000, at 150 (reporting the prediction by economists that interest rate increases will slow housing production).
70. See, e.g., Robert Samuelson, "A Global Glut of Greenbacks," *Newsweek,* Dec. 29, 2003/Jan. 5, 2004, 67.
71. Richard Briffault, *The Local Government Boundary Problem in Metropolitan Areas, Symposium Surveying Law and Borders,* 48 Stan. L. Rev. 1115, 1150 (1996). See, in a different context of shared self-interest as an incentive to work against exclusion, Sheryll D. Cashin, *Privatized Communities and the "Secession of the Successful": Democracy and Fairness Beyond the Gate,* Tenth Annual Symposium on Contemporary Urban Challenges Redefining The Public Sector: Accountability and Democracy in the Era of Privatization, 28 Fordham Urb. L.J. 1675, 1691 (2001).

14

Commentary on the Affordable Housing Presentations with a Practitioner's Perspective

Dwight H. Merriam

I just knew this was going to be a great conference when Dan Mandelker, as only Dan could, started the planning some two years ago. He asked me to take on the job of responding to Tony Downs (Chapter 12) and Professor Charles Daye (Chapter 13), two of the country's leading thinkers on affordable housing and inclusionary zoning. I agreed for three reasons. First, because it was Dan and whatever Dan asks me to do, I will always do. Second, the faculty he selected was simply outstanding. I looked forward to, and have now been rewarded by, the thoughts of an extraordinary group of people who, while not always of the same values, are committed to land-use law as an intellectual pursuit and a means to implement societal good. Third, I wanted to spend a little more time with Tony Downs and finally meet Charles Daye.

I have known Tony Downs by reputation for decades and personally for several years since becoming a Counselor of Real Estate. I have heard him speak many times, enjoying each occasion immensely. I've also heard some of his jokes before but, having forgotten the punchlines, they never fail to entertain. More importantly, Tony is such an insightful speaker and writer that I listen to every word he has to say.

Charles Daye arrived at the University of North Carolina School of Law the same year I did, in 1972. Charles came to teach at the law school and, just back from three tours in Vietnam, I came to teach in the Navy's Reserve Officers' Training Corps program and work on my master's degree in regional planning. I learned about Charles Daye shortly after I arrived on campus but, in all the years—these 33 years—I had never met him in person. A great attraction for me in participating here today was the chance to hear him speak and to spend time with him. My expectations have been met several times over.

I have three jobs to do here: I need to summarize what our speakers have said. Then I need to tell you a little about what I know of these issues as a day-to-day practitioner in order to add my observations, to the small extent that I can, to what you have learned from their writings and talks. My final role is to pull this all together and fill in the gaps in the process of melding our speakers' two compelling perspectives.

What jumps out at me most strongly from Tony Downs' article and his talk today is that 21 percent of households have an affordable housing need or problem. It is safe to say that Tony believes that one simply can't trust local governments to solve the problem. There is not enough money; there is an absence of affordable housing, especially in affluent suburbs; housing costs vary tremendously from region to region; and gentrification is a continuing, exacerbating problem.

In very broad terms, Tony identifies two forces affecting the market. First are the structural impacts from citizen involvement in the regulatory process, particularly the use and abuse of environmental law, the homeownership bias of our federal housing policy, and the fragmented and often purely local control over land use. I don't see how we can complain much about that last point; I've made a career of riding on the back of the fragmented control of land use.

The second force that Tony sees driving the affordable housing market is what he labels "dynamic." This dynamic includes growth itself and the newly minted "smart growth initiatives," which he doesn't seem to like in the least. Overarching these two forces, and a driving dynamic in its own right, is the phenomenon of the wealthy protecting their assets. Tony points out the attempts to implement policies that have tried a two-pronged approach: increasing buying power on one hand and decreasing housing prices on the other. These attempts, Tony concludes, have never worked.

So, what to do? In the first instance, Tony believes we must try to reduce the fear that existing homeowners have of affordable housing and suggests a type of insurance against decreases in housing values. The idea, as I understand it, is this: If upper middle class, suburban homeowners could be provided with insurance that their housing prices would not decline when lower-income people move into their neighborhood, then those well-to-do (affluent) folks would embrace their new neighbors.

I'm not buying the concept. I've lived in central cities—first in New Haven and then in Hartford—from 1975 until just four years ago when I moved to the suburbs, voting with my feet like so many others to find schooling for my two youngest children. I can tell you from my perch in the suburbs that these folks are not as concerned about protecting their property values as they are about maximizing the increase in those values.

I am pleased to report that I see few problems of race or ethnicity. It is about issues of economic class, if at all, although I know full well of the strong linkage between economic class and race/ethnicity. Even with that, I am really quite surprised and gladdened to find my suburban neighbors open to friendly relations with people from broadly diverse economic backgrounds. In our own neighborhood, with the same elementary school, there are homes ranging in value from $125,000 to $1.5 million. This is as good a mix as market forces may ever yield in the suburbs.

My guess is that, as a practical matter, the idea of insurance would backfire. I can't imagine going to a group of neighbors in an established suburban neighborhood and saying, "We're going to develop a few units of affordable housing here for some families moving out from Hartford. They are diverse— African American, Latino, and Asian—and, while they may not have much money, we think it's the right thing to do, to have them in our town and to open our town and our schools to their families. We know you might be afraid that housing prices will go down if people move into affordable homes in your neighborhood, so we've created and we're going to give you an insurance policy that guarantees your housing price won't go down, or will increase by at least some percentage of the region's normal increase [I can't even begin to figure out how to write this formula . . .], so you should feel more comfortable with their moving in."

However, Tony also suggests something that I embrace entirely: the production of smaller, cheaper units. He talks about manufactured housing, which can include everything from a single-wide mobile home to a grand home of several thousand square feet that just happens to be manufactured offsite.

He also identifies a role for accessory apartments and I completely agree. An increasingly significant part of the housing stock in our suburbs is becoming physically, functionally, and economically obsolete—it's too big, too old, and too expensive for the families who are there, particularly the aging individuals that comprise one- and two-person households. Carving up these houses to create an additional accessory apartment can provide a great benefit to the homeowner and to the residents of the accessory unit.

I also had occasion recently to consider new-construction accessory apartments as part of a large development, intended as a strategy to provide more affordability. Though my developer client chose not to pursue that alternative, new-construction accessory apartments of 500-700 square feet for a single person or couple, whether for the young or the elderly, could be a wonderful addition to many of our more exclusive communities. It would allow older people of limited means to stay in town in their homes, and young singles and couples to continue living in the town and community where they grew up. From the perspective of the fiscally burdened local governments, accessory apartments have a tremendous benefit. They provide a strong tax ratable without throwing large numbers of children into the school system where most of local fiscal burden is created.

Tony also has written and has talked about legalizing small houses. I was involved in that myself in the case of *Builders Service Corporation, Inc. v. Planning & Zoning Commission of the Town of East Hampton,*[1] where we established that in Connecticut, as a matter of state constitutional law, it was illegal to require nonoccupancy-based minimum floor areas. This is the extremely pernicious use of large minimum floor areas to artificially drive up housing prices and exclude people of limited and modest means.

We determined in our investigations that more than a third of Connecticut cities and towns had a minimum floor area of at least 1,000 square feet. So we found a plaintiff and a town, and then we developed a cause of action and brought a lawsuit, and eventually won. The Connecticut Supreme Court held as a matter of Connecticut constitutional law, as about a half dozen other states have also done under their own constitutions, that you cannot use minimum floor areas without reference to occupancy in order to artificially maintain high housing prices.

It would have been wonderful if the net result was a flood of new small units, but it simply hasn't happened. Builders build what will return the most profit. There is not enough money to be made in houses of 1,000 square feet or less, so the builders continue to build to the market. The market in my suburb says, "Give me at least a 2,000- or 2,500-square-foot house, certainly nothing smaller, and more often something much bigger," as we see in the McMansions appearing virtually everywhere.

My own family home, built by my house painter father and stay-at-home mother in 1940, safely and comfortably housed six children, with five at home most of the time. It had a 24-by-32-foot footprint—a classic World War II-era Cape Cod house of 768 square feet, which accommodated a later addition of a dormer with two small bedrooms and a half bath. When my father died four years ago and we sold the place, it became the victim of the "scrape off" phenomenon. That house, built with the lot for $5,000 on 7,000 square feet of land (do the numbers: that's a density of six units to the acre!), was unceremoniously demolished and scraped off by its buyer who paid a third of million dollars so he could build a new, much bigger home, which we assume sold for around $750,000.

I must say that my father would not have regretted that at all. Sitting at the front window of his house, looking out at the other houses in our little neighborhood as they were scraped off and replaced with McMansions, he said, "New families need new homes."

However, I submit that there aren't any house painters with six children and stay-at-home wives who are buying new houses in suburban Boston where I grew up because they don't have the money or the borrowing power to afford a $750,000 home or even the rundown place that was scraped off. It is those people, like my working-class parents, who we need to think about and accommodate because, in the end, as I will comment on shortly, the ultimate way to a democratic and egalitarian society is to provide equal physical—and I emphasize *physical*—access to the resources available in the suburbs and elsewhere.

Finally, Tony suggests concerted political action by powerful groups. This is a hard proposition with which to disagree. The plain fact remains, however, that those families who would move to the well-to-do suburbs are virtually disenfranchised. They don't live there. They have no constituency there and there is no one out there in the well-to-do suburbs who will stand up and speak for them. No, instead we need to think about a political infrastructure that will create constituencies for those who are disenfranchised.

Tony goes on to present eight points to consider as part of an inclusionary zoning remedy:

1. Housing goals;
2. Planning procedures;
3. State review of local plans;
4. State review of local regulatory rules;
5. State review of affordable housing targets;
6. Financial incentives;
7. Support of developer suits; and
8. Statewide mandatory programs.

I have been to the well of inclusionary zoning and what is there is at best brackish. In 1984, I coedited with my friends David Brower and Philip Tegeler a book entitled *Inclusionary Zoning Moves Downtown*,[2] which we wrote with a grant from the American Planning Association, to honor the life of Paul Davidoff, who was dying of cancer at the time. We were blessed with his presence and participation in the workshop, all of which ended up in the book we produced, just as this book will include our workshop, articles, and edited commentary.

The "bottom line" for inclusionary zoning is that mandatory programs are largely unworkable. They are too risky; there is fear among developers of marketing failures; there is way too much delay in the process; and there are several sides with competing interests, including local government, the developer, housing advocacy groups, and neighborhood opposition. Most often with these competing interests, the result is lawsuit piled on top of lawsuit—a dog pile of litigation that is tremendously wasteful of our societal resources.

What strikes me as troubling with most of these suggestions by Tony Downs—no, I'll say with all of these, even the incentivized inclusionary zoning programs—is that they only benefit the middle class and lower middle class. They seldom—and never in my experience—ever reach the truly poor because they can't. There are not enough internal subsidies built in or available through density bonuses and the like in mandatory and voluntary inclusionary zoning programs to generate housing that is cheap enough for the working poor.

We are deluding ourselves if we think that we are reaching the full range of economic classes in mandatory or incentivized inclusionary zoning programs. The only way the working poor and truly poor can ever be accommodated is with direct public subsidies and public construction of housing, which fortunately can be (though regrettably seldom is) constructed on a scattered-site basis throughout the suburbs. The portability of housing assistance payment contracts under Section 8 provides some help in this area but nowhere near enough.

Professor Charles Daye has a profoundly different perspective. He starts out by saying that he is growing cynical and wonders whether there really is a housing problem. Rather than turn to the statistics and the numbers as Tony does, Professor Daye disassembles the housing problem into five component parts. He says that housing is:

1. Shelter;
2. A home that provides safety and status;
3. Part of a neighborhood that provides physical access to important cultural resources such as schools;
4. An economic investment; and
5. A source of capital.

What a wonderful way to think about housing: to take it apart into its components and build a model up from that!

Professor Daye makes four main points, all of which deeply resonate with me. As I said at the outset, I knew this was going to be a worthwhile event, but I never realized how much so and how enlightening and stimulating these two speakers would be.

Professor Daye says first that housing plays a central role in social justice. As I hear him, physical access to housing resources is critical, and that was my experience as a child of a working-class family growing up in an affluent suburb. I never would have had access to great public schools and to the cultural and social experiences that encouraged and prepared me to move up. He is right on the mark.

We can only overcome racial, ethnic, and economic exclusion and break the tragic cycle of poverty by physically opening up communities everywhere so that all people and all families can have equal physical access to these resources, tangible and intangible. In short, without saying so directly, Professor Daye suggests that we enable African American, Latino, and Asian moderate- and low-income flight, just as we enabled white flight from the central cities to the suburbs a half a century ago. Let these people vote with their feet to attain the physical, social, and economic environments within which they want to live, and within which they want to raise their families.

Professor Daye's statement of the central role that housing plays in social justice makes me think that there is a need for direct government action, and not incentive programs or even the mandatory percentages of inclusionary zoning, which fail to reach the lowest economic stratum. No, instead there is a compelling role for government, perhaps something like the former Urban Development Corporation in New York, to make sure that housing for all economic classes, and for all races and ethnic groups, will be available everywhere. The key to success, I think, has to do with a scattered-site strategy, involving perhaps the acquisition and, as necessary, the conservation of older homes.

If we are to preserve and expand the stock of affordable housing, it must be in accordance with the "plan" but modified from our usual practice. The plan should be both top down and bottom up—state plans with a housing element should inform substate regional and local plans, and local plans should move up in the other direction and inform the substate regional and statewide plans. Communities should have an obligation to see that housing is provided for and, where they fail to do it, we should not be reluctant to use the power of government, because government and planning work best when there is market failure, and when they come in and make sure that the housing is built.

Professor Daye's second major point is that there are positive externalities, real and measurable benefits, from solving the race, class, and housing problems. He points out that the private optimum level of consumption/production often differs from the social optimum. His key point is that we can capitalize on the externalities of solving these problems as a society. Although he overmodestly eschews the expertise of an economist, he certainly seems to hit the mark here. The plain fact is that ameliorating the race, class, and housing problems, which are so damaging to our society, will have multigenerational benefits as we break the cycle of poverty and allow the most disadvantaged to move up and contribute to society.

Third, Professor Daye addresses the ownership and investment advantages of providing homes for all classes, races, and ethnic groups everywhere. This is self-evident but bears stating directly. The late Paul Davidoff once told me how much he truly believed in the theory of "trickle down" and how he had wished that, instead of fighting only for affordable housing in the suburbs, he had simply fought for more housing, to loosen up the market and allow people to move throughout the economic range of housing.

Regrettably, some of the perverse economics of our suburbs have resulted in "trickle up" or gentrification, ensuring that lower-income classes and racial and ethnic minorities are displaced. Crude regulatory techniques like housing preservation ordinances are little more than the Dutch boy's thumb in the dike, are bound to fail in the end, and are unable to resist overpowering market forces. Instead, we must work to solve the supply side; to design and build more housing that is functionally, physically, and economically suitable for families of modest and limited means.

As a corollary to his point of housing for all, everywhere, Professor Daye observes that healthy regions will help all. I guess we would call this the theory that a "rising tide raises all ships." It is true. If we do it right—and, in doing so, do the right thing—we all benefit. The enormous fiscal drain in the central cities, where the subsidies and money must come from federal and state government and indirectly from the wealthy in the suburbs, can be abated if housing opportunities improve; those who have the desire, the motivation, and the capability to succeed have the support and facility to do so by having direct, physical access to the resources of all of our communities.

Professor Daye ends with a discussion of the race, class, and housing dilemma and a social efficiency analysis. His approach encourages me to put his principles in context, just as I tried to do with those of Tony Downs, from the perspective of a practitioner who has a good understanding about what works and what doesn't, albeit limited by the fetters of being a lawyer for hire.

First, we must admit and acknowledge directly that expectations have changed. Fifty years ago, the normal aspiration for a typical suburban household, at least in my experience, was that the family would have one car, one black-and-white television set, no central air conditioning, one telephone, no computer, one bathtub (with a shower and a curtain that always seemed to channel water onto the floor), no electric dishwasher, no garbage disposal, and no clothes dryer. I remember my mother bringing in the sheets frozen hard from the clothesline in the backyard, and nothing that you can get from a box beats the sweet smell of air-dried sheets. It's not just that we expect to have clothes dryers, either. The restrictive covenants on the lot where we built our new house prohibit drying clothes outside!

We have watched the size of houses steadily increase so that the one I was brought up in, which was a standard for the time, is about the area of the master bedroom suite for a McMansion. We, as a society, are profoundly more footloose. Magnet schools draw our children away from their neighborhoods (not a bad thing in many cases) and the Internet and other communications technologies have shrunk our world to a fraction of its size. In short, these expectations and the ability for people from all classes to see what others have, right from their own living rooms on their televisions, have caused many to want and demand more, to be satisfied with less, and to be more frustrated by exclusionary regulation and development.

One overarching principle is that we must approach this problem incrementally and practically, recognizing the political realities. Tony Downs wants dramatic action and so do I, but it is unlikely to happen. Here are some of my own thoughts on an agenda for action.

We must break the cycle of poverty. It will take time. It will require the creation of constituencies. Government action will be necessary. Regulation alone will not even come close to solving this problem.

Following the model of the Urban Development Corporation, states should have a statewide affordable housing authority that can develop, own, and operate affordable housing, particularly on a scattered-site basis. These authorities should be able to delegate their power to certified development agencies and individuals, just as many states now delegate certain environmental responsibilities to certified environmental professionals—private practitioners who work for the public good and are managed through a state process.

The name of the game today is joint ventures and public-private partnerships. Rather than simply giving developers the crude and bludgeoning club of overriding local zoning by state statute, which does have some real advantages, why not allow the state to team up with developers and identify sites, shape projects, and then provide those private developers with the authority to override local zoning where necessary?

Regrettably, some of our affordable housing regulatory override programs in this country have been grossly misused by a small minority of the development community to leverage their way into development approvals that they never should receive, affordable housing component or not. Having public-private partnerships and state-level certification of a project before handing over the club of the zoning override would result in better designed, more effective developments.

Next, these programs must be adequately funded. The two-tier property tax system in Vermont—although I don't like it myself because I pay a premium on my taxes for my house there in order to support the education system in poor towns—has done an effective job of shifting wealth. Ironically, the taxes I pay as a resident of one of the so-called "gold towns" (Ludlow) goes to one of the poorest towns of the state (Glover) where my family lived for generations. Should wealthy, exclusionary municipalities assume a greater burden in funding affordable housing programs? I think so.

We need regional tax-base sharing so that local governments don't fight over tax ratables. We need a progressive income tax at the state level with the wealthiest paying the cost of government intervention and production of affordable housing in the most exclusionary towns. We need the largest consumers of land and materials—and here I target the McMansions—to be taxed at higher levels to fund the cost of affordable housing. In many communities, we may need to consider the legality and political acceptability of impact fees to build housing either directly or through a housing trust fund.

I don't believe that we have come anywhere close to fully realizing the potential of housing trust funds. I had a project recently where I thought that our developer client, and the host community, could benefit by contributions to a housing trust fund, which could then be used for the acquisition of older homes elsewhere in town, and the imposition of rental and resale restrictions to preserve that housing stock.

It is enormously expensive and inefficient to build new, affordable housing, but there is good, used housing stock that is sold at somewhat of a discount as people move out (again, I do embrace the theory of trickling down). We need to capitalize on that by stopping the scrape-off of these older houses that are torn down to allow McMansions to be built, preserving those homes as affordable housing alternatives when needy households enter the marketplace.

My experience as a practitioner is that there is no monistic or single-minded regulatory approach that will work, nor is there any financing or programmatic or planning "silver bullet." Instead, we must always orchestrate techniques. Here are just a few that we might use, some in small measure and some in large measure:

- Rent subsidies
- Mortgage subsidies
- Shared equity
- Nonamortizing mortgages
- Leased land
- No-down-payment loans
- Maintenance assistance
- Weatherization and energy programs
- Housing trust funds

I think we need to focus especially on the elderly. I say this as somebody within shooting distance of age 60. The elderly are generally house-rich and cash-poor. We should enable older Americans to help us fashion a solution for younger, upwardly mobile families. What if we negotiated with these older people for resale controls on their homes and shared-equity arrangements in return for reduced or eliminated tax payments and reverse annuity mortgages that would put money into their pockets? They could remain in their homes in the suburbs and they would be able to do so with money and security. Their homes would be preserved as part of the affordable housing stock. This can be applied on a scattered-site basis.

Elderly homeowners are an ideal group to work with to create new accessory apartments that will provide them with a source of income, security, and assistance in day-to-day tasks (e.g., mowing the lawn, raking the leaves, cleaning the gutters, and, for those of us up north, shoveling the inevitable snow). What a great opportunity to provide housing for young singles, young couples, empty nesters, and retirees while taking care of the older people in our suburbs who will inevitably age in place!

Only about 5 percent of the elderly, who have the financial resources and who can make potential use of assisted living, ever move into assisted living facilities. Why? Because they would prefer to age in place, just as my father did until he died at 93, taking in two or three men by renting rooms in his house, all in violation of local zoning. It enabled him to stay on in the house he had lived in for more than 60 years. Why shouldn't we legalize that, instead of making our elderly become willful violators of the zoning laws? I once heard that there were more illegal accessory apartments on Long Island than legal ones. I believe it.

I sometimes think of how great it would have been to have my father's house preserved as a small, affordable unit in the now-pricey suburb where I grew up and, in doing so, to have funded my father's retirement by reducing his taxes and providing a reverse mortgage.

As Martin Luther said, "It matters whose ox is gored." It is the empty nest-ers and retirees who are getting pushed out of their ever-more exclusive sub-urban communities by rapidly escalating housing prices and real estate taxes. These people are part of the housing constituency that must be addressed.

In talking about the empty nesters and retirees, I must add a comment on an omission by our speakers, probably because it was outside the intended reach of their writings. Common interest communities have a much greater exclu-sionary effect through their covenants and restrictions than all the zoning reg-ulations one might muster. As private agreements, they go much farther than public regulation in walling out those deemed undesirable. We need to take a long, hard look at how much exclusion we will allow by private agreement and assess just how pervasive and pernicious these exclusions really are.

My experience is that accessory apartments and duplexed homes will be resisted. People who have achieved the status of single-family, detached own-ership don't like the idea of "two-family" homes in their neighborhoods. I have a strong preference for small, scattered-site efforts to overcome this natu-ral resistance to intensifying existing housing and neighborhoods. Distancing and separation requirements might help.

I would like to try auctioning resale restrictions. What would happen if you put an advertisement in the newspaper that said everyone who has a house with a market value of $100,000 or less, and who is willing to restrict the resale or rental of that house to some affordable limits, would be given a pay-ment based on what they were willing to take in exchange for that restriction. Why, maybe we can even get these on eBay!

There are many people who are, as I said, house-rich and cash-poor. I sus-pect that a large number of them would jump at the chance to get $5,000 or $10,000 in cash in return for a restriction on resale or rental, knowing that the next time their house is sold will probably be after they are dead and buried.

Local governments and developers ought to consider buying existing homes at market, encumbering them with resale and rental restrictions, and then reselling them. You could buy an existing house at $100,000, place an encumbrance on it, and then sell it for $90,000 or $95,000. For $5,000 to

$10,000, you have permanently preserved an older, more affordable house from expansion, conversion, or scrape-off and McMansionization.

We need to get new legal tools into our bag. As I said, I like the idea of creating a statewide authority and delegating some of the responsibilities to certified affordable housing developers. That requires legislation.

On the purely technical, legal front, there is a lot we could do to shift the burden of proof from the housing advocate to the municipality. We could abandon the American rule in favor of the English rule by making the recalcitrant local government pay the affordable housing developers when an affordable housing developer wins its case. Affordable housing developers ought to get head-of-the-line privileges and have their applications processed ahead of others.

In the end, my experience has been that more often than not (but not always), the one with the greatest staying power wins. If a private developer is a certified affordable housing developer with a state-approved plan, then maybe that developer ought to have state financial support in order to keep up the battle with the hold-out municipalities. Maybe the state's attorney general could provide representation.

I'm not entirely comfortable with this idea of bolstering staying power because I represent developers, municipalities, neighborhood opposition groups, and projects with affordable housing elements. However, with the most difficult legal issues, I suspect there would be a lot less litigation if the losing party had to pay the winning party's legal fees in whole or in part from the beginning or after some point in the proceedings.

There are indeed big issues remaining. Present programs provide a housing benefit for a very narrow stratum (i.e., those capable of paying the rent or getting a mortgage) but at the same time not making too much money. This narrow band of lower-middle-income households receives a considerable advantage; that's fine, but in the end it is to the detriment of the even lower-income classes and those who really need the housing. A significant problem is that those who first qualify to buy often advance economically but continue to occupy the affordable units to the exclusion of those who are needier.

As a retired Navy Captain who spent 30 years as a surface warfare officer, solving the affordable housing problem makes me think of the famous story of Lord Nelson. Lord Nelson was probably the greatest naval tactician of all times. During the 1794 battle at Calvi in Corsica, he lost the sight in his right eye. Years later, Lord Nelson retired, but he was brought out of retirement to fight the Armed Neutrality in the Baltic Sea in 1801. Under the command of Admiral Parker, he sailed his ship into Copenhagen harbor and engaged the enemy. Nelson's ship, *Elephant*, was ahead of Parker's. Admiral Parker, believing Lord Nelson would soon be overwhelmed, hoisted the recall signal ordering Nelson to retreat. An aide told Lord Nelson of the recall signal and handed him his long glass. Lord Nelson put the long glass up to his right eye and said, "I see no signal." He then went on to win one of the most important victories in his long career.

There are so many problems and so much danger, yet there is so much to be gained by aggressive action on the affordable housing problem. I challenge all of us to turn a blind eye to the risks in proceeding aggressively and expansively with a variety of innovative approaches and techniques because, in the end, we might . . . we just might . . . win a brilliant battle.

POSTSCRIPT

Two months after our conference and after I had finished up revisions to my commentary, I sat in my youngest son's fourth-grade class in our suburban town (10 miles from Hartford) and listened to the children read essays on a wide variety of subjects.

Destinee Santiago, age 10, of Hartford, who attends our local elementary school under a limited program that brings children out from Hartford, wrote the following essay. It is stunning in its directness, insight, and simplicity. It brings to the ground what Tony Downs and Professor Daye are saying, and it moves me to pick up yet another lance and charge at this windmill once again. If we could just help one or two or three more children like Destinee, we will have accomplished something good and useful for individuals like her, for society in general, and for generations to come.

Hartford Kids Should Get To Go Other Schools

Do you live in Hartford? Do you want to go to another school or does you parent or parents want to move to another school? Do you live too far away? Well I think Hartford kids should get to go to other schools because schools in the suburbs are safer, have a better education, and have parents that help a lot.

Schools like Latimer Lane in the suburbs are safer then Hartford schools. There are fewer bullies and more teachers around. In Latimer Lane, there are only two floors so you can see every one on the first floor. The teachers and other people who work at Latimer Lane School know you by name because there are fewer children to keep track of.

Another reason why Hartford kids should get to go to different schools is because they get a better education. The teachers do not stress the children about CMT'S.[3] The children that go to great schools like Latimer Lane can concentrate more on learning. The teachers give one on one attention and are expected to do their best! The schools have many fund raisers to help the homeless too. Latimer Lane has great ideas like birthday clubs, Scholastic News, and the list the teachers make for books they suggest for that grade.

Last but not least, parents at Latimer Lane School are very helpful. The parents help the after school program, fundraisers, and volunteer in classes. Many parents put in a lot of time because they want to, not because they have to. Parents also help with projects. They also bake and show up for hay rides, survivor, and other activities.

No matter where you live or where you or your parents want to send you, you should be able to go to different schools.

Destinee Santiago, age 10

DWIGHT H. MERRIAM NOTES

1. 208 Conn. 267, 545 A.2d 530 (1988).
2. Dwight Merriam, David J. Brower, and Philip D. Tegeler (eds.), *Inclusionary Zoning Moves Downtown* (Chicago: American Planning Association, 1985).
3. "CMT" stands for Connecticut Mastery Test (in furtherance of federal legislation, "No Child Left Behind").

Evaluating the Impacts of State and Local Programs

15

Land-Use Law in the Courts: One Judge's Observations

Shirley S. Abrahamson

Good morning. I am delighted to be part of this excellent symposium and panel. I, like the other speakers, am here because Professor Daniel Mandelker called in all of his chips.

I first met Dan in the spring of 1956 in Indianapolis. I was graduating from Indiana University School of Law–Bloomington Division and was at a dinner party at the Indianapolis campus where Dan was teaching. He and I sat next to each other and made small talk. When I told him I was going to Madison, Wisconsin, where my husband had a postdoctoral fellowship in the genetics department, Dan inquired whether I had a job. I did not.

Dan suggested I work with University of Wisconsin Law Professor J. Willard Hurst, the founder of the field of American legal history. I thought not. The position would not allow me to spend the year doing nothing too intellectual or too taxing. Well, the next day, Professor Hurst telephoned me. At Professor Mandelker's suggestion, he was offering me a tax-free fellowship. Well, there I was—trapped. I didn't have a job and the offer was for a substantial sum of money, somewhere between $4,500 and $5,000. So I arrived at Dan's alma mater, the University of Wisconsin Law School in Madison, for the year and, as it turned out, for the rest of my life.

This experience led to two consequences: I am forever indebted to Professor Mandelker for a chance dinner conversation, and I always sit next to strangers at every function I attend. You can never tell when lightning is going to strike again.

In spite of my debt, when Dan called about this symposium, I tried to beg off because of my time constraints and my lack of expertise on the subject. He reassured me that my task was not going to be difficult. He wrote, "The objective is to get your perspective as a justice deciding cases on planning. Your paper will not take a great deal of research. What we want to hear from you is your view of the land-use field based on your years on the court. What are the issues you see in land-use planning and regulation, and what direction should reform take, not only in legislation, but in case law and practice? This will not require extensive case or other research from you, although you can reference your own experience from the bench." Thus lulled, I accepted the invitation.

When I began to prepare the paper, the assignment initially appeared an easy one that could be accomplished quickly. Clearly, land use in Wisconsin is rapidly changing. Farms are becoming housing developments; downtowns are being rejuvenated; condominiums are rising; affordable housing is the catch phrase; regional and strip malls are multiplying; vacant lakefront lots are fast disappearing; billboards remain controversial; adult, sexually oriented businesses with opaque windows and alluring advertisements are in local neighborhoods.

My sense of the ease of the task quickly gave way to a deep sense of unease. There was a lot of case law and legislation out there. After much research and considerable thought, I make 10 overlapping and interrelated observations.

OBSERVATION #1:
JUDGES TAKE A CASE-BY-CASE APPROACH

Professor Mandelker erred in thinking that an appellate judge is the right person to give an overview of land-use cases in appellate courts generally or in her own jurisdiction specifically. I realized that I, like most judges I know, consider cases as they reach us, one at a time. We explore the law surrounding the limited issues raised in a case, write the opinion, and go on to the next case. We try to understand each case in the context of a particular subject while attempting to foresee the ramifications of each case. Most of the time, the parties do not put the case in a broad context or explain possible ramifications, except in hyperbole describing slippery slopes or horrendous, unintended consequences.

The real-life significance of each case is, therefore, not always clear to the court. A court is often the last to know whether its decision has made a difference in real life. Cases that seem significant to a court during the decision-making process often turn out not to be significant because interested persons have taken steps to cope with the decision no matter which way it comes out. Other cases appear significant only to the parties but turn out to be "sleepers" affecting far more people than anticipated.

Only after several cases raising substantially the same issue—say, for example, zoning variances—do patterns emerge. Only then do courts likely see patterns and think about the issue more globally. Often patterns and emerging doctrine are pointed out by law review articles or amicus briefs after the individual cases become numerous or significant enough. Nevertheless, here I am.

OBSERVATION #2:
LAND-USE CASES FIT INTO MANY LEGAL CATEGORIES

Having said that, my initial, overall impression that the dockets of appellate courts do not include a significant number of land-use cases is dead wrong.

When I went to law school, the law school curriculum did not have land-use or land-planning courses, so I tend to pigeonhole land-use cases into subjects with which I am familiar, namely property, torts, nuisance, environmental law, municipal government law, or constitutional law. This may account for my initial conclusion that our docket does not include many land-use cases. I imagine many judges' law school experience has given them a perspective similar to mine.

On reflection, I see that land use encompasses a vast array of topics from annexation to zoning, including but not limited to nonconforming uses, variances, conditional use permits, easements, extraterritorial platting, Tax Incremental Financing Districts (including state constitutional debt limitations), environmental impact statements, condemnation, inverse condemnation, regulatory takings, public use, nuisances, pollution, agricultural districts and farmland preservation, navigable waters, wetlands, floodplains, estoppel of state and local governments, and siting facilities such as prisons, community-based treatment facilities for sexual predators, and ball parks.

Considering all these topics, and looking at a 15- to 20-year span of Wisconsin cases, I conclude that an appellate court decides many land-use cases and that land-use cases are a significant part of state appellate court business.

OBSERVATION #3:
INDIVIDUAL RIGHTS AND
COMMUNITY WELFARE ARE BALANCED

Courts are the bulwark between the government and the individual and between public interests and private interests. Courts perform this traditional judicial function in land-use cases. The decisions in land-use cases often walk a tightrope between safeguarding the rights of private property owners and protecting the public's interest in creating safe, healthy, and livable communities.

A battle rages between two major ideologies regarding property rights and government regulation affecting property. One ideology emphasizes individualism and unhampered private property rights; a second emphasizes environmental considerations and communal health and welfare.

Simply put, the first value system advocates individualism, a free market, business, commerce and industry, and profit-making. This ideology rests on the right to own and use land. Necessary to a realization of this value system and ideology, state and federal compensation must accompany any regulation of land use that goes too far. Of course, the key words are "too far." Advocates of this position recognize that a property right, like any right, may be restricted.

The second value system advocates that private property rights are subordinate to the rights of society. Societal interests justify restraints on individual conduct regarding land use. Regulation will be upheld (without compensation) if it furthers public purposes and leaves a property owner with an economically viable use of the property. Property owners are not ensured the most profitable use; they are ensured a reasonable use.

Advocates of the first value system often cite Justice Brennan's dissent in the 1981 *San Diego Gas* case, in which Justice Brennan wrote, "After all, if a policeman must know the Constitution, then why not a planner?"[1] Justice Brennan wrote that property may be taken for public use by police power regulation within the meaning of the Fifth Amendment and that "once a court established that there was a regulatory 'taking,' the Constitution demands that the government entity pay just compensation."[2]

However, Justice Brennan appears to have taken a different view of the police power of a state encompassing the authority to impose conditions on private development in his dissent in *Nollan v. California Coastal Commission*. In this dissent, Justice Brennan appears to favor land-use control over private property rights. Justice Stevens enjoyed reminding Justice Brennan of his change of position, writing, "I like the hat that Justice Brennan has donned today better than the one he wore in *San Diego*, and I am persuaded that he has the better of the legal arguments here."[3]

Private property is a protected individual right that will at times give way to public welfare. The question is, "When?"

A sentiment seems to be growing that favors private property rights over public welfare. See, for example, the recent Oregon Measure 37,[4] which requires that landowners be paid compensation for reduced property values caused by land-use regulation. This Oregon measure was recently reported in *The New York Times*.[5] *The New York Times* wire service is picked up by newspapers around the country. Legislators read local newspapers. I would expect that state legislators across the country will read about Oregon and request that bills be drafted duplicating Oregon's Measure 37. Ultimately, this legislation will come to the courts.

On the one hand, advocates of this kind of legislation say it will keep planners in check because government will have to pay to regulate private interests. It will create incentives for government to design rules more carefully. On the other hand, detractors say that in times of fiscal difficulties this legislation may chill government regulation.

What is clear, however, is that legislation affecting individual property rights is fodder for the courts.

OBSERVATION #4:
GROUPS SEEK REMEDIES OUTSIDE THE COURTS

Commentators, land-use practitioners, and interest groups should explore a comparative institutional analysis of the courts, the legislature, and administrative agencies in the field of land use.

Professor Brian W. Ohm of the University of Wisconsin Department of Urban and Regional Planning reported in 2000 that the Wisconsin Supreme Court's decisions in an increasing number of land-use cases encouraged interest groups to go to the legislature. Professor Ohm wrote that courts decide land-use cases on a narrow reading of the statutory requirements and avoid appraising the value judgments expressed in the local actions. Professor Ohm's take was that the diverse interest groups decided that it was better to go to the legislature than to rely on case-by-case decisions in the Wisconsin courts. Professor Ohm says that we got smart growth legislation in Wisconsin (which Professor Ohm helped draft) as a result of Wisconsin cases (which, he writes, did not establish any bold, new legal theories but brought to the fore problems with the state's existing land-use laws).

The Wisconsin smart growth legislation resulted from a consensus-building process in mid-1998, bringing together many diverse interest groups such as representatives of counties, cities, and villages; the building industry; planners; Realtors; 1000 Friends of Wisconsin, a grassroots, land-use advocacy organization; and University of Wisconsin faculty (who served as neutral facilitators).[6]

Apparently, some view the legislature as a better venue than the courts for addressing land-use issues.

OBSERVATION #5:
"SMART GROWTH" LITIGATION IS IN WISCONSIN'S FUTURE

Smart growth legislation is sweeping the country, and the phrases "smart growth" and "growing smart" are key words in land-use and land-planning circles. These are not widely known terms in Wisconsin courts. I checked the databases for Wisconsin appellate cases and I found only two cases (one in the Supreme Court and one in the Court of Appeals) that referred to the 1998 statute or used the words "smart growth." There were, of course, many cases (in

Wisconsin and in other states) that used the words "smart" and "growth," but these cases were irrelevant to "smart growth" legislation.

Wisconsin's smart growth legislation does not fully kick in until 2010, so cases mention it only as an aside. Smart growth legislation is still in its gestation period in the Wisconsin appellate courts.

OBSERVATION #6:
ALTERNATIVE DISPUTE RESOLUTION COULD
RESOLVE INTERGOVERNMENTAL DISPUTES

The court system handles an increasing number of disputes between local governments and between local and state governments. These disputes pit a locality, like a town, against a larger unit of government, like a county or a state agency such as the Department of Natural Resources. Each unit of government has land-use powers under state law, but these units have competing interests and may seek different remedies. Consequently, the courts wind up settling intragovernmental disputes.

I often think, "Why are two units of government coming to the third branch of government to settle their disputes? Why can't these units of government negotiate their differences without expending limited government resources on in-house or private counsel to fight in court?"

I suggest these disputes may be better resolved through alternative dispute resolution than in the courts.

OBSERVATION #7:
LITIGATION BY ADVOCACY GROUPS IS ON THE RISE

My sense is that, in prior years, litigation typically involved private property owners thwarted by government action. They sought help from the courts. Today, courts see an increasing number of cases in which groups of neighbors and associations of landowners or environmental interests come into court to challenge a pro-individual-property-owner decision by a trial court or an administrative agency. Thus, the court sees individuals pooling their resources to afford the costs of prolonged litigation.

OBSERVATION #8:
STATE AND FEDERAL CONSTITUTIONAL LAW
ISSUES ARE INVOLVED IN LAND-USE CASES

Constitutional law—federal and state—will be playing a larger role in land-use disputes in state courts because regulatory takings have been, and will continue to be, a major issue presented to the state courts. Furthermore, First Amendment, due process, and equal protection issues arise in land-use cases.

The Wisconsin Constitution, like other constitutions, includes a clause similar to the United States Constitution's protection against the taking of private property for public use without just compensation.

The U.S. Supreme Court cases are forcing the state courts to rethink regulatory takings. State courts are reshaping their state precedent to fit U.S. Supreme Court cases. Furthermore, to the extent that the federal constitution is not interpreted as requiring compensation for land-use regulation, property owners will go to state courts, asking that state courts give broader protection to property owners under the state constitution takings clauses than does the federal constitution.

As you all know, a state constitution can grant greater protection than the federal constitution. One of the next emerging areas in state constitutional law, I predict, will be takings law.

OBSERVATION #9:
NEW PROPERTY RIGHTS AND FORMS
OF OWNERSHIP ARE EMERGING

New forms of property and property protection will emerge in the context of land use. For example, Wisconsin recently had a case involving "dockominiums." A dockominium uses condominium law to sell slips for boat docks. Property owners "condominiumized" a marina, selling slips. The Wisconsin case was fought on the public trust doctrine, but the majority of the court did not get there. Our court said this use did not fit within the traditional concept of condominium law.

The right to farm is another new kind of property interest that has spawned legislation and cases. All 50 states have some form of "right to farm" statutes attempting to protect farmers. For example, these statutes protect farmers from nuisance suits by neighbors objecting to odors or insecticides. Cases are beginning to challenge what some see as government legalization of farm nuisances that are takings of neighboring nonfarm land.

OBSERVATION #10:
COMMON APPELLATE ISSUES APPEAR IN LAND-USE CASES

My last observation is that, in many of the land-use cases, the standard run-of-the-mill appellate court issues appear and may be outcome determinative.

• Just like in nonland-use cases, state and federal constitutional issues requiring constitutional interpretation arise in land-use cases. These include home rule provisions, due process, and equal protection. Concepts of original intent, a living constitution, and similar doctrines play a role.

• Legislative interpretation is a major issue in land-use cases, including local ordinances and statutes as well as administrative rules and regulations. Disputes about standard interpretive doctrines are evident.

• Judicial review of decisions of local and state administrative agencies invokes disputes about the principles governing such review. A court often must determine whether an administrative action is quasi-legislative or quasi-judicial; different rules of judicial review and judicial deference apply. To the extent that administrative decision-making is viewed by the courts as quasi-judicial, courts may require more and more formality at the administrative agency level, with written findings of fact and conclusions of law.

Here's the problem: In many instances, local administrative land-use agencies are untrained volunteer boards, with members of varying experience and sophistication. The smaller the locality, the more issues of conflict of interest and local favoritism are likely to arise. Some agencies will go into closed session and come out with an unexplained result; sometimes a transcript of proceedings makes matters even worse. I suggest that time and effort must be spent training local administrative agencies and providing them with legal assistance.

Speaking of training, I have seen few education programs for judges on land-use issues. Perhaps the American Planning Association (APA) should consider presenting judicial education programs sponsored by state judicial education entities, the National Judicial College, and the American Bar Association.

• State courts tend to look at their own state laws and cases and do not explore the law of other states. Appellate courts can learn from other states' experiences, even though differences exist in the statutes and case law. The Wisconsin Supreme Court has had a number of zoning variance cases determining what "unnecessary hardship" means. When I prepared for this symposium, I found a rich literature on the issue that was not called to our Court's attention, including case law, academic commentary, and articles written by planning and land-use practitioners and scholars. Training is necessary not only for the volunteer boards and judges but also for lawyers who are not land-use specialists but periodically handle these cases.

• Amicus briefs are very helpful to a court if they take a different perspective than that taken by the parties. Amicus briefs should put the case into a broader perspective of planning and land use. In a number of cases, either the Wisconsin chapter of the APA or an association of lake property owners has filed a very useful friend of the court brief. I encourage the APA and its local chapters to continue writing briefs in state court cases. I know brief writing is a time-consuming and expensive project, but these briefs are very worthwhile.

CONCLUSION

Let me conclude by saying that I have, to a large extent, relied on the appellate court workload in Wisconsin, as Professor Mandelker instructed. I paraphrase Garrison Keillor, from our neighboring state of Minnesota and his "Prairie Home Companion" radio program, to remind you that in Wisconsin, all the women judges are strong, all the men judges are good looking, and all of our decisions are above average.

Thank you for giving me this opportunity to speak with you today.

SHIRLEY S. ABRAHAMSON NOTES

1. *San Diego Gas & Electric Co. v. San Diego*, 450 U.S. 621, 661, n. 26 (1981) (Brennan, J., dissenting).
2. Id. at 653, 658 (Brennan, J., dissenting).
3. *Nollan v. California Coastal Comm'n*, 483 U.S. 825, 867 (1987) (Stevens, J., dissenting).
4. Ballot Measure 37 (2004) (available at http://www.oregon.gov/LCD/ measure37.shtml#Text_of_the_Measure).
5. Felicity Barringer, "Property Rights Law May Alter Oregon Landscape," *The New York Times*, Nov. 26, 2004, A1.
6. Brian W. Ohm, *Reforming Land Planning Legislation at the Dawn of the 21st Century: The Emerging Influence of Smart Growth and Livable Communities*, 32 Urb. Law. 181 (Spring 2000).

16

State and Local Planning Programs Have Had Quite an Impact; Perhaps It Is Time for a Rest

Michael M. Berger

It has been almost a quarter of a century since the late Supreme Court Justice William J. Brennan, Jr., challenged the planning profession with his famous query: "If a policeman must know the Constitution, then why not a planner?"[1] It's not that Justice Brennan was unsympathetic to the goals and tribulations of land-use planners. After all, his constitutional gauntlet was thrown down shortly after he had authored the Court's opinion in the *Penn Central* case[2] (generally lauded in planning circles), upholding New York City's Landmarks Preservation Law.

Rather, Justice Brennan had a keen understanding of how easy it is for those in authority—particularly those well-meaning people whose motives are to advance the public weal—to lose sight of the impact of their actions on individuals who happen to be in the way. His message should have been clear: Even as they advance the public weal, they cannot occupy the moral high ground by climbing there on the backs of innocent victims who are pauperized by their actions.

This conference was probably not timed to coincide with any anniversary of Justice Brennan's pithy comment, but it is an appropriate time to take a hard look at how planning is practiced, and to ponder the significance of comparing the constitutional impact of decisions made by young law enforcement officers, who are often compelled to make split-second decisions on dark streets in life-threatening situations, and those made by professional planners with time to reflect and obtain the advice of both colleagues and legal advisers (not to mention copious input from the general public and specific interest groups) before they act.

TWO BIASES REVEALED

My Personal Bias (Or, At Least, Viewpoint)

The late Justice William O. Douglas wisely noted that people with "axes to grind" should reveal that fact when they enter the scholarly lists so their readers will know through what color spectacles their advisors view the problem.[3] He was right, so you are entitled to the following information that has necessarily colored my views no matter how much I try to balance them.

First, I have spent the last 35 years representing landowners and developers, generally in litigation against government agencies that either wanted to condemn their property openly (but pay as little as they could get away with) or subject their property to restrictive regulations that left little or nothing productive to do with the land.[4]

That is, by the way, a broad cross-section of people with ownership interests in land. Landowners and developers, for example, are not the same thing. Landowners are often farmers or individuals, people who have either held land in family ownership for years and finally seek to adjust to changing times and population pressures by converting it to other uses, or people who bought land for their retirement (either to use for themselves or to hold as an investment).[5]

Developers, by contrast, come in all sizes and shapes. Earlier in this program, people heard from Alan Bornstein (another speaker at this conference), who explained the viewpoint of a wealthy landowner/developer—the kind that can afford to simply hold title and wait for the regulatory climate to change if it is temporally unfriendly.[6] Others, however, don't have that luxury. Time is not only money; sometimes it is survival.

The second bit of background coloration comes from my base of operations: California. It is a wonderful state, but every waking moment and every activity seems to be planned and regulated by some official agency. If not today, someone is working on it for tomorrow. Elsewhere in this volume, my fellow Californian, Tony Downs, explains some of the severe regulation in California and its adverse impact on the ability to provide adequate housing (see Chapter 12).[7]

Even after spending prodigious sums and making an enormous effort to draft "general" (California's word for "comprehensive") plans and zoning ordinances, planning agencies rarely approve development proposals that seek to develop land *precisely* in accordance with the applicable planning and zoning. They always demand something less.

The *Del Monte Dunes* litigation, which took years to conclude and which had to go all the way to the U.S. Supreme Court for finality, is a paradigm. There, the 37.6-acre rectangular, undeveloped parcel bordering the Pacific Ocean in Monterey had for many years been planned and zoned for multi-family housing at a density of 29 units per acre. I'll do the math for you: It comes to more than 1,000 homes for the property. That level of development was in keeping with the commercial and multifamily development bordering the parcel. The developer would certainly have been within his rights to pro-pose a 1,000-unit condo development, but he didn't. He sought only 344 sin-gle-family detached homes. The planners turned him down because—at one-third the density of the official plan—it was deemed too dense. They told him to submit a revised plan for 264 units; they turned that one down and sug-gested 224. Then it was 190. Nothing passed muster. That's when the courts got involved.

Here's the planning essence: What's the point of comprehensive plans and zoning ordinances if landowners and developers cannot rely on them as at least rough guides of what they will be allowed to do? Planning and zoning is not cheap, not easy, and (at least in California) not done overnight. Enabling legislation requires intensive analysis involving housing, traffic, geology, the environment, and more, along with multiple public hearings for public input—often by planning commissions as well as governing bodies. After all that, shouldn't it be reliable?[8] However, that's our system and it is why some landowners and developers chafe at it.

The regulators have been actively abetted by a judicial system that is pro-regulation.[9] It's an open secret. People from other parts of the country have acknowledged for years that California is a very difficult place to operate as a land developer. One could present extensive quotes and lists, but the com-ment of two noted planners, Richard Babcock and Charles Siemon, should suffice:

> "California has always been notorious for being the first jurisdiction to sustain extreme municipal regulations. Practitioners in other states have joked about why a developer would sue a California community when it would cost a lot less and save much time if he simply slit his throat."[10]

Thus, my conclusion may be heresy at a conference largely populated by planners—and in a volume of proceedings published by the American Plan-ning Association (APA)—but here it is: We already have too much planning; we need less, not more. Perhaps all that is needed is to take a leaf from the APA's recent labeling success and urge that what we need is "smart plan-ning," not additional layers of more of the same. From the vantage point of landowners, the title of this conference is apt. Planning, as it is practiced, needs reform.

The Organized Planning Community

Justice Brennan's message has apparently fallen on deaf ears in the planning community. Planners, or at least the organized planning community, seem to treat property owners as one of three things: (1) enemies; (2) adversaries; or (3) widgets. One needs to look no further than the presentations at this program and the contents of this volume for proof:

• In a paper handed out at the conference, Stuart Meck (see Chapter 3) referred to a group of homeowners who were opposed to a new Illinois regulatory scheme as the local equivalent of a "white citizen's council." When that line was delivered at the conference, the audience nodded and chuckled.

• Another speaker (see Robert Freilich, Chapter 6) referred to some rural opponents of planning in a derogatory tone, noting that they seemed to view planning and zoning as "commie threats," something designed to force the farmers into Stalinist-type "collective farms"—without any hint of understanding that some people (particularly those less sophisticated than the generality of the planning community) might feel threatened by controls being imposed from outside by people unfamiliar with (and seemingly unconcerned about) their own local and individual needs. Planners in the audience laughed.

• Gerrit-Jan Knaap (see Chapter 7) opined that most planners are Democrats and the audience seemed in agreement. Indeed, at times, the conference seemed like a Democratic Party pep rally, with the assumption being that only Republicans could oppose "good" planning.

• Other speakers at the conference produced lovely graphics, showing population densities, development trends, and the like. Planners like dealing with such charts and statistics. There is nothing wrong—indeed, much right—in doing so, but there is also the tendency to lose sight of the fact that the dots on those charts actually reflect individual people. When planners treat those people as interchangeable items, mere widgets, or ball point pens that can be shifted around as it suits them, the people represented by those dots begin to take umbrage.[11]

Why would people not trust planners? Here are a few current illustrations:[12]

1. *Kelo v. City of New London* is one of the cases pending before the U.S. Supreme Court for decision in 2005. *Kelo* is a case about the abuse of eminent domain, but it all started with planning.

The City of New London, Connecticut, in difficult financial straits, decided it needed to change some land uses on its waterfront. The goal was to attract the sort of redevelopment that would increase the property tax base and provide more jobs. It's hard to quarrel with the goal. The method chosen was to re-plan the area. That was probably fine for part of the land (it was governmentally owned anyway); however, part of it was in an older residential community with people whose families had spent their lives there. These New England homes had been there for generations. They were not blighted. They were not nuisances. They were merely old and small. Their only sin was that they produced little in the way of property taxes—and the city wanted more.

When the owners refused to sell, the city resolved to condemn the homes in order to implement the plan. The properties would be acquired and then leased to a developer for $1 per year so the city's plan could be carried out. After years of bitter litigation, the matter is now before the highest court in the land where a decision will be made on this fundamental planning issue: Can eminent domain be invoked in order to force a change of use from one private development to some other private development that city hall would rather have there, even though the current use is lawful and innocuous? The Connecticut courts upheld the power to force such a conversion.

In light of the *Kelo* experience, perhaps the farmer's comment about the fear of being forced onto "collective farms" by planners becomes more understandable.

2. Oregon has had great success with urban growth boundaries. Those strictly enforced restrictions on "sprawl" (the trendy curse word for outward municipal expansion) have worked to contain Oregon's urban growth in tightly defined areas. Planners—viewing the issue from 20,000 feet and moving land uses around on their giant game boards—generally see this as having been beneficial to the state's residents except, perhaps, for those who own property on the outside of those lines. Those people—individuals who don't like being singled out at random to provide benefits for others at their own expense—have been chafing for years as they watched nearby land being sold and developed for valuable uses while they were compelled to maintain their land undeveloped and economically unproductive so they could continue to provide the bucolic backdrop that others found desirable.

Payback came in November, just before this conference convened. The Oregon electorate passed Measure 37, a very "red state" kind of thing to do in a very "blue state." Measure 37 was an initiative aimed at loosening the death grip that Oregon's land-use regulatory regime has held on property owners on the urban fringe (i.e., those just beyond the urban limit lines).

The new law is quite simple and straightforward. It deals with land-use regulations that reduce the fair market value of property. In contrast to efforts elsewhere (including the U.S. Congress a few years back), this statute does not deal in numbers or percentages; in other words, it does not set any mathematical threshold. Where other statutes (or proposed statutes) required some specific reduction before the remedy would kick in, the new Oregon measure applies to all land-use regulations that have "the effect of reducing the fair market value of the property."

Oregon's law applies to new regulations and new applications of old ones, and it offers the regulating entity this option: Pay compensation to the owners for the reduction in fair market value or remove the restriction. Either way, the owners can get on with life instead of sitting on the sidelines watching life pass by while others enjoy it.

The initiative overwhelmingly passed, garnering some 60 percent of the votes cast, and cannot be dismissed as a fluke. Four years ago, a similar initiative was passed as a constitutional amendment. The Oregon Supreme Court struck it down for procedural reasons having to do with its manner of adoption, not its substance; now it is back again.

The greatest lesson from Oregon may be that it is time to take some of the rigid, centralized control out of land-use disputes. It is also time for those who draw arbitrary lines on the ground, enriching people on one side and impoverishing those on the other, to start viewing those who are directly affected by land-use planning as individuals rather than interchangeable dots on a map or mere elements in bars on a graph. The result of current practices is a lack of trust in those with the power to draw the lines. The upshot is initiatives like Measure 37 that take some of the planning control away from the planners.[13]

3.   Just before this conference convened, a jury in Santa Barbara, California, returned a stunning $5.6 million verdict against the county's planning department. How could that happen and why? The jury was convinced that local planners were playing games with the regulatory law they administered in order to achieve their goal of preventing development. In this case, it wasn't conversion of farmland to condominiums; it was merely using farmland . . . for farming. The planners wanted no use at all, but the county made no effort to buy the land to ensure absence of use. It preferred regulatory stultification.

The jury concluded that the planners had conspired to designate the property as a protected wetland, which would then allow them to prevent any use. The jury apparently found that the planners had engaged a "willingly incompetent consultant," someone they had apparently chosen to rubber stamp the desired conclusion, to tar the property with a "keep out" label.[14]

This should not be shrugged off as aberrational. Although most public servants are well meaning and law abiding, there are others (not merely in the Santa Barbara County Planning Department) who share the zealotry of those involved in that litigation and who believe that good ends *do* justify whatever means are needed to achieve them. They are wrong, of course, and this may be the beginning of catching up to them.

The twin lessons of the Santa Barbara litigation are that:

• The Fifth Amendment (specifically, its guarantees against uncompensated takings and against takings without due process of law) was designed to ensure that only legal means are used to achieve even legitimate goals; and

• Events like this will continue to cast all planners in a suspicious light.

4.   As discussed in more detail later, Californians are currently facing a group of state planners who believe that it is good policy to allow the Pacific Ocean to act "naturally" (i.e., to erode the coastline). This "back-to-nature" concept pits the planners against the owners of coastal properties who want

to construct protective devices so their homes or other improvements (or even vacant land) won't fall into the sea. Some of the planners involved in this effort work for the federal government, so the idea will not remain localized to California, while others want to allow more than just that part of the Pacific Ocean to run wild. What's next?

Confronting landowners by telling them that their investments mean nothing, that their homes mean nothing, and even (because some of the landowners are government agencies) that their streets and bridges mean nothing[15] is not a way to engender warm feelings, or trust, or confidence in the planning community. If anyone wonders why people hurl epithets, these examples should provide some of the reasons.

5.   Everyone favors environmental protection. That isn't an open issue. Any time someone places a generally worded matter on a ballot, or takes a poll of citizens, the answer will come back that the overwhelming majority of people favor environmental protection. Now ask the hard question: Who should pay for it? It is very easy to vote in favor of someone else paying for it. It was easy in Oregon, for example, to say that those people who own rural property should preserve it because the rest of us like the idea of driving through it, or looking at it from our office windows, or having it as the background for our new homes at the far end of the urban limit line. It is more difficult when voters are asked whether they would tax themselves to buy land to preserve it.

A number of years ago, a law professor, who had spent the early part of his legal career as a county staff lawyer, put the matter in stark perspective:

> "The fundamental question that should be faced, and which deserves a rationally developed legislative response, is not *whether* these costs will be paid; it is *who* will pay them, in accordance with *what* substantive and procedural criteria, and through *which* institutional arrangements."[16]

Environmental protection is important, but planners will not serve either themselves or their communities if all their input comes from the local chapter of the 1000 Friends of Whatever or other single-issue organizations. By definition, the planning community must serve a broader constituency, one that includes those who will be asked to forego their own plans for the good of the rest of us. At bottom, if the rest of us aren't willing to pay for the privilege of "preserving" land for our own enjoyment—land that, under our system of constitutional government, is owned by others—then perhaps we need to question the propriety of preserving it at all. Planners, at least, ought to consider the total cost of such measures and make informed decisions accordingly.[17]

6.   The APA's posture is a problem. The APA routinely opposes legislation helpful to property owners and just as routinely supports legislation restrictive of property owners' rights.[18] The same is true of litigation involving planning issues. Judged by its actions, you'd think that the APA was a hired gun for local government. Taking an inventory of land-use cases in the U.S. Supreme Court, it seems there is nothing that local government can do that the APA doesn't support—no matter how outrageous or injurious. The APA knee-jerkly files briefs asking the Supreme Court to support the government action du jour.[19]

The APA even supported local government in *Del Monte Dunes*,[20] where the city's lawyer made the planning profession look like a collection of fools by telling the Supreme Court that a "process" in which the landowner was compelled to submit five different, complex, and expensive proposals with 19 different site plans over a five-year period was "not atypical" of the way city planners act. The Court was outraged, and rightly so, but the APA supported Monterey.[21]

In *Suitum*,[22] where the Tahoe Regional Planning Agency (TRPA) fought strenuously to keep an 80-year-old widow from using her land and from litigating her case on the merits, the APA candidly—and rightly—told the Court that the current ripeness rules[23] are unfair and abuse the rights of landowners. In spite of that conclusion, however, the APA asked the Court to side with the government. Adding insult to injury, when that brief was later cited to a congressional committee considering legislation to change the ripeness rules that the APA had criticized as being unfair and abusive, the APA's then president (Eric Damien Kelly) wrote to the chairman of the House Judiciary Committee to "repudiate" the argument in the brief!

More recently, the APA literally crowed about the decision in *Tahoe-Sierra*, calling it, among other things, "the best legal victory for planning in more than a decade."[24] Well, since it was the *only* Supreme Court win for the government side in more than 15 years,[25] the relief expressed in that statement may be understandable. However, for the APA to also assert that what happened in that case was a victory for "fairness and justice,"[26] or that "all parties"[27] benefit from the decision, is a display of moral nonsense.

The facts behind the headlines need to be understood. Lake Tahoe was changing and the problem—a loss of some of the lake's storied clarity—was at least in part due to the increasing development in the area around the lake. California and Nevada decided they needed a new plan for development and preservation in the area and authorized the TRPA to prepare it.

In response, the TRPA enacted a freeze in 1981 on the development of land it considered hazardous to the lake's clarity. The properties frozen in limbo were quarter-acre, single-family, residentially zoned lots. They were scattered throughout hillside (not lakeshore) subdivisions that had already been partially developed in the 500-square-mile Tahoe basin. In other words, there were no large, cohesive tracts involved. There were no major developers involved—just moms and pops who wanted a home for vacation or retirement.

That initial freeze lasted two years but it wasn't enough for the TRPA to complete its job. Two subsequent freezes (one formal, one informal) extended the period to 32 months. That brings the story down to 1984. At that point, the TRPA adopted its new plan for the region, which made the "temporary" freeze on these parcels permanent. However, because the rest of the 1984 plan granted additional development rights to others in the area, a federal court enjoined its operation. That injunction remained in effect until 1987, when the TRPA adopted another plan. That plan still exists and continues to prohibit the use of virtually all of the lots that were involved in the *Tahoe-Sierra* litigation.

Twenty-three years and counting . . . *that* is the "temporary" period that the individual victims of the TRPA's planning activities have suffered. So the next time someone says that the delay was "only" temporary, keep in mind that the problem is definitional. A significant number of the people who began that litigation in 1984 died waiting for the temporary freeze to end. The rest will follow in due course now that the courts have refused them any remedy.

Ignoring, for the moment, what actually happened to the people who were involved in the *Tahoe-Sierra* litigation, I have to tip my figurative cap to the APA and the others who participated on the government side of the case. They sold the Supreme Court a bill of goods. The Supreme Court thought it was making the world safe for the planning community. That's what the briefs filed by the APA and the other governmental apologists deserve credit for: convincing the Court's swing voters that "good planning" was at stake. Thus, the majority opinion is filled with platitudes and generalities about the need for good municipal planning.

No one ever questioned the propriety of good planning. Indeed, it could easily be argued that a win for the landowners would have been more supportive of "good planning" than the actual result. Such a holding would have explained how planning should take place in a measured and thoughtful way, not under emergency circumstances that require lengthy moratoria to allow last-minute "planning" to take place. That isn't planning; it is damage control. As two commentators put it, "Moratoria should not be used as a crutch in place of long-term planning . . ."[28] or, as a land-use text expanded:

> ". . . moratoria are not an acceptable substitute for consistent advance long-term planning. Moratoria are enacted, in most cases, because comprehensive plans and land development regulations have not been prepared or kept current with changing conditions. If they were, development applications which are unwanted and the kind of 'emergency' planning studies which engender moratoria would be avoided."[29]

The *Tahoe-Sierra* litigation was not about ends but about means. The question was *how* to go about good planning in a constitutional democracy that prides itself on protecting individuals, not *whether* we should have planning at all or whether it should be "good."

The Bill of Rights (including its protection of the rights of property owners) was designed to protect individuals against the collective will of the state—

not the other way around. No provision of the Bill of Rights protects the government against individual citizens. Justice Brennan thought planners ought to know that. It doesn't seem to have sunk in yet.

In a post-*Tahoe-Sierra* release to planning leaders throughout the nation, the APA stressed that "good planning" is "outcomes of planning which are desired by our citizens"[30]—an admirable thought but constitutionally irrelevant. That is *precisely* why the Bill of Rights was enacted: to protect the interests of minorities from majoritarian oppression, even when the majority's desire is to do something "good." For example, while the majority of urban dwellers may be in favor of aggressive police activity to rid residential neighborhoods of crime, that hardly justifies disregard of the Fourth and Fifth Amendments. Similarly, Nazis and Klansmen are protected in their disruptive activities, and confessed murderers are given scrupulous judicial attention—not because the majority wants it, but because the Bill of Rights demands it.

There is nothing in the Supreme Court's opinion about the resulting cost or who would have to bear it. In fact, the Court's disembodied statement that there is some "reciprocity of advantage" because the moratorium protects the interests of everyone is just so much eyewash. Nothing in the opinion explains how people whose land has been *de facto* confiscated for more than two decades obtained any benefit whatever. For a decision by the so-called liberal, or progressive, wing of the Court, the opinion is curiously devoid of any concern for individuals. It is a bloodless, lifeless, soulless bureaucratic screed, callously nullifying cherished constitutional rights of individuals who have done nothing wrong.

I noted earlier that there are three constitutional planning cases pending in the Supreme Court as this goes to press. What posture will the APA assume? At the time of this conference, the APA had already filed a brief in *Lingle v. Chevron*, siding with the regulators in a case seeking to keep courts from judging whether regulations are designed to (or will, or even can) substantially advance legitimate state interests.[31] In *Kelo*, the briefs challenging the city's action of condemning an innocuous group of homes so the area's tax base can be upgraded had already been filed when the conference was held. The APA did not join that group.[32] Briefs supporting the city were yet to be filed and I confidently predicted that the APA once again would side with the government. Predictably, the APA did.

None of the briefs had yet been filed in *San Remo Hotel*, a case dealing with the Supreme Court's ripeness rules about when (and even whether) a landowner can sue for a regulatory taking in federal court. The APA *could* again have made the argument it did in *Suitum* (i.e., that it is unfair to compel landowners, alone among constitutional claimants, to sue in state courts); it could have taken the position it did in the congressional hearings and disown its *Suitum* position in favor of once again supporting the government; or the

APA could choose to just sit this one out. Since the conference, the APA has taken the government side.

It is time for the planning profession to develop a more balanced agenda—one that accounts for the interests of the regulated as well as the regulators. Bob Freilich's paper echoes this thought. Instead of constantly fighting with landowners, the planning community along with government agencies responsible for land regulation ought to be looking for ways to involve the markets to help achieve goals that serve all parties. We will, I am convinced, get better planning, happier citizens, and more justice.

SOME RECENT CASE STUDIES

To flesh out the discussion, the remainder of this paper consists of some recent case studies in planning that I think illustrate much of what is wrong with planning today. A number of them arise in California. I like to use California as an exemplar, not only because I live there, but because California is something of a national laboratory. Things that start there eventually end up infecting the rest of the country.

New "Environmental" Initiatives Aim to Revert California to What It Was

A few years ago, there was a movie called "Back to the Future" about a crazy scientist who invented a time machine that had no trouble running backwards but developed problems returning to where it began. Don't look now, but there is a growing cadre of folks who are trying to turn the clock back to the 19th century and even earlier—a group of modern-day Luddites, in the name of protecting the environment, wants to send us all back and leave us there.

There is, for example, a project currently underway by the California Resources Agency, dealing with the state's entire 1,100-mile coast. The effort is aided and abetted by a number of traditional environmental groups. The question is: What should be done to protect coastal development (both public and private) from the ravages of the sea? The new environmentalists' answer is "nothing."

If that sounds like an exaggeration, here's a recent illustration that illuminates the point. There is a cliff at a place called Pleasure Point, overlooking Monterey Bay. There is a road on top of the cliff and on the inland side of the road there are homes. The ocean has had such an erosive impact on the base of the cliff that the cliff has been disappearing at a rate of about a foot each year. The Corps of Engineers, the city, the county, and the folks who live on top of the cliff want to erect a seawall to stop the erosion. The new environmentalists "believe nature should be allowed to take its course, even if it means losing East Cliff Drive and the houses opposite the bluff."[33] They call this process "managed retreat" (i.e., they would permit no "artificial" protection to be built and let the chips—or houses or roads—fall where they may).

It's easy for them to say. They don't own a home being slated for catastrophe nor are they responsible for maintaining a public street that is in danger of falling into the sea. Their only concern is in returning the coastline to the way it was before people decided that the coast was a pleasant place to live. One way or another, that dispute will be resolved. Either East Cliff Drive will survive or the locals will be treated to the spectacle of watching first the street and then the homes plummet off the cliff. If you've never seen such an event, it's not a pretty sight.

As noted, however, this is only illustrative of a far larger problem. The campaign against "armoring" or "hardening" the coast is in full swing in Sacramento and, in typical political fashion, it is being waged in a semi-clandestine fashion. If the proponents were being honest, they could have simply introduced legislation that said, "Henceforth, there will be no construction in the coastal zone, nor shall there be any protective devices built or maintained to protect construction that already exists. The ocean shall be allowed to attack the coast at will, unimpeded by manmade protective devices." Put bluntly, it just might be too harsh to sell, but that's not the program that is being put forward in writing. Instead, the program is being advertised as one that merely deals with "coastal erosion planning." The plan, however, has the potential to wipe out much of the development along the coast that has been built up over the last century.

Here's one proposed provision: "Barriers to natural sources of sand leading from coastal watersheds to beaches shall be reduced or eliminated and sand flow currently restricted by dams or other structures shall be reestablished." Ponder that one: How would one "reestablish" sand flow (to replenish beaches and reduce coastal erosion, of course) that is currently restricted by dams or retention basins? The only logical answer is to eliminate the existing dams and retention basins that now disrupt sand flow to the coast but, in the process, protect inland developments from severe flood damage. To be sure, the provision says this should be done "whenever feasible," but by whose definition of feasibility? Judging by the public comments of those in favor of such legislation, feasibility would have nothing to do with protecting the investments of individuals and government agencies and everything to do with "letting nature take its course."

The plan to revert the coast to the days of yore is not the only such plan afoot today. There is also Yosemite National Park, one of California's—if not the nation's—favorite places to visit. In late 1996, the park was struck by the worst flood in 80 years. It scoured the valley, leaving much destruction in its wake. Damages were estimated at $178 million, and Congress soon appropriated slightly more than that to reconstruct the facilities so the park could once again be a tourist mecca.

However, the Park Service has a different idea. Its plan is to restore the park's "natural environment" (i.e., put it back the way it was before explorers and settlers appeared on the scene). In the Park Service's view, they would not use the appropriated funds to rebuild the facilities that had served more than four million visitors before the flood, but would instead "restore the natural habitat and 'hydrological processes' of the river."[34]

If the Park Service succeeds (this "restoration" plan has been in the works since the Carter administration, and the 1996 flood gave its sponsors an excuse to implement it), the plan will radically limit the public's access to the park as well as the public's ability to use the park. The plan calls for the reduction in the amount of shelter available for overnight campers, along with the removal of bridges, roads, and parking lots. That suits some in the so-called environmental community just fine (i.e., those who believe that the nation's public lands are only to be enjoyed by those who can hike in to see them). That cuts out an awful lot of taxpayers who foot the bill for these publicly owned facilities.

Finally, there is California's plan for trees. Californians love trees. They love them when they are growing and they love them when they are converted into lumber. At the present time, however, they are trying to have it both ways. While California regulations make it more and more difficult for local timber growers to harvest trees (resulting in another historic reversion by forcing forested areas that have been used as croplands for years to revert to their primeval state), Californians are using more lumber than ever through what some have called "economic imperialism": we import it from Canada. Thus, while Californians can feel smug about restoring their historic forests, they needn't concern themselves about what their consumptive desires are doing to Canada. It's too far away to worry about.[35]

In a nutshell, if you like living in the 21st century, watch your back. There is a movement afoot to reverse the steady march of progress and regress to an earlier (easier?) time. While there may have been much that was good in the way things were in the past, it is not realistic to attempt to turn back the clock—particularly when it comes to how and where people make use of their land. "Their land" is used here, of course, in an individualistic sense; unless we want to further burden an already overweight state budget with the cost of buying an awful lot of land in order to "revert" it to nature, time would be far better spent in deciding how to house our population and protect the large public and private investments that already exist. Pipe dreams about "letting nature take its course" are just that—pipe dreams—and are not realistic.

State Coastal Commission "Gives" Malibu New Land-Use Plan

For nearly its entire existence (now more than a quarter of a century), the California Coastal Commission has been at war with coastal communities and coastal property owners. Some would undoubtedly say that it shows the commission's success and that the whole idea of establishing the commission in the first place was to control the thoughtless ways that those in local charge of the coast were dealing with it.

However, the commission, in the time-honored way of zealots, went overboard. One of its cherished policies, for example, has always been to have a public beach that stretches from Mexico to Oregon. In pursuit of that goal, the commission routinely demanded that any coastal landowner seeking a permit to do anything must "dedicate" an easement over the sand to the public. Seventeen years ago, the U.S. Supreme Court struck down that tactic, calling it not a "gift" but "extortion."[36]

Most recently, the commission took aim at an entire city in one gulp. Malibu is something of a cheap-shot target for populists. It's trendy, flashy, and populated by rich people—the kind of folks it's fun to poke with a stick, sort of the modern-day equivalent of placing a banana peel on the ground in front of the fat guy in a top hat. (At least that's the image from outside.) Who can work up any empathy for people like that? "They" are not, after all, "us."

Anyone who doubts the ease with which one can poke fun at Malibu doesn't read Garry Trudeau's "Doonesbury" comic strip. For those who missed it, one of Trudeau's targets has been people who own homes on the beach in Malibu. His weapon of choice for this foray is Zonker Harris, former professional tanner, who roused the rabble to storm the beachfront citadels of the rich and famous. That's a bit of a digression but useful local folklore nonetheless.

For all coastal communities except Malibu, land-use plans are drawn up and controlled by local political leaders, which sometimes presents its own problems, but at least any complications are homegrown. Here, the legislature (for what it believed were good reasons) decided to wrench control from the Malibu City Council and assign the task of deciding Malibu's land uses to an agency controlled by the state legislature itself.[37] Two-thirds of the commission's voting members are appointed by the speaker of the assembly and the chairman of the Senate Rules Committee.[38]

Locals—ranging from elected officials to small lot owners—have lived in fear while state officials they did not elect and can neither influence nor control debated their fate. Now they've done it: After a stunning and salty two-day hearing, the commission adopted a plan and told Malibu to enforce it. That's the commission's way of "returning" control to the city: adopting a plan and cramming it down the city's municipal craw.

What's the problem, one might ask? Good planning is good planning, isn't it? What difference does it make which agency officially draws up the plan? From the standpoint of Malibu property owners, the difference is between the devil you know and the one who drops in for the weekend. As much rancor as local landowners sometimes experience with their elected officials, at least they know where those officials live and that their names will be on a ballot sometime in the near future. If they displease too many people, the time-honored remedy is to throw the rascals out.

From the standpoint of Malibu's governing officials, they have been evicted from one of a municipality's most important tasks: deciding land-use issues. Nothing hits closer to home than issues regarding housing and local commercial development—especially at a time when California as a whole is producing tens of thousands of housing units fewer than needed each year to keep up with the growing population. Local government wants, indeed needs, to have its hand on the controls. When a city council drafts its own land-use ordinances, it has hopefully benefited from input from the local citizens and usually has both a sincere interest in local problems and a deep knowledge of local conditions.

Not so with the Coastal Commission's roving band. They dropped in for a visit, drew up their ukase about permissible land uses, and ordered the local officials (who are then expected to face the wrath of those being controlled) to enforce it. They also set policies involving such locally sensitive issues as how and where to establish beach access points (touchy issues related to traffic, safety, sanitation, and the like that local folks will have to deal with long after the nomadic coastal commissioners have gone on to other pastures) without either being intimately familiar with the local concerns or having to live with the consequences afterward. (Anyone who doesn't think this particular issue is touchy needs to check out those Doonesbury strips—or the pending lawsuit that inspired them, in which a prominent local record producer sued the Coastal Commission, trying to prevent it from opening a beach access path on his property.)[39]

From the landowners' point of view, one of the largest bones of contention deals with the commission's designation of half or more of the city as an "environmentally sensitive habitat area." That is a problem for those who own such land because it is not just a benign, generic description; it is a legal term of art that has strict restrictions. As applied by our courts, one who owns land so designated can make virtually no productive use of it. None. Zip. Nada.[40]

Thus, by slapping that label on a large swath of Malibu, the commission has essentially doomed large numbers of landowners to either hold open space for the rest of the community to enjoy (at no cost to the public but substantial expense to the individual) or engage in protracted, expensive litigation in an effort to free themselves from that yoke. On lots that are already developed, but now designated as environmentally sensitive, must homes be removed? If not, can they ever be expanded or repaired? Current case law doesn't address these issues; neither does the Coastal Act. The parties have been in litigation and the future for more seems assured.[41]

As either a sop to landowners or an effort to be scrupulously fair (depending on your point of view), the commission included a provision that permits landowners to ask the city to declare that the new regulations do not permit an economically viable use on a particular lot. The monkey is first placed on the landowner's back to prove the absence of economically viable use and, if she can, the burden shifts to the city to either deviate from the plan that the city didn't want in the first place or buy the property. (Note that, even though it is the commission's plan, it is the city that will bear the burden of acquiring properties deemed constitutionally taken by its harsh terms. There is no reason why the commission would have placed that burden on itself or some other state agency.)

Any deviation, of course, will certainly be appealed to the Coastal Commission. Yes, in the wonderful world of the Coastal Act, the plan that the commission itself drafted for Malibu is ultimately overseen by the commission itself. Thus, anyone who thinks the city either caved in too easily (because it never liked the plan in the first place) or showed too little moxie in defending it can appeal to the commission so it can decide whether its plan is being properly maintained. In the quaint realm of California's Coastal Act, if no one else appeals, the commissioners themselves can appeal such a decision and then sit in judgment on their own appeal. Honest.[42]

If a landowner somehow survives this gauntlet and emerges from a Coastal Commission hearing with either a permit or cash from the city, the only certainty is that the same folks who appealed to the commission will sue the commission to overturn the approval. That's what passes as a remedy for landowners in coastal California.

The commission's action was only the first shot in a war—a salvo toward Fort Sumter, if you will. The stakes are too high for either the city or its residents to meekly accept this dictat from on high.

Change Happens. Get Used to It.

Explaining the recent denial of a land developer's request to rezone property so it could be subdivided and improved, the head of the governing board in Oconee County, Georgia, said, "Who likes change? A wet baby. That's the only person who likes change."[43] Short-sighted? Sure, but if such views were restricted to bucolic locales in the rural south, it wouldn't be worth mentioning. They're not.

By now, everyone is accustomed to seeing those who have acquired their home in the hills (or in the suburbs, or at the beach, or pick your own favorite destination) attempting to keep others out, or to "preserve" open buffer zones to separate them from the rest of the world. The sponsors of such measures generally talk the talk of environmentalism; it is pure coincidence that it maintains their own upwardly mobile home values.

Another movement has been gaining momentum lately: historic preservation. It is hard to be "against" historic preservation (just as it is hard to be "against" environmental protection). At bottom, there is nothing wrong with the concept of historic preservation. It is a wonderful thing that New York City's Grand Central Terminal was preserved.[44] The same goes for the Willard

Hotel in Washington, DC, sometime home of U.S. presidents and others of similar international rank.[45] Doubtless, everyone has his or her favorite example of a timeless treasure preserved. The issue often at the bottom of such cases, however, is economic: Should the current owners of the building be required to maintain it at their own expense for the greater benefit of society at large?

As with other issues that buzz around the Fifth Amendment's Just Compensation clause, the courts have tended to decide such issues on an ad hoc, case-by-case basis, sometimes (as in *Penn Central*) telling the owners to come back if they can no longer make a living with the preserved property (factually erroneous with respect to Grand Central Terminal, but that story is too long to tell here[46]), and at other times (as in *Benenson*) compelling the government to bear the cost of preservation. However, this discussion isn't so much about the taking of property without compensation as it is about the abuse of the concept of historic preservation that is made by some who are simply trying to influence land-use decisions rather than actually preserve historic sites.

One is reminded of the great San Fernando Valley car wash flap where a group of citizens waged a long (although ultimately unsuccessful) battle to have the City of Los Angeles declare a Ventura Boulevard car wash "historic" to prevent its owner from converting the site to a more profitable use. How about the folks (also in the San Fernando Valley) who urged the city to designate as a historic site a vacant parcel that was once the site of the procreative exertions of a prize Hereford bull named Sugwas Feudal?[47]

On the other side of the country, what was sometimes called the Third Battle of Manassas (or Bull Run, depending on whether your progenitors wore blue or grey uniforms) took place in Virginia a decade ago over land use around the historic battlefield—not on the battlefield itself, mind you, but on neighboring territory. A group of historians proclaimed themselves outraged that anything touching the hallowed ground might contain any kind of modern development. They were particularly offended that the Disney organization (whose historic credentials were questioned) announced its intent to create a historical theme park in the vicinity. When the dust settled, Disney withdrew, apparently preferring to avoid the public relations impact of such a fight. Thus, the answer to the question, "Who lost the Third Battle of Bull Run?" was "Disney."[48]

More recently, the decision by the National Trust for Historic Preservation—usually a pretty level-headed organization—to designate the entire State of Vermont as an endangered historic site has caught the headlines.[49] That's right; the entire state is endangered. Usually, the National Trust focuses on specific buildings, sometimes on physical landmarks, but an entire state? What's the threat? It seems that there is an army poised on Vermont's borders, imminently waiting to invade. As described on the National Trust's Web site,[50] Vermont was placed on the endangered list because "it now faces an invasion of behemoth stores that could destroy much of what makes Vermont

Vermont." The National Trust for Historic Preservation has declared war on Wal-Mart. Nothing personal, mind you; it's just that the folks at the National Trust have different ideas about land-use planning than the businesspeople who direct the nation's largest corporation.

This is not a plea for corporate control of land-use planning or a concession that organizations like the National Trust for Historic Preservation (i.e., organizations that have a discrete axe to grind) are the best source of general land-use planning advice. Both corporate landowners and tightly focused interest groups have a kind of tunnel vision that allows them to provide valuable input into the planning process, but they are too self-centered to be controlling.

So what is it about Wal-Mart that offends the National Trust (setting aside the possible political proclivities of its leaders)? Land-use issues. Again, according to the National Trust Web site, the issues range through traffic, environmental impacts, the compatibility of new structures with old ones, and the threat that building one big-box retailer is "sure to attract an influx of other big-box retailers."[51] (The number of such stores that the National Trust believes Vermont's 600,000 residents can support are not mentioned.)

The remaining objections appear to be political, including a presumed "erosion of the sense of community that seems an inevitable by-product of big-box sprawl"[52] and the assertion that "there are communities all over America whose downtowns have been devastated by the arrival of big-box retailers."[53] Maybe, maybe not; those are matters of opinion, not fact.

The National Trust has accomplished some good things over the years, but its focus currently seems to have reached a bit afield. In addition to placing the State of Vermont on its endangered list, the group also wants to preserve the historic Bethlehem Steel Plant in Pennsylvania: a once-vibrant part of industrial America but currently a rusty derelict that, in the National Trust's words, "lies dormant and threatened with demolition."[54] With all respect, *shouldn't* such a decaying hulk be threatened with demolition? Who will pay to take it over and preserve it in amber as a museum piece?

Before leaving the National Trust, don't miss the recent issue of its magazine that seems to wax poetic about the beauty of the skies revealed last August when the North American power grid failed, plunging much of the northeastern part of the country into blackness.[55] Will next year's list of most endangered sites include the night sky? To "preserve" that, do we return to the Stone Age?

Returning to first principles, there is nothing intrinsically wrong with historic preservation. However, the concept needs to be tempered by reality. Contrary to the Georgia politician quoted earlier, it isn't just wet babies who like change; more than that, it isn't just wet babies who need change. When facilities outgrow their usefulness and decay (like the Bethlehem Steel plant), they need recycling. When historic structures are worth preserving for all of us to enjoy, then all of us ought to figure out a way to finance their preservation. When land-use planning is being proposed for an entire state, it ought to be based on more than distaste for an obviously popular mode of commerce.

San Francisco Makes Innovative Use of Rent Control to Affect Land Use; Courts Order It to Loosen Its Grip on Landlords

San Francisco has long used rent-control ordinances as land-use control devices to maintain what city government views as the appropriate housing balance. Indeed, it has a knack for adopting landlord/tenant ordinances that raise constitutional eyebrows, even when courts uphold its actions.[56] Recently, the Court of Appeal held that the city may have pushed too hard again and remanded a case for trial of a constitutional takings challenge that could result in either invalidation or compensation, or both.[57]

Cwynar involved an initiative measure that restricted (and, in some cases, forbade) landlords from either occupying units in their own buildings or having relatives do the same. The provisions of the ordinance were written in the context of preventing landlords from compelling existing tenants to vacate the premises. In a nutshell, the ordinance did three things:

1. It commanded that only one building owner could live in the building at one time. As soon as one owner obtained possession of a unit by asking a tenant to leave, no other owner could ever seek to occupy another unit. Thus, if a building had more than one owner, as soon as the first of them became an occupant of the building, the others were foreclosed.

2. The ordinance said that a landlord could recover possession of a unit for a family member to occupy only if the owner was either residing in the building already or was seeking a unit for him or herself. Thus, unless the owner intended to live in the building, no family member could be placed there.

3. The ordinance precluded eviction of tenants who were old, disabled, or catastrophically ill, and who had lived in the building a specified period of years.

A number of San Francisco landlords (all owners or part owners of small, three- to six-unit apartment buildings) and three trade associations sued, challenging the constitutionality of the ordinance. The trial court sustained the city's demurrers without leave and the Court of Appeal reversed.

The plaintiffs were an interesting group, obviously designed to raise difficult and concrete issues for decision. Plaintiff Cwynar, for example, was part owner of a three-unit building. Because a co-owner already occupied a unit in the building, the plaintiff was forbidden to move into a second unit and also forbidden to move her sister into the third unit. Plaintiff Cox, a retired disabled schoolteacher with AIDS, bought a six-unit building along with his friends, the Crotwells. Each of the co-owners intended to combine two of the small apartments into a single unit (thus ousting four of the existing tenants) and live there. As Mrs. Crotwell was a nurse, she would be able to care for Mr. Cox. Plaintiff Salma bought a six-unit building so that each of his four children could have his or her own apartment. However, as Mr. Salma did not intend to live in the building, he was prohibited from moving *any* of his children into it. There were others, but the picture should be fairly clear by now that the group illustrated with bright lines and vivid colors the problems the ordinance caused to rental housing owners.

The Court of Appeal first held that the ordinance could result in a coerced permanent physical occupation of private property and thus be a taking that would require compensation. The court had to deal with the U.S. Supreme Court's decision in *Yee*[58] but had little trouble doing so. *Yee* involved a challenge to a rent-control ordinance that permitted existing tenants in a mobile home park to sell their units to incoming tenants and prohibited raising rent at that time. *Yee* was a purely economic challenge. The landlords complained about their inability to choose their tenants but only because of the impact that it had on their ability to charge market rents. Here, by contrast, the landlords wanted to move either themselves or family members into properties that they owned and the ordinance forbade it.

The Court seemed to have no trouble concluding that the situation was brought about through government coercion, as the ordinance plainly set up its goals and responded to them. There seemed to be some question in the Court's mind whether the occupation was permanent; however, that also seemed possible to prove and indeed, it should. Although the opinion failed to mention it, the rudiments of "permanency" in this context were amply explained by a federal appeals court in *Hendler*.[59] There, in dealing with environmental cleanup problems involving the Stringfellow Acid Pits, the government took indefinite possession of neighboring property.

The government claimed in *Hendler* that its occupation was not permanent, but the court would have none of it. "In this context, 'permanent' does not mean forever, or anything like it." The court went on to explain that the intent to remain indefinitely sufficed and that a governmental command that third parties be allowed to use private property at will was a permanent governmental taking. Indeed, on the facts before it, the Court of Appeals reversed a judgment favoring the government and remanded with directions to enter summary judgment for the property owner. That analysis should provide substantial assistance on the remand of *Cwynar*.

The *Cwynar* court also held that the ordinance could be a regulatory taking under each of the extant theories supporting such a cause of action. Such a taking occurs if:

1. The regulation fails to substantially advance a legitimate state interest[60]; or

2. If it denies the owners economically productive use of their land[61]; or

3. If, on the examination of a series of factors (including the economic impact on the owners; interference with their distinct, investment-backed expectations; and the character of the governmental action) the totality of circumstances demonstrates that the owners are contributing more than their fair share to the general welfare.[62]

Undoubtedly, the theory the city felt most confident about was that its ordinance substantially advanced a legitimate state interest. It claimed to be maintaining a reasonable balance of owner-occupied and rental housing; preserving affordable housing; and avoiding the displacement of the old, the sick, the poor, and the disabled. Although the court agreed that the goals were legitimate, that was not the issue. The issue was whether this ordinance was a means that substantially advanced those goals.

The court was unable to reach that conclusion as a matter of law. It was not clear that the ordinance would preserve a "reasonable balance" or that it would preserve "affordable" housing. This was not, after all, a rent-control ordinance but an occupancy ordinance. In any event, it could not be said that either the "one owner per building" rule or the family occupancy restriction rule had anything to do with any of these goals. Trial will be needed.

With respect to balancing the series of factors to determine whether the plaintiff is being asked to contribute more than a fair share to the community, the court noted the seriousness of the owners' charge that they were being singled out to forfeit their own homes in order to create public housing. The right to occupy one's own property is a weighty one and cannot be dealt with in a cavalier fashion. After all, the U.S. Supreme Court has repeatedly noted that one of the most important of the rights we call "property" is the right to possession, including the right to exclude others. The strength of that right is such that it prevails even when the intrusion is minimal and has little, if any, economic impact.[63]

Nor does the fact that the owners still retained property of significant value undermine their takings case. The California Supreme Court has noted that takings can occur despite that, particularly where—as here, with the right to live in one's own building—the regulation extinguishes a fundamental attribute of ownership.[64]

A SUMMING UP

Plainly, state and local planning initiatives have had an impact. Contrary to the impression one might gain from the foregoing, I don't believe it has all been bad. However, there is an unfortunate zealousness that tends to permeate city halls in this field and I'm hard pressed to say that Houston looks any worse than Los Angeles.

MICHAEL M. BERGER NOTES

1. *San Diego Gas & Elec. Co. v. City of San Diego*, 450 U.S. 621, 661, n. 26 (1981) (Brennan, J., dissenting).
2. *Penn Central Transp. Co. v. City of New York*, 438 U.S. 104 (1978).
3. William O. Douglas, *Law Reviews and Full Disclosure*, 40 Wash. L. Rev. 227, 228-230 (1965).

4. I represented the property owners in the U.S. Supreme Court cases of *Tahoe-Sierra Preservation Council v. Tahoe Regional Planning Agency,* 535 U.S. 302 (2002); *City of Monterey v. Del Monte Dunes,* 526 U.S. 687 (1999); *Preseault v. I.C.C.,* 494 U.S. 1 (1990); and *First English Evangelical Lutheran Church v. County of Los Angeles,* 482 U.S. 304 (1987); and prepared amicus curiae briefs in many of the Supreme Court's remaining significant takings cases during the past quarter-century. I have, for example, prepared amicus curiae briefs supporting the landowners' position in three cases pending in that Court at this writing, slated for decision in 2005: *Kelo v. City of New London,* case no. 04-108; *Lingle v. Chevron U.S.A., Inc.,* no. 04-163; and *San Remo Hotel v. City and County of San Francisco,* no. 04-340.

5. In *Tahoe-Sierra,* for example, the hundreds of landowner/plaintiffs consisted of individual owners of quarter-acre lots, not owners of large land holdings. In addition to being subjected to a severe moratorium by planners, the owners found their interests discounted by the courts because they held their land for retirement rather than immediately seeking to develop it.

6. Some have commented, for example, that they would just leave the land to their grandchildren to deal with, anticipating that time would change regulatory viewpoints.

7. California adds more than half a million people to its population each year, but planning and zoning regulations—most local, but some (like those of the California Coastal Commission) come from the state level—prevent construction of housing to match that increase (e.g., Miguel Bustillo, "Democrats Urge $1-Billion Plan to Ease Chronic Housing Shortage," *Los Angeles Times,* May 5, 2000, A22; Joel Kotkin, "Locked Out of a House," *Los Angeles Times,* Sept. 22, 2002, M3). Because of the continuing lack of available housing, the Southern California Association of Governments gave a D+ housing grade to the counties of Los Angeles, Orange, Riverside, San Bernardino, Ventura, and Imperial (Laura Coleman, "Southern California Cities Fail to Make the Housing Grade," *California Real Estate Journal,* Oct. 6, 2003, 16). What kind of planning is that?

8. In *MacDonald, Sommer & Frates v. County of Yolo,* 477 U.S. 340 (1986), the U.S. Supreme Court even suggested that a developer, whose plan for a residential subdivision was rejected, needed to try again with a lesser development on pain of having his vision—wholly in keeping with the existing planning and zoning—dubbed "exceedingly grandiose."

9. *Del Monte Dunes* was not decided in California's courts. When suit was filed in 1984, California's courts were so unsympathetic that they provided no compensation remedy for regulatory takings. The only remedy was to seek invalidation and, if successful, to try again with a different plan. (Compare Justice Brennan's comments on this sorry situation in *San Diego Gas,* 450 U.S. at 655, n. 22.) That situation didn't change until the *First English* decision in 1987. Thus, that litigation took place in federal court and ultimately in the U.S. Supreme Court.

10. Richard F. Babcock and Charles L. Siemon, *The Zoning Game Revisited* (Cambridge, MA: Lincoln Institute of Land Policy, 1985), 293. Things haven't changed much since those words were written.

11. Indeed, that umbrage is sometimes reflected in epithets like "commie," as noted above.

12. The latter portion of this paper contains more detailed case studies.

13. This brings to mind the whole issue of "ballot box planning." I have often wondered why the organized planning community hasn't risen up en masse to protest this clear invasion of the planners' world; if it has happened, I confess I have missed it. Indeed, my own anecdotal litigational experience has been that planning groups have supported such practices which, until Measure 37, generally restricted the ability of owners to use their land.

14. The story is reported in the *Los Angeles Daily Journal,* Nov. 30, 2004, 1. An earlier appeal in the case resulted in an "unpublished" appellate decision (one of the judiciary's little *1984* aspects) that can be found online as *Adam Bros. Farming, Inc. v. County of Santa Barbara,* 2002 WL 31053937, remanding the case for the trial that recently concluded. My earlier comment

about California's generally unfriendly courts referred to judges, not juries. When jurors are allowed to hear about the kind of shenanigans practiced here, they respond accordingly—as they did in this case and in *Del Monte Dunes*. Perhaps that is why those on the regulatory side in *Del Monte Dunes* fought so hard in their unsuccessful effort to convince the Supreme Court that juries should not be allowed to consider government liability in these cases.

15. Honest. The discussion appears later in this paper.

16. Arvo Van Alstyne, *Just Compensation of Intangible Detriment: Criteria for Legislative Modification in California*, 16 U.C.L.A. L. Rev. 491, 543-544 (1969). [Emphasis in original.]

17. For earlier discussions, see Michael M. Berger, *Do Planners Really Chafe at Being Fair?* 41 Land Use Law & Zoning Digest 3 (April 1989); Michael M. Berger, *The State's Police Power Is Not (Yet) the Power of a Police State*, 35 Land Use Law & Zoning Digest 4 (May 1983).

18. *Planning* magazine routinely contains reports of either national policies or local chapter actions regarding such legislation. To my observation, the reports are uniformly pro-regulator and anti-landowner.

19. To be fair, I am aware of one case in which the APA filed a brief in the U.S. Supreme Court opposing government action. The case was *Bersani v. E.P.A.*, 850 F.2d 36 (2d Cir. 1988), U.S. Supreme Court no. 88-902, *cert. denied.* I filed the brief on the APA's behalf. Note, however, that the agency was not state or local government, and the issue was not traditional planning and zoning. The agency was the federal Environmental Protection Agency and the issue involved a nonsensical policy requiring individual landowners seeking development permission to show that there were no alternative locations for their projects, even though the applicants owned no other property and other alternative locations were not for sale.

20. *City of Monterey v. Del Monte Dunes*, 526 U.S. 687 (1999).

21. Although the author of the APA's brief has emphasized to me that the brief only dealt with the standard of review, not the city's treatment of the landowner, the fact remains that the brief was filed in support of the city, and sought reversal of the judgment and contained no hint of criticism of the city's actions. It always seemed to me that this was an appropriate case for the APA to take the high road and condemn the sort of planning that went on in Monterey, but it didn't. By the way, after the decision came down affirming judgment against the city, the city attorney was asked how the city's practices would change. His response: "Will it change anything? No. It was clear we complied with the law then. We comply with the law now." Kristi Belcamino, "Monterey Loses Long Court Battle," *The Herald* (Monterey County), May 25, 1999, at A10. Note that no court agreed with his conclusion.

22. *Suitum v. Tahoe Regional Planning Agency*, 520 U.S. 725 (1997).

23. This is no place to discuss such legal arcana. Those who are interested are invited to peruse, *inter alia*, Michael M. Berger, "The 'Ripeness' Mess in Federal Land Use Cases, or How the Supreme Court Converted Federal Judges Into Fruit Peddlers," in *Institute on Planning, Zoning, and Eminent Domain* (New York: Matthew Bender & Co., Inc., 1991), Chapter 7; Michael M. Berger, "Supreme Bait & Switch: The Ripeness Ruse in Regulatory Takings," in *A Festschrift in Honor of Daniel R. Mandelker*, 3 Wash. U. J.L. & Pol'y 99, Chapter 3 (2000); Michael M. Berger and Gideon Kanner, *Shell Game! You Can't Get There From Here. Supreme Court Ripeness Jurisprudence in Takings Cases at Long Last Reaches the Self-Parody Stage*, 36 Urb. Law. 671 (2004).

24. American Planning Association press release, April 23, 2002.

25. Note how a win for the government became translated as a win for "planning." The facts belie that conclusion. Read on.

26. Note 24, *supra.*

27. Id.

28. Wendy U. Larsen and Marcella Larsen, *Moratoria as Takings Under Lucas,* 46 Land Use Law & Zoning Digest 3 (June 1994).
29. Michael A. Zizka et al., *State & Local Government Land Use Liability* (Eagan, MN: West Group, 2000), § 4:4, 4-14.
30. American Planning Association, "Talking Points" accompanying press release entitled "U.S. Supreme Court Decision: A Solid Win For Planning," April 23, 2002. Additional overstatements in that release are commented on in Dwight Merriam, *Tahoe Sierra: A Takings Time Warp?* 25 Zoning & Planning Law Report 41, 47 (June 2002).
31. That requirement was established and applied in a series of Supreme Court decisions including: *Agins v. City of Tiburon,* 447 U.S. 255, 260 (1980); *Hodel v. Irving,* 481 U.S. 704, 718 (1987); *Nollan v. California Coastal Commn.,* 483 U.S. 825 (1987); and *City of Monterey v. Del Monte Dunes,* 526 U.S. 687 (1999). See also *Tahoe-Sierra,* 535 U.S. at 334.
32. To their credit, a number of prominent law professors who are also APA members joined a group that filed a brief challenging the city's action.
33. David L. Beck, "Foes Envision Rough Ride For Plan to Protect Cliff," *San Jose Mercury News,* May 12, 2003.
34. Sara Foster, "Park Wars," *World Net Daily,* May 12, 2003.
35. See Tom Knutson, "Timber Firms Chafe at Rules," *Sacramento Bee,* May 8, 2003.
36. *Nollan v. California Coastal Commn.,* 483 U.S. 825 (1987).
37. Cal. Pub. Res. Code § 30166.5.
38. Cal. Pub. Res. Code § 30301. Until recently, those members served at the pleasure of the legislative appointers—a happenstance that caused a trial court and an appellate panel to declare the commission itself unconstitutional because the legislative control violated the separation of powers provision in the constitution. The matter is presently pending in the California Supreme Court. *Marine Forests Society v. California Coastal Comm'n,* Case No. S113466.
39. See Patt Morrison, "Breaching the Great Wall of Malibu," *Los Angeles Times,* May 25, 2005; Steve Lopez, "A Concerted Effort to Free Malibu Beaches for the Rest of Us," *Los Angeles Times,* July 17, 2002.
40. See *Sierra Club v. California Coastal Com.,* 12 Cal.App.4th 602 (1993); *Bolsa Chica Land Trust v. Superior Court,* 71 Cal.App.4th 493 (1999).
41. See *City of Malibu v. California Coastal Commn.,* 18 Cal.Rptr.3d 40 (Cal. App. 2004), refusing to allow the citizens of Malibu to have a referendum election on the commission's local land-use plan. Citizens of all other cities have the right of referendum on local land-use plans.
42. See Cal. Pub. Res. Code § 30602.
43. Anne Berryman, "Developer Hits Homeowners in the Nose," *Los Angeles Daily Journal,* June 24, 2004, 9.
44. See *Penn Central Transp. Co. v. City of New York,* 438 U.S. 104 (1978).
45. See *Benenson v. U.S.,* 548 F.2d 939 (Ct. Cl. 1977).
46. It can be found in Gideon Kanner, *Making Laws and Sausages: A Quarter-Century Retrospective on Penn Central Transportation Co. v. City of New York,* 13 Wm. & Mary L. Rev (forthcoming 2005).
47. Southern California—where else? Both incidents are described in Gideon Kanner, "Southland Is Living Up To Its Quack-Pot Reputation," *Los Angeles Daily News,* June 20, 1993.
48. See Sandy Grady, "Rest Easy, Stonewall," *Baltimore Sun,* Oct. 6, 1994; Don L. Burrows, "Mickey Mouse Walks Away From a Fight," *U.S. News & World Report,* Oct. 10, 1994.
49. Pam Belluck, "Preservationists Call Vermont Endangered, by Wal-Mart," *The New York Times,* May 25, 2004; Alan Solomon (AP), "Look out, Vermont! Historic group worried by Wal-Marts," *USA Today,* May 24, 2004.

50. National Trust for Historic Preservation (http://www.nationaltrust.org).

51. National Trust for Historic Preservation press release, May 24, 2004.

52. Id.

53. Id.

54. Id.

55. Anne Matthews, "Beyond the Glare and the Blare," *Preservation*, May/June 2004.

56. See, e.g., *Terminal Plaza Corp. v. San Francisco*, 177 Cal.App.3d 892, 912 (1986) [ordinance upheld because it was "onerous" but not "confiscatory"]; *Bullock v. San Francisco*, 221 Cal.App.3d 1072, 1101 (1990) [ordinance invalidated because it required "payment of ransom" by landlords to escape its harsh terms].

57. *Cwynar v. San Francisco*, 90 Cal.App.4th 637 (2001).

58. *Yee v. City of Escondido*, 503 U.S. 519 (1992).

59. *Hendler v. United States*, 952 F.2d 1364 (Fed. Cir. 1991).

60. *Agins v. City of Tiburon*, 447 U.S. 255, 260 (1980).

61. *Lucas v. South Carolina Coastal Council*, 505 U.S. 1003, 1015 (1994).

62. *Penn Central Transp. Co. v. City of New York*, 438 U.S. 104, 124 (1978).

63. E.g., *Loretto v. Teleprompter Manhattan CATV Corp.*, 458 U.S. 419 (1982).

64. *Kavanau v. Santa Monica Rent Control Bd.*, 16 Cal.4th 761 (1997).

17

Lessons to Take to Heart

Vicki L. Been

First, let me thank Professor Daniel Mandelker for organizing this confer-ence and bringing together such a thoughtful group of scholars, policy-makers, and practitioners to think about the lessons we've learned over the past few decades about the role of planning. More importantly, I want to thank Professor Mandelker for being the revered dean of the land-use and planning community. Professor Mandelker is unparalleled in his energy, gen-erosity of spirit to his colleagues, mentorship and leadership of junior faculty, and intellectual ambition and depth. That so many of us at this conference can attest to the difference that Professor Mandelker's many kindnesses made in our careers is proof positive of the power that one remarkable person—with vision, character, and goodness of heart—can make across a nation.

I also want to thank Michael Berger (see Chapter 16) and Justice Abraham-son (see Chapter 15), upon whose paper and talk I am privileged to be asked to comment. Michael and I are frequently on opposite sides of an argument, and I always come away from conversations with Michael having learned a great deal. I admire Michael's willingness to engage in debate even when the sentiment in the room is stacked against him, his genuine efforts to listen as well as to persuade, and the care and craft that he brings to his arguments. I am honored to be on the panel with him.

Justice Abrahamson is part of my professional family, because the New York University School of Law was lucky to have her son as a student, and continues to be lucky to have her guidance and support as a member of the board of our Institute for Judicial Administration (IJA). I'm pleased to report that the IJA has provided education for judges on land-use matters and agrees with Justice Abrahamson about the need for further efforts to train judges about the land-use regulatory system.

The presidential election of November 2004, the startling blue cities/red suburbs and towns cartograph that Gerrit Knaap (Chapter 7) has shown us, the passage of the property rights "takings" initiative in Oregon,[1] the Supreme Court's grant of certiorari in *Kelo*,[2] jury verdicts like the Santa Barbara verdict that Michael mentions in his paper, and the increasing tension between affordable housing advocates and the environmental and land-use communities all are wake-up calls to planners and to everyone else who cares about the quality of our built and natural environments. What are the lessons we should take to heart from that call?

1. We should focus more on *getting the prices right* and then let people make choices about how they want to live as long as they pay the full social costs of those choices. Much of what has gone wrong with urban form is a result of subsidies for sprawl. End those subsidies—make the market price of housing in sprawling areas approach its true social costs—and we'll start to see real change. However, the change will come without our interfering with people's freedom to choose among various lifestyles and environments. Those who value large lots and low density, for example, more than they value alternative uses of the money they'll spend on those large lots, are free to choose to use their resources as they wish. As long as those consumers are paying for the true cost of the housing they want, we have no grounds to complain.

As several of the papers and the discussion at this conference have made clear, the only thing Americans hate worse than sprawl is density. I understand that the only things they will hate worse than density are higher prices for what they've been able to buy at a subsidized discount in the past. I'm not proposing that we go to the voters and ask them to approve a "true social cost pricing" initiative, but we already have the tools to go some distance to correct the market price: impact fees. In many communities, those fees are underused or not used at all; in others, they are underpriced. Impact fees won't get at the massive federal subsidies that underlie sprawl; however, if well-designed and carefully calibrated to the real cost of providing services to development, impact fees will bring the market price of different urban forms and types of housing closer to its social costs.

2. We must understand that the need for better pricing requires *more attention to the tools of cost/benefit analysis.* For too long, environmentalists and others concerned about the costs of development have taken a "head-in-the-sand" approach to the use of cost/benefit analysis. Because cost/benefit analysis is seriously flawed and doesn't capture many of the important values at stake in decisions (as Professor Charles Daye's paper in Chapter 13 shows us), some have believed that policy-makers and advocates should refuse to engage in such analysis, but that is a luxury we can't afford.

Those who are concerned about the development of our cities and countryside have to do a better job of trying to quantify both the costs and the benefits of various urban forms and of proposed land-use policies. That task requires enormous creativity, as Professor Daye's analysis so cogently reveals. It requires that we seek to improve the tools of cost/benefit analysis and then use those tools offensively to show the potential efficiency gains of better development practices and of better urban design.

3. We have to care more about *the individuals affected by land-use policies.* As Michael quite rightly points out, there are people behind the numbers and the lawsuit's caption. These people have dreams of a better life; many have worked two or three jobs at a time and have told themselves and their children "no" countless times so that they could save the money to buy a house—one of the most important symbols of success in America.

However, much of what planners and environmentalists do in their attempt to secure better development and better urban design means that, as soon as many people get close to finally achieving their goal, it is jerked from within their reach. In effect, we tell the young families, the recent immigrants, and the racial and ethnic groups long denied the same housing opportunities as the white middle-class has received: "Sorry. This environmental concern or that concern about preserving agricultural land means that you can't have what you've worked so hard for all these years." We tell them: "You can't have what we already have, because environmental or other values are now so important to *us.*" We have to keep those people front and center in our thinking about land-use policy. We have to respect their dreams and their hard work, and be more conscious about not shaping policies that allow existing residents to exercise the drawbridge mentality that pervades so much of land-use policy.

4. We have to take with more seriousness the responsibility of *reshaping the American Dream into a more sustainable one.* We have to do better at ensuring that good planning, good land-use policy, and good environmental policy helps the first-time homebuyers and other real people that Michael rightly reminds us are behind legal controversies to achieve the dream of homeownership in homes and communities that they'll be proud to pass on to the next generation.

We shouldn't mortgage our children's future or ruin an environment that our children will never be able to recover in the service of an ideal that no longer fits the reality of a crowded planet with rapidly diminishing resources and increasingly troubling signs of environmental damage. We must be sure that people do not achieve the American Dream only to come to the sad realization that the homes and communities they've worked so hard for came at the high price of long and stressful commutes, undrinkable water, polluted skies, and massive debt piled upon infrastructure deficits and crumbling bridges.

5. We must *find better ways to communicate.* Of course, we need to think harder about the "packaging" game. As Peter Salsich (another speaker at the conference) mentioned, at its best, packaging is a matter of recognizing that calling something "workforce housing for police and teachers" may get a different reaction than calling it "moderate income housing." At its worse, packaging is a race to the bottom. Michael Berger decries the duplicity of environmentalists who call their measures "coastal erosion planning" rather than revealing that (assuming Michael's version of the facts) the measures would prevent further coastal development. We can debate whether Michael's charge of duplicity is accurate; however, if we want to play the packaging game, I could retort, for example, that maybe the environmentalists should take a page from the current administration and call the bill a "clean beaches initiative."

Such a focus on packaging or "spin" alone is not a sustainable strategy. Let's focus instead on doing a better job of "telling it like it is." We should, for example, take notice of the incredible force of the visual representation of sprawl contained in Gerrit Knaap's slides. Showing, rather than telling, people about the consequences of bad land-use policy is critical. We need to do so much more to develop and use technologies that will show people what their neighborhood will look like if we implement this plan or policy, and what it will look like if we don't.

We also need to find better ways to communicate about the relationship between property rights claims and subsidies. For example, Michael raises the question, "What should be done to protect coastal property owners from the ravages of the ocean?" I don't know the particular controversy to which Michael refers, so I can't speak to the specifics of his claims. However, those who are decrying the "callousness" of environmentalists who seek to prevent rebuilding on erosion zones, flood plains, steep slopes, or other dangerous but beautiful locales often want public money to be used to safeguard the homes built in such risky environments and to insure homeowners against the inevitable losses that accompany risk.

We have to find better ways of talking about the callousness of a public policy that subsidizes the construction of such homes (which often are inhabited by the upper middle class and the rich), absorbs the risk those homeowners are happy to take but don't want to pay for, and allows the concomitant destruction of the environment, rather than investing in better education, better healthcare, and better housing for the nation's children. Planners, environmentalists, and liberals all have at times spoken out of both sides of their mouths, to be sure, and we should not sanction such duplicity. The call of property rights' advocates for the free market rather than for government intervention except when it subsidizes their home purchases, subsidizes the infrastructure for those homes, subsidizes the cost of driving their automobiles to those homes, and on and on, should not go unchallenged.

6. We have to care about, and remind people of, the *distributional consequences of their choices.* Michael properly decries Americans who want to preserve their forests but don't want to give up or pay more for the products those forests yield and instead exploit other countries' resources. His criticism is well taken. We should pay more attention to the issues of globalization and fair trade that his criticism raises, but those who are concerned about the hypocrisy of our "have-our-cake-and-eat-it-too" mentality have to be taken to task in turn for the hypocrisy of complaining about that mentality while resisting calls to make the production processes of the goods obtained through free trade more transparent or calls to ensure that products are priced at their true social cost. We should be concerned about the distributional implications of all land-use policies, both within and without our borders. We have to acknowledge the racial, ethnic, and class implications of each and every one of our policies, and work to ensure that land-use policy furthers, rather than limits, equality of opportunity for all citizens.

7. We should talk about issues in a way that *address people's concern about how this will affect them and their pocketbook.* As Professor Daye and Anthony Downs so eloquently pointed out, we should focus on the benefits that better integration by race and class and better land-use policy of all types will bring to voters: how it affects the values of their homes, the quality of their schools, the availability of the workforce from which they draw, and the character of their neighborhood.

8. *We have to admit when we've made a mistake.* Heavy regulation doesn't equal good regulation or good land use. We shouldn't be wasting our time defending rent control. We have to recognize that land-use planners, variance boards, and the people who implement land-use policies make mistakes, don't anticipate some consequences, overreach, and sometimes take out petty grudges or prejudices on the applicant before them. We need to find new ways of addressing those mistakes and abuses by structuring incentives to help encourage better decision-making and better policy. We need to provide easier, fairer ways of resolving conflicts. Professor Nolon's discussion of alternative dispute mediation (see Chapter 1) is crucial. Litigation doesn't solve problems; it hardens positions and forever scars its participants.

Michael has, as he always does, provided a sobering critique of planning and land-use policy. He is right that there is much to make us step back and take stock. We have an opportunity in this new century to do so much better and, because necessity is the mother of invention, I am optimistic that we *will* do better.

VICKI L. BEEN NOTES

1. 2004 Oregon Laws Init. Meas. 37, Or. Legis. I (I.P. 36) (2005).
2. *Kelo v. City of New London*, 843 A.2d 500 (Conn. 2004), *cert. granted*, 125 S.Ct. 27 (2004).

Observers

18

Frameworks for Thinking about Reform

Robert C. Einsweiler

THINKING ABOUT PLANNING REFORM

Will "Specificity" in Enabling Legislation Lead to Appropriate Planning?

Stuart Meck's argument (see Chapter 3) that state legislation authorizing planning should be "specific" raises several concerns about the effect of this specificity on the ability of a community to make appropriate choices regarding its plan form, plan content, planning process, and regulatory schema, especially since smart growth can produce a very large agenda.

The first concern is how these specified items relate to the community's issue agenda. Fred Bosselman's retrospective view of the planning situation in 1904 (see Chapter 2) constitutes an indictment of the City Beautiful movement with its three-dimensional, physical-spatial emphasis that failed to take account of the issue agenda of that day—the need for better sanitation and adequate worker housing in the new industrial age. By 1904, he notes, the engineers had taken over from the planners/urban designers (with the City Practical) to address sanitation, and housing was advanced by various social and nonprofit organizations.

In passing, one might note that the urban designers (my academic education) seem to rise up about once every 50 years—City Beautiful in the 1890s, urban renewal in the 1940s, and now new urbanism at the end of the 20th century—and, a short time later, drop again from national prominence. With each succeeding appearance, the concerns addressed are broader but still less than the issue agenda of the day or the potential agenda of smart growth.

The second concern about specificity is the California approach cited by Meck. By the 1960s, that law's specified contents of the plan were often producing, in a geriatric allusion, "hardening of the categories." The emphasis on individual elements often detracted from or wiped out a focus on the whole.

The third concern about specificity is how it relates to the process of urbanization and how that in turn relates to appropriate forms of planning and regulation. John Nolon's oral presentation (see Chapter 1) cited the concept of Murray Gell-Mann's "complex adaptive systems," which the author describes as "systems that learn or evolve by utilizing acquired information"—an apt characterization of the process of urbanization, and of Nolon's prescribed organizational process to manage it with its need for feedback loops to deal with new issues, and connectedness among the actors/stakeholders at all levels of government with land-use authority.[1] Contrast this with the dominant view of a plan that describes the community in physical-spatial terms, presenting how the community should look at some future date (usually 20 years ahead), with chapters covering various topics or facets of development, followed by simple, standard regulatory tools. How can this latter format manage the process of urbanization described above?

An Alternate Framework

In my experience, the choice of an appropriate planning process, plan content, plan form, and regulatory schema is *situational* starting with Nolon and Gell-Mann's dynamic interactive views and other factors, not a free choice without consequences. The choice depends on:

1. The issue agenda;
2. The rate of growth;
3. The location of the community on the spectrum of pro developer to pro community in its attitudes toward land-use regulation; and
4. The capability of the planning staff and legal assistance.

The Issue Agenda

This is not the planner's view of what should be addressed, but that of the elected officials and citizens. The issue agenda may become the chapter headings of the plan.

Rate of Growth

If growth is slow, the physical-spatial, end-state plan and a less inclusive organizational process will work as will simple zoning and subdivision regulations. In Gell-Mann's terms, the system is less complex and there is time for adaptive learning if the plan is in error, as it surely will be, since, in this framing, the developer decides on the timing and location of development, and for affected but excluded parties to make their concerns known.

If growth is faster, a growth management system is a better choice as the focus is on managing each incremental decision and the government decides the timing and sequencing of development. Further, it may draw on all its legal powers (e.g., contract, eminent domain, and regulation/exaction) and fiscal powers (e.g., tax, fee, capital investment, loans, and subsidies) and not just zoning and subdivision regulation or new urbanism techniques to manage change.[2] The organizational arrangements should also be more extensive and dynamic as the spillovers on others will come with less time to react. Only with such a system can one bring a semblance of order to an often chaotic process.

When the rate of growth is very fast, strategic planning is often required as the issues of prime concern to the citizens—including traffic congestion (not just physical streets), quality of schooling (not just the number and location of school buildings), state of health of the environment (not just the location of open space to be preserved), and quality of life—often supersede discussion of the more typical topics of traditional planning. Further, these citizens may want an annual check on the plan and its actions using indicators tied to their issues to show whether the government is making headway on their concerns.

Pro Developer or Pro Community?

In his unmatched work, Norman Williams describes and arrays the states of the country by the tendency of their zoning decisions to be pro developer or pro community, the nexus mentioned by Chief Justice Abrahamson (see Chapter 15).[3] Some years ago, Fred Bosselman described this part of Williams' work in forceful imagery by saying, as I remember it, that in California it is appropriate for the planner to tell the landowner that he may plant avocados but he may not plant artichokes, while in Illinois it is appropriate for the planner to stand up and salute the developer when he enters the court room. This is the central issue in all land-use regulation, and appropriateness requires that the planner understand where his/her community resides on Williams' spectrum. This is discussed more fully below.

The alternatives for controlling development can be grouped into three major categories:

1. Systems that control geography, that use spatial bounding, and that focus on location (including traditional land-use zoning systems, new urbanism, and the State of Oregon system that is zoning writ large);

2. Systems that control infrastructure and use it to grow from nodes of existing development (Ramapo[4] is the tightest example); and

3. Systems that control compatibility by specifying performance of development or mitigation of impacts.[5]

The first category provides the least flexibility for the developer but the greatest certainty, and places the greatest burden on the planner to outguess the future. The third category gives the developer the greatest freedom but the least certainty if standards are not clear; the planner has the least need to outguess the future but the greatest burden in administration of the three categories. These choices, like the earlier ones for the planning process, are situational and relate directly to the pro developer or pro community values reflected in prior court decisions for the area.

Quality of Staff and Legal Assistance

Even the traditional systems—physical/spatial plans with simple, traditional regulatory tools—require more knowledge and skills than they often receive. Many planners lack a good understanding of land economics, including the concept of the land rent gradient, or how and why the value of land varies across the community; even fewer understand the economics and finance necessary to execute the more entrepreneurial and laudable joint development activities described by Bob Freilich (see Chapter 6). Therefore, the most appropriate planning process and regulatory schema for a community may be beyond the reach of its staff.

One final consideration: Each of the new planning approaches over the decades was designed to overcome the weaknesses of what went before. Unfortunately, each ignored the strengths of that preceding approach. Growth management focused on the failings of the physical/spatial, end-state plans without giving consideration to design. Most recently, new urbanism has emphasized design without recognizing the strength of growth management to address rapid incremental change. Some communities have wisely combined both, but that is still rare.

Summing up, specifying plan contents may cause planners to lose sight of the above considerations in choosing an appropriate approach for their community, and especially of Nolon's call to think about the appropriate connectedness of their community to all other political entities and stakeholder groups. Smart growth does not emphasize these considerations either.

A FRAMEWORK FOR THINKING ABOUT DEVELOPMENT REGULATION

Chief Justice Abrahamson noted in her oral remarks that, in land use, the courts are the bulwark between public and private interests in property. As a precedent to the courts performing this vital task, the planners reviewing a rezoning request or a development proposal take the first crack at this public-private nexus, which is, at bottom, about the moral sense of the community. This is the most central relationship of all planning and land-use regulation; it is one of the very few settings in which the appropriate balance between the rights and obligations of an individual and the community is openly argued and settled.

The following conceptual framing is designed to enable me to explain my sense of this relationship more fully. It is based on various data points, research using portions of the framework, extensive literature covering some aspect of the whole frame, and related writings on the whole. The four columns set out the four significant, different conceptual ways in which individuals see their relationship to their community:

A. Community *over* individual	B. Individual *in* community	C. Individual *over* community	D. Individual, *no* community

At the outset, note that an individual may occupy different "boxes" in this diagram on different issues or at different times, because his/her personal diagram may be weighted in one box but also extend across portions of another box or boxes.

- "A" encompasses those individuals (e.g., EarthFirst!) who place the community values/rights in the environment or natural ecology of a property above any individual rights to make economic use of it.

- "B" individuals see the community as something sufficiently valued that they restrain their conduct when it would violate social norms.

- "C" includes those whose guiding light is individualism and the current "right" in national politics in which the individual view is placed ahead of community, although recognizing it in a more limited form than "B."

- "D" includes the individual maximizing self-interest as in capitalism and economics with no consideration of community. In this category "in the economic sphere, efficiency trumps community. Maximizing returns comes before family or personal loyalty."[6]

As "B" and "C" encompass the overwhelming majority of U.S. voters, and the individual vs. community framing of interest to this conference, they are the focus here, but "A" and "D" cannot be ignored. "A" was stronger in the peak of the environmental movement; it still arises in specific antigrowth actions; "D" has been growing stronger over the past 25 years as the federal government has moved ever farther in giving preferential treatment to the private sector through deregulation, free trade, and privatization.

Daly and Cobb make a thorough and persuasive case for the "B" (individual *in* community) framing.[7] Unlike "economic man" optimizing self-interest, individuals in this view act to achieve their own interests and those of the community, too. This view predominates in the European countries and many parts of, and individuals in, the U.S. today. In the last two presidential elections, this framing encompassed more Democrats than Republicans. Its other-regarding moral perspective is captured by Lakoff as "the most fundamental form of morality concerns promoting the experiential well-being of others and the avoidance and prevention of experiential harm to others or the disruption of the well-being of others."[8]

From this view flows the support for those less fortunate and for U.S. social programs. Most traditional or mainstream religions fall into this category. A somewhat similar framing occurs in the rule of thumb that I learned in my first encounters with zoning. It is a three-part set of queries:

1. If the proposal benefits the developer/property owner and also benefits the community, it is "thumbs up."

2. If the proposal benefits the developer/property owner and does not harm the community, it is "acceptable."

3. If the proposal benefits the developer/property owner and harms the community, it is "thumbs down." Property rights are not absolute in this view but they are valued.

This framing is part of a relationship that philosophers have pursued in part at least since Plato's *Republic* and Aristotle's *Politics* under the rubric of "one and many."[9] It lies behind the founding fathers' discussion that led to *e pluribus unum* (from many, one) as the relation between the individual states and the United States. Plato, Aristotle, and the founding fathers saw community (including the nation) as a unity; so, too, does the term "community" in this framing. It is not just an aggregation of individuals as capitalism, economics, and markets see them; it is something more.

The "C" (individual *over* community) perspective is distinctly different; community is just an aggregation of individuals, not something more. It, too, has a moral basis often seldom understood by those in the "B" category. There are different subsets here that share much of the framing with some differences. Conservatives and others on the far right—although strong supporters of capitalism, free trade, and "economic man" based on extreme individualism—do not use its morality as in type "D." Rather, they generally express their morality as the individual being responsible for himself, his gains, and his losses, but with limited obligations to others, especially those less fortunate.

In contrast to "B," it is self-regarding (i.e., placing one's personal interests above that of others or one's city interest above that of other jurisdictions), or, as President George W. Bush's statements and actions imply, the U.S. interest above that of other nations of the world community. This view comes from the Middle Ages and from 19th century social Darwinism enhanced by more recent shifts in the U.S. version of capitalism.[10] They see those in lesser circumstances as not assuming responsibility for themselves. It is this mindset that objects to welfare programs, foreign aid to less developed countries, or public housing for the poor, but often is generous to those harmed by "acts of God." Newt Gingrich provides an apt example in discussing proposed health savings accounts: "The higher the deductible, the lower the insurance premiums. Make your choice, take your bet, live with the consequences."[11]

A second subset is a stream that draws on medieval religion. Unlike mainline religions of today, the prime objective then and for these followers today—the new evangelicals—is to save one's soul, not to focus on doing good to others, although many do that, too.[12] Also common to most of the religious in this perspective is the biblical challenge to have dominion over and to subdue the earth, thus their positions on land and its use and the environment: land as commodity. These are the strong property rights people.

In my experience, the "B" framing was the dominant view during the Great Depression, during World War II, and in the 1950s. As the economy heated up and the younger generation began to pursue its own thing, the individualism of "C" became stronger. In recent years, this trend has been substantially reinforced by:

- The more dominant role of corporations and capitalism;
- The suburbanization and exurbanization of the country, which has enabled leaving the wider, multicultural, multiethnic community of greater diversity for one of more like-minded individuals;
- The products of technology that diminished the family togetherness of listening to the radio or watching television when computers, iPods, portable game devices, and more emerged, which enabled or required individuals to entertain themselves;
- The elimination of the balanced reporting or fairness doctrine in broadcasting, which ended everyone listening to the same news and instead led to the emergence of right-wing talk radio, Internet news, and more; and
- The public schools that have yielded to charter schools, more private or religious schools, and home schooling, each further narrowing the experiences of children living with a cross-section of the community.

Today, individuals can choose to spend their nonwork time in a self-absorbed world with those technologies or information sources that require no interaction with others or no one but like-minded individuals that reinforce their own views.

In summary, these two major, different perspectives—individual *in* community and individual *over* community—often closely parallel the pro community/pro developer perspectives in court cases.[13] Current trends may be reinforcing the "individualism" group "C" with more property rights legislation and more testy arguments on development permission and rezonings, just as individualism is reshaping the political agenda at the national level.

SOME APPLICATIONS OF THE FRAMEWORK

Oregon's Proposition 37

This decidedly flows from a type "C" perspective with a dose of type "D" thinking. The property owners are demanding compensation for any loss in land value occasioned by the community. One might remind these proponents of the views of Henry George in which he made clear that there was nothing a property owner could do to increase the value of raw land.[14] He demonstrated that all the value increase was owing to the community—those individuals who developed homes and businesses near the site, thus increasing the value of the vacant site, or the improvements built by the government (e.g., sewers, roads, schools, and parks) that added to the land's value. Therefore, he proposed his land value tax wherein the community would levy a tax to capture all the economic rent of the land, driving its value toward zero. However, there would be no tax on improvements, the work of the owner's hands. The idea was to achieve social justice by rewarding those who did something with the land and penalize those who just sat on it, who prevented its use by others, and who captured its increased value although they had no moral right to it.

Today, the land value tax is used in Taiwan, South Korea, and South Africa, among other places. It appears in truncated form in the British betterment-detriment system. It is used in part in South American countries (a legacy of Spain) where national constitutions require the government to capture all the value, *plus valia*, attributable to public improvements. This concept is also the basis for our impact fees. Pittsburgh uses the two-rate concept in which the land is taxed more heavily, although not enough to capture all economic rent, and improvements are taxed more lightly.

Should the Proposition 37 landowners challenge Henry George's calculations, a mind game could be suggested in which they take their highly valued land and transfer it to a remote desert island in the South Pacific where the value would drop toward zero. Put another way, as all the value increase rightly belonged to the community as its creator, the Oregon community was merely reducing its own created value in the interest of other community purposes. Or, as a former colleague of mine once explained, private property is less fully owned that some think. Try to go without paying your property taxes and see how government can confiscate your land. From that perspective, a private property owner can be said to possess something closer to a "lease" for which the "lease" payment is the annual property tax.[15]

Lake Tahoe, Again

In Michael Berger's paper (see Chapter 16), we find a person incensed by the outcome of this latest case and the American Planning Association's role in it. Using the framework above, Berger's perspective is category "C" thinking. His argument, not without substantial merit, is that the *Tahoe-Sierra* case should have been seen at worst as a type "B" case, but it was justified more as type "A," with the community interests rated far above the interest of individuals who had waited for 20 years for the opportunity to use their land.

It calls to mind Fred Bosselman's characterization of land-use regulation in California cited earlier. There is no single rule that applies across the country equally. Norman Williams' state diversity is alive and well, and frustrating to those who ignore or disagree with it. Those thinking type "B" individuals ought to see this as a failure of good planning that refused to address the inequities created for property owners on the slopes.

The Nature of Land and Its Treatment in Regulation

Those with a "C" perspective (individual *over* community) would view land as commodity, treating it in the standard fashion where price determines what can be done with it. Planners in such settings must really know their land economics. Those with a "B" perspective (individual *in* community) might well see land as ecology, treating it as Sanibel,[16] the Pine Barrens,[17] and others have done in which the site and its ecological sensitivities determine what development can be allowed or the degree of care that must be taken with it. Planners in these settings must really know their environmental science. Paul Sedway[18] once proposed a layered approach to land regulation with the land and ecological considerations being the first layer, use being the second layer, and the three-dimensional improvements housing the use as the top layer. While some have used the concept, in this day of geographic information systems, it is less used than it should be as a way to put a more solid systems-grounding basis into each of the three aspects of development.

Gerrit-Jan Knaap's Unexplained Commuters

In his very interesting and challenging paper, Knaap (see Chapter 7) notes a survey of the increasing acceptance of people living in developments based on greater densities. One survey revealed that 55 percent would support a smart growth community ("B" type people?), while 45 percent would choose sprawl with over a 45-minute commute ("C" type people?). If you estimate from the last national election how many fit the "B" and "C" perspectives, the percentage of commuters seems remarkably similar.

Looking over the long time period of suburbanization since World War II, we would find that the first suburbanites were not fleeing the city. The factors behind their moves were:

1. The amortized mortgage created during the Depression as a consequence of all those who lost their housing;

2. The fact that lenders required a higher down payment for existing housing than new (riskier in the city than in new suburbs); and

3. All the savings that households amassed during World War II when every able-bodied person was working and all major expense items were prohibited, especially new houses and new cars.

Later, there was the push of "white flight" with desegregation. Further decentralizing is occurring to the exurbs and to the "out beyond."

I suspect if one had the data, one would find that increasingly these were "C" individuals moving to less multicultural settings than the cities from which they moved, to places with more like-minded residents and special interest groups—not communities as the term is used here.[19] As such, Knaap should not expect them to behave like communities rather than the individualist, special-interest groups that they are. This applies to the limits of new urbanism or smart growth that assumes people of type "B" perspective, when a significant part of the population is type "C." I would expect to find the "C" perspective in new developments on the Front Range of the Rockies where individualism and property rights have always been strongly held and expressed.

Affordable Housing

Both Anthony Downs (see Chapter 12) and Charles Daye (see Chapter 13) address this issue of increasing importance. The tragedy and the challenge in this field is to find some technique like Henry George's land value tax, which captures all the value increase of raw land—a value created by the community—and prevents its capture by the landowner who has no moral right to it, or to find a way to ensure that the impact fee rightly falls on the landowner and not on the developer or the ultimate occupant of the housing. Each would make housing more affordable to more citizens and make urban development more just. The most charitable solution would be a method to make incomes more equitable, a divergence that has been increasing for the past 25 years as a result of national policies that highly value individualism.

CONCLUSIONS

State enabling legislation, while pursuing the argued benefits of specificity, should ensure that the many ways in which local communities differ can be accommodated through differing issue agendas, rates of growth, attitudes toward (and court histories of) leanings toward the community (acting in light of others), or toward the individual (acting in their own self-interest) in land-use decisions, including housing choices and appropriate alternative planning and regulatory elements to meet the needs of these differences.

Local communities should be aware of the need for different planning and regulatory approaches based on these same factors in relation to the capabilities of their staffs.

Both would benefit from a framework (as in the section herein entitled "A Framework for Thinking About Development Regulation"), or one of their own design, that better enables them to facilitate making tough choices between competing views by legitimating those contending interests and where they are "coming from." While in court, it may be necessary to argue from legal precedent; in political decisions, it is better to argue from differing legitimate views of how each party believes the world does or ought to work.

ROBERT C. EINSWEILER NOTES

1. Murray Gell-Mann, *The Quark and the Jaguar: Adventures in the Simple and Complex* (New York: W.H. Freeman and Company, 1994).

2. Robert C. Einsweiler and Deborah Miness, *Managing Growth and Change in Urban, Suburban and Rural Settings* [hereinafter "Einsweiler/Miness" with page reference] (working paper) (Cambridge, MA: Lincoln Institute of Land Policy, Oct. 1992), 37-39.

3. Norman Williams, Jr., and John M. Taylor, *American Land Planning Law* (St. Paul, MN: Thomson-West, 2003).

4. Michael E. Gleeson, Robert C. Einsweiler, Robert H. Freilich, et al., *Urban Growth Management Systems,* PAS Report Nos. 309, 310 (Chicago: American Society of Planning Officials, 1976), 22, 23; David R. Godschalk and David J. Brower, *Constitutional Issues in Growth Management* (Chicago: American Planning Association, 1979), 227-242.

5. Einsweiler/Miness, 47-50.

6. William Greider, *The Soul of Capitalism* (New York: Simon & Schuster, 2003), 35.

7. Herman E. Daly (an economist) and John B. Cobb, Jr. (a theologian), *For the Common Good* [hereinafter "Daly/Cobb" with page reference] (Boston: Beacon Press, 1989).

8. George Lakoff (a cognitive scientist), *Moral Politics: How Liberals and Conservatives Think* (Chicago: University of Chicago Press, 2002), 41.

9. These texts are most readily accessed from the 54-volume *Great Books of the Western World,* Encyclopedia Britannica (Chicago: University of Chicago, 1952). The idea of "One and Many" is Chapter 63 of Vol. II, "The Great Ideas: A Syntopicon of Great Books of the Western World." From that, one can find: Plato's *Republic,* Book IV, 343c-344a, and Aristotle's *Politics,* Book I, Chapters 1-2 and other selections. On this subject, the Syntopicon also lists citations for many more authors.

10. See John Dewey, *Individualism Old and New* (Amherst, NY: Prometheus Books, 1999), 37; Daly/Cobb, 15-16.

11. Steve Lohr, "Health Care's Unlikely Surgeon," *The New York Times,* Jan. 16, 2005.

12. Dewey, loc. cit.

13. Another book addressing this set of value differences is Charles Wolf, Jr., *Markets or Government: Choosing between Imperfect Alternatives* (Cambridge MA: The MIT Press, 1994).

14. Henry George, *Progress and Poverty* (New York: Robert Schalkenbach Foundation, first published in 1879).

15. A frame-jogging analysis by Joan Youngman of the Lincoln Institute of Land Policy, Cambridge, MA.

16. John Clark, *The Sanibel Report: Formulation of a Comprehensive Plan Based on Natural Systems* (Washington, DC: The Conservation Foundation, 1976).

17. "The Pinelands: A Radical Experiment Works," in Richard F. Babcock and Charles L. Siemon, *The Zoning Game Revisited* (Cambridge, MA: The Lincoln Institute of Land Policy, 1985), 135-157.

18. Paul Sedway and Bonnie Lloyd, "Building Block Zoning Provides a New Flexibility," American Institute of Planners, *Practicing Planner,* Sept. 1977; see also Paul Sedway, "What is Framework Zoning?" *Urban Land,* April 1998.

19. Writers about computer use in the 1980s used the term "special interest groups" (SIGs) to denote those who met on certain Web pages, etc. Today, these writers call these gatherings "communities." They are not in the sense used here; they remain SIGs. The distinction is important when it comes to patterns of urbanization where the like-minded locate together, rather than in a community encompassing the range of residents of the country. Robert D. Putnam in *Bowling Alone; The Collapse and Revival of American Community* (New York: Simon & Schuster, 2000) includes both groups in his use of community, but his purpose is to show participation in civic life and politics. Here we are interested in how individuals locate in space and what perspective they bring to political and land-use decisions.

19

A View from the Outside: The Role of Cross-National Learning in Land-Use Law Reform in the U.S.

Rachelle Alterman

In this brief paper, I offer a few observations about American land-use law as viewed from the outside. These thoughts are based on my ongoing comparative research into planning law and practice in various countries. I hope that this comparative view might add an additional perspective to the discussion of directions for reform in American land-use law in the 21st century. I will comment on the legal instruments and not on substantive policies.

Most of the proposals for reforming American land-use law aired in this symposium did not suggest "reengineering" the entire framework—and rightly so.[1] Had a similar debate taken place in some other (democratic) country, one would have frequently heard the phrase "a different planning system." The term "planning system" is not part of the professional vocabulary in the U.S. for good reason: The U.S. does not have "a planning system" where most elements that regulate the use of land are expected to link into a single, overarching concept. In the U.S., planning law emerged through evolution, not revolution. Reforms are therefore likely to be partial, either issue led or location led.

THE CROSS-NATIONAL TRANSFER OF PLANNING LAWS

The vast majority of nations in the world today have national legislation that regulates land use and development. Each and every pre-2004 member of the European Union (EU) had a specific national law for regulating planning well before it entered the EU (EC 1997-2000).

The formerly communist countries, some of them members of the EU since 2004, have already adopted a national planning law (some, such as Poland, have gone into the second round of planning-law reform). Many of them did not have "planning" (or "land-use") laws as we know them until the collapse of the communist regimes. Even China joined the "haves" of planning law in the late 1990s.

Many nations across the world legislated their planning laws during the first half of the 20th century, often importing or adapting British or German models that emerged in the late 19th and early 20th centuries (Sutcliffe 1980). The newer planning laws are often a mixture of these older models with newer concepts about the roles of plans, public involvement, institutions and hierarchies, and implementation instruments. Although each country's planning law differs from other countries'—not only in name but in substance, too[2]—planning laws do have enough in common for the readers of this book to say, "We'll know one when we see one."

The remarkable spread of planning laws has been aided by cross-national transfer of full or partial models or of particular instruments of planning regulation. This process reflects a growing "export and import trade" across the globe in planning-law concepts.

Some countries have largely been on the "export" side of this process. Germany initiated land-use and planning law at the local level in the latter years of the 19th century, and some elements of its format were exported abroad. Britain took these ideas much further: It pioneered land-use and planning law at the national level (in 1909), created the first academic degree in planning, and established the planning profession. Through its colonial powers, Britain was able to introduce planning law into many countries in various parts of the world (Home 1997, 1993; Alterman and Haddadin 2005). Most other countries have been on the "import" side.

The U.S. is an exception. Its land-use and planning law is largely home grown. During the latter 19th and early 20th centuries, U.S. planners did import many ideas from Europe, but their interest tapered down in later years (see Yaro 2002: 211). Since then, the "traffic" of planning and especially planning-law ideas to and from the U.S., in both directions, has in most years been relatively low. However, I shall later show why I think that such exchange has increased in recent years and will continue to rise.

The challenge of reforming American land-use law in the 21st century might benefit from a look from the outside inward. Such a perspective would enable legislators, planners, and legal scholars to recognize the unique attributes of American land-use law and to appreciate the opportunities for creating two-way traffic of planning-law ideas. Whereas writers on comparative planning usually point out what Americans may learn from planning laws elsewhere—especially from Europe (see, for example, Faludi 2002 and Yaro 2002)—I shall argue that there are opportunities for *mutual* learning. In comparative terms, U.S. planning law has both "strengths" from which others may wish to learn and "weaknesses" that might encourage the import of ideas from other countries. (I have placed these terms in quotes to indicate that, of course, this paper does not presume to do what even comprehensive research can hardly do: critically evaluate a country's entire planning "system.")

THE BOTTOM-UP EVOLUTION OF AMERICAN LAND-USE LAW

The potential for transfer of ideas to and from American planning law is grounded in the manner by which that law emerged. From an international perspective, American land-use law is in a class almost of its own. It is special both in its manner of evolution and in certain aspects of its structure and content. Whereas in most countries planning law was initiated "top down" through national legislation, in the U.S. it emerged largely "bottom up." While the U.S. is not the only country where planning law started out in particular cities (for example, such a process occurred in Frankfurt, Germany, in the latter years of the 19th century), in most other countries this process culminated in national legislation. The federal structure of the U.S., its sheer size, and the central role played by its Constitution all make the U.S. story special.

The bottom-up process in the U.S. occurred gradually during the first decades of the 20th century. With New York City pioneering in 1916, scores of other municipalities in many parts of the country began to regulate land use by initiating their own local bylaws. "Zoning" and the "master plan" both emerged in this manner. Zoning made its way through the hierarchy of courts until it finally obtained constitutional clearance from the Supreme Court in 1926 in the famous *Euclid* decision (Cullingworth and Caves 2003: 64-74).

Americans may view this bottom-up process as natural but, from an international perspective, the evolution of land-use regulation in the U.S. has been a rather unique process. Only after zoning had taken root in many localities did states across the country begin to enact "enabling" laws that authorized local governments to apply zoning and related tools. In the absence of federal-level legislation, these laws might have turned out to be highly different from each other, yet state land-use laws in most U.S. states do share distinctive similarities. These are due to the initiative of the federal Department of Commerce to draft two model acts in the 1920s. The model act for zoning had great influence on the states; the model act for planning was less successful (Meck 2002; Lewyn 2003).

Another force that has worked to moderate the "bottom-up" emergence of American planning law is, of course, the role that the Supreme Court has played in molding key issues related to land-use and planning law (among them the "takings issue" or the limits to "aesthetic controls"; see Lewyn 2003). From a cross-national comparative perspective, U.S. planning law has had a more direct interface with the Constitution than in most other countries, where national statutory law mediates between the constitution and the legality of on-the-ground planning decisions.

However, the federal model acts and the Supreme Court decisions could not entirely account for why most states adopted similar land-use laws. An intensive cross-town and cross-state learning process must have occurred with considerable success (without the availability of today's communication media). Mutual learning among local governments and states characterizes the evolution of American land-use law to date. It is aided not only by electronic communication, but also by a growing body of academic research and nongovernmental organization briefs that report on and evaluate various practices that have emerged "bottom up" (and, for that matter, "top down" as well).

During the last decades of the 20th century, several states initiated new state planning laws. This trend in state legislation has been tagged "The Quiet Revolution" (Bosselman and Callies 1972; Callies 2002) or second-generation legislation as "growth management" (Meck, in Chapter 3, counts nine such states). This revolution produced a set of innovative, state-level, land-use and planning laws, each different from the other, and the body of evaluation research about how these have performed is growing (see, for example, Freilich 2000 and Meck's excellent survey in Chapter 3). Compared with the traditional state land-use laws, the new state laws bear greater similarity in structure to planning laws prevalent in Continental European and most other countries than to traditional U.S. state planning laws. The newer state laws usually call for an additional institutional echelon above the local level, and they usually grant greater legal weight to plans than traditional land-use law had given them (see Sullivan, Chapter 9). Interestingly (to a foreign observer), the new state laws for the most part left the underlying layer of zoning regulations intact, rather than creating a new "planning system."

THE STRENGTHS AND WEAKNESSES OF U.S. LAND-USE LAW AND PRACTICE AS OPPORTUNITIES FOR CROSS-NATIONAL LEARNING

From my (admittedly subjective) point of view, the process whereby American land-use law emerged gave birth to both strengths and weaknesses. Some of the strengths have served as the basis for the "export" of U.S. land-use and planning ideas overseas, while the weaknesses might be candidates for cross-national learning towards reform.

Strengths and Potential Targets for "Export"
Some of what I view as strengths of U.S. planning law are easy to guess; others may seem counterintuitive.

The Absence of a Federal Law Allows Room for Local Innovation

When planning laws are fashioned nationally, they often entail a long process of debate and negotiation among national institutions and civic groups before they are legislated. The stakes are high because national planning laws in most countries are not just "enabling"; they usually lay down obligations that the lower echelons must carry out. There is only one law at a time at the national level—a single experiment. Once enacted, this law is not likely to be revised frequently and, over time, usually becomes inadequately responsive to transformations in the economy and in society.

Because national laws normally entail high political and professional exposure, their designers often seek "elegant" institutional and plan-hierarchy structures. They tend to be more optimistic about the value and validity of formal plans than real-life experience has supported. National laws also tend to be high on hierarchies and obligations and low on "hands-on" tools for implementation.

By contrast, the decentralized American planning-law structure, while low on elegance and on systems, has provided room for many concurrent "experiments" in land-use and planning laws. Over the decades, decentralization has led to a pageant of U.S.-grown innovative tools.

A Process of "Survival of the Fittest"

The second strength gained from the evolution of American planning law is the built-in *competition* among alternative instruments. The U.S. has tens of thousands of municipalities, 50 states, and a multilayered hierarchy of courts. In order for a land-use instrument to last over time and gain recognition beyond its local birth place, it must survive many political and legal challenges.

The combination of decentralized innovation and high competition has probably acted as a mechanism of "natural selection," whereby the most fit instruments have survived. Becoming known beyond their place of origin, they were imported by other local or state governments. Although over the decades many locally grown innovations may have disappeared, those that survived the policy competition process and court challenges have been imbued with a high degree of resilience to challenge and adaptability to change. The "survival of the fittest" process from time to time elevates a set of locally conceived tools to become good candidates for transfer to other legal-institutional contexts.

A Growing "Export Trade" in Market-Friendly, Locally Grown Land-Use Regulation and Incentive Instruments

Instruments that are both resilient to challenge and adaptable to change are obvious candidates for "export" to other countries. In my various research projects—some already published; others in the making—I encountered many American-grown instruments that have crossed the oceans.[3] To do so, these instruments have had to be rather "footloose," so that someone overseas could disconnect them from their home context and implant them in a totally different planning system. My list includes:

- Impact fees and "linkage"[4]
- Transfer of development rights[5]
- Purchase of development rights
- Development agreements[6]
- Incentive zoning[7]
- Tax increment financing[8]
- Design review instruments[9]
- Environmental mitigation instruments[10]

The majority of the tools on my list are market-based—they manage to harness market forces to propel the implementation of the planning policy.[11] You may also notice that they tend to be relatively "neutral" in terms of social and ideological values. These tools deal with challenges shared by planners in any country where there are private property rights, a dynamic economy, and government financial shortages. The strengths of most of these tools are that they represent a new way of packaging together market forces, property rights, property values, planning, and public finance.

The trend to import market-friendly planning instruments from the U.S. seems to be on the increase in recent years—perhaps due to better communication, more international professional organizations in the planning-related field, and, of course, "globalization" of the economy and the increasing mobility of developers across national borders. Some of these American-bred instruments have found their way to the United Kingdom (U.K.), several to western European countries, some to the new democracies in Central and Eastern Europe, and a few to Far East nations. Importing these tools may at times require an amendment to the national land-use and planning law. Thus, ironically, some of the locally grown U.S. tools may become featured as elements in a new national-level land-use law in another country.

The Innovativeness of Comprehensive Plans

The discussion in this section is likely to seem counterintuitive. The picture regarding comprehensive plans in most U.S. states is rather ambivalent. On the one hand, their legal status is weak (and I shall dwell on this issue later); on the other hand, the American city-wide "comprehensive plan" (also called "master" or "general" plan and, more recently, "strategic plan") have a longer history than their counterparts in most other countries (except the U.K., Germany, and a few other countries). Initiated by many local governments in the 1920s and 1930s, the comprehensive plan has become part of expected practice by local authorities.

Due to the sheer scale of the U.S., the experience gained in the preparation of comprehensive plans across thousands of municipalities has created innovative formats and functions. Some American planners have been savvy in drawing into plan-making new concepts in planning theory, such as public participation, advocacy, conflict mediation, and communicative planning. Americans may not be aware that some of these ideas have crossed the oceans and have influenced the conceptions and formats of plans in many other democratic countries (Alterman 2001). Paradoxically, in some countries, these innovative concepts and formats of plans and the planning process were given the legal status that they lacked in their place of origin.

The Role of U.S. Federal Legislation in Selected Environmental Topics

In a book on cross-national comparative research of national-level planning in 10 democratic countries, I classified the U.S. among the countries with the lowest degree of institutionalization of land-use regulation and planning at the national level (id). However, as Kayden (2001) has convincingly argued, this does not mean that the U.S. has no national land-use policy or planning. Although the U.S. Congress never adopted a general national land-use law—having rejected such a proposal in 1970—it would be incorrect to say that the U.S. does not have national-level laws that relate to land use.

The U.S. does in fact have a wide array of laws at the national level that pertain directly or indirectly to land use (Mandelker et al., 1986). These deal with several sectorial topics, such as transportation, economic development, and housing. Most significant, from an international perspective, are the set of U.S. federal environmental laws, many of which were globally innovative at the time they were enacted. American environmental policies and regulations have been high on the "export trade" to other countries, including the "environmental impact statement," which is now well integrated into regulative practices in many other countries, including at an EU-wide level (Williams 1996: 184-203; Redman 1993). One might conjecture that the very absence of general land-use legislation at the federal level may have allowed space for specialized innovative laws to be created at the national level.

Weaknesses and Potential Targets for Using "Imported" Ideas

Alongside its strengths, the American style of land-use law also has some weaknesses. In some cases, these are the "antonyms" of its strengths.

The Absence of a Federal Land-Use Law

While the lack of a nationwide land-use law has a positive side (as noted above), the fact that the U.S. is one of only a few countries without such a law should at least raise some questions. The constitutional demarcation of powers between the federal and state levels cannot provide the full answer. One example is Germany, also a federal country, which has a federal land-use law that structures the division of planning powers between the *Bund* (the federal government), the *lander* (the equivalent to states), and the municipalities (Schmidt-Eichstaedt 2001).

The absence of a federal land-use law jeopardizes the ability to take a nationwide view of land-use and environmental priorities and to resolve key conflicts. Without federal legislation, regional planning has become one of the weakest links in the American "nonsystem." Several of the writers in this volume and many other analysts stress this weakness and agree that it is unlikely to improve. Those states that have only traditional state enabling legislation usually lack regional-level land-use regulation and planning altogether. Some of the more innovative state laws do have a form of regional land-use planning, but many researchers agree that this element is weak on implementation. States also need federal help in coordinating with neighboring states. More effective state- and regional-level planning and land-use regulation are essential for "growth management" and "smart growth" to reach their major goals.

By comparison, Europe has taken significant steps towards regional and trans-national planning. Without requiring specific legislation, EU member countries have come together to prepare a joint European Spatial Development Perspective (EC 1999). Many other supra-national policies—in transportation, environment, economic development, and interregional equalization—have been adopted and implemented (Williams 1996; Faludi 2002).

The Potential for the Introduction of a Federal Land-Use Act: Learning from Other Democracies

Is there any chance that a federal land-use act would be passed? Is there a better chance in the coming years compared with the failed 1970 "Jackson Bill" (Kayden 2001)? Despite the pessimism of authors in this book and many others, my inclination is to say that a future opportunity may arise.

Modest optimism on this topic is grounded in my study of national-level planning in 10 democracies. There, I identified several triggers that may help to explain why planning emerged at the national level in each of the countries at a particular time. These explanations include external circumstances, such as nation-building; national security or disaster threats; the need to reduce interregional disparities; the goal of environmental mitigation; or the need to comply with a supra-national directive or incentive (such as from the EU).

There may also be political-ideological triggers, such as a party change that regards more government intervention as legitimate for achieving its vision. To my surprise, I have discovered that political-ideological attitudes towards national-level planning no longer abide by our entrenched notions of "left" and "right." I have even conjectured that in some countries, there are signs of the "death of ideology" in determining whether the decision-makers choose to strengthen or dismantle national-level planning (Alterman 2001).

Most of the triggers that have propelled the introduction of national-level planning in other democratic, advanced-economy countries are not likely to occur in the U.S.; however, there are two potential triggers that might provide the necessary boost in the future. One is some major crisis (perhaps regarding home security or natural disasters); the second is stronger public endorsement of the importance of a sustainable environment.

I'd like to conjecture about the second potential trigger. The early U.S. environmental movement of the 1960s and 1970s was able to bring about the enactment of several federal environmental laws in the 1970s and, subsequently, several incentive-based federal laws to encourage sustainable development (Kayden 2001). These were very daring at the time and, as noted, some were worldwide innovations. Since then, public endorsement of environmental goals has increased, not decreased. Recent setbacks such as Oregon's Measure 37,[12] some Supreme Court decisions, and other trends noted by Knaap (see Chapter 7) should not be allowed to cloud the longer-range trend. Is it inconceivable that, at some future political point, political leaders might be able to harness the same momentum that underlies the environmental movement for an appropriately repackaged federal law tagged "Environment and Land-Use Act" or "Sustainable Land-Use Act"?[13]

The Weak Status of Plans

In most U.S. states, the major tools that regulate development are zoning and subdivision regulations (along with some more recent tools such as planned-unit development (PUD)). The legal and institutional gap between zoning and planning that exists in many U.S. states is lamented by several authors in this book (Meck, Freilich (Chapter 6), Weitz (Chapter 5), Sullivan, Pelham (Chapter 10), and Stroud (Chapter 11)), which does not make much sense to an observer from the outside.

The decoupling between zoning and planning in the U.S. may not have been intended by the early designers of U.S. land-use enabling legislation (Mandelker 1976). The model acts stated that zoning should be enacted "in accordance with a comprehensive plan" and most states incorporated this phrase in their legislation. In his classical 1976 paper, Mandelker argued that this phrase should have been interpreted to mean that the comprehensive plan should serve as the "constitution" that guides zoning decisions (Mandelker 1976). However, over the years, the courts in many U.S. states adopted interpretations of this phrase whereby the "plan" did not have to actually exist as a separate document but could be subsumed to be folded into the zoning regulation (Haar 1955a and 1955b; Cullingworth and Caves 2003: 74-78; Mandelker and Payne 2001: 535-537). Sullivan reports (in Chapter 9) that today, in some states, plans are more influential than in the past, but there is still a long way to go. If one remembers that zoning regulations are amended frequently—a process that Mandelker (1971) has tagged "the tail wags the dog"—the notion of an imaginary plan becomes even more problematic.

What Americans Could Learn from Other Countries about Alternative Legal Statuses for Plans

Given that so many policy-makers and researchers agree that plans should have a more effective legal status, they might wish to broaden their search to include not only U.S. models and experiences, but those of dozens of other countries as well.

In most countries, the function of assigning different permitted land uses and development rules to particular zones and parcels of land is usually assigned to the lower, more detailed level of statutory plans. Because each nation's "planning system" has a different name for this level, Crow (2002) suggests calling it the "determinative instrument." It is usually the lowest in a hierarchy of two or more echelons of plans (or is a quasi-plan, such as the U.K. and Ireland's "planning permission"). There are no "zoning" bylaws underlying these plans—the hierarchy of plans covers the function of planning (national, regional, country, local, or sublocal) and, at the same time, the functions fulfilled in most U.S. states by zoning, subdivision regulation, PUDs, and related instruments.

In democratic, advanced-economy countries, legally anchored plans—known in international planning lingo as "statutory plans"—are part of most land-use planning practice. Their specific names, legal status, and functions often differ from one country to another, but they are usually there as a major and essential component to provide the rationale for land-use regulation (Alterman 2001). Beyond this common denominator, statutory plans come in many legal shapes and colors. Researchers could view this variety as providing a large-scale laboratory.

American planners, lawyers, and legislators frequently debate about whether the preparation of plans should be compulsory or discretionary. The set of EU countries, for example, provides a wide range of options along this range (EC 2000).

Americans—including several authors in this book—also debate the issue of "consistency" of plans with the regulatory zoning and development-control instruments. For example, with the introduction of a clear hierarchical relationship between zoning and plans in Florida came the need to interpret "consistency" (see Pelham in Chapter 10). This type of question—in various forms—has engaged legislators, planners, and the courts in many other countries. In continental European lingo, this issue is usually discussed under the concepts of "certainty" versus "flexibility" (EC 2000: 44-46). Lower-echelon plans—the "determinative instrument" noted above—are usually fully binding and rather inflexible. The higher-echelon plans encompass a range of degrees and types of "consistency." Some are binding on all private actors as well as on government actors; others, in the same or a different country, may be binding only on government entities (Alterman 2001).

Statutory plans also differ in their legally permitted (or mandated) contents. In some countries, plans are authorized to deal only with "physical" land-use goals; in other countries, more recent legislation provides for a broader incorporation of social and economic goals. Some types of statutory plans cover a large geographic scale; others are project specific. Plans also differ in their degree of inherent flexibility to accommodate change. Some are drafted in very general terms to apply to a variety of detailed demands (and, at the same time, they may or may not be binding); other types of plans may be specific and rigid in order to decrease uncertainty. European planning "systems" have in recent years shown a tendency to innovate with a growing variety of approaches to resolve the age-old planners' conundrum of how to reconcile the need for certainty with the need for flexibility to accommodate change. (For an EU overview, see EC 2000: 45-47; for a German example, see Munoz 2005).

Despite the many difficulties of cross-national research, the pool of experiences with the variety of types of statutory plans in the set of democratic, advanced-economy countries could provide American planners and lawyers with potential "take-home" insights.

The Large Differences Among "The Quiet Revolution" State Laws

The dozen or so states that have adopted innovative state planning laws, as a group, bear greater similarity to continental European planning laws than traditional state laws, but they differ from each other in significant ways. For example, plans may have a more secure legal status than in the traditional state enabling laws, but their formats, scopes, and functions differ as much as among countries outside the U.S. I would assume that this great variety in a single country also has its "down side."

The clients of land-use regulation who would like to receive services from two or more states may feel the burden of having to learn the inevitably complex "rules of the game" of each of the states. The advantage of the traditional state land-use laws (alongside their many "down sides") is their general similarity across state boundaries. Developers may at times feel as if they are moving across international borders, even though they are within a single— though federal—country.

Of course, many differences among national planning laws exist in Europe as well. However, there, unlike the U.S. Federation, each country has its own constitution and statutory national planning law. I noted above that in the U.S., the Constitution plays a more direct role than in most European countries. In the EU, a new constitution is under discussion. Might that lead to a uniform land-use planning law to apply to each of the member countries? Although much progress has been made in Europe towards an overall coordinated European planning *policy* (see Williams 1996 and Faludi 2002), the idea of a uniform statutory *law* is likely to be unrealistic in the near future.

Yet the emerging body of EU constitutional law is beginning to play a role somewhat similar to the role played by the U.S. Constitution. The European Charter of Human Rights already plays a partial constitutional role. Various planning-related issues (some regarding property rights; others related to what Americans call "procedural due process") can potentially reach the European Court of Human Rights in Strasbourg. However, to date, only a few such cases have reached that court—partly due to the immense cost of exhausting all echelons of potential remedies and partly due to the length of time required (estimated by the European Council of Ministers to be five years on the average) (Crow 2002).

Some analysts expect—or fear (Litwinska 2005)—that many more such cases will emerge to the extent of incrementally creating a body of European land-use law. The future of the proposed European constitution that might have served to strengthen such a trend is presently in doubt. Following the French and the Dutch referenda on this issue that delivered a "no" in May and June 2005, the prospects of a European constitution look dim.

In the U.S., imposition of a uniform format for state planning legislation is of course legally and politically unfeasible. Perhaps Americans should return to the successful model of the model acts drafted in the 1920s. Such an idea is being pursued by the "smart growth" initiative (as reported by Meck in Chapter 3). Although the success rate to date is reported to be low, the model act direction is worth following as a key element in a proposal for legal reform (perhaps repackaged as "environmental land use," as suggested above). A more favorable political situation and public opinion might provide momentum in the future.

The Low "Import Rate" of Planning Law Concepts from Overseas

I noted that "The Quiet Revolution" and "smart growth" state land-use planning laws are more similar in their conception to planning laws in some other countries (usually a different set of countries is relevant to each state or issue). There are now opportunities for Americans to be on the "import" side of cross-national learning. When designing or interpreting the newer state legislation, American planners, lawyers, and the courts could benefit from learning from planning-law concepts that have been developed in other countries.

THE ROLE OF CROSS-NATIONAL
EXCHANGE AMONG RESEARCHERS

While doing my doctoral research in the 1970s, I came across Dan Mandelker's 1971 book, *The Zoning Dilemma: A Legal Strategy for Urban Change*. I had been trying to develop ideas about how to theorize and measure plan implementation. Mandelker's book was about zoning law and practice in the U.S., while my research was about planning law and "outline plans" in Israel—two very different countries in size, location, and legal-institutional systems—yet the concepts and methods in Mandelker's book were major inputs to my thinking. In subsequent years, I have found that a cross-national research prism often provides me with the most lucid view.

All countries face the need to plan and regulate the use of land, but I have yet to find a country where there is general satisfaction with the system in place. As much as their legal, political, economic, and social structures may differ, the legal mechanisms for the regulation of land use in countries across the world share basic traits. Setting up mechanisms for land-use regulation that work well seems to be an almost intractable task. Therefore, planners and lawyers could learn much by pooling experiences and by conducting systematic, cross-national comparative research. However, the field is barely charted, and only a handful of contributions can as yet be cited (among them Kushner 2003; Alterman 2001; Schmidt-Eichstaedt 1995; and EC 2000).

Most fields of science and professional knowledge have an international academic society. This is not true for scholars in planning and land-use law. For the past 20 years, North American, European, and other scholars of urban and regional planning have been working hard to create an international academic community that could offer regular academic conferences and journals and encourage comparative and collaborative research. An example is the global collection of prize-winning papers jointly published by the world's academic planning associations (Stiftel and Watson 2005).

The field of planning law—a specialized, complex area of law and policy that could benefit so much from cross-national exchange—has yet to take an initiative in this direction. To date, there is no academic organization of researchers in the field. Although the American Planning Association's Planning and Law Division has played an important role in linking planning and law for the American planning profession, it has not evolved into an academic community of scholars, nor is there such a group under the canopy of the Association of Collegiate Schools of Planning. An embryonic Planning and Law "thematic group" is in the process of being established under the canopy of the Association of European Schools of Planning, and hopefully later under the Global Planning Education Association Network, but it has a long way to go before it turns into a real international academic society.[14]

American scholarship in planning law is unparalleled in any other country or set of countries, in breadth, depth, and quality. Although the number of books (I estimate several dozen) and academic papers (many hundreds) in this field may seem small when compared with other areas of law or policy, it is many times larger than in any other country. Establishment of an international academic group of scholars in land-use and planning law would benefit greatly from the participation of the American scholars in the field. As Americans consider planning-law reform in the new century, the benefit would likely be mutual.

RACHELLE ALTERMAN NOTES

1. Instead, the speakers raised a variety of issues—some related to the "property rights" debate over the "takings" issue that currently rages in the U.S.; others focused on housing and social exclusion; still others spoke about the instruments for "growth management" that might reduce the notorious appetite of American towns and cities for consuming land and natural resources.

2. A major piece of comparative research commissioned by the EU's European Commission in 1997-2000 is the first to undertake an in-depth analysis of each of the member countries' "planning systems" using common concepts and terms to enable comparison. See EC 1997-2000.

3. Given the scope of this paper, I won't provide citations to the many references or applications of each of the tools in the literature and legislation in other countries. I will only cite my own work where I discuss some of these tools.

4. Importing impact fees has been recently discussed in Britain. In Alterman (1988a and 1988b), I discuss a variety of American exaction tools from a cross-national perspective. In Alterman and Kayden (1988), we classify and discuss American terminology for various types of exactions to enable cross-national comparison. Linkage is analyzed in Alterman (1989). The transferability of various types of American-style exactions, including impact fees to Britain, is discussed in Alterman (1990a). In another paper (Alterman 1990b), I discuss exactions in Israel and compare them with the U.S. practices.

5. The innovativeness of transfer of development rights (TDR) and purchase of development rights as tools for open-space preservation is discussed in my six-country research on open-space preservation policies (Alterman 1997). Their transferability to the Israeli context is discussed in Alterman and Hann (2004). An especially interesting and successful example of TDR policy can be found in divided Nicosia, Cyprus. Since the mid-1990s, TDR has been used extensively in the southern (Greek) part of Nicosia for historic preservation of its walled town and other low-rise conservation areas; the transferred rights may be bought by developers in other parts of the city. As a member of a team of experts invited by the United Nations in June 2005 to assess the implementation of the joint master plan for the two sides of the city, I recommended that a similar approach be applied in the northern, Turkish side of the city. These examples highlight the extent to which TDR is transferable to very different legal, administrative, economic, and social contexts.

6. A comparative analysis of development agreements is offered in Alterman with Vitek (1996) and Margalit and Alterman (1998).

7. Id.

8. While I don't have a publication to cite, I can report that the tax increment financing concept has influenced the thinking of the Ministry of Construction and Housing in Israel when it conceived a new urban regeneration program in recent years.

9. In a paper in preparation, a colleague and I analyze design control or review tools in a cross-national comparative perspective (Alterman and Corren 2005).

10. The idea that there are many ways by which developers could be asked (or required) to mitigate environmental depletion is in process of entering planning practice in many countries.

11. An example of the "export trade" of ideas is a conference to be held on September 15-16, 2005, in The Netherlands, titled "Property Rights and Private Initiatives," to be organized jointly by the University of Nijmegen (research team Governance and Places) and the Netherlands Institute for Spatial Research.

12. See Howe et al., 2004, and Howe 2005, "Oregon's Tsunami: Measure 37 and the Disaster It Has Wrought."

13. I have used these terms because, as an outside observer, the terms "growth management" and "smart growth" seem a bit euphemistic to me.

14. I am the initiator of the group, announced on the Association of European Schools of Planning (AESOP) Web page (see http://www.ncl.ac.uk/aesop under "Working Groups"). The precursor has been the Planning and Law Track, which Professor Benjamin Davy of Dortmund, Germany, and I initiated in 1999 at the AESOP annual conference. Since then, this track (with name variations and several co-chairs) has been held consistently at each AESOP annual conference and has drawn an increasing number of participants from many countries.

RACHELLE ALTERMAN BIBLIOGRAPHY

Advisory Committee on City Planning and Zoning, U.S. Department of Commerce. A Standard City Planning Enabling Act. Washington, D.C.: U.S. Government Printing Office, 1928.

Advisory Committee on Zoning, U.S. Department of Commerce. A Standard State Zoning Enabling Act, rev. ed. Washington, D.C.: U.S. Government Printing Office, 1926.

Alterman, Rachelle. 1988a. *Exactions American Style: The Context for Evaluation.* In R. Alterman, ed., *Private Supply of Public Services: Evaluation of Real-Estate Exactions, Linkage and Alternative Land Policies,* 321. New York: New York University Press, 1988; paperback ed., 1990.

Alterman, Rachelle, ed. 1988b. *Private Supply of Public Services: Evaluation of Real-Estate Exactions, Linkage and Alternative Land Policies.* New York: New York University Press, 1988; paperback ed., 1990.

Alterman, Rachelle. 1989. *Evaluating Linkage, and Beyond* (monograph). Cambridge, MA: Lincoln Institute of Land Policy. Also published as Alterman, Rachelle. 1988. *Evaluating Linkage and Beyond: Letting the Windfall Recapture the Genie Out of the Exactions Bottle.* 32 Wash. U. J. Urb. & Contemp. L. 3-49.

____. 1990a. *Developer Obligations for Public Services, American Style: Lessons for British Planners.* In Patsy Healey and Rupert Nebarro, eds., *Land and Property Development Processes in a Changing Context,* 162-174. Aldershot, Hampshire: Gower Publishing Co.

____. 1990b. *Developer Obligations for Public Services in Israel: Law and Social Policy in a Comparative Perspective.* 5 J. Land Use & Envtl. L. 3:649-684.

____. 1992. *A Transatlantic View of Planning Education and Professional Organization.* 12 J. Plng. Ed. & Res. 102-117.

____. 1997. *The Challenge of Farmland Preservation: Lessons from a Six-Country Comparison.* Awarded the JAPA Best Paper award for 1998. 63 JAPA 2:220-243.

____. 2001. *National-Level Planning in Democratic Countries: A Cross-National Perspective.* In Rachelle Alterman, ed., *National-Level Planning in Democratic Countries: an International Comparison of City and Regional Policy-Making,* Chapter 1, 1-42. Liverpool: Liverpool University Press, Town Planning Review book series.

Alterman, Rachelle and Nurit Corren. 2005. *Reviewing Design Review: An International Perspective* (working paper). Technion City, Haifa, Israel: Center for Urban and Regional Studies.

Alterman, Rachelle and Munther Haddadin. In preparation. *Transfer and Adaptation of Planning Laws: How British-Based Planning Legislation Has Persevered in Israel and Jordan* (working paper). Technion City, Haifa, Israel: Center for Urban and Regional Studies.

Alterman, Rachelle and Iris Hann. 2004. *Instruments of Open Space Preservation: What Can Israel Learn from Other Countries?* Technion City, Haifa, Israel: Center for Urban and Regional Studies and the Neaman Institute; with Jerusalem: Jewish National Fund (Hebrew).

Alterman, Rachelle and Jerold Kayden. 1988. *Developer Provisions of Public Benefits: Toward a Consensus Vocabulary.* In R. Alterman, ed., *Private Supply of Public Services: Evaluation of Real-Estate Exactions, Linkage and Alternative Land Policies,* 22-32. New York: New York University Press, 1988; paperback ed., 1990.

Alterman, Rachelle with Miri Vitek. 1991 (1996). *From Expropriations to Agreements: Methods for Obtaining Land for Public Services*. Technion City, Haifa, Israel: Klutznick Center for Urban and Regional Studies, 1991 (1st ed.); 1996 (Hebrew ed.).

Bosselman, Fred and David Callies. 1972. *The Quiet Revolution in Land Use Control*. Washington, DC: Council on Environmental Quality.

Callies, David L. 1994. *The Quiet Revolution Revisited: A Quarter Century of Progress*. 26 Urb. Law. 197.

____. 2002. *The Quiet Revolution Redux: How Selected Local Governments Have Fared*. Pace Envtl. L. Rev. 277.

Commission of the European Communities. 1999. *European Spatial Development Perspective: Towards Balanced and Sustainable Development of the Territory of the EU*. Luxembourg: Office for the Official Publication of the European Communities.

Crow, Stephen. 2002. *Catching Up with Europe? The European Charter of Human Rights and Planning Process in the United Kingdom*. Paper presented at the 2002 Annual Conference of AESOP—Association of European Schools of Planning, Volos, Greece, in July 2002.

Cullingworth, Barry and Roger W. Caves. 2003. *Planning in the USA: Policies, Issues and Processes*. 2d ed. New York: Routledge.

European Commission (EC). 1997-2000. *The EU Compendium of Spatial Planning Systems and Policies*. Luxembourg: Office for Official Publications of the European Communities (15 national volumes and one overview volume).

Faludi, Andreas, ed. 2002. *European Spatial Planning*. Cambridge, MA: Lincoln Institute of Land Policy, 209-216.

Freilich, Robert H. 2000. *From Sprawl to Smart Growth: Successful Legal, Planning, and Environmental Systems*. Chicago: Section on State and Local Government Law, American Bar Association.

Haar, Charles. 1955a. *In Accordance With a Comprehensive Plan*. 68 Harv. L. Rev. 1154, 1174.

____. 1955b. *The Master Plan: An Impermanent Constitution*. 20 Law & Contemp. Probs. 353.

Hofstad, Christian. 2005. *Planning and Zoning—a Comparison of Urban Development Projects in the Cities of Madison and Oslo*. Paper to be presented at the 2005 Annual Conference of the Association of European Schools of Planning, Vienna, in July 2005.

Home, R. K. 1993. *Transferring British Planning Law to the Colonies: The Case of the 1938 Trinidad Town and Regional Planning Law*. Third World Pl. Rev. 15(4): 397-410.

____. 1997. *Of Planting and Planning: The Making of British Colonial Cities*. London: Spon Press.

Howe, Deborah. 2005. *Oregon's Tsunami: Measure 37 and the Disaster It Has Wrought*. Paper to be presented at the 2005 Annual Conference of the Association of Collegiate Schools of Planning, Kansas City, in October 2005.

Howe, D., C. Abbott, and S. Adler. 2004. *What's on the Horizon for Oregon Planners?* JAPA 70(4): 391-397.

Kayden, Jerold S. 2001. *National Land-Use Planning and Regulation in the United States*. In Rachelle Alterman, ed., *National-Level Planning in Democratic Countries: An International Comparison of City and Regional Policy-Making*, Chapter 2, 44-64. Liverpool: Liverpool University Press, Town Planning Review book series.

Kushner, James A. 2003. *Comparative Urban Planning Law*. Durham, NC: Carolina Academic Press.

Lewyn, Michael. 2003. *Twenty-First Century Planning and the Constitution*. 74 U. Colo. L. Rev. 651.

Litwinska, E. 2005. *Uniform Methods of Planning for All Europe?* Paper to be presented at the 2005 Annual Conference of the Association of European Schools of Planning, Vienna, in July 2005.

Mandelker, Daniel. 1971. *The Zoning Dilemma: A Legal Strategy for Urban Change*. Indianapolis: Bobbs-Merrill.

____. 1976. *The Role of the Local Comprehensive Plan in Land Use Regulation.* 74 Mich. L. Rev. 899.

Mandelker, Daniel, Jules Gerard, and J. E. Thomas Sullivan. 1986. *Federal Land Use Law.* New York: C. Boardman.

Mandelker, Daniel and John M. Payne. 2001. *Planning and Control of Land Development.* 5th ed. Charlottesville, VA: The Michie Company.

Margalit, Lirit and Rachelle Alterman. 1998. *From Fees to Agreements: Methods for Encouraging Developers to Participate in the Supply of Public Services.* Technion City, Haifa, Israel: Center for Urban and Regional Studies, with the Israel Center for Local Authorities (Hebrew).

Meck, Stuart (gen. ed.). 2002. *Growing Smart[SM] Legislative Guidebook: Model Statutes for Planning and the Management of Change.* Chicago: American Planning Association.

Munoz, Gielen D. 2005. *Possibilities to Use Legally Binding Land Use Rules in a Strategic Way.* Paper to be presented at the 2005 Annual Conference of the Association of European Schools of Planning, Vienna, July 2005.

Redman, Michael. 1993. *European Community Planning Law.* J. Plng. Envtl. L. 999.

Schmidt-Eichstaedt, Gerd. 1995. *Land Use Planning and Building Permission in the European Union.* Germany, Deutscher Gemeindeverlag Verlag W.Kohlhammer (in English and German).

____. 2001. *National-Level Planning Institutions and Decisions in the Federal Republic of Germany.* In Rachelle Alterman, ed., *National-Level Planning in Democratic Countries: An International Comparison of City and Regional Policy-Making,* Chapter 6, 127-147. Liverpool: Liverpool University Press, Town Planning Review book series.

Stiftel, Bruce and Vanessa Watson, eds. 2005. *Dialogues in Urban and Regional Planning 1.* London and New York: Routledge.

Sutcliffe, A., ed. 1980. *The Rise of Modern Urban Planning, 1980-1914.* London: Mansell.

Williams, Richard H. 1996. *European Union Spatial Policy and Planning.* London: Paul Chapman.

Yaro, Robert D. 2002. *Epilogue: Implications for American Planners.* In Andreas Faludi, ed., *European Spatial Planning,* 209-216. Cambridge, MA: Lincoln Institute of Land Policy.

Contributors

SHIRLEY S. ABRAHAMSON

Chief Justice Shirley S. Abrahamson became the first woman on the Wisconsin Supreme Court when she was appointed in 1976. She was elected to a 10-year term in 1979 and was re-elected in 1989 and 1999, and has served as chief justice since 1996. She earned an A.B., *magna cum laude*, from New York University in 1953, a J.D. with high distinction from Indiana University Law School in 1956, an S.J.D. in American legal history from the University of Wisconsin Law School in 1962, and holds 14 honorary doctorate of law degrees.

Before her appointment to the court, she practiced law in Madison for 14 years, taught as a faculty member of the University of Wisconsin Law School, and lectured at Marquette University Law School. Chief Justice Abrahamson is president of the Conference of Chief Justices, chair of the board of directors of the National Center for State Courts, a member of the council of the American Law Institute, and a member of the board of directors of the Institute of Judicial Administration at New York University. She is the author of numerous articles on such topics as state constitutional law, victims' rights, juries, and judicial independence. She is an elected fellow of the American Academy of Arts and Sciences, the American Philosophical Society, and the Wisconsin Academy of Arts and Sciences.

RACHELLE ALTERMAN

Professor Rachelle Alterman holds the David Azrieli Chair in Town Planning at the Faculty of Architecture and Town Planning, Technion—Israel Institute of Technology. With degrees in planning and law from the University of

Manitoba (Canada), the Technion—Israel Institute of Technology, and Tel-Aviv University, Dr. Alterman is internationally recognized as an authority on comparative land policy, planning law, and planning theory. In Israel, many of her publications have been cited and applied by the Supreme Court and district courts, and she often advises the Knesset and government bodies on planning law, land policy, and planning methods. She holds the academic seat on the statutory National Planning and Building Board.

Rachelle Alterman has been a Visiting Professor at the urban planning programs of the University of North Carolina at Chapel Hill, New York University, University of Wisconsin–Madison, University of Michigan–Ann Arbor, and in the law school of the University of Florida at Gainesville. She has also been a Visiting Fellow at the University Tsukuba in Japan, Princeton University, and the Lincoln Institute of Land Policy in Cambridge, Massachusetts. In 2005, she will be a Visiting Professor at the University of Wageningen and the Catholic University of Nijmegen in The Netherlands.

Alterman's cross-national comparative research includes many papers and several books. *Private Supply of Public Services: evaluation of real-estate exactions, linkage and alternative land policies* (New York: New York University Press, 1988) presents an international comparison of exactions policies. Her paper on linkage, *Evaluating linkage and beyond: Letting the windfall recapture the genie out of the exactions bottle* (Wash. U. J. Urb. & Contemp. L., 1988), has been highly cited in the U.S. A coedited book with Goran Cars, *Neighborhood regeneration: An international evaluation* (London: Mansell Pubs., 1991), presents a comparison of neighborhood regeneration programs in nine countries. Her paper, *The challenge of farmland preservation: Lessons from a six-country comparison* (JAPA, 1997), won the 1998 Best Paper award of the JAPA. Alterman's book, *National-Level Planning in Democratic Countries: an International Comparison of City and Regional Policy-Making* (Liverpool: Liverpool University Press, Town Planning Review book series, 2001), is a 10-country comparison of national-level land-use institutions and policies.

VICKI L. BEEN

Vicki Been is the Elihu Root Professor of Law at New York University (NYU) School of Law, where she has been a member of the faculty since 1990. She is the director of the Furman Center on Real Estate and Urban Policy, a joint research center of NYU's School of Law and Wagner School of Public Service. Professor Been teaches courses in land-use regulation, property, and state and local government, as well as seminars on the takings clause, environmental justice, and empirical issues in land-use and environmental law. She also co-teaches an interdisciplinary colloquium on the law, economics and politics of urban affairs. Professor Been received a B.S. with high honors from Colorado State University in 1978 and a J.D. from NYU School of Law in 1983, where she was a Root-Tilden Scholar. After graduation, Professor Been served as a law clerk to Judge

Edward Weinfeld, United States District Court for the Southern District of New York (from August 1983 to July 1984) and as a law clerk to Justice Harry Blackmun, United States Supreme Court (from August 1984 to August 1985). She was an associate at the firm of Debevoise & Plimpton in New York City for one year, then served as an associate counsel at the Office of Independent Counsel: Iran/Contra in Washington, DC.

Professor Been joined Rutgers University School of Law in Newark as an associate professor in August 1988. She has written extensively on the Fifth Amendment's Just Compensation clause, environmental justice, impact fees, housing affordability, "smart growth," and other land-use topics, and is a coauthor of *Land-Use Controls: Cases and Materials* with Robert C. Ellickson (New York: Aspen Publishers, 2005).

MICHAEL M. BERGER

Michael M. Berger is a partner in the Los Angeles office of Manatt, Phelps & Phillips LLP. He has specialized in land use, eminent domain, and other varieties of real property litigation since 1969 and is a member of the American College of Real Estate Lawyers. Active as both a lecturer and legal commentator on land use and eminent domain, Mr. Berger devotes most of his time to appellate practice. He is co-chair of his firm's Appellate Practice Group, a founding member and past-president of the California Academy of Appellate Lawyers, a fellow of the American Academy of Appellate Lawyers, and is certified as an appellate specialist by the State Bar of California, Board of Legal Specialization.

Mr. Berger wrote the briefs and presented oral argument on behalf of the property owners in *First English Evangelical Lutheran Church v. County of Los Angeles*, 482 U.S. 304 (1987); *City of Monterey v. Del Monte Dunes*, 526 U.S. 687 (1999); *Preseault v. ICC*, 494 U.S. 1 (1990); and *Tahoe-Sierra Preservation Council v. Tahoe Regional Planning Agency*, 535 U.S. 302 (2002). He filed amicus curiae briefs in support of the property owners in such cases as *Kirby Forest Indus., Inc. v. United States*, 467 U.S. 1 (1984); *Nollan v. California Coastal Commission*, 483 U.S. 825 (1987); *Lucas v. South Carolina Coastal Council*, 505 U.S. 1003 (1992); and *Yee v. City of Escondido*, 503 U.S. 519 (1992), as well as three cases being decided by the Supreme Court in 2005. Berger obtained his J.D. in 1967 from Washington University Law School and his LL.M. in real property law in 1968 from the University of Southern California.

FRED BOSSELMAN

Fred Bosselman, FAICP, is professor of law emeritus at the Chicago-Kent College of Law. Prior to joining the faculty in 1991, he practiced law with the firm of Burke, Bosselman and Weaver in Chicago and Boca Raton. His most recent article is *A Dozen Biodiversity Puzzles* (12 N.Y.U. Envtl. L.J., 364 (2004)). He is working on the second edition of a law school casebook entitled *Energy,*

Economics and the Environment with four coauthors. He is a former president of the American Planning Association (APA).

CHARLES E. DAYE

Charles E. Daye expresses appreciation to Kenneth M. Achenbach, UNC Law Class of 2006, who provided very valuable work on his article as a research assistant; and to his colleagues, Scott Baker and William Marshall, for reading and commenting on drafts of this article. Any errors, omissions, or bad ideas, of course, are exclusively Mr. Daye's.

Charles Daye is a Henry P. Brandis Professor of Law, School of Law, at the University of North Carolina at Chapel Hill (UNC-CH). He received his B.A., *magna cum laude*, from North Carolina Central University (NCCU) in 1966; his J.D., *cum laude*, from Columbia University in 1969; and an honorary LL.D. from Suffolk University School of Law in 1999.

Professor Daye began his legal career with the Wall Street law firm of Dewey, Ballantine, Bushby, Palmer and Wood. In 1970, he served as a law clerk to the late Honorable Harry Phillips, chief judge of the U.S. Court of Appeals for the 6th Circuit. Professor Daye was the first African American law clerk in that circuit. Daye then practiced as an associate with Covington & Burling in Washington, DC. He joined the faculty at UNC-CH School of Law in 1972, and was its first African American tenure-track professor. In 1980, Professor Daye became the first African American at UNC-CH to progress from entry-level through the ranks to full professor. He served four years as dean of NCCU School of Law (1981-85) and he rejoined the UNC-CH law faculty in 1985.

For over three decades, Professor Daye has taught torts, housing and community development, and administrative process and advocacy. He is senior editor of *Housing and Community Development* (3d ed.) (Durham, NC: Carolina Academic Press, 1999), and is coauthor (with Mark W. Morris) of *North Carolina Law of Torts* (2d ed.) (Charlottesville, Va.: LEXIS Law Publishing, 1999). He is a fellow of the American Bar Foundation, chair of the board of the North Carolina Fair Housing Center, and a member of the board of Triangle Housing Development Corporation (after serving 16 years as president for the nonprofit corporation that operates federally subsidized housing for low-income elderly).

He is legal affairs vice president of North Carolina Academy of Trial Lawyers (2002-2004), has served as president of the Law School Admission Council (1991-1993), and served 20 years as executive secretary of the North Carolina Association of Black Lawyers (1979-1999). He has also served the Association of American Law Schools, the American Bar Association, the North Carolina State Bar, and the North Carolina Bar Association. He has been admitted to the bars of North Carolina, New York, the District of Columbia, and the United States Supreme Court.

JOHN J. DELANEY

John J. Delaney, AICP, is a former assistant county attorney for Montgomery County, Maryland, and a founding partner of the Bethesda, Maryland, law firm of Linowes and Blocher LLP. For the past 42 years, he has represented developers, institutions, public sector entities, and public utilities in a wide variety of land-use matters before Maryland agencies and courts, the federal courts, and the U.S. Supreme Court. He is a member of the adjunct faculty at American University Washington College of Law, and coauthor (with Stanley D. Abrams and Frank Schnidman) of the book *Handling The Land Use Case: Land Use Law, Practice & Forms* (3d ed.) (Rochester, NY: Thomson-West, 2005). His most recent publication is *Addressing the Workforce Housing Crisis in Maryland and Throughout the Nation* (33 U. Balt. L. Rev., 153 (2004)). Mr. Delaney is a graduate of Georgetown University and the Georgetown University Law Center.

ANTHONY DOWNS

Anthony Downs is a senior fellow at The Brookings Institution in Washington, DC, where he has been since 1977, and a visiting fellow at the Public Policy Institute of Cal ifornia in San Francisco from July 2004 to February 2005. Before 1977, Downs was for 18 years a member and then chairman of Real Estate Research Corporation, a nationwide consulting firm, advising private and public decision-makers on real estate investment, housing policies, and urban affairs.

Dr. Downs has served as a consultant to many of the nation's largest corporations; major developers; government agencies at local, state, and national levels (including the Department of Housing and Urban Development (HUD) and the White House); and to many private foundations. President Lyndon B. Johnson appointed him to the National Commission on Urban Problems in 1967, and HUD Secretary Jack Kemp appointed him to the Advisory Commission on Regulatory Barriers to Affordable Housing in 1989.

Dr. Downs is a director of General Growth Properties and the National Association for the Advancement of Colored People's Legal and Educational Defense Fund. He was also a past director of the Mass Mutual Life Insurance Company, Bedford Property Investors, the Urban Land Institute, Essex Property Trust, the National Housing Partnership Foundation, Penton Media Inc., and the Counselors of Real Estate.

Dr. Downs received a Ph.D. in economics from Stanford University. He is the author or coauthor of 24 books and over 500 articles. His most famous books are *An Economic Theory of Democracy* (New York: Harper, 1957), translated into several foreign languages, and *Inside Bureaucracy* (Glenview, IL: Scott Foresman and Co., 1967). Both are still in print. His latest books are *Still Stuck in Traffic: Coping With Peak-Hour Traffic Congestion* (Washington, DC:

Brookings Institution Press, 2004) and *Growth Management and Affordable Housing: Do They Conflict?* (Washington, DC: Brookings Institution Press, 2004).

ROBERT C. EINSWEILER

During his career, Robert C. Einsweiler, FAICP, has focused primarily on urban growth management, strategic planning, environmental policy, and transportation planning. He worked in the public sector for 13 years (Twin Cities Metropolitan planning and Metropolitan government), ran a national consulting practice in urban growth management and strategic planning for 25 years, both paralleled by teaching (University of Minnesota and the Lincoln Institute of Land Policy). He is a past president of the APA. Throughout his career, he has been engaged simultaneously in research, teaching, and practice using the insights from each to inform the others.

Among the accomplishments in which he played a leading or key role are: the first national pilot project to integrate metropolitan land use and transportation planning; creation of the first multicounty metropolitan government in the U.S.; metropolitan tax-base sharing; the first comparative description and analysis of growth management systems in the U.S.; creation of the graduate planning degree at the University of Minnesota; and, most recently, as a leader in global teaching and research in the study of national, state, and local "value capture" systems around the world. These systems span the total capture of the "economic rent" of land (including Taiwan, South Korea, and South Africa); the British betterment-detriment system; Spain and its legacy in South American national constitutions of *plus valia*, capturing all the land value increase from government provided infrastructure; and impact fees in the U.S.

Mr. Einsweiler produced numerous publications in all the fields identified above. Academic honors include: Gargoyle (architectural honorary), Tau Beta Pi (engineering honorary), and Bronze Tablet (highest honors at the University of Illinois). Among his practice honors are: Who's Who in America, Who's Who in the World for the 20 years preceding retirement in 1996, and Fellow of AICP.

ROBERT H. FREILICH

Robert H. Freilich, AICP, professor of law and special land-use counsel in the nationally recognized law and planning firm of Paul, Hastings, Janofsky & Walker LLP in Los Angeles, California, is at the forefront of land-use law, planning, and litigation. During his distinguished career, Dr. Freilich has represented more than 200 cities, states, and counties, as well as countless private developers.

Dr. Freilich received his A.B. degree from the University of Chicago, holds a J.D. degree from Yale Law School, an M.I.A. degree from Columbia University School of Public Administration, and LL.M. and J.S.D. degrees from

Columbia University School of Law. In 1968, he became Professor of Law of the University of Missouri–Kansas City School of Law. He has served as visiting professor of law at Harvard Law School (1984-1985), the London School of Economics (1974-1975), and the University of Miami School of Law (1996-1997). Dr. Freilich specializes in smart growth and growth management, development of master planned communities, financing of capital infrastructure, and regulatory taking litigation, and he frequently serves as an expert witness. He is the author of *From Sprawl to Smart Growth: Successful Legal, Planning and Environmental Systems* (Chicago: American Bar Association, 1999), the coauthor (with David L. Callies and Thomas E. Roberts) of *Cases and Materials on Land Use* (4th ed.) (St. Paul, MN: West-Thomsen, American Casebook Series, 2004), and the forthcoming *A 21st Century Land Development Code* (Chicago: American Planning Association, 2006) (with S. Mark White).

Dr. Freilich is national editor of The Urban Lawyer, the national quarterly journal on state and local government law of the American Bar Association; director of the Annual Planning and Zoning Institute, American Center for National and International Law; past-chair of the Planning and Law Division of the APA; and a member of the Federalism Committee of the International Municipal Lawyers Association, the Advisory Board of the Land Use and Environment Law Review, the Urban Land Institute, Congress of New Urbanism, Lincoln Institute of Land Policy, and the American Institute of Certified Planners. Dr. Freilich is a member of the California, Florida, Missouri, and New York Bar Associations.

GERRIT-JAN KNAAP

Gerrit-Jan Knaap is professor of urban studies and planning and director of the National Center for Smart Growth Research & Education at the University of Maryland. He earned his B.S. from Willamette University, his M.S. and Ph.D. from the University of Oregon, and received post-doctoral training at the University of Wisconsin–Madison, all in economics.

Knaap's research interests include the economics and politics of land-use planning, the efficacy of economic development instruments, and the impacts of environmental policy.

DANIEL R. MANDELKER

Daniel R. Mandelker, FAICP, is the Stamper Professor of Law at Washington University in St. Louis, where he teaches land-use law, state and local government law, and environmental and land-use litigation. He is the author of treatises on *Land Use Law* (5th ed.) (Newark, NJ: LexisNexis Matthew Bender, 2003) and *NEPA Law and Litigation* (2d ed.) (Eagan, MN: West, a Thomson business, updated annually), and coauthor (with J. Payne, Q. Salsich, and N. Stroud) of a law school casebook, *Planning and Control of Land Development* (6th ed.) (Newark, NJ: LexisNexis Matthew Bender, 2005).

Professor Mandelker is a frequent lecturer at conferences and workshops on land-use law and has consulted nationwide on land-use problems. He was the principal consultant to the APA's Growing Smart^SM project, which has published new model legislation for land-use planning and regulation, and was the principal draftsman of the chapter on the administrative and judicial review of land-use decisions. He has B.A. and LL.B. degrees from the University of Wisconsin (Madison) and a J.S.D. degree from Yale University.

STUART MECK

Stuart Meck, FAICP, was until recently a senior research fellow with the APA. From 1994 to 2002, he was principal investigator for the APA's Growing Smart^SM project, a long-term effort to draft and implement the next generation of model planning and zoning legislation for the U.S. The project was based in APA's Chicago Research Department, where Meck participates in other research initiatives, including planning statute reform studies for Montana, Michigan, and the Czech Republic, and two major reports, *Regional Approaches to Affordable Housing* (Chicago: American Planning Association, Planning Advisory Service Report No. 513/514, 2003) and *Model Smart Development Codes* (Chicago: American Planning Association, Planning Advisory Service Report, forthcoming in 2005). A former APA national president, Meck was also a commissioner of the American Institute of Certified Planners, the professional institute of the APA. He is also a fellow of the AICP.

Meck holds a bachelor's degree and a master's degree in journalism and a master's of city planning degree from Ohio State University. He also holds a master of business administration degree from Wright State University and is a registered professional community planner in the State of Michigan and a licensed professional planner in the State of New Jersey. Meck has 33 years of professional experience. He has served as assistant city manager and planning director of Oxford, Ohio; on the staffs of the Miami Valley Regional Planning Commission in Dayton, Ohio; and on the Memphis and Shelby County Planning Commission in Memphis, Tennessee. He has also been a planning consultant.

Meck is an adjunct instructor in urban history in the Goucher College Master of Arts in their Historic Preservation program and has taught planning and public administration at several Ohio universities. He has written widely on planning and land-use issues for many years. In conjunction with Professor Kenneth Pearlman of the Ohio State University graduate planning program, he has coauthored (with Kenneth Pearlman) *Ohio Planning and Zoning Law* (Eagan, MN: Thomson-West, 2005), a treatise published annually and which has been cited numerous times by the Ohio Supreme Court, Ohio Court of Appeals, and the Ohio Attorney General.

DWIGHT H. MERRIAM

Dwight H. Merriam, FAICP, represents local governments, landowners, developers, and advocacy groups in land development and conservation issues. He is the senior land-use lawyer with the 240-lawyer firm of Robinson & Cole LLP, with offices in Boston, NewLondon, Hartford, Stamford, White Plains, New York City, and Sarasota.

Mr. Merriam has published over 180 professional articles on land-use law, coedited *Inclusionary Zoning Moves Downtown* (Chicago: American Planning Association, 1985) and coauthored (with Robert Meltz and Richard M. Frank) *The Takings Issue: Constitutional Limits on Land Use Control and Environmental Regulation* (Chicago: Island Press, 1999). His newest book is *The Complete Guide to Real Estate Zoning* (Columbus, OH: McGraw-Hill, 2005).

He is a Fellow and past president of the American Institute of Certified Planners, a former director of the APA and a previous chair of APA's Planning and Law Division. Mr. Merriam is also a member of the American College of Real Estate Lawyers and The Counselors of Real Estate, and he teaches land-use law at Vermont Law School. He received his bachelor's degree in sociology, *cum laude*, from the University of Massachusetts at Amherst, where he was also elected to Phi Kappa Phi. He received his master's of regional planning degree from the University of North Carolina at Chapel Hill and his J.D. at Yale Law School.

JOHN R. NOLON

John R. Nolon is a professor of law at Pace University School of Law where he teaches property, land-use, and environmental law. He is also counsel to the Land Use Law Center, director of the Joint Center for Land Use Studies, and a visiting professor in environmental law at Yale School of Forestry & Environmental Studies.

Professor Nolon received a Fulbright scholarship to develop a framework law for sustainable development in Argentina, where he worked from 1994 to 1996. He has been designated several times as the recipient of the Charles A. Frueauff Research Professorship, and, with that support, published several law review articles and books on land-use and environmental law. Professor Nolon was selected by the Pace University Law School faculty to receive the first annual Richard L. Ottinger Faculty Achievement Award in 1999. He is the coauthor of a leading law school casebook on land use, *Land Use Cases and Materials* (6th ed.) (St. Paul, MN: West, 2004).

Professor Nolon received his J.D. from the University of Michigan Law School, where he was a member of the Barrister's Academic Honor Society. He has served as a consultant to President Jimmy Carter's Council on Development Choices for the 1980s, President Bill Clinton's Council on Sustainable Development, and as a member of New York Governor George Pataki's Transition Team.

Professor Nolon's writings include three books on local land-use and environmental law. These are *New Ground: The Advent of Local Environmental Law* (Washington, DC: Environmental Law Institute, 2002), *Open Ground: Effective Local Strategies for Protecting Natural Resources* (Washington, DC: Environmental Law Institute, 2002), and *Well Grounded: Using Local and Land Use Authority to Achieve Smart Growth* (Washington, DC: Environmental Law Institute, 2001). Professor Nolon wrote articles in both 2002 and 2003 that were selected by a national peer-review process as among the 10 best publications in the area of land-use and environmental law.

THOMAS G. PELHAM

Thomas G. Pelham, AICP, is a partner in the law firm of Fowler White Boggs Banker, P.A. He is a land-use lawyer and certified planner who concentrates his practice in land-use planning law. He is also an adjunct professor at the Florida State University College of Law, and a former professor of law at Southern Methodist University School of Law. He received his bachelor and J.D. degrees from Florida State University, his master's degree from Duke University, and his LL.M. from Harvard University.

Mr. Pelham served from 1987-1991 as the secretary of the Florida Department of Community Affairs, the state land-planning agency with responsibility for supervising implementation of Florida's state and local comprehensive planning laws. He is currently chair of the Land Use Committee of the American Bar Association's Section on State and Local Government. He is a past chair of the Florida Bar's Section on Environmental and Land Use Law and Section on City, County and Local Government Law, and a past president of the Florida Chapter of the APA.

ROLF J. PENDALL

Rolf J. Pendall, AICP, is an associate professor in the Department of City and Regional Planning at Cornell University, where he teaches courses in land-use planning, growth management, environmental planning, affordable housing, infrastructure planning, and quantitative methods. His current research includes two projects sponsored by the Brookings Institution's Center on Urban and Metropolitan Policy on Upstate New York and local land-use regulations in the 50 largest U.S. metropolitan areas. He is currently working on two projects funded by the U.S. Department of Agriculture and the National Science Foundation on the patterns, causes, and consequences of low-grade "rural sprawl" in upstate New York. Professor Pendall holds a Ph.D. in city and regional planning from the University of California at Berkeley, a master's degree in community and regional planning, a master's degree in Latin American studies from the University of Texas at Austin, and a bachelor's degree in sociology from Kenyon College in Ohio. Professor Pendall is also a member of the American Institute of Certified Planners.

NANCY E. STROUD

Nancy E. Stroud, AICP, is a shareholder with the firm of Weiss Serota Helfman Pastoriza Cole & Boniske, P.A. and heads its Municipal Land Use Group. She concentrates her practice on the representation of local government in land-use law and growth management matters. Her clients include cities, counties, special districts, school boards and community redevelopment agencies in Florida and in other states. Ms. Stroud has a master's degree in regional planning and a law degree from the University of North Carolina. She is a member of the American Institute of Certified Planners.

Ms. Stroud has extensive experience in the defense of local government in state and federal courts and in administrative hearings on issues such as comprehensive planning, civil rights, zoning, and developments of regional impact. She regularly speaks to professional organizations and has authored numerous publications in the areas of her practice, including First Amendment issues, impact fees, quasi-judicial hearings, traditional neighborhood development, regulatory takings, and comprehensive planning.

EDWARD J. SULLIVAN

Edward J. Sullivan is an owner in Garvey Schubert Barer in Portland, specializing in planning, administrative, and state and local government law. He also teaches planning law at Northwestern College of Law and Portland State University. In addition, he has edited all five editions of the Oregon State Bar's *Continuing Legal Education Publications on Land Use.* Mr. Sullivan has written numerous law review articles on land-use and administrative law. He has also been the associate editor of and writer for the Oregon State Bar's *Real Estate and Land Use Law Digest* since its inception in 1979.

He received an M.A. (Political Thought) from the University of Durham, 1999; a diploma in law from University College, Oxford, 1984; an LL.M. from University College, London, 1978; an urban studies certificate from Portland State University, 1974; an M.A. in history from Portland State University, 1973; a J.D. from Willamette University, 1969; and a B.A. from St. John's University in New York, 1966.

He has taught planning law and administrative law at the undergraduate, graduate, and law school levels since 1972. In addition, Mr. Sullivan has serves as 9th Circuit North regional vice president (2002) of the International Municipal Attorneys Association (IMLA). He has also served as chair of the Land Development Planning and Zoning Section of IMLA. Mr. Sullivan is also a member of the Executive Committee and serves as Vice-Chair to the Council of the American Bar Association Section on State and Local Government Law. He chairs the section's Comprehensive Planning Subcommittee.

Sullivan has been assistant county counsel (1969-70) and county counsel (1971-75) for Washington County, advising the board of county commissioners and county boards, commissions, and departments on legal matters. From

1975-1977, he was legal counsel to the governor of Oregon. Since 1978, he has been in private practice. He is city attorney for the Cities of Oregon City, Island City, and Rivergrove, and acts as special counsel for other local governments. He is frequently involved in major land-use controversies in the state, acting on behalf of local governments, appellants, or opponents. The author gratefully acknowledges the assistance of Carrie Richter in the preparation of his chapter.

JERRY WEITZ

Jerry Weitz, AICP, has a master's degree in city planning (land use and environmental planning) from Georgia Tech, and a Ph.D. in urban studies (growth management and policy analysis) from Portland State University. He is the author of *Sprawl Busting* (Chicago: American Planning Association, 1999), *Jobs-Housing Balance* (Chicago: American Planning Association, 2003), coauthor (with Leora Waldner) of *Smart Growth Audits* (Chicago: American Planning Association, 2003), and author of numerous articles on growth management published in planning journals.

Dr. Weitz is a consulting city planner in Alpharetta, Georgia, and president of Jerry Weitz & Associates, Inc., Planning & Development Consultants. His firm was hired by the APA's Growing Smart^{SM} project to prepare the user manual for *Growing Smart^{SM} Legislative Guidebook: Model Statutes for Planning and the Management of Change* (Stuart Meck, gen. ed.) (Chicago: American Planning Association, 2002). In 2000, Professor Weitz won the Distinguished Professional Achievement in Planning Award from the Georgia Planning Association (GPA). Two of his clients have won outstanding plan implementation awards from the GPA. Professor Weitz is also the current president of the GPA and editor of the American Institute of Certified Planners' publication, *Practicing Planner.*

Index

Minneapolis-St. Paul, urban form of, 114–115

Minnesota
planning authority in, 96–97
smart growth planning reform in, 119
urban form in, 114–115
urban growth in, 8, 20

Missouri
planning history in, 24
smart growth planning reform in, 119

Mixed-use projects, 98, 99, 115

Moby Dick Corp., Willapa Grays Harbor Oyster Growers Ass'n v., 171–172

Modern Civic Art, or the City Made Beautiful (Robinson), 25

Montgomery County, Hyson v., 65, 87

Montgomery County, Maryland, urban form of, 114–115

Moore, Terry, 44

Moratoria
abuse of, 59, 77–79, 86–87, 268
authorized use of, 96–97

Musgrove, Machado v., 158, 171

National Association of Realtors, 116, 189, 195, 197

National Center for Smart Growth Research & Education, 117

National economic well-being interest, 222, 226–227

National Land Use Planning Act, 4

National Trust for Historic Preservation, 276–277

Natural Resources Defense Council, 104, 112

Natural selection, 308

Neighborhood infill, 99. *See also* Housing

Neighborhood plebiscites, 68

Neighborhoods. *See also* Communities
characteristics of desirable, 211
citizens defending, 193
housing as, 218–219, 220, 239
promotion of specific, 123–124

Nelson, Arthur, 44, 46–47

Nelson, Horatio, 245–246

New Jersey
housing affordability in, 45–46, 189, 206
housing policy in, 131
permit review and appeals in, 46–47
smart growth planning reform in, 118

New London, Connecticut, 263–264. *See also* Connecticut

New Mexico
legislation review in, 36–37
smart growth planning reform in, 119

New urbanism, 98, 104, 296

New York City
historic preservation in, 98, 163, 260, 275–276
planning history in, 24
population growth in, 113
zoning history in, 35–36

New York (state)
affordable housing in, 240
case studies, 12–16
early land-use legislation in, 137
intermunicipal planning in, 10–11
local planning in, 11
state-level regulation in, 16–17
waterfront protection in, 6

The New York Times, 254

NIMBY (Not In My Back Yard), 4, 89, 94, 210

Nolen, John, 23

Nollan v. California Coastal Commission, 254

Nolon, John R., 3–22, 26, 289, 294, 296

North Carolina, smart growth planning reform in, 119

Not In My Back Yard (NIMBY), 4, 89, 94, 210

Ocala, Florida, housing prices in, 192. *See also* Florida

Oconee County, Georgia, development opposition in, 275. *See also* Georgia

Ohm, Brian W., 255